DATE DUE	
ILL 5-11-92	
JUL 2 3 1992	
OCT. 1 5 1993	
ILL 11-29-94 NOV 1 4 1996	

BRODART, INC.   Cat. No. 23-221

Blackfeet and Buffalo

Memories of Life among the Indians

BLACKFEET

Memories of Life among the Indians

EDITED AND WITH AN INTRODUCTION BY

NORMAN AND LONDON

AND BUFFALO

by James Willard Schultz *(Apikuni)*

KEITH C. SEELE

UNIVERSITY OF OKLAHOMA PRESS

Library of Congress Catalog Card Number: 62–10762

ISBN: 0–8061–1700–1

Copyright © 1962 by the University of Oklahoma Press, Norman, Publishing Division of the University. Manufactured in the U.S.A. First edition, 1962; second printing, 1968; third printing, 1980; fourth printing, 1983; fifth printing, 1988.

Wide brown plains, distant, slender, flat-topped buttes; still more distant giant mountains, blue sided, sharp peaked, snow capped; odor of sage and smoke of camp fire; thunder of ten thousand buffalo hoofs over the hard, dry ground; long drawn, melancholy howl of wolves breaking the silence of night, how I loved you all!

James Willard Schultz, *My Life as an Indian*

Introduction

THE WRITER OF THESE LINES has read thirty-three of James Willard Schultz's thirty-seven books in the last two years. While he has long been convinced that the first one of all, *My Life as an Indian,* is an American classic of the old West, he sees now more than ever that *Apikuni*—to refer to Schultz by his Blackfoot name—will forever be remembered as the greatest interpreter of a noble Indian people to all who are capable of appreciating them. *Apikuni,* however, in contrast to many of the distinguished writers who in their turn have added to our knowledge and understanding of Indian life and history, has permitted the Blackfeet—more strictly the Pikunis (Piegans), southernmost branch of the great Blackfoot Confederacy—to interpret themselves in their own words. Without being a journalist he has been a reporter, and a very faithful one, on the daily life and conversations as well as the deeper side of the Indian as revealed by his prayers, his religious ceremonies, and his unswerving conviction of the indwelling presence of the Above Ones in all his acts.

Apikuni's reporting is unique for the reason that, though a white man, he was also truly an Indian. He was married to a remarkable woman of the Pikunis, Fine Shield Woman *(Mutsi-Awotan-Ahki,* the lovely Nätahki of *My Life as an Indian),* who became the mother of his son, Hart Merriam Schultz (Lone Wolf), noted artist of Tucson, Arizona. He learned the difficult Blackfoot language at the age of eighteen and spoke it constantly with his family and Indian relatives and friends for more than fifty years. Thus he not only spoke Blackfoot, he *thought* it as well. Moreover, from the beginning of his life as an Indian, in 1877, he made excellent use of his talents and opportunities. He not only listened to the stories of their lives and adventures told by famous men and women story tellers like Crow Woman, Earth Woman, Hugh Monroe, Tail-Feathers-Coming-Over-the-Hill, Many-Tail-Feathers, Three Suns, and others; he kept notebooks in which he recorded their stories. He spent countless evenings before the lodge fires of his friends, hearing from different ones their versions of the same events, until many of their stories were burned into his memory.

With the death of Fine Shield Woman in 1903, Schultz considered his life to be finished. The buffalo had gone, the Montana plains were fenced and overrun with cattle and sheep, and now the passing of his beloved wife removed his will to live. Yet, he had met George Bird Grinnell in the eighties, they had named many of the mountains and glaciers in the near-by Rockies, and he had begun to contribute stories to Grinnell's *Forest and Stream*. Life was over in 1903, but thirty-seven books and much additional writing were ahead of him and he was to play an important role in the creation of Glacier National Park, which he and Grinnell had conceived long before. Soon he would be world famous as *Apikuni* the storyteller.

One of the most extraordinary aspects of *Apikuni*'s books, in my estimation, is the fact that nearly all of them were published for youthful readers. I have read most of them for the first time after reaching the age of sixty. Why were they published for young people? First of all, they were fit for young people to read—more than can be said for much that is published today. But most of all, they are youthful in spirit; they breathe the wholesome atmosphere of the mountains and the plains; they tell of a clean, decent, high-minded race—the terrible Blackfeet, the "savages," the cruel and bloody "raiders of the northwest plains," who turned out to be wholly human, kindly, generous, friendly, hospitable, joking and laughing, loving and lovable. Yes, they were stealers of horses, yet they were honest and truthful; they were relentless killers of their enemies, but a Blackfoot was certainly killed by a white man before he became a killer of white men.

Apikuni lived this Indian life and understood it as none before him and few at any time. *He was a storyteller, but he never set himself up to be a historian or scientist.* It is of the utmost importance that the historian and searcher after facts neatly verified not look to him for definitive historical truth. This was not his forte nor his aim. What appears in this book has, however, something of the indispensable value of a George Frederick Ruxton in *Life in the Far West*. As such, it may have that same atmospheric value for an interpretation of Indian life that Ruxton's recaptured lingo and adventures of the mountain man of a century and a quarter ago have for an interpretation of life in the Far West.

Apikuni listened to the Indian storytellers, and he became one of the best of them. But, unlike them, he could transfer their stories of the lodge fires to paper for thousands to enjoy forever. His literary style is unique; it is Blackfoot talk in English words and sentences. He is an artist of narrative and a master of suspense. One follows his stories with breathless interest and deplores the thinning pages at the end of the book. If only there were more and more and more! If only his books were not so few—only thirty-seven. But now there is another—this wonderful volume of reminiscences and stories.

There are a few discrepancies in *Apikuni*'s stories. Sometimes his memory failed him where his notes were incomplete. Not infrequently the same tale was related by different persons at long intervals, so that the details and at times even the participants varied. (In this connection it must be recalled that one and the same Indian bore several different names in the course of his life; renaming after an important exploit was a commonplace. *Apikuni*'s name was given to him by Running Crane, who had been *Apikuni* in his youth.) Nevertheless, his stories are for the most part historical. Few events related in the books and shorter works did not actually take place. In rare instances, *Apikuni* narrated in the first person an episode in which he had not personally participated. The only example in the present volume is "Cut-Nose" (Chapter 15). This is a true story of a tragic event such as *Apikuni* had himself witnessed, but he related "Cut-Nose" in the first person as a vivid literary device. He was always intent on verifying the facts which he reported and never ceased his attempts to clarify in his own mind the smallest detail of every adventure which he chronicled.

Schultz was, like all humans, not wholly free from prejudice. He was not infallible and never pretended that he was. At times he drew mistaken conclusions from the incomplete facts at his disposal—most conspicuously, perhaps, in his estimate of Major Young, agent on the Blackfoot reservation during the "Starvation Year" of 1883–84. Recent research seems to prove that Young attempted to obtain from Washington the help required to save his charges from starvation. He may not, therefore, have been quite the dishonest, lying wretch that he was painted in *My Life as an Indian*. However, my own inquiries among the Blackfeet on the reservation at Browning plainly show that Major Young was regarded as anything but a sympathetic and understanding "father" to his Indian children. They may have had their natural prejudices against the white overlord who tyrannically controlled their destiny in those awful months of 1883–84, but, in view of the fact that some five hundred of them died for want of food, I am convinced that such prejudices were based on more than mere misunderstanding. Realizing that there still remain marked differences of opinion of this subject—sometimes influenced by whatever source a person has consulted—I should like personally to re-examine all those faded letters directed by Major Young to Washington before coming to positive conclusions on the relation of the Major to his charges.

There are historical facts in this book which have been, and will be, disputed by other authors. Thus, notably, in Chapter 2, "Buffalo Robes," Chief White Calf is represented as having been unaware of the two executive orders which deprived the Pikunis of their lands between the Yellowstone and Marias rivers. And in Chapter 24, "A Bride for Morning Star," mention is made of the story of Running Eagle, the famous Pikuni woman-warrior. Schultz places her warring activities "in the very long ago"; but another view places Running Eagle's exploits after 1856, the time of Schultz's story.

I believe it is of the utmost importance to retain these seeming discrepancies in Schultz's work. As a storyteller, he undoubtedly took some liberties with factual history, and yet he *lived* most of the history that he relates in this book, and thus should have known it well. Perhaps these discrepancies will be a challenge to readers and scholars to undertake additional investigation to discover who is right and who is wrong.

A number of the tales herein have been previously published as short stories in popular magazines and newspapers. Nearly all were first seen in the Great Falls Tribune, and one was in the *Los Angeles Times Magazine. American Boy, Youth's Companion, Open Road for Boys, St. Nicholas, Cavalier, True Western Adventures*, and *Boy's Life* all carried earlier, and sometimes shorter, versions of the stories which the author has to tell. But *Apikuni* had during his later years entertained the intention of bringing them together into a book. His death in 1947 prevented this. It has thus remained for his wife, Jessie Donaldson Schultz—affectionately known as *Apaki* to innumerable Indian and white friends—to collect the papers and prepare them for publication. Without her selfless and tireless devotion the book could never have advanced beyond the planning stage in which it was when *Apikuni* was laid to rest in the Indian burial ground in Two Medicine Valley on the Blackfoot reservation. More than anyone else she has shared with *Apikuni* those memories of the long ago. Now, solely because of her determination and industry, the reminiscences are a reality.

The stories contained in Part II of this volume were all related to Schultz by his Indian friends. Thus, though they are genuine in every sense of the word, their contents must, of necessity, bear some of the stamp of *Apikuni's* organizational ability and flavor.

This latest book of James Willard Schultz is going to recall their boyhood days to many of his avid readers of thirty years ago. We *know* Nätahki and Crow Woman and Tail-Feathers-Coming-Over-the-Hill and many more of *Apikuni's* friends of the eighties, for he made them our friends as well. What fine people they all were, and what a privilege to have known them! We have been parted from them for a whole generation, but now we come together once more to talk over old times.

Actually, only two or three of them are still alive, and I proudly count my connection with one of the noblest of all, my adopted father, Chewing Black Bone, who is identical with the *Ahko Pitsu* of this book.

KEITH C. SEELE

Chicago, Illinois

Contents

Map

Part I: *Autobiographical Narrative*

CHAPTER ONE

Some Adventures at Old Fort Conrad[1]
(1878–79)

"I AM WHITE DOG, ASSINIBOINE"

Fort Conrad! What memories I have of it: the busy days of trade; the quiet peace; the stirring adventures there and thereabout in the long-ago days of the buffalo. A well-patronized trading post for the Blackfoot Indian tribes, it stood on a south high bank of the Marias River, close above the mouth of its Dry Fork, eighty miles northwest of Fort Benton, then the metropolis of Montana Territory. The ever-changing current of the river long since cut out its bank, the land upon which it stood; and its logs rotted upon the sandbars of the Marias, the Missouri, and Mississippi rivers, perhaps all the way down to the Gulf of Mexico.

The connecting log cabins of the fort formed three sides of a square 150 by 150 feet. Its east side was a high stockade of logs, with a plank doorway wide enough to permit passage of wagons. Adjoining the west side was the stable and corral for our horses.

Charles Conrad, a member of the St. Louis–Fort Benton firm of Indian traders, built Fort Conrad in 1875, and it was named for him. In 1878 my friend and employer Joseph Kipp—called by the Blackfeet *Mastúnopachis*, "Raven Quiver"—bought the fort and promptly, with a large stock of trade goods, we moved into it, the whole outfit of us: Kipp and his family, Chief Clerk Hiram D. Upham and family (their wives were Pikuni[2] women), some of their Pikuni relatives, and a youth of nineteen years—myself.

1 Adapted from *The Great Falls Tribune* (November 8 and 15, 1939).
2 True form of the tribal name usually corrupted to "Piegan."

Kipp was a born Indian trader, in the most literal sense of the word, for his father was that intrepid Captain James Kipp of the American Fur Company who in 1831 built Fort Piegan near the mouth of the Marias River, in order to take the trade of the Blackfoot tribes—the Blackfeet, the Bloods, and the Pikunis—from its northern rival, the Hudson's Bay Company; and his mother *Sahkwi Ahki,* "Earth Woman," was the fine daughter of that Mandan Indian chief *Mahtotopa,* of whom George Catlin wrote so admiringly in his letters.[3] At an early age son Joseph had become an employee of his father's company at Fort Benton, then later of Carroll and Steel, who took over the fort when, in 1865, the American Fur Company went out of business. Still later he had continued in the trade for himself and had done exceptionally well at the posts he had built in Alberta, Fort Standoff, and, later, Fort Kipp on Belly River. During those years, chiefly because of his sagacity and kindness of heart, he had attained great influence with the Blackfoot tribes. Up to the time of his death in 1913 they made no moves of importance to them without first obtaining his counsel and advice.[4]

During the winter of 1878–79 we had a good trade with the Blackfoot tribes, the Pikunis, Blackfeet, and Bloods, getting from them two thousand buffalo robes and several thousand deer, wolf, beaver, and antelope hides. Came spring and the tribes left, the Blackfeet and Bloods returning to their reservations in Alberta Province, Canada, and the Pikunis going to summer hunt along the foot of the Rockies, seventy-five miles to the west of us.

A hundred yards below our fort was the Marias River crossing of the Fort Benton–Fort Macleod, Alberta, wagon road. All of the supplies for that northern fort and other southern Alberta settlements came on steamboats up the Missouri River to Fort Benton, and from there were carried on to their destinations by bull trains, horse trains, mule trains. In June, John Haney's outfit of three horse-teams, eight spans of horses and two wagons per team, en route with goods for Fort Macleod, made camp one evening at Pend d'Oreille Coulee,

[3] George Catlin, *North American Indians* (Edinburgh, 1926), I, 104, 118, 129–32, 163–74.
[4] For a longer sketch of the life of Joseph Kipp, see James W. Schultz, *Friends of My Life as an Indian* (Houghton Mifflin Company, 1923), chap. V.

twenty miles south of us, and during the night a war party of Indians made off with all of his horses. A few nights later, at Rocky Springs, thirty miles north of us, a war party attacked Henry Hagan's wagon train, making off with most of his horses and killing two of his teamsters. Then in quick succession and in like manner several smaller freighting outfits lost their horses here and there along the road, with the result that the Royal Canadian Mounted Police began patrolling the Alberta part of the road, and the commanding officer at Fort Shaw, on Sun River, undertook to make safe our Montana part of it.

So came from Fort Shaw one day a company of mounted soldiers of the Third United States Infantry, led by First Lieutenant J. H. Beacom, and made camp several hundred yards out from our fort. Very white and neat were their Sibley tents, their rows of canvas-covered pack saddles; quite gay and heartening, the calls of their bugler to this and that detail of their activities.

Came Lieutenant Beacom to confer with Kipp. "Who are these raiding, killing war parties?" he asked.

"Some of them, without doubt, the Assiniboines. Most likely Crees or Crows or Yankton Sioux, the others," Kipp replied.

"Yes, and very likely some of the war parties of the Blackfoot tribes."

"Oh, no! No!" Kipp exclaimed. "They would not think of raiding the whites right here in their own country. They are raiding their Indian enemies, and with good success. Only the other day a Pikuni war party passed here with more than a hundred horses and five scalps that they had taken in a fight with the Assiniboines at the mouth of the Milk River."

"Well, how can I find and punish these war parties?"

"A slim chance for you ever to run onto one of them. They travel only at night, lie securely hidden in the daytime, with several of their scouts ever on watch. But they are afraid of you white soldiers. I advise you to ride south on the road, north on it, occasionally down the valley of the river. Any war parties hereabout will be sure to see you and turn back whence they came."

Said the Lieutenant, sighing, "Yes, that seems to be all that I can do. Thanks for the advice."

And after a little: "How terribly handicapped we soldiers are in this kind of work. Conspicuously clothed and mounted, we ride about in close formation for these war parties to see us from afar, and so avoid us. Small chance that we can ever meet up with one of them, red-handed from an attack upon a freighting outfit. How I would like to go after them with a party of men of your experience. I am sure that with some of your hunting and trapping friends you would soon make this road safe for the travel on it."

"Yes, maybe we could," Kipp modestly replied.

We had not many horses, only a four-horse wagon team, a dozen saddle horses, including two fast, well-trained buffalo horses, one of them mine. For transporting our buffalo robes, furs, hides, and trade goods we had a large bull train, three teams of eight yokes of bulls (steers), and two wagons each. Long John Forgy was our wagon boss; and Kipp's brothers-in-law, Takes-Gun-at-Night, Red Eyes, and Comes-with-Rattles, our bullwhackers. All three were young Pikuni men of not more than twenty years. At this time the train was not in use, the bulls grazing at will in the next river bottom below the fort. The horses were kept in the corral at night, and at sunrise were turned out to graze.

As Lieutenant Beacom and his men had to use their saddle horses daily, they were turned out with the pack mules to graze of nights, with chain and leather hobbles, and herded by two shifts of men, the first one until midnight, the other one until daybreak, when they were unhobbled and driven in to camp.

Came a rainy, winter night and, early in the morning, someone pounded on the door of our office, in which I slept. I sprang out of bed and let him in, Lieutenant Beacom, all out of breath and dripping wet. He sank down in a chair before the fireless stove and gasped:

"I must see Kipp. Show me where he sleeps. Better still, will you please awaken him and ask him to come in here?"

I dressed, threw a slicker over my shoulders, ran across the court and into Kipp's quarters, found him up and building a fire in the cookstove.

"Lieutenant Beacom is in the office, plenty worried, wants to see you," I said.

"*Ha!* What's wrong that he would come in this early?" he wondered.

As we entered the office Beacom sprang up to meet us and cried:

"Oh, Joe! I want your advice, your help. Last night five of my horses were stolen. Yes, stolen right out from under my herders' noses, as it were. You know what that means for me if we can't recover them. I will be the laughing stock of my regiment for as long as I live."

"Perhaps they just strayed off," Kipp suggested.

"Oh, no. No! Just in defiance of us the thieves left a pair of our hobbles, neatly rebuckled and tied to a long stick, in a thick growth of sage. Now, my men and I are no good at trailing. Won't you, please, try to trail and overtake the thieves? We will follow you, do whatever you say."

"Sure. I'll do what I can, but you know as well as I do that it will be hard to find, to overtake them, this heavy rain washing out their trail about as fast as it is made," Kipp replied. And at that, refusing to have breakfast with us, Beacom hurried back to his camp.

As soon as we could get ready, Kipp and I mounted our buffalo horses and joined the Lieutenant and his waiting men, and we all rode up the Dry Fork's narrow valley to where, at dawn, the two herders had rounded up the big band of army horses and mules to drive it to camp, and found that five of the horses were missing, one of them the Lieutenant's favorite horse. They showed us, too, the stock to which the pair of hobbles had been tied. But even in that short time the rain had washed out all tracks of the herd in the heavily grassed bottom land, and, if anything, the rain was coming down harder than ever, driven by a stiff northwest wind.

Leaving the Lieutenant and his men, Kipp and I circled and re-circled the bottom and failed to find any trace of the missing horses. Useless, too, to look for tracks of them along the Dry Fork, now a fast-rising torrent of muddy water. So, returning to the command, Kipp said:

"Well, Lieutenant, it's just as I thought it would be. Absolutely, the rain has washed out the tracks of the stolen horses. No way of knowing which way the thieves went with them."

"But I have to make an attempt to recover them, so what do you advise?"

"Well, the war party may be from any of a half-dozen different tribes, but more than likely they are Assiniboine Sioux. If so, they no doubt crossed the Marias not far below here, and are heading to pass the south foot of the Sweetgrass Hills on their way home. Slim chance to overtake them but you can try it."

"Will you go with us?"

"Yes," Kipp replied. And then to me: "Best that you go back to the fort. Tell my brothers-in-law to ride out and see how our bulls are doing."

I was glad enough to get in out of the wet. Comes-with-Rattles, Red Eyes, and Takes-Gun-at-Night grumbled when I gave them Kipp's message—said that the bulls were all right, did not need looking after—but, scolded by their sister, Double-Strike Woman, Kipp's wife, they saddled their horses and rode off down the valley.

The storm lessened into a windless drizzle of rain. Early in the afternoon our bull herders came hurrying in, greatly excited. In the second, southside river bottom below, they had found one of the bulls killed with an arrow, and its tongue, liver, and some of its ribs missing. Then, near it, in the heavy timber, they had come upon a war lodge, a temporary shelter of poles and brush, in which a war party had rested and broiled the meat. The beaded pattern of a pair of worn-out moccasins that they had found in the lodge proved that, without doubt, the party had been Assiniboines, and also without doubt, the ones who had made off with the army horses.

So Kipp had been right in his conjecture that the horse thieves were Assiniboines. It was possible that he might lead the soldiers onto them, and they would fight. Kipp's wife, his fine Mandan mother, and her close companion, Crow Woman, got together and prayed Sun to keep him safe. The afternoon dragged on. Dark night came and the drizzling rain continued, and still he did not appear. More and more anxiously, fervently, the women prayed for his safety.

Lieutenant Beacom had left a few of his men to guard his camp and the pack mules. Near nine o'clock one of the men came to the gate of our stockade, shouted for admittance and said, when we had let him in, that the company's second sergeant, down in camp, was very sick, suffering from stomach cramps, and could we do something for him?

I knew from experience with them that Kipp's mother, *Sahkwi Ahki*, "Earth Woman,"[5] and Crow Woman were good medicine women. They had cured me of several illnesses. They readily agreed to do what they could for the sick one, and, hurriedly pouching their medicines, they accompanied the soldier and me out to the camp. The sick one was humped over, groaning. Earth Woman quickly brewed a concoction of black roots, white roots, gave him several cups of it, and he soon stretched out upon his bedding and, with a sigh of relief, said that the pain was lessening. The women smiled, and Earth Woman told me to tell him that, after a little, she would give him another drink of the cure and he would suffer no more.

The night was windless, but rain continued to fall, faintly pattering upon the roof of the tent. A Sibley stove in its center gave out genial heat, and a lantern afforded us sufficient light. We smoked, talked a little—Earth Woman worrying about her son, out with the soldiers in the cold wet night; wondering where they were and when they might return.

The sick sergeant was in charge of the camp, and his six men were, in shifts of two each, herding the hobbled horses and pack mules closely. One of the present shift came hurrying into the tent to hover over the stove and warm his hands, so numb, he said, that he couldn't light his pipe. Said the sergeant to him: "Well, be quick about it, them mules and horses, they got to be closely watched."

And then, in the Blackfoot language, and plainly, we heard not far off shouting: "Listen! Listen! Me, I am White Dog. Last night I took five of your horses. Now I have taken five of your bigears. I am White Dog. Come and get me!"

And then, as Earth Woman was wailing "White Dog! He has come again!" and the soldiers were crying "Who's that? What's he

[5] More exactly, *Ksakwi-Oyis-Ahki*, "Earth-House-Woman."

saying?" guns boomed and several bullets ripped through the tent.

"He is White Dog, an Assiniboine. Says that he took your horses last night, and now has five of your mules," I shouted to the soldiers as I made a grab for the lantern to put out its light. They snatched up their rifles and ran, all but the sick sergeant. I said that I had not brought my rifle, and he told me to take his Springfield. After some fumbling I got it, felt my way to the tent doorway and out of it, to bump against one of the soldiers. The night was very dark, so dark that we couldn't see the near mules, snorting and stamping about on their hobbled feet, still frightened by the shooting. And we could hear the hoofbeats of the stolen ones, becoming fainter and fainter as the thieves rode them off, heading toward the mouth of the Dry Fork.

The soldiers shouted to one another, to obtain their different positions. I told them that the war party would not be back that night, so it was useless for us to stand out in the rain. Returning to the tent, I relighted the lantern, put some wood in the stove. The women were talking about the daring of White Dog. The sergeant moaned: "This is bad luck for me; I'll sure get a scolding for this when Lieutenant Beacom returns."

He had me call in four of his men. Earth Women gave him another dose of her medicine, and he said: "This White Dog! He sure has gall, yellin' to us that he has swiped five of our mules. What about him, anyway?"

White Dog, I explained, was an Assiniboine who for years had cunningly pestered the Blackfoot tribes. Years back, he had captured a woman of the Pikuni-Blackfoot tribe, had made her one of his wives, had learned somewhat of her language, and had a child by her, a boy.[6] But she had hated him, had run off with the little one, and had managed to return to her people. From that time, White Dog, always with a few chosen followers, had preyed upon all three of the Blackfoot tribes—killing now and then one and another of their unwary hunters; raiding their horse herds at nights; always, when feeling safe, shouting defiance of them, boasting that he, White

---

[6] Many-Tail-Feathers had a different recollection of the way in which White Dog learned his boastful Blackfoot words. See *Friends of My Life as an Indian*, 232–33.

Dog, was the raider. War party after war party of the tribes had tried to put an end to him; several of them had come near doing it, but always he had managed to outwit them and get away.

"Well, why was he yelling his defy of us? He knew that we were not Blackfeet," the sergeant said.

"He no doubt thought that some of us of the fort would be here with you, and understand his defy," I answered.

"Sure a slick one. Here he comes with his men, camps, kills one of your bulls, steals five of our horses, leaves no trail of his going, and comes back the next night and takes some of our mules. Gosh! How I would like to trail him, meet up with him before Lieutenant Beacom gets back, and here I am too weak to move," the sick one said.

Said one of his men: "What's the use of your talkin' that way? You know darn well that we have to stick right here and herd the stock." And to that there was no answer.

I proposed to the women that we go home. No, they would remain where they were until day came. The sergeant offered to have four of his men escort us to the fort. "But no. White Dog and his Cutthroat followers might still be near, and against them four white soldiers would be as nothing," Earth Woman declared.

The rain ceased just before dawn, and the sun was rising in clear blue sky as we neared the fort and were met by our three young bullwhacks, rifles in hand. They had heard the shooting out at the soldiers' camp and had stood on watch until we appeared, not knowing what might happen. They were more than vexed when we told them of White Dog's second raid on the soldiers' stock.

Said one of them, Comes-with-Rattles: "What a uselessness: Raven Quiver (Kipp) far-riding with the soldiers in search of White Dog, and he close hidden here to take this time some of their bigears."

I had breakfast, took to my couch in the office, and slept for a time. Kipp and the soldiers returned in late afternoon. They had ridden far down Marias River Valley, out along the foot of the Sweetgrass Hills, but found no signs of the raiders. When we told them what had transpired during the night, Kipp laughed, said that White Dog was the wiliest, most successful horse thief that he had ever known. But Lieutenant Beacom was grim enough. He paced up and down in our office, frowning, snapping his fingers, muttering to himself, and at last said: "Kipp, this is terrible hard on me. What, oh. what am I to do about it?"

"I think that you should go with your outfit down to the Assiniboine camp—it is somewhere near the mouth of Milk River—and make White Dog give back your stock, and then arrest him, maybe kill him," Kipp replied.

"But that is impossible! Impossible!" Beacom cried. "My orders are that I must camp here; do my utmost to protect the travelers on this road. Were I to go down there with my detachment I would surely be court-martialed."

"Well, then, why not write your commanding officer, ask him to go round up White Dog and your horses and mules?"

"Yes, that is the only thing for me to do. When does the mail stage go south again? In ten days? Ha! Two weeks for my letter to reach Fort Shaw. And oh, what snickering there will be when it is read!"

"Now, now, don't take it so hard," Kipp advised. "Not your fault nor your men's fault that White Dog got away with your stock. All was against you: the dark, rainy nights, and the smartest horse thief that ever rode these plains."

Said the Lieutenant as he strode for the door: "Maybe my C. O. will see it as you do, but I doubt it."

Soon after sunrise of the following morning, a war party of seven Pikunis, led by Many-Tail-Feathers, arrived to pass the day with us. They were afoot and had traveled all night from the tribal camp up near the foot of the Rockies. They were going south, to raid the horse herds of the Crow Indians, they said, but had come first to us to trade some beaver hides for a good supply of cartridges. We told them of White Dog's raid upon the soldiers' stock, and they were loud in their hatred for the Cutthroat and all his kind.

Said one: "It must be that the Cutthroats' gods most powerfully protect some of them. This White Dog, always he has his way with us. He makes off with our horses and we fail to trail him. When, rarely, we do manage to get near him, though we aim so carefully, our bullets fail to strike his body."

Said Many-Tail-Feathers: "Five times have I sought that White Dog and failed to get him. I have vowed to Sun that I will kill him, the killer of my father, my grandfather, and my mother from grieving for my father. So now I will again try to find him and make an end of his killings and stealings."

So it was that Many-Tail-Feathers and a few of his friends offered to travel the long journey to the camp of the Cutthroats in search of Lieutenant Beacom's horses and bigears, hoping to this time find White Dog and make an end to his raidings.

Said Lieutenant Beacom as the little party was ready to leave: "I hope you and your friends are going to have luck getting White Dog's scalp. And if you can recover the horses and mules that he stole from me, I will do something for you all."

When I had interpreted that to the others, Many-Tail-Feathers said: "Tell him this: 'Soldier Chief, if we can possibly take your horses and bigears from the Cutthroats, you shall have them.' "

With that they were off, Kipp setting them across the river in the ferryboat.

Many weeks later they came into camp, a bedraggled, despondent group. They had seen the Assiniboine camp, had been close to it, when they had met up with a Pikuni hunting party, learned that White Dog was not in the camp of his people, had taken off for the west side of the Backbone. They had taken only the horses they were riding, could not get into the camp of the Cutthroats, were seen, had a bad time escaping. They would try again when White Dog returned to his people. Lieutenant Beacom strode up.

"No," said Many-Tail-Feathers, "we did not bring your horses and bigears to you. We did not even see them. We will go after White Dog when he comes back across the mountains. Next time we will find him, kill him. We might find your horses, too. We will try."

"Too bad. Too bad," muttered Lieutenant Beacom and turned on his heel and left.

WELL, MANY-TAIL-FEATHERS finally did achieve his purpose, that of killing his and the Pikuni's enemy, White Dog, but not until several years had passed, and he failed to find and return to him the horses and mules of Lieutenant Beacom. On this last and successful war trail, went with him Bear Head, my good friend, and many a night I have listened to him tell of the events of that long journey to the camp of the Cutthroats.

"*Apikuni*," he would say, "you remember how many times Many-Tail-Feathers had tried to kill his enemy. How he had once been close to him, had killed his horse, had shot White Dog in the arm, but never would his bullets kill him."

"I have heard that story many times; but tell it again, Bear Head. Tell all that happened to you and the others in the war party."

This, then, is Bear Head's story:

There were six of us, experienced warriors of from thirty to forty summers: Weasel Tail, Heavy Runner, White Antelope, Little Otter, and me, led by Many-Tail-Feathers who was both warrior and medicine man.

We set off down Marias River Valley on a well-worn trail. Some of us carried Henry repeating rifles of .44 caliber, the others, '73 Winchesters like mine. Each had his war sack, his war bonnet in a fringed and painted parfleche case, plenty of cartridges, and a lariat for roping enemy horses.

Many-Tail-Feathers was the owner of the sacred elk-tongue pipe. It and the many other things that went with it—different kinds of animals, bird skins, buffalo stones, rattles, drums, and whistles—made a bundle that was a load for a horse. But certain very small parts of the bundle—sweet pine and sweet grass for incense, the feathered skin of a raven, some native tobacco, and a black stone pipe—he carried in a painted parfleche pouch at his back. We were, as usual, traveling on foot.

I asked Many-Tail-Feathers to tell us his plan for the raid. We would, he said, follow down this river to where, at the mouth of

Black Coulee, it turned southward. Then keeping on due east, and passing along the north foot of the Bear Paw Mountains, we would in due time strike Little (Milk) River, and somewhere along it, perhaps where it joined Big River, we would be sure to find the camp of White Dog and his Cutthroat people.

A long way for us to go. We would have to travel anyway eighteen nights in order to reach the enemy camp; that is, if we traveled twenty miles each day.

Our trail cut across the bends of the river, so we were sometimes traveling along the timbered bottoms and again out over the plain. The night was clear; an almost full moon was shining. After we had gone ten or twelve miles from the fort, we began frightening game resting or grazing along our way: elk, deer, antelope. Near and far wolves were howling, coyotes shrilly yelping. Good sounds they were. We had no fear of attack by the wolves or the coyotes.

When in the east the sky began to whiten with the first faint light of day, our leader told me to go on ahead and kill something. I was not long in finding a few antelope, killed a buck, and was butchering it when my friends came down to help me. We turned off into the thick timber and willows bordering the river, and over a fire, almost smokeless, broiled and ate our fill of the fat meat.

Our early meal ended, Many-Tail-Feathers named Weasel Tail to go up onto the rim of the plain and watch for the possible approach of any enemies until noon when he was to come in and waken me for the afternoon watch. With that our leader went off by himself, in quiet to smoke to the gods and pray them to give him, as he slept, a vision of what might be in store for us—whether of danger to be avoided or overcome, or of our safe advance. We others, after smoking a couple of pipes, put out the fire and slept.

The day passed uneventfully. Near evening we all got together for another meal of broiled antelope meat, Many-Tail-Feathers reporting that he had not been given a vision of any kind. Well, he, because of his ownership of the sacred pipe, had great favor with the gods. If danger threatened they surely would have given him warning of it. Dusk came and we took to the trail again.

On our third morning out from the fort, we camped at the mouth of Black Coulee, and in the evening left the river and struck off northwesterly upon the plain. Three mornings later we stopped for the day in a grove of pines on the north slope of the Bear Paw Mountains. Silently, glumly, we sat around our little fire as we broiled and ate portions of a yearling buffalo that we had killed the morning before. What wrong had we done that the gods seemed to have deserted us? Was it that we were heading straight to our end at the hands of the enemy?

Many-Tail-Feathers named me to take the morning watch, and then as always went off by himself to pray for a revealing vision and sleep. I drank from the little spring near by, went down and sat in the lower edge of the pines. To the north were a few buffalo and antelope, peacefully grazing, resting, some of them going for water.

Came noon. I went up in the pines, awakened Little Otter to go on watch, told him that, so far, no enemies had come in sight. Then I stretched out where he had lain, to sleep and forget my troubles. Late in the afternoon loud singing awakened us. Many-Tail-Feathers, happily singing the wolf song, the good-luck song of warriors, came dancing toward us, and we all sat up and stared at him. Then, ending his song, he shouted to us:

"Take courage, my friends. Take courage. The gods favor us. They heard my prayers; they gave me a vision. It was that, as we were traveling, we discovered some enemies. We attacked them; some of them fell. Then I awoke. But that was enough, my friends. You all know as well as I do that a vision of falling, dying enemies means success for us."

"It does! It does!" Heavy Runner cried. And all began happily talking, telling of visions that had proved to be true. And hotheaded White Antelope said: "Well, now that we are to have success, let's broil and eat what little meat we have left and then be on our way."

Said Many-Tail-Feathers: "No. My vision does not free us from being ever cautious. We will raise no more smoke here on this high place for enemies, possibly wandering about, to see. Besides, except for antelope, game is scarce. We were lucky to find that buffalo yearling. No. We will not eat the meat we have left."

We all moved down to the edge of the pines to sit until it would be dark enough for us to resume our way. As the sun was setting, suddenly a raven, hoarsely croaking, came flying toward us from the east, circled over us several times, and still croaking, flew back eastward. Then came back, again circled over us, and flew eastward and disappeared. Silently, breathlessly, we watched it and now we knew that it, wisest of birds, true friend of the warriors, had come to urge us to keep on. Many-Tail-Feathers was the leader of the Raven Carrier band of the All Friends Society, the warrior's society of the Blackfoot tribes, so we knew the raven had come especially to give him its message.

Said he: "Now I know that we are to kill that worst of all Cutthroats, White Dog."

"But how are you going to find White Dog in the big camp of his people," I asked. "How know him?"

"Know him," almost shouted Many-Tail-Feathers. "Three of us here, Little Otter, White Antelope, and I, have twice fought the man and his companions, and twice he got away from us. So, well we know him, his appearance, his shouting to us in our own language, 'Me, I am White Dog.' So, when we find the Cutthroats' camp, we will, in the early night, while the fires are burning, look into lodge after lodge until we find him, kill him, and run for the horses that we have already taken."

"And what will we others be doing while you three seek him?"

"That you should ask a so nothing question. Of course we first go into the camp and take some of the fast buffalo horses there tied before the lodges of their owners every night. Then you others will hold them in readiness for our getaway while we seek out and kill our enemy."

So there we had it, our leader's plan for the raid. It didn't look good to us. To prowl about in the camp and lead out the horses that we needed would be dangerous enough. But for our leader, Little Otter, and White Antelope to go from lodge to lodge drawing aside, however slightly, the door curtains and peeking in looking for White Dog, well, that, we thought, was craziness. They would surely be discovered by some of the people, of evening visiting about from lodge to lodge. And then what chance for us all to get away? But we must do our best to follow our leader's orders.

Said Little Otter: "How unlucky for us if they should start out on another raid before we can get there, the way White Dog did when we came after the soldier chief's horses and bigears."

"*Ha! Ha!* How strange. You spoke my very thoughts," said White Antelope. "But on that raid, the plains were black with buffalo. And now we are lucky to find a lone yearling."

"I am thinking," said Weasel Tail, "that we should hurry to get to Little River and begin following it down. The Cutthroats may be camped well up it, right in our own country."

"True. True. Let us strike out for it right here. Follow this Little Antelope Creek down to its junction with it," White Antelope proposed, and to that we all gave quick assent.

Dusk came. We dropped into the willows along the creek, ate heartily of meat that we broiled, and moved on northeasterly in the valley of the little stream that would take us to Little River.

Dawn found us at the edge of the wide, timbered valley of our Little River, that stream that runs on top of the plain instead of a deep badlands cut like our other rivers. Near and far the antelope were quiet, a good sign that no enemies were about. We descended the short slope from the plain to the floor of the valley, entered its timber, raised a whitetail buck. It gave a few leaps, then stopped to stare at us. I shot it and we were soon broiling and eating each our favorite cuts of the meat.

Many-Tail-Feathers asked me to take the morning watch. "Not long now," he said. "Only four long nights' travel to the mouth of the river by way of its winding course."

Three mornings later, at dawn, we stopped where the river was running south instead of easterly as heretofore; and my companion said that, on the following morning, we should arrive at, or anywhere near, its junction with Big (Missouri) River. So far we had seen no enemies, nor any signs of them since leaving the Bear Paw Mountains. But now Many-Tail-Feathers, appointing Heavy Runner to take the morning watch, said to him: "Be very alert this morning. Constantly keep looking at the plain and the valley, far and near. It is that we may be close to the camp of the Cutthroats. If so, you should discover riders out from it in quest of meat."

Taking up his rifle, Heavy Runner at once set out for the rim of the plain, and Many-Tail-Feathers as always strode off into the timber to rest apart from us. We others smothered the fire and stretched out to sleep.

The sun shining hotly on my face through a parting in the tree branches awakened me. Very thirsty, I went to the river to drink and was surprised by Many-Tail-Feathers coming and joining me on the shore. Stepping noiselessly across the sand and to my side, he startled me. Looking up, I knew at once from the worried expression of his face that something was wrong with him. "*Kai yiwahts?*" ("What troubles you?") I asked.

"My vision. It was bad. I heard women wailing for their dead. It was night. The lodges were just dim shapes in the darkness. Though I could not see them, I could plainly hear the women mourning for their dead. You know what that means. It is warning that there is trouble ahead for us."

"But your good vision, your vision of us killing enemies; and then the raven circling over us, beckoning us eastward—all that, you said, meant good luck for us."

"So it did, but this, my new vision, brings all that to nothing; it is sure warning that we are heading into danger."

"Well, what are we to do about it?"

"Be more than ever cautious, watchful; pray now, all of us. Pray to the Above Ones to keep us safe, to give us success against our enemies," he answered. With that he led back to our sleeping companions, awoke them, told of his bad vision; and soon we were gathered in a circle, smoking in turn his pipe, singing his elk-tongue pipe songs after each of his fervent prayers to the sky gods for our safety and success. And so to the last one of his songs:

> *Raven says, my medicine, it is strong, it is powerful.*
> *Enemies I seek. I have found them.*
> *Dead on the ground they lie.*
> *My medicine, it is powerful.*

The brief ceremony ending, we were all happy again, alert, nerved up to meet whatever danger might be in store for us.

As we were about to try to get more sleep, came Heavy Runner hurrying in to us from the rim of the plain and exclaiming: "Riders to the south of us! Many riders running a herd of buffalo on the plain to the east of the river. So not far below there must be the Cutthroats' camp!"

Exciting news. We all wanted to see the enemy hunters, so, sheltered by the timber and then the tall sagebrush, we moved into a patch of cherry trees on the edge of the plain, and from there had a good view of them. All of forty men, some three miles off, down from their horses butchering their kill. And then came many women riding in to help them with their work. Proof enough that the Cutthroats' camp could not be far below us.

Said Many-Tail-Feathers: "Tonight, the Above Ones helping us, we kill that worst of them, White Dog, and get off with some of their horses. So now, all of you, lie down, sleep, so that you may be strong for what you have to do. I will, myself, keep watch upon the Cutthroats, and later on, call upon one of you to take my place."

We found it impossible, there so near our enemies, really to sleep. We dozed at times, often sat up to look at them, and at last, in mid-afternoon, saw them string back down the valley, their horses loaded with meat and hides.

Then Many-Tail-Feathers said: "Remember this, all of you. Our one and hard undertaking is to kill our worst enemy, White Dog."

After that, none spoke for a long time. Serious were our thoughts. We were this coming night to enter the enemy camp, and with what results? Well we knew the danger of it. I knew that each of my companions was praying as I was. I touched my sacred helper in the little bag at my breast and whispered: "Hear me, Sacred Helper. Help me. Give me to survive this night."

Said Many-Tail-Feathers then: "Take care. Let us go."

The sun was still an hour or so from setting. Many-Tail-Feathers leading, we started on, keeping just within the edge of a long grove bordering the river. It ended well above a sharp bend of the valley, so we were obliged to keep on in the open until we could reach the shelter of another grove. As we were about to round the bend we heard singing below it, men singing a high-keyed song strange to our ears, undoubtedly a war song. It brought us to sudden stand, made our hearts beat fast.

"Enemies! A war party! Coming up!" Many-Tail-Feathers cried. He turned, looked back at the grove we had left, shook his head, muttering: "Too far. Too far." Then pointing to a grove of rose-brush and sage to our right, he told us to hurry into it.

In no time we were kneeling in it peering through the tops of it at the bend and wondering how many of the enemies we were so soon to see coming up around it. Many-Tail-Feathers saying this to us: "Now, my friends, mind this that I tell you. Though they be only a few, we must not shoot into them unless they discover us here. It is that we must not spoil our chance for finding and killing White Dog this night."

Ha! He had no more than said that when a lone man appeared rounding the bend. A tall man walking swiftly, easily, wearing a white blanket capote, a fur cap, carrying a gun, its barrel resting in the crook of his left arm, a bulging pouch at his left side. Well back of him, down around the bend, the shrill singing continued as though the singers had come to a stand or were dancing.

Said Many-Tail-Feathers, excitedly: "*Ha!* He appears to be White Dog, this oncoming man."

"He is White Dog," Little Otter exclaimed.

"Yes, White Dog himself," White Antelope hissed.

"Mine. Mine alone at last to kill," our leader declared.

"You must not shoot him now, Many-Tail-Feathers," said Weasel Tail. "We have first to see his followers. They may be too many for us to fight."

Our leader's answer to that was quickly to aim his rifle at the man and fire. The bullet broke his left leg between ankle and knee, for we saw the foot flap as he went down upon his knees.

Yelling triumphantly, Many-Tail-Feathers sprang up, fired again, hit him somewhere in the body, ran toward him, we all following him. Like us, White Dog had a Henry rifle and though grievously wounded he managed to fire it at us three times, his first shot killing

Little Otter, his third tearing the muscles of my left arm just below the shoulder. Then as he weakly dropped the rifle, Many-Tail-Feathers was at his side, picked up his gun, struck him with it, told him how long he had sought him, that now he must die, now after all his killings of the Pikunis, of Many-Tail-Feather's father, his grandfather, his other relatives.

"Heavy Runner, my long-time friend, you may take his scalp. I have done with him."

Heavy Runner grasped the top hair, cut White Dog's scalp across the back of his head, yanked it forward and severed it at the forehead —long, shining hair braids and all.

Many-Tail-Feathers gave the groaning one a finishing shot just as his followers, fifteen or twenty of them, rounded the bend and began shooting at us as they came running on, almost at once killing White Antelope.

But we remained right where we were, returning their fire, and had far the best of it in that our weapons were repeating rifles; theirs, most of them, single-shot Springfield rifles. They could not keep on against our rapid, withering fire. Almost at once we killed four of them, and then one more as they abruptly turned and ran back out of our sight around the bend.

"The dog-faces! The bad dog-faces! They have killed brave Little Otter, brave White Antelope. Come on. We must take the scalps and the guns of our kills," Heavy Runner said.

"No. They will be coming up along the rim of the plain, there safely to shoot at us. We must get back up into that grove above," Many-Tail-Feathers replied, as he took up White Dog's rifle and stripped off his cartridge belt and pouch.

Said Heavy Runner, and angrily: "Go then. Desert me. I shall count coup on our kills off there, take proof of this that we have done to them, take scalps for the poor widows and children of our killed friends to dance with."

"Too dangerous," Many-Tail-Feathers argued. "Scalp enough, that of White Dog." But Heavy Runner was gone.

"Useless to argue with him, the strong-minded one," said Many-Tail-Feathers. "Well, Weasel Tail, Bear Head, take up the guns, the belongings of our poor, dead friends. Oh, too bad, too bad that we can't bury them."

My wound was bleeding, painful. Before we were halfway back to the grove I was feeling faint. Many-Tail-Feathers called a halt, relieved me of my rifle and pouch, and was binding my wound with a piece of my shirt when, down on the rim of the plain, guns boomed, and we saw Heavy Runner fall, then jump up and start shooting.

"Not killed," said Many-Tail-Feathers. "Not far enough on his way to get the scalps, either. Now he may join us again."

The Cutthroats did not come on after us, well knowing what we could do to them with our repeating rifles and not knowing that we did not have others close by. They went back up on the plain, doubtless to send one of their number down to their camp for help, and to keep watch on us.

The sun had set when we got back to the grove and sat down to talk over our situation, the while we watched for our enemies along the rim of the plain. Heavy Runner joined us, sullen at his foolish act, not wounded severely. We would have to leave the grove before the whole force of the Cutthroats could come up and surround it, Many-Tail-Feathers said. They would expect us to try to escape them by going up the valley, keeping well within the timber. But we would not do that. We would, instead, cross the river and travel northward on the plain until break of day, then lie hidden until night when we could safely strike out for our camp.

"But, Chief, we are not to try to raid the Cutthroats' camp, take some of their fast horses?" Weasel Tail asked.

"No. Failing to find us here, they will keep close watch upon their horses for many nights to come. So is it that we are going home on foot."

"Going home," I growled. "Our two good friends killed, two of us wounded, we here in a most dangerous situation. Many-Tail-Feathers, what now of your good-luck vision, the good-luck coming and calling of the raven?"

"True they proved to be. I killed White Dog, worst one of all our enemies, did I not? That our friends were killed was by no fault of mine. Somehow they failed to get the protection of the Above Ones."

Even though we well knew that our enemies were out on the rim of the plain, or closer, keeping watch upon our grove, we could not see them. When night came, they would, we thought, move to the upper end of it, expecting us to leave it there. Of us all, Many-Tail-Feathers was alone cheerful, confident that all was to be well with us.

Worriedly we others sat, expecting, dreading to hear, to see, a horde of Cutthroats arrive from their camp and surround the grove. We ate the last of the broiled meat that I had saved.

Dusk came at last. We moved to the river, found a shallow crossing, and when it was really dark took off our moccasins and leggings, waded noiselessly to the other shore, dressed, and slowly, silently stole through the tall sagebrush across the valley, then into and up a coulee. As we neared the head of it, we heard a horde of Cutthroats, yelling and singing, ride into the valley and, apparently, on to the grove that we had left.

Said Many-Tail-Feathers: "There they are, my friends. I knew that they would come. My sacred medicine warned me of it. Just in time we left the timber. All for nothing will be their search for us. *Ha!* It is for us to laugh."

"Not I. Our two friends killed. It is not for me to laugh," I answered him.

"Nor I. Nor I," the others mumbled, for our hearts were low.

Well, we saw no more of the Cutthroats. Came morning. We had traveled all night over the plain, and well out from the river, and with the dawn we turned down into the valley, shot a deer, feasted on it, and slept—I, somewhat uneasily because of my wound. However, it proved to be not very painful. From there on, night after night, we traveled our homeward way, and on the seventeenth morning of it, we neared Fort Conrad, Many-Tail-Feathers urging us to join him in singing the victory song and dancing, waving White Dog's scalp, and shouting that he had killed the worst one of the Cutthroats.

Came running the women, the men more slowly, to meet us. There was rejoicing for what Many-Tail-Feathers had done. But came, too, the widows of White Antelope and Little Otter. And there was mourning in the camp. Alone, our leader was happy over this, our raid on the Cutthroats; but all of us knew that we had done what had to be done to rid the Pikunis of their long-time enemy White Dog.[1]

[1] In 1939, Mr. and Mrs. Schultz visited the Assiniboine Indians at Fort Belknap and there became acquainted with an old Assiniboine named Returning Hunter, who had been a member of White Dog's party at the time of his death. Returning Hunter was actually one of the few who escaped with his life. *Apikuni* and Return-ing Hunter re-enacted the drama of the battle and the killing of White Dog, each speaking his own language (*Apikuni*'s knowledge of Blackfoot was extraordinary) and gesticulating dramatically and dynamically, as Mrs. Schultz looked on. They were agreed on the details of the action, and *Apikuni* took advantage of the oppor-tunity to verify the facts of that famous exploit, to fix the exact location, and to ascertain the precise details of the action from the Assiniboine point of view.

CHAPTER TWO

Buffalo Robes

FORT CONRAD consisted of two long rows of connecting log buildings paralleling the river and about fifty feet apart, with a stable and corral running from one to the other at their west end. In the south row were the office, trade room, warehouse, and one living room. The remainder of the living quarters was in the north row. In the summer of 1879 these were occupied by Kipp and his wife, Double-Strike Woman; their adopted children, William and Maggie Fitzpatrick; Kipp's mother, Earth Woman, and her close and constant companion, Crow Woman; Hiram D. Upham, clerk, and his wife, Lance Woman; Frank Pearson and Charles Rose, half-blood employees; and my wife, Fine Shield Woman,[2] and myself, I fallen sadly from grace. Two years before I had obtained permission from my mother and my guardian to go west for a buffalo hunt, with the distinct understanding that I would return in the autumn to continue my studies at Peekskill Military Academy, preparatory for entering West Point. But I had broken my word; the wild, free life of the West had so entranced me that I could not go back.

In this summer of 1879, the Pikunis, by our Indian Bureau misnamed Blackfeet, were camped at and around their agency on Badger Creek, thirty miles to the west of us. Their brother tribes, the Bloods and the Blackfeet, were in Alberta—the former on Belly

---

[1]Published in *The Great Falls Tribune* (April 7, 1935).

[2] *Mutsi-Awotan-Ahki*, the Nätahki of James W. Schultz, *My Life as an Indian* (Doubleday, Page & Company, 1907).

River, the latter on Bow River. A few lodges of the Pikunis were camping near us and subsisting on antelope still plentiful in that part of the country. In the previous winter Kipp had camp traded with the Pikunis in the Bear Paw Mountains (Little Rockies) with fair success, and now, in August, came White Calf, Little Dog, Running Crane, Little Plume, and other prominent ones of the Pikunis to plan with him for the coming winter hunt and trade. Some were for going again to the Bear Paw country; others suggested the Cypress Hills; but most were in favor of wintering on Judith River, as a war party of Pikunis, recently returned from a raid upon the Crows, had reported plenty of buffalo from Arrow Creek to the Judith, and south of it to the Yellowstone. So, after long talk, interspersed with many rounds of the big stone bowl, the long-stemmed council pipe, it was decided that Kipp should build a trading post on *Otokwi Tuktai* (Yellow River, the Judith) at the mouth of *Kaksimi Tuktai* (Sage Creek, as the whites had also named it), and that the tribe would winter near it and trade only with him. Also, the chiefs readily agreed to Kipp's proposal that this Yellow River post should be a dry, no-whisky, trading post.

Kipp had a bull train—three eight-yoke teams and six wagons; Long John Forgy, wagon boss—that was freighting profitably between Fort Benton and Helena and Fort Macleod, so he decided not to use it in this new undertaking. Thus, leaving our womenfolks to winter at Fort Conrad, Hiram Upham in charge of it, on a day late in August we set out with five four-horse teams and wagons for the Judith. Two of the teamsters were half-brothers of Kipp's wife, and Dick Kipp and Billy Upham were along. Yes, and good, brave Crow Woman and her handsome adopted daughter of sixteen, Flag Woman, came along to cook for us. And Frank Pearson's wife made such a howl about being separated from him that she came, too.

In those days, the itinerant fur traders were known either as I. G. Baker & Company men or T. C. Power & Brother men, according to which one of the firms they favored. Kipp was one of the former kind, so at I. G. Baker & Company's store in Fort Benton we loaded our wagons with trade goods and various necessities for cabins and kitchen. Then, reinforced by Politte Pepion and his four-horse team, we ferried across the river and proceeded on our way, on Shonkin Creek passing the sheep ranch of Paris Gibson, who was later to be the father of Great Falls city. A fine man, a real man he was. At Arrow Creek—oh, welcome sight!—we discovered ahead of us several buffalo herds, whereupon Crow Woman in her Arikara language broke into prayers of thanks to the gods.

Hers had been a life of terrible experiences. When a young woman, a member of a Crow war party, swooping in on a small camp of Arikara buffalo hunters, had captured her, and had kept her for some years, more as a slave than as one of her captor's three wives. Then, in a fight between the Crows and the Bloods, she had been seized by one of the latter tribe, Spotted Elk, and she became his fourth wife and a drudge for his three Blood wives. Many years passed, unhappily for her, and then, one day when the Bloods were trading in Fort Benton, she had come face to face with Kipp's Mandan mother. Though of different tribes, they had been close friends in their girlhood days. So now they hugged and kissed one another, and with tears Crow Woman told of her years of suffering under one and the other of her captors. Said Earth Woman when she had finished her tale: "Dear friend, here and now your troubles end. You shall not live with that Blood man another day. I will take you from him, to live with me."

With that Earth Woman went straight to Spotted Elk about it. He laughed, said Crow Woman was a fine worker, very useful to him; he would not for any consideration let her leave him. Earth Woman offered him a new many-shots gun (Henry rifle) for her. No, she was worth many rifles, many horses to him. To which Earth Woman replied: "Either you take the rifle and let her go, or I will have the white seizers (soldiers), for your stealing of her, shut you up for many winters to come."

"No. No. Go not to them about it. Give me the many-shots gun and she is yours," he quickly answered.

Herds of buffalo, numerous bands of antelope, fled from us as we neared the junction of the Judith River and Sage Creek, and we saw a number of elk and deer when we crossed the river to make camp in the timber just above the mouth of the creek. While the others were busy with that, I, with willow pole and line, hook baited with grasshoppers, hurried to the river and was soon yanking from a deep pool my first Montana trout, a beauty of a pound or more; these were trout so different from those trout of the Adirondacks of New York, in which I had spent many a vacation. I deeply regretted that I had not brought west my light fly rod, reel, and book of flies, for bait fishing was not sport to me. I caught, cleaned, and fried crisply brown two panfuls of trout, and then, to my surprise, Kipp alone joined me in eating of them. It was, I learned, that the Blackfoot tribes believed fish to be the property of the dread *Suyi Tupi* (Water People), monsters of human form who inhabit the rivers and lakes and at every opportunity seize unwary swimmers and draw them down to their underwater homes, there to kill them.

Early on the following morning, we began cutting and hauling logs for our post, building it in the large cottonwood grove in the forks of the river and the creek. We completed the work early in October. One cabin, sixteen by forty feet, was our trade room and storehouse; the other cabin of three rooms was our kitchen, occupied by Crow Woman and daughter, and by Pearson and wife; Kipp and I had the third room. Our teamsters, when present, slept in the warehouse. Rude our post but sufficient for our needs.

The Pikunis and a few lodges of the Bloods arrived soon after we completed the post, and came, too, one who was to become and always remain a close friend of mine, Eli Guardipee, named by the Pikunis *Isinamakan*, "Takes Gun Ahead." He was of that family for which so many places in the north are named, as, for instance, the Guardipee Crossing of Bow River. His keen-witted, handsome mother was a Shoshoni woman. He was but a year older than I; tall, slender, very intelligent, kind of heart, brave to a fault; and the most successful hunter, the surest shot that I have ever known.

The fur of the buffalo did not become prime until November so we would not be getting any tanned robes over our counter until December. But with the arrival of the Pikunis we began buying from them daily a hundred and more hides of deer, elk, and antelope, so plentiful were they upon the near plains and mountains. We gave one dollar's worth of merchandise for a hide. We had no scales, no wrapping paper, no paper sacks; our customers furnished their own receptacles for their purchases. A pint cup, not a pound, was our standard of measurement. Sugar was twenty-five cents per cup; coffee, fifty cents; tea, fifty cents; flour, three cups for fifty cents; and so on. Tobacco was two dollars a pound; cartridges, two dollars a box; and other merchandise that we had in stock—red trade cloth, blue trade cloth, calico, gingham, needles and thread, baking powder, Chinese vermilion, axes, knives, pots, and frying pans—went at better than 100 per cent profit. Our prices exorbitant? No. The Pikunis were rich; meat was their staff of life, and they had plenty of it. All that we traded to them for their buffalo robes and furs were —except cartridges, knives, and axes—luxuries that they did not need.

White were the four hundred new, buffalo-leather lodge-skins of the Pikuni camp; those of the Sun priests, medicine men, painted in vivid colors with symbols of their sky gods, sun, moon, and the stars, and the birds and animals of their visions, their dreams. At the rear top of every lodge-skin was painted in red and black a small figure resembling a Maltese cross. It was the symbol for the butterfly, believed to be the giver of good dreams.

So long as they had plenty of buffalo for the killing of them, no people anywhere on earth were happier, more content, than those of the Blackfoot tribes. Meat was *nitápi waksin*, "real food"; all other eatables were *kistapi waksin*, "nothing foods." As meat and hides were needed, the men hunted. That was not work; it was exciting sport. To the women fell all of the lodge work, yet they had much leisure time; none worked as hard as the average white farmer's wife.

With the break of day, the women started their lodge fires, and the men, wrapped only in robes or blankets, herded their boys, from three-year-olds up, to the river to bathe. In summer, in winter, regardless of the weather, that was their daily custom. When unable to find open water, they dropped their wraps and rolled in the snow, then hurried home to dress. The baths, they said, inured them to the cold; enabled them to hunt and butcher their kills in severest weather without even freezing their fingertips. In summer the women daily flocked to the stream for a swim; in winter they had sweat baths in small lodges built for that purpose alone.

In the daytime, save for the shouting of children at play, the great camp was quiet; but with the setting of the sun it livened up. Men began shouting invitations to their friends to come and feast and smoke with them. Members of the various branches of the *Ikuni Kahtsi* (All Friends warriors society) got together to sing and dance. At once in a hundred lodges there were various social gatherings—gatherings of old men, young men, old women, young women, chiefs and leading warriors, Sun priests. Evening always found me joining one or another of the lodge-fire circles to listen to the talk, and so I heard great tales of war, of hunting, and of the wondrous doings of the gods. In greatest demand were the tellers of humorous stories; they had so many invitations to social gatherings that they were rarely found at home. And theirs was clean humor; one never heard any obscenity in the lodges of the Blackfoot tribes.

What George Catlin had to say of the Mandans he visited in 1832 —that they were kindly, courteous hosts—was equally true of the old-time Blackfeet. A man giving a feast-and-smoke stepped outside his lodge and shouted his invitations. One by one the guests came and were seated according to their standing in the tribe. The more prominent a man was—such as chief, Sun priest, warrior—the nearer he would be placed to the host. When all were seated, the women of the lodge placed dishes of food, the choicest that they had—boiled or broiled buffalo tongues, buffalo dorsal ribs, berry pemmican, stewed berries—before them, and the host, not eating, began cutting finely a mixture of tobacco for the smokes. At the same time he started the talk about something of general interest, or, perhaps, called on a certain one to tell of some thrilling experience he had had in hunting or at war; or, as often happened, a Sun priest would talk about the gods or relate a powerful vision that the gods had given him in the night. As the talk went on, all ate slowly, moderately, and in most pleasant manner, of their portions. Contrary to the general opinion of them, the Indians, anyhow the Blackfeet, were not gorgers of great quantities of food.

When all had finished eating, the host passed the filled big-stone bowl with its long stem to someone of the circle to light from the fire—always a Sun priest if one were present—and he, touching a coal or burning stick to the mixture, blew a whiff of smoke to the sky, exclaiming: "Oh, Sun! Oh, Above People! Pity us; help us." Then another whiff to the ground with: "Oh, Earth Mother! Pity us; help us." With that, he leisurely drew a few whiffs of smoke from the pipe, inhaling deeply, and from him the pipe went from hand to hand straight to the end man of the row, then from him to be smoked by the others in turn until it returned to the host. So was it smoked from east to west, thus imitating the daily courses of the sun. Sun priests in the row of guests grasped the stem of the pipe with both hands when taking, smoking, and passing it on, imitating the actions of the bear, sacred animal, when seizing anything. No others were privileged to do that. (Then, too, the Sun priests' special name for the bear was *páksi kwoyi*, "sticky mouth." The common people called the animal *kaiyo*, "lost.")

The pipe smoked out, the host cleaned the bowl, allowed it to cool, then refilled it, and it went again the length of the row of guests. Generally, it was filled and smoked three times in the course of an hour or so of pleasant talk. Then at last, ostentatiously knocking the pipe bowl upon his tobacco cutting board, the host loudly exclaimed, "*Kyi! Itsinitsi!*" ("There! It is burned out!"). Whereat the guests arose, filed out of the lodge, and went their several ways. What a boon that would be to civilized hosts so at will to dismiss their guests!

Persistent hunting and killing of cow buffalo began in November, and the women were soon busily converting the heavily furred hides into well-tanned robes. It was arduous work. The hides were fleshed; that is, cleaned of all adhering scraps of meat and fat, then laced into lodgepole frames, where they dried as stiff and firm as thin boards. Then, standing upon the hide, smooth side up, the tanner, with an elkhorn-handled, steel-bladed instrument the shape of a hoe, chipped it to about one-half its original thickness and rubbed it with grease. When that was thoroughly soaked in, the hide was then well smeared with a mixture of boiled liver and brains, folded and rolled, and laid away for several days in order for the mixture to neutralize its glue. Then came the hardest of the work: the tanner for an hour or so at a time rubbed and seesawed the hide against upright, stretched thongs of rawhide, until, at last, it became almost as soft and pliable as velvet. The result: a well-tanned cow buffalo robe for which we gave five dollars worth of trade goods.

Persistent hunting of the buffalo herds caused them to drift ever farther eastward from us, until, by the beginning of January, the nearest of them were from Armell Creek eastward. From that time on, the hunters, with their accompanying women helpers, had to go farther and farther eastward and southward to make their kills—hard work in the intense cold and quite deep snow. In early February, when returning from a hunt, one member of a party froze to death, and others were so badly frosted that they were crippled for life.

Beginning in December, we daily had a good trade for buffalo robes. Since we had no whisky, some of our customers occasionally went up to Reed and Bowle's place (Reed's Fort) for a spree. So was it that one day, in a drunken row up there, our friend Bear Chief killed a Red River half blood named Flory.

Ours was a contented, prosperous camp when, early in March, dire disaster came upon us. Arrived one afternoon from Fort Benton, Lieutenant Crouse with a dozen mounted infantrymen, and he tremblingly announced that he had come at once to escort the Pikunis back to their own country, to their agency on Badger Creek. This he gave out at a gathering of the Pikuni chiefs and warriors, with Kipp as interpreter. It was, he said, that "Colonel" Henry Brooks (a rancher close above us) complained that the Pikunis were killing his cattle. That, of course, could not be allowed. Therefore the Pikunis must go.

Roared Chief Running Crane: "That white man is a liar. We have killed none of his white horns (cattle). We would be foolish to kill them when we have constantly all the real meat (buffalo) that we want."

Said the head chief, White Calf: "Our hunters have seen this white man's white horns grazing with our buffalo even as far down as Bear River (Musselshell). That is where his white horns have gone."

Then Little Plume: "Soldier chief, are you crazy? You say that we must return to our country. This, right here where we are, is our country."

Lieutenant Crouse: "Not yours, this part of the country. Your country is from Marias River and Missouri River north to the country of the Red Coats."

White Calf: "Soldier chief, you are mistaken. Twenty-five summers ago, where this river and Big River come together, we made treaty with men that Your and Our Grandfather (the president) had sent to us. That treaty was put in writing. Those men signed it; our fathers signed it, put their names to it. I, myself, saw them sign it. That writing said that from the Red Coat's country south to Musselshell River, and from the Backbone (Rocky Mountains) east to the mouth of Little River (Milk), all was our country. Right here, we are in our own country. We will not move up to our agency; no buffalo up there; we would starve."

When Kipp had interpreted that to Crouse, the poor fellow fairly trembled, and after long thought, replied: "Mr. Kipp, have they never been told that President Grant by executive order opened to settlement the country between the Missouri and the Yellowstone, and that President Hayes, also by executive order, opened the country from the Missouri north to the Marias River?"

"No, they know nothing about it," Kipp replied, "and I won't tell them of it for God knows what might then happen."

"Then what am I to do? What can I do?" Crouse whimpered.

"Just tell them that your orders are your orders; that they will have to pack up and go. Then I, myself, will tell them something that I think will work," Kipp answered.

Lieutenant Crouse: "Yes. Tell them this: 'My friends, I feel very sorry for you. I know that it will be great hardship for you to go back north, away from the buffalo, but I can't help it. My chiefs have ordered me to escort you up there. You will have to pack up and start tomorrow.' "

Barely had Kipp finished interpreting that when the big crowd of men surrounding us began to yell: "We will not leave here. We must kill these soldiers." "This is our country. We will not leave it." "Hurry, get your guns. We will kill these dog-face soldiers."

But Kipp had sprung up, shouting and signing: "Listen. Listen to me." And when all had quieted down he turned and said to the chiefs: "White Calf, Little Dog, Little Plume, Running Crane, be wise. Well you remember what white soldiers did to a camp of Pikunis on Marias River, ten winters ago? Without cause, without reason, they sneaked up to it while they slept and killed nearly all of them there, men, women, and children alike.[3] If now you refuse to do what this soldier chief asks of you, hundreds and hundreds of their kind will come, with their big-mouth guns (cannons) and kill you all off."

Said White Calf to the other chiefs: "My friends, this that Raven Quiver tells us is true. Because of our helpless ones, we cannot fight the white soldiers, killers that they are of women and children, even newborn ones at their mothers' breasts. So is it that we have to do as this soldier chief tells us. Say you not so?"

"We are powerless to do otherwise," Little Dog answered. The others sadly nodded assent. "Then go, scatter out, calm our young men, our hotheads, lest they get us into trouble," White Calf advised them, and turning to Lieutenant Crouse, said: "Because you and your kind are killers of women and children, we have to do as you say. But we cannot possibly move tomorrow. We must have at least three days to pack up our belongings, make ready for the long trail back to our agency." To that Crouse readily agreed, and the conference ended.

A little later, White Calf came into our trade room and said to Kipp: "This soldier chief, what did he mean by saying that this is not our country?"

"Will you promise, if I tell you that, to make no trouble now about it?" Kipp asked. And the chief nodded assent. Kipp continued: "My friend, it is that one of Your and Our Grandfathers gave to his white kind all of your country between Big River (Missouri) and Elk River (Yellowstone). And then, not long ago, another of Your and Our Grandfathers did the same with your country between Big River and Bear River."[4]

At that White Calf all but collapsed; he fairly groaned; and after a little, muttering, "Oh, what thieves, what liars are the whites,"

[3] See "The Baker Massacre," chap. XX of this volume.
[4] For information about the executive orders see James M. Hamilton, *From Wilderness to Statehood* (Portland, Oregon, Binfords & Mort, 1957), 190–91; J. W. Schultz, *Sahtaki and I*, 232–39.

he turned and left us. There was no singing, laughing, happy chatter in the camp of the Pikunis that night, nor for many a night thereafter.

Myself, I personally knew several of those greedy ruthless Montanans who, working through equally venial senators, congressmen, and officials of the Indian Bureau, caused that 1855 "Stevens Treaty" with the Blackfeet, Gros Ventres, and other tribes to be twice broken. But, for the sake of their living descendents, I will not name them. However, I somehow cannot believe that President Grant and President Hayes knew what they were doing when they put their signatures to the papers authorizing the thefts, the two greatest wrongs that our government ever perpetrated upon its Indian wards. For some years the Blackfeet, Pikunis, have been trying—so far in vain—to be recompensed for the vast territory that was stolen from them.

The northward trek of the Pikunis began on time, and we went with them, for during the winter our four-horse teams and wagons had hauled our buffalo robes and furs to Fort Benton about as fast as we had traded for them. In all we had taken 1,800 buffalo robes; 3,000 elk, deer, antelope hides; and a few fox and beaver skins. Our progress was slow, for the long, constant, and far hunting of the Pikunis had worn most of their horses to skin and bones. More than two hundred of them died before we arrived at Fort Benton. I happened to be present when Lieutenant Crouse met his commanding officer, Colonel Moale, on the street. At once the Colonel began scolding him for his delay in bringing the Indians in. Crouse interrupted with: "Great Caesar's ghost, Colonel, I could not help it!" At which Moale roared: ". . . you, Crouse, if you can't swear like a man, don't swear at all!"

On our way from Fort Benton to Fort Conrad, about two hundred more of the Pikuni horses died from exhaustion. There the Pikunis remained with us for several months, tanning and trading to us their remaining buffalo hides and the skins of the antelope and deer that they daily killed.

No sooner were we home than Kipp began planning for the next winter's trade. He talked with the Pikuni chiefs about it, then, mounting a good horse, went north to consult with the Bloods and

Blackfeet. Agreement was soon made that we should build a post on the Missouri, not far above the mouth of the Musselshell River, and that all three tribes would winter thereabout and trade with us.

FINAL HUNT ON THE GREAT HERDS (1880–1881)[1]

So CAME JUNE, 1880. We at Fort Conrad were none too cheerful; we were, for the last time, to build a trading post, get the last of the buffalo robes that the Blackfoot tribes could tan; for the end of the buffalo herds was near. The center of the remaining herds was approximately the junction of the Missouri and the Musselshell rivers. The Blackfeet and the Bloods of Alberta had promised *Mastún-opachis* ("Raven Quiver," Joseph Kipp) that wherever there in that last-of-the-buffalo county he would build a fort, there they would come to hunt and trade with him.

Kipp decided that he would locate at Carroll, some thirty miles above the mouth of the Musselshell, where, some years previously, Colonel Broadwater, Matt Carroll, and others had attempted to organize a short freight line from the Missouri River steamboats to Helena. The attempt had been short-lived. Early in June, Kipp went with his bull train, Long John Forgy, train master, to Fort Benton, and there loaded it with trade goods and other necessaries and sent it on to that point, then returned to Fort Conrad.

On June 10 we ourselves set out for that point with three four-horse teams and wagons, with Charles Rose (Yellow Fish), Frank Pearson (Horns), and Comes-with-Rattles as drivers. Kipp, his mother Earth Woman, Crow Woman and her adopted daughter Flag Woman, Eli Guardipee and I were passengers. We left Hiram Upham in charge of the fort, and Kipp and I left our wives there. We feared to take them down into that wild country.

Arriving in Fort Benton, the teams were loaded with trade goods and sent on—Kipp, Guardipee, and I going down later on the steamboat *Red Cloud* with more trade goods. Genial, fearless Charles Williams was the captain of the I. G. Baker & Company boat. We

[1] Originally published in *The Great Falls Tribune* (November 3, 1935).

left Fort Benton early in the morning. At the mouth of Arrow Creek we first saw buffalo, a small herd of them, and from there on herds of them were constantly in sight.

For many miles below the mouth of Marias River the narrow valley of the Missouri is a miniature Grand Canyon, its cliffs weirdly carved by winds and rains. Kipp, Guardipee, and I sat with Captain Williams on the upper deck enjoying the impressive scenery—Guardipee with his rifle at his side. As we neared the mouth of Eagle Creek, we saw a bighorn ram standing on the shelf of a sheer cliff, interestedly looking down at the swiftly moving boat.

"I'll kill it," Guardipee exclaimed.

"Too far. You can't," I said.

The ram was all of 250 yards above us. Without answer Guardipee raised his rifle, sighted, fired, and the ram leaped, plunged from the cliff down into the river with a resounding splash. Captain Williams ran to the pilothouse, himself took the wheel, and shouted to his roustabouts. They soon had the ram on deck, his pilgrim passengers to have their first, and probably last feast of juicy bighorn steaks. I have said before, and I say again, that Eli Guardipee was the most accurate rifleman I ever knew.

Late in the afternoon we arrived at Carroll, tied up at a twenty-foot cut bank in which was a narrow, sloping trail running up onto the upper part of the bottom. That was a sagebrush flat; below was a large grove of cottonwoods in which Long John Forgy and his bullwhackers were getting out logs for our post. Of the Broadwater-Carroll buildings none remained. At the extreme upper end of the bottom was a small log building owned by Augustus Tyler, who had some trade with the wood-hawks located here and there up and down the river, furnishing cordwood to the steamboats. At the time he was in Fort Benton having a good spree. I went up into the cabin and there on its floor was his assistant—I will not name him—dead drunk. He was a Virginian, a gentleman; his one failing, drink. Later Kipp pitied him, cared for him for years until he died in the Fort Benton hospital. He was but one of the old-timers whom Kipp fed, clothed, and cared for until they died. As I have said, Kipp's Black-

foot name was Raven Quiver. It should have been Great Heart. He
was ever a father to the poor and afflicted.

By September 1 our trading post was finished. The main log, earth-
roofed building was one hundred by forty feet with a partition at
the upper part, twenty-five by forty feet, which was our trade room.
In its southwest corner Kipp and I had our bed; beside it was an old
Wells-Fargo safe, its door-like brass key quaint and large. There
were two counters; back of them were shelves loaded with groceries
and dry goods. Behind this building was one of three rooms, our
kitchen and dining room, and quarters for our cook and several
employees. In our warehouse, as we called the greater part of the
post, was a $6,000 stock of trade goods. An upriver steamboat from
St. Louis brought us sixty barrels of good, blue-ribbon whisky that
Kipp had ordered. We were afraid of the United States marshal and
dared not have it in our post; hence we built a separate cabin for it
and had a man named Hewie in charge of it. When the Indians arrived and wanted whisky as a part of their purchases, we gave them
an order to Hewie for it. We built another small cabin for smoking
buffalo tongues.

North and south of us the plains were black with buffalo herds.
Daily they came down into our bottom to drink at the river and
turn back onto the plain to graze again. It was their mating season,
and from afar we could hear the coming of a herd by the deep moaning of the bulls. Like deep thunder it was, so different from the
bellowing of domestic bulls. Now and then a herd in this mating
season would come down off the plain at a swift run, plunge into
the river, cross it, and wander up onto the plain on its other side. With
some of our spare boards I had built a skiff. One day I said to Kipp:
"When the buffalo are crossing the river, let's go out and catch
some of the calves and raise them."

"*Ha!* Where's the milk, where the hay to feed them? And even
if we could raise a few, what good to us?"

I could not answer. But in that same year, Charles Allard and
Michell Pablo caught a few buffalo calves, drove them over into
the Flathead country, with the result that the Canadian government

paid $40,000 for the herd. It was the foundation of the famous Wainright, Alberta, herd, now numbering many thousands. Yearly some of them are shipped into the far north, the Peace River country, to interbreed with the huge black buffalo of that woody section. There they thrive under the watchful care of the Northwest Mounted Police.

First of our friends to arrive were the Blackfeet. We saw their mile-long caravan heading into the bottom across from us, and I hurried in my skiff to meet them. A number of the leaders of the tribe were down off their horses gathered on the sandy shore. Well clothed, well armed they were—men of impressive dignity. Springing from the skiff, I said: "I come as a messenger from Raven Quiver. He asks Crow Big Feet to come smoke and eat with him."

Stepped forward from the row of them the most keenly, intelligently featured Indian I have ever known—not tall, not heavy, but of a wonderfully dignified appearance. Taking my hand, he said: "You speak our language well, young white man. I am eager to visit with my close friend Raven Quiver. Let us go."

I was eying a white man in the group—slender, dark, bewhiskered, wearing buckskin trousers and blanket capote. Said he to me in Blackfoot and excitedly: "We are in danger. We hear that the Cutthroats (Assiniboines), many of them, are coming with intent to wipe us out."

Said Crow Big Feet to him: "You, Three Persons, absolutely close your mouth. Should the Cutthroats come to fight us, we shall, as we ever have done, make them to cry." And with that he signed to me, "Let us cross."

Two lesser chiefs of the tribe got into the skiff with Crow Big Feet. When we landed Kipp was on the shore to greet them. He and Crow Big Feet embraced, rubbed cheeks, said how pleased they were to meet again. The two others likewise greeted him. We strolled up into our kitchen-dining room where the smoke-and-feast was awaiting our coming. As soon as I could I said to Kipp: "Who is the white man across, named Three Persons?"

Smiling, he answered: "He is a Frenchman named La Rue. Was studying to become a priest; got let out because of a mix-up with a woman. Ever since has been trailing around with the Blackfeet. Tried to convince them that there are three gods only: Father, Son, and Holy Ghost. So deridingly they named him Three Persons."

Swimming their horses, rafting their belongings, the tribe crossed the river that afternoon and camped close back of our post. Before they moved out on the Musselshell, Kipp and Crow Big Feet had some serious talks. Kipp convinced him that the buffalo were going fast—a year or two more of them, and then no more.

"And when they, our real food, are gone, what then for us?" he asked one day.

"You will have to take to the white man's ways. Raise grains and white horns for food," Kipp answered.

"*Haiya, haiya!*" the chief exclaimed. "What a nothing existence that will be. Better that, when our buffalo pass, we pass too."

Next to arrive were the Kainahs (Bloods), about a thousand of them under chiefs Running Rabbit and Far-Off-in-Sight. After camping a few days close above our post, they moved out on Big Crooked Creek to hunt.

We did a thriving trade with these two tribes for elk, deer-, antelope, wolf-, and beaver skins until late fall, when they began bringing plenty of new, tanned, prime-furred buffalo robes. They were soon joined, to our great surprise, by Louis Riel and about one hundred families of his Red River, French-Cree mixed bloods, and a thousand or so Crees, led by their chief, Big Bear.

These Red Rivers and Crees arrived when both the Blackfeet and the Bloods had moved in to camp at our post for a few days to trade with us. Both of these tribes were enemies of the Crees. At once the different bands of the *Ikuni Kahtsi* (All Friends warriors society) of each tribe began painting and arming themselves, shouting that they would now completely exterminate the dog-face Crees. Well we knew that, if they did fight, our trade, so prosperously begun, would be ruined. Our hearts were low as Kipp sent word to the Blackfoot, Blood, and Cree chiefs to come and counsel with him. They soon arrived, and so for the first time I saw Big Bear: heavily, dumpily built, face coarse and unintelligent, poorly clothed. So different from the tall, fine-featured, alert, well-dressed chiefs of the other tribes. He could speak Blackfoot fairly well. For all his un-prepossessing appearance he was undoubtedly a man of dominating character and brave, else he could not have been a chief.

The meeting of the Blackfoot and Blood chiefs with Big Bear was apparently fairly friendly. As soon as they were seated, Kipp served to each of them a drink of whisky, then handed to Crow Big Feet to light a big stone pipe, long-stemmed, which he had ready for the occasion. All smoked it by turn, and that was encouraging. Food was set before them and they ate and talked of inconsequential matters. There was another round of whisky. The pipe was refilled and smoked, and then Kipp said to his guests: "My friends, you are camped here in the midst of the last of the buffalo herds. Soon they will be no more. That you may live well upon them so long as they do last, I urge that you camp and hunt in peace with one another. I speak, too, for your women and children. Well you know that your fighting makes widows and orphans of them."

As he spoke, we could hear the young hotheads in the Blood and Blackfoot camps singing war songs and shouting to one another.

Said Crow Big Feet: "I am for peace between us and your Crees, Big Bear. What say you?"

Said Big Bear: "We knew that you all were here, but we had to come or starve, for there was no place else for us to go. I am all for peace. You are many; we are few. I ask you to have pity for us."

Then Running Rabbit: "Hear them out there, singing make-ready-to-fight songs. Let us go quiet them. At once go."

Out they went without further words, Kipp and I close trailing them. First into the Blackfoot camp, where Crow Big Feet briefly said to his warriors that, positively, they were not to fight the Crees. If any disobeyed his order, they would later have to fight him, himself.

From there we hurried to the Blood camp, where Running Rabbit gave like instructions to his warriors, and surlily they listened. Then, as we neared the Cree camp, all hurried out to meet us, and I noted how strained, how anxious was the expression of their faces. But after Big Bear spoke to them they were all smiles and turned back to their various affairs happily chatting and singing.

Although we feared that this peace agreement would soon be broken by some of the young hotheads of the Blackfeet or Bloods, it actually did last so long as the three tribes remained in that part of the country—until, in fact, they crossed back into Canada. During that winter of 1880–81, they separately camped and hunted on the plains south of the river, coming frequently to trade their buffalo robes to us and, camping close by our post, having a hilarious time of it.

Louis Riel's French-Crees, with their high, one-horse, two-wheel, homemade squeaking carts, roamed the plains close about, some of them, and others built and lived in cabins in the river bottoms below us. The men were good hunters and trappers, their women fine tanners of buffalo robes. We liked their trade but did not like them. They were, in fact, more than disliked by all Indian tribes, save the Crees, and by the whites of their country and ours, too. I myself could hardly bear to stand behind the counter and trade with them, for, in their bastard French, they were always reviling us, all the *"sacre Americaines."*

One, however, their leader, Louis Riel, we did not dislike; we pitied him. He often came to trade and to tell Kipp and me of his troubles and his plans. Riel was rather short, rather heavily built, quite white, blue-eyed, with whiskers of almost auburn hue. He had been educated in some Catholic institution for the priesthood but somehow had never been ordained. He had good manners, except that his greetings and his au revoirs were excessively polite. As a leader of his French-Cree people in their quarrel with the Canadian government, he had killed a government official, and, fleeing across the border, had come to the United States and become a naturalized citizen. Now he was planning with Big Bear and his Crees as allies to lead his French-Cree people back there and to occupy the lands in question. Kipp and I repeatedly told him that that could only lead to war. Well, he said, they were all of them going back well armed, with plenty of ammunition, and they were good, experienced fighters; they could overcome the Northwest Mounted Police.

"If necessary, troops would come from England to subdue you," I one day told him, but to that he only laughed.

43

So, for all his education, Riel was a visionary, a dreamer. He was sure that he could accomplish whatever he set out to do. He once said to me that he was a second Moses, that, like the Moses of the Bible, the Lord was with him; he would surely lead his people out of bondage.

And so came Riel's Rebellion of 1884, with the result that he was hanged and Big Bear imprisoned for the rest of his life.

There where we were, and afterward in Canada, Riel often importuned Crow Big Feet (Crow Foot) to join him with his warriors in fighting the Red Coats. He steadily refused. For that, and for his constant friendliness to them, the Canadians erected a handsome monument in memory of him. Today a circle of cemented stones and a bronze tablet, on a bluff overlooking Bow River, mark where stood the lodge in which Crow Big Feet died.

All through the winter some of the Indians of the three tribes were camped close to our post, and at times they were all there, trading in their buffalo robes, resting from their strenuous hunting. We paid, in trade, five dollars for a well-tanned, head-and-tail cow buffalo robe. A family would often bring in five to ten robes at a time. The man would count the one-dollar brass checks that we gave for them and, reserving a few of them for his own use, give the rest to his women. Their purchases would be mainly sugar, tea, flour, baking powder, cloth for gowns, beads, thread, and needles. With his checks, the man would buy tobacco, cartridges, and an order of whisky. But not always whisky. Many of the men of each tribe did not drink at all. Crow Big Feet was one of them. But enough of them did imbibe to make the camps very lively of nights. In dozens of lodges there would be large gatherings of men and women, drumming, singing, dancing, telling stories.

By turns during the winter Kipp, Eli Guardipee, and I took a few days off to visit in the Blackfoot or the Blood camp, out on the plain, and to hunt. On a day in March when Kipp was visiting in the Blackfoot camp, he took part in the run of a big herd of buffalo in which a young hunter killed a big, spotted cow. Its head and its tail were pure white; there was a white strip running from its neck back along the length of its belly; and there was a large round white spot on its flanks. The young man carefully removed its hide, gave it to his father, old Spotted Eagle, and he told Kipp that, when it was tanned, he should have it. At once one of the Sun priests (medicine men, sacred pipe men) made objection. White buffalo belonged to Sun. Accordingly, when, in the summer, the Sun's lodge would be built by the sacred-vow woman, the tanned robe would have to be tied to its center post, presented to Him Above. To which Spotted Eagle replied that this was not a white buffalo; it was only white spotted, therefore not Sun's own. Sun would not want it. Therefore Raven Quiver (Kipp) should have it.

So, on a day in April, when we were apprised that old Spotted Eagle and his family were coming in with the spotted robe, as Kipp directed, we hurried to pile on the floor of the trade room some presents for him: a sack of sugar, five hundred cartridges, fifty pounds of flour, two blankets, one Winchester carbine, five pounds of tobacco, a gallon keg of whisky, little things for women.

Came in the old man, his son, his two wives—the old man with his robe on his arm. "As I promised you, Raven Quiver, here it is," he said, handing it to Kipp.

"Good. And there are a few presents for you all," Kipp replied, pointing to the pile of things on the floor. The old man stared at them, clapped hand to mouth in pleased surprise, exclaimed: "*Puhts ikahksaps nituka, Mastúnopachis!*" ("How generous is my friend, Raven Quiver!"). The son and the wives were equally happily surprised; they all but ran to the pile—the son to take up the carbine, the women to kneel and fondle their knicknacks. Said the old man to them: "At once wrap that keg in a blanket."

The robe was perfectly tanned, as soft as velvet; and on its flesh side the old man had painted some pictographs of enemies he had killed, enemy horses he had stolen, and encounters with grizzly bears. Said Kipp when we had extended and pinned it to a wall of the trade room: "It is the only pure-white-spotted robe that I have ever seen. And it is worth something. Anyhow a hundred dollars."

Word that we had a white-spotted buffalo robe spread all up and down the river. On a day in August, when Kipp was in Fort Benton, the *Red Cloud*, St. Louis bound, tied up at our landing, and Captain Williams and his passengers came in to see the robe.

"How much?" asked one of them.

"A hundred dollars," I answered.

"There you are," he said, laying two fifty-dollar bills upon the counter.

I learned afterward that he was a Montreal man, and have often wondered if he had been generous enough to give it to some museum. When he had gone with it, I began to feel very uneasy about selling it. Kipp had said that it was worth a hundred dollars, and I had been paid that price for it. Still, perhaps I should not have let it go.

I was right in my misgivings. When Kipp returned, he stopped just within the doorway of the trade room, stared at the bare wall, roared: "Where's that spotted robe?" I meekly answered that I had sold it for a hundred dollars. "Oh, my God," he groaned. "I had a hunch somehow that you were likely to do it, so I hurried back. Why, Charlie Conrad, you know, told me that I ought to get at least five hundred for that robe."

The first steamboat of the season, on its return from Fort Benton, landed the fur buyers who were to bid for our buffalo robes. They were Charles E. Conrad for I. G. Baker & Company, Thomas Bosier for T. C. Power & Brother, A. E. Rogers for Broadwater, Pepin & Company, and John Goewey for a Boston firm. All day long for about a week they sat in a row with pencils and pads of paper, counting each robe as we showed it to them—first the fur side, then the inside, marking it "No. 1" or "No 2," according to the color of the fur and softness of the tanning. That done, they handed in their bids for the lot: 4,111 robes. John Goewey's bid was the highest: $7.11 per robe. He handed Kipp a check for $29,229.21 and that was that. He also bought our deer, elk, antelope, wolf, beaver, fox, and other hides. I forget what he paid for them. I. G. Baker & Company got our more than a thousand smoked buffalo tongues at forty cents each. Some thousands of pounds of dried buffalo meat and pemmican went to a trader at Standing Rock Agency. Yes, we had had a very successful winter trade.

In the warehouse we built a robe press, a plank box three by four feet. Into it were laid at a time ten folded robes, which were then pressed down with strong lever and attachment and bound with rawhide strands. That itself was a long task. The steamboat *Red Cloud* carried them and all of Goewey's other purchases down to St. Louis.

Now was come summer. Out on the plain to the south the men of the three tribes were hunting only enough to keep their families supplied with meat and hides for various uses, and the women were tanning buffalo cow leather for new lodge-skins. A passenger on an early downriver steamboat had been a certain missionary who had taken it upon himself to come to look after the spiritual welfare of our heathens, so he said. Though long-since dead, I will not name him; simply call him Sacred Talker. Kipp, always so generous, told him to live with us, ever to help himself to such of our supplies as he might need. And, since we were not to use our smokehouse until fall, Kipp gave him that to live in, after lining it with muslin and putting in a bed and other conveniences. He would have had our liquor house except that it had burned. No longer fearing the coming of a United States marshal, we now kept our liquor and beer in our warehouse and handled it ourselves.

Kipp left for Fort Benton and Fort Conrad, leaving me in charge of the post. Somewhere out in the badlands, we never learned just where, Big-Nose George and his gang of horse thieves had their headquarters, and they bought their supplies from us. We feared them, did not want their trade. I expected any night to be awakened by a pistol against my ribs and to be told to open the safe and lose no time about it. Big-Nose George we never saw. Always he sent one or another of his desperadoes for the goods that he wanted.

Came with saddle horse and pack horse one of the gang, on a day when many lodges of Crees were camped close back of our post. A young, quiet, good-looking man he was; neatly dressed; armed with a Winchester rifle and a holstered six-shooter at each hip. He wanted a drink of whisky. I led him into the warehouse, gave it to him from the barrel. He drank two more as fast as I could fill the glass. I put his list of groceries, whisky, and cartridges in canvas sacks that he furnished, and he lashed them upon his pack horse, then came in for another drink. I gave it to him, followed him to see him mount and leave. As we came to the doorway of the trade room, a young Cree and his wife, a beautiful woman, were just passing. Said the desperado to me: "See me kill that damned Injun!"

Even as he spoke he snatched out his right six-shooter, fired, and ran to his horses. The Cree, with a shriek of agony, fell and writhed, shot through his kidneys. The wife, knife in hand, ran after the murderer, but he was in the saddle and fast leaving with his pack horse. Sacred Talker helped me carry the wounded man to his lodge, and there we did all that we could for him—Sacred Talker praying for him, I filling him with whisky. Within an hour he was dead. A company of mounted infantry was encamped a few miles above us. I sent a Cree with a note to the commander, Colonel Bartlett, telling him of the murder, asking that he try to trail and overtake the murderer. The reply that I got read: "I have nothing to do with civil cases. If you want the man arrested, send to Fort Benton for Sheriff Healey."

That, of course, was out of the question. The murder, however, ended the gang's coming to us for supplies; we never again saw any of them. If I rightly remember, Big-Nose George was later hanged somewhere in the Yellowstone country.

The widow of the murdered Cree was very beautiful, of perfect features and figure, her heavy braids falling down her back almost to the ground. Now that she was single, many wanted her, particularly one of our white employes whose Indian name was Long Whip. But in vain he courted her, besought her to marry him. To our great surprise she became the companion of Sacred Talker.

Kipp returned from Fort Benton by steamboat, bringing a fine stock of goods, except whisky, for our next winter trade. The whisky, sixty barrels of it, came later from St. Louis on the *Helena*. Soon after Kipp's return, a medicine man of the Crees had a vision (dream). It was that the Crees should go to camp by themselves and no longer mingle with the Blackfeet and Bloods, lest they get into trouble. Talking it over, Big Bear and his lesser chiefs decided that they would move down to the mouth of the Musselshell, and, if we would not send down there a man with stock of goods for their convenience, they would go still farther: down into the Cutthroat (Assiniboine) country and to the traders there. Useless to argue with them; naught for us to do but comply.

We got ready about a thousand dollars worth of goods, a tent, stove, etc., to send down there by steamboat, a French-Cree employee, one Archie Amiott, to be in charge of the outfit. Since we did not implicitly trust him, Kipp asked Sacred Talker, as a great favor to us, to accompany Archie and see that he attended strictly to business and worked solely for our interest. Sacred Talker was loath to go, and well we knew the reason why: it would never do for him to be seen on the boat with his beautiful Cree companion. Reluctantly, after many feeble excuses, he consented to go. Just before leaving he took his companion to our good old Crow Woman and instructed her to keep her close until he returned. To him Crow Woman merely grunted. But to me, later, she said: "I do not want that Cree in my house. She is not fit to associate with my good daughter."

Crow Woman had not to worry long about her charge; within a week after Sacred Talker's departure, the young Cree widow became Long Whip's companion. A couple of weeks later, a war party of Crees, returning from a raid upon the horse herds of the Crows, arrived, expecting to find their tribe still with us. They went on down to the mouth of the Musselshell and there told that the widow had married Long Whip. The next upriver steamboat brought a letter from Sacred Talker to Long Whip in which he denounced Long Whip at some length for stealing his companion. He signed his name and then added: "P.S.: By Heaven. If I find this is true, you shall repent."

Time passed. Somehow the head of Sacred Talker's denomination got word of Sacred Talker's misdeeds among us. Came a letter for him by a downriver steamboat, and we forwarded it on. It was, as we later learned, a demand that he return at once and report to his superiors. When the next upriver steamboat arrived, I was waiting upon some Blackfoot customers. Long Whip came hurrying in, said that Sacred Talker had arrived, and, going behind a counter, took up one of our ever-ready six-shooters under it, and stood waiting for whatever was to happen. In came Sacred Talker, stared angrily at Long Whip, and then said to me: "When I first arrived here, I left a purse with you that contained one hundred and three dollars. I want it."

I thought to myself: "Here's where he will put one over on me." I stepped to the safe, took out the long, shabby purse, gave it a flip, and showered the floor with one-dollar bills that had never been wrinkled. One by one I took them up, one hundred and three of them, put them back in the purse, and handed it to him. Without a word he turned to leave; at the door he turned, stopped, glared at Long Whip, and said to him: "I shall see you again."

"Yes, I will probably meet you in hell," Long Whip answered.

"Well, that is said to be a central point," Sacred Talker replied, and with that he was gone.

Late in August we got an unexpected setback to our bright prospects of another big winter trade. The Blackfeet and the Bloods suddenly decided to return to their Canadian reservations, in order to receive the five dollars per person annually due them from that government. They had left there the previous summer before the payment was due and now had two payments coming to them. Kipp had a long talk with Crow Big Feet and Running Rabbit. He urged them to remain where they were, in the midst of the buffalo herds. What good would ten dollars per person be, he asked. In a few days the money would be spent, and then all would suffer from want of food. Here they would have plenty of meat and robes constantly to sell.

To which Crow Big Feet sadly replied: "Raven Quiver, that you have said to us is true. I do not want to go back up north, nor does our friend here, Running Rabbit. But for once we are powerless against our children. All they can think of is ten round pieces for each of them to spend. They will not listen to us. We have to go."

Go they did. Well, we still had the Crees, also Riel and his French-Crees. We would, anyhow, get some robes.

Buffalo Robes

PASSING OF THE HERDS (1881–82)[1]

IN THE SUMMER OF 1881, at Carroll, when the Blackfeet, Bloods, Crees, and Louis Riel's French-Crees were camped well out upon the plains, Eli Guardipee and I often took advantage of the slack times of trade to go hunting. Sometimes on foot, in the river bottoms or pine-clad breaks, for deer, and again on our well-trained buffalo horses, for the exciting run of a herd. Eli (*Isinamakan*, "Takes Gun Ahead") was such a wise hunter and sure shot that I had great pleasure in hunting with him.

We set out one day to hunt deer in the big grove below our trading post and were following a dusty game trail when we glimpsed three deer speeding through the brush, heading to cross the trail ahead of us. They came on in single file, and as each one leaped into the open of the trail, Eli fired at it with his '73 model Winchester repeater. He fired three shots about as fast as I could count them, with the result of three dead bucks lying within a yard or two of one another. Some shooting!

Of fat cow buffalo meat and buffalo tongues we always had plenty. Deciding that we would like to have some fat antelope ribs for a change, we set out to hunt on the plain to the south of our post— Eli riding a small, slow mare, and I on my fast buffalo horse. We ascended parallel ridges of the long, steep badlands of the valley, planning to get together up on the rim of the plain. I arrived on top just in time to see Eli riding out from the head of a pine-timbered coulee, going as fast as his little mare could carry him, and pursued by a huge grizzly bear. He was shooting back at it, apparently without effect, and with long, swift leaps it was gaining on him. I was too far away to be of any help—all would be over in one way or another before I could reach him—but anyhow I set out to try to do the impossible, my heart all aflutter with anxiety for him. Oh, why, why hadn't he ridden a good horse? I groaned as I saw the huge bear, regardless of his shooting, fast overtaking him, and he always such an accurate shot. Never having experienced it, I did not realize that to shoot straight back with sure, killing effect from a swift-

[1] First published in *The Great Falls Tribune* (December 10, 1935).

running horse was something that could not be done. Watching the bear gain upon him sickened me. I realized that with, at most, three more leaps it would be upon his horse's back and mauling him. And then, just as the bear was making that last leap, he fired again, and what was my relief as I saw the huge creature flatten down upon the grass and lie still.

When I rode up to Eli, he was down off his horse, looking at his kill, and calmly chewing gum. "Well! What a narrow escape you had. I thought it was to be the end of you," I managed to stutter.

"*Sa! Matsikiwa* (No, it was nothing)," he said in Blackfoot, adding in English: "I knew that I could kill her when she came close."

It was, he explained as we got out our skinning knives, that he had ridden onto her cubs in the edge of the pines, and they, squalling from fright, had caused her to take after him. She was, indeed, a huge grizzly, and so fat that we had great difficulty in getting off her hide. It was too heavy and fat for us to carry, so Eli went for it and its carcass with team and wagon on the following day. Rendering out the fat, we got ten gallons of pure, white bear oil that we later sold to a St. Louis druggist for $75.00.

One afternoon in September, no Indians being in to trade, Eli and I strolled down into the grove below our post looking for deer. We were midway between the outer edge of the grove and the shore of the river and about thirty yards apart when Eli sighted a white-tail deer and shot it. We were unaware that at the time a herd of about a thousand buffalo were at the shore of the river, straight in from us, to drink. At the report of Eli's rifle they instantly turned and came with a rush to get back up onto the plain. Their thunderous pounding and rattling of feet and smashing of willows warned us of our danger before we could see them. I sprang onto the trunk of a big, newly fallen cottonwood tree that lay directly across the front of the oncoming herd, and, dropping my rifle, climbed for a few feet up one of its slender, upright branches and hung on. I glimpsed Eli standing close against a tree no larger in diameter than himself. And then, with a rush like a wide brown torrent of heaving water, the buffalo were smashing past us, snapping off the branches of my tree, and lunging against the one to which I clung with fast weakening grip, as they leaped over the trunk. I expected it to break, let me down to be trampled, torn to pieces by a thousand hooves. I have no words to express my fright. And then, as suddenly as they came, they were gone. As I dropped, weak and dizzy, to sit upon the tree trunk, I heard Eli shoot, saw a tail one of the herd, a young cow, fall.

"You all right?" he asked, coming over to me.

"All right, but somehow tired," I answered.

"Gosh, a close call for us. Why, they kept brushing against my sides. I expected every minute to be knocked away from my tree and made hash of. And I worried about you, hanging onto your branch; thought you would break it off; its a wonder that you didn't when they brushed against you," he said. And then: "Oh, look! Look! We can see the river."

Sure enough, the running herd had trampled the willows and rose brush in their course as though it had been cut down by a giant scythe. We could plainly see the shimmering river, two hundred yards away. We went to the deer that Eli had killed and shivered at what might have been our fate; it was a shapeless mass of hashed meat, bones, hide, and entrails. We butchered the cow, to be come for later, took up the grove for home, and there had a big drink of whisky and a smoke to quiet our nerves.

With the coming of November, when the fur of the buffalo was at its best, Kipp detailed Guardipee to hunt them for their hides, which, later on, we would have softly tanned. So, with a four-horse team and wagon, three fast buffalo horses, and a camp outfit and cook, Eli set out to make his killings. Several weeks later, when he was camped on Armell Creek, with my own fast buffalo horse I joined him for a couple of days of the sport. On the following morning we sighted a large herd of buffalo grazing at the head of a long coulee putting into the creek. We set out to make a run of them—Eli on Jerry, Kipp's buffalo horse, the fastest, most enduring, best-trained buffalo runner that any of us had ever known. I was riding my own horse, whom I called Dick. Each of us was carrying a rim-fire, .44 caliber Henry repeating carbine, short, light, easy to aim and fire with one hand, best of all weapons for running buffalo.

We rode up the coulee, keeping out of sight of the herd until, at the head of the coulee, we charged out and right in among them. They instantly ran, gathering compactly together, and we, choosing the cows that we wanted, always those with rounded hips and rump and therefore fat, turned our horses after them. And our horses were as eager for the chase, for the killings, as were we. With ears set fiercely back, they did their best to get us close up to the left of the cows, so that we could put a single, killing shot into their lungs or hearts. The pace at which we were going seemed to us like the swiftness of lightning. Well we knew that, at any moment, our horses might step into a badger hole and we go down to be trampled to death; that a hard-pressed bull might turn and gore us. It was that danger, that constant risk, that made the chase so exciting, so fascinating. Oh, how we loved it all: the thunderous pounding and rattling of thousands of hooves; the sharp odor of the sage that they crushed; the accuracy of our shooting; the quick response of our trained horses to our directing hands. Always the run was over all too soon. Never was a horse that could keep up with a frightened buffalo herd for much more than a mile. When I had shot my sixth cow, my horse was all in, winded, and wet with white foaming sweat. I brought him to a stand and sat watching Eli, still going on Jerry, and frequently shooting. Then he, too, stopped, turned, came slowly back; and, equally slow, I rode to meet him. "How many?" I asked.

Grinning, he answered: "Eighteen. Eighteen cows with eighteen shots." Hard to believe, but there were the proofs of it, blackly strewn upon the yellow-grassed plain. To select, chase, and kill eighteen cows in the run of a buffalo herd was something to talk about, to be remembered. I have never heard of anyone's equaling the feat.

The Blackfoot tribes' name for Armell Creek is *Itsískiotsop Ituktai*, "It-Crushed-Them Creek." For, the story goes, in the long-ago, some women were gouging red-paint earth from the foot of a high cut bank along it, when suddenly the bank fell, burying them deeply beneath it, so deep that their bodies were never recovered. About ten miles up from the mouth of the creek, and some thirty yards west of it, is the *Aístikokukim Mutsískum*, "Rub-Their-Backs

Spring," of the Blackfeet. It bubbles up in a deep recess in a ledge of dark, conglomerate rock. About two feet high in the rear of the recess, the roof slopes upward and outward at an angle of about twenty degrees, and, from the height of a small deer or antelope to that of a mature buffalo bull, it is as smooth and lustrous as polished mahogany from the various animals' rubbing their backs against it through how many centuries of time. A most interesting place. I visited it several times during my brief outing there with Guardipee.

With the help of the cook, we were nearly two days in taking the hides from our twenty-four cows and properly pegging them out to dry. It was hard work. It quenched for the time my desire to make another exciting run of a herd.

After the Missouri froze over, early in December, Guardipee hunted north of it, out toward the Little Rockies, the *Mahkwiyi Stukists*, "Wolf Mountains," of the Blackfoot tribes. Returning to our post one day with a wagonload of cow buffalo hides, he mentioned that he had found, in the valley of Rock Creek and close up to the mountains, two dead elk, their antlers interlocked. I thought that the antlers would be well worth having, so went out with Eli to get them, my conveyance a one-horse, homemade sled. Strange enough, we found that the wolves had not touched the two elk. They had fought, and inextricably interlocked their antlers in a grassy park close to the creek. There they milled around, unable to graze or go to the near, murmuring stream to drink, until, after days of horrible suffering, they had fallen from exhaustion and slowly died.

We cut off their heads, thoroughly cleaned them of brains and meat. At our post, six men tried to pull the two sets of antlers apart but failed. In the following spring I sent them downriver and on to my friend C. Hart Merriam, and he, in turn, presented them to the Smithsonian Institution.

It was a severe setback to our prospects for another big winter trade, when, late in this summer of 1881, the Blackfeet and most of the Bloods returned to their reservations in Canada. Turned their backs upon our buffalo country in order to obtain the annual five dollars per person due from their treaty with their Grandmother, the Queen. So now we had trade only with Big Bear's thousand or so Crees, Louis Riel's four or five hundred French-Crees, and thirty lodges of Bloods. Incited by our big trade of the previous winter, of more than four thousand buffalo robes, and unaware that the Blackfeet and Bloods would be leaving the country, other traders had built near us. Broadwater and Pepin, old-timers, at Rocky Point, a few miles upriver; and at Carroll, two tenderfeet, Jim Massie and Mitt Marsh, had gone in with Gus Tyler, much to his sorrow as was afterward proved. And, too, we now had at Carroll fiery Tom Burns, who, a part of the time, with four-horse teams and a wagon traded in the camps of the Indians and the Red Rivers and when at home ran a poker game. His wife Susette was a beautiful young French-Cree, of whom more later.

We now knew, positively knew, that this was to be our last winter's trade for buffalo robes. All the buffalo herds that remained were within 150 miles of Carroll. To the south, white hide-hunters, putting out from the Yellowstone, up which the Northern Pacific Railway was building, were slaughtering thousands of buffalo with their high-power Sharp's rifles. To the east, the Assiniboines and other Sioux were getting their share of them. The Gros Ventres and Pikunis hemmed them in on the north and west. Our hearts were low. I said to Kipp one day: "What are we to do, what can we do when the trade ends here?"

"Huh! Go back to Fort Conrad and a nothing life," he growled.

As I have said, the Crees and Riel's Red River mixed bloods were good hunters, and their women expert tanners of robes. And now, constantly urged on by Big Bear and Riel, they hunted harder than ever, tanned more robes than ever, in order to buy rifles and cartridges, plenty of them, for their coming war upon the Canadians for the lands that they claimed. And, as always, they laughed at Kipp and me when we tried to convince them that they could not possibly win their cause. But at times, ignoring the commands of their chiefs, they would come in to camp close to us, trade their robes for *uskiti waubu*, "fire water," and have a grand spree. Well, one thing to our credit, the whisky that they got from us was pure; we drank it ourselves. Strange it was, a thousand Indians, men and women, drinking, chatting, singing, dancing around their evening fires, and quarreling not at all. All winter long we had no trouble with them except that, one morning, when our good Crow Woman was standing on a buffalo hide, chipping it for tanning, a drunken Cree came along, picked her up, and started off with her. Just then I came from the cookhouse, saw what he was doing, struck him with all my strength, smashed in two knuckles of my hand, but did not even jar him. The pain in my hand was so great that I was powerless. The Cree let Crow Woman go, took up a heavy stick, came at me, and I had to run, heading for the doorway of our trade room. Kipp, happening to look out of the window, saw my plight and, taking up a bottle of beer, came running out; he passed me, and, as the Cree rounded the corner of the building, he brought the bottle down upon his head. He fell as though struck by lightning but after an hour or more got up and staggered to his lodge, never to come to our post again.

Early in March we traded off the last of our blankets, much in demand by the Crees, so, with John Hudson, a sturdy, dependable English-Cree, I set out for T. C. Power & Brother's trading post at the mouth of the Judith River in order to try to replenish our stock of them. Each of us supplied with horse and sled, rifle, bedding, and food, we traveled on the frozen river, cutting bends not at all. Pausing at Rocky Point for a drink or two with Al Rodgers, in charge of the Broadwater & Pepin post, that evening we made Cow Island and camped in an abandoned cabin of some pretensions, standing upon a little rise at the mouth of Cow Creek, the *Stahktsikye Tuktai*, "Middle Creek," so named because it flows to the Missouri between the Bear Paw and the Little Rocky Mountains. It was here that, in 1877, the Nez Percés had, in their flight for Canada, killed a few whites and captured Joe Pickett's mule train, burning the wagons. With that in mind, the builder of the cabin had run, as we discovered, a tunnel from the cellar, under the kitchen, out to a dense stand of brush fifty yards away. And, as it proved, he had had no use for it as a means of escape, as no more trouble with Indians had occurred there.

During that day we passed several small herds of buffalo in the river bottoms, but on the following day saw none, not even a lone bull. Cow Creek seemed to be the western limit of them. Starting on early in the morning, we nooned in a deserted wood-hawk's cabin that had some unique homemade furniture, particularly an easy chair, its frame of cherry, its seat and back a buffalo hide that, put on green, had dried in conformity with the sitter's body. It was the most comfortable, restful chair that I ever sat in. Many years afterward, visiting with my good friend Charles Bucknum in Los Angeles, I spoke of that trip and mentioned the chair. "Why, boy, I made that chair!" he exclaimed. "I built that cabin, wintered there, had some wood-hawks working for me, did some trading with the Piegans."

(All Fort Benton old-timers will remember Charlie Bucknum and his good wife, sister to the Mee brothers, blacksmiths there in the long-ago. Owner of a large orange grove near Riverside, California, Charlie died there in, I think, 1915.)

Near evening of our second day out, we arrived at our destination to find that the manager of the post, "Diamond R." Brown, was in Fort Benton. But his wife and daughter welcomed us, and we had a pleasant visit with them until Brown returned three days later. Then, our sleds loaded with bales of blankets, we set out for home. "Diamond R." was feeling pretty blue. Though the Gros Ventres and Pikunis had promised to come and trade with him during the winter, not a single Indian of them had appeared.

Again, from the mouth of the Judith down, we saw no buffalo until, as we neared the mouth of Cow Creek, we discovered a herd of them coming swiftly down the creek bottom, heading to cross the river. That worried us; well we knew that, at that time of year, buffalo never ran except when frightened by their great enemy, man. Even as they dashed across the snow-covered ice of the river, we saw, a half-mile up the creek, a caravan of Indians, a whole tribe of them, riding down the steep slope from the plain. Then we were alarmed, for we thought that they might be Assiniboines, and if so, we were in for trouble. During the winter their bad chief, Little Mountain, and his followers had killed several white wood-hawks and trappers along the river. Said Hudson: "Let's go! Down the river as fast as we can."

"No. Too late. They have seen us and on their buffalo horses can soon overtake us. We will try to get to that tunnel cabin before they can and stand them off," I answered.

With ready rifles, and lashing our slow sled horses, we left the river and headed for the cabin, jouncing over the hummocky bottom land. A number of riders had left the caravan and were coming swiftly on; with sinking hearts we saw that they would cut us off from the cabin. Hudson, ahead of me, brought his horse to a stand and said, as I drew up beside him: "Well, if we got to die, we're going to die fighting."

"Yes," I answered, and we got down behind our sleds with rifles cocked and ready. On came the Indians, so swiftly and so many; and I, looking at the determination of them, quirting their horses to ever swifter speed, thought how soon our end was to come. So, as I cocked my rifle and made ready to raise it, imagine my surprise, my relief, when the lead rider shouted: "*Ha! Apikuni, unook! Kitsikipah anom?*" ("*Ha!* Far-off-White Robe,[2] himself. What do you here?").

He was my good Pikuni friend, Red Bird's Tail. Yes, and there were Little Plume, Running Crane, and many others—all my good friends. We exchanged news. I said that I was going to the cabin to camp for the night. Roared Red Bird's Tail: "No, you will not. You and your companion will stop in my lodge." That we did and had a pleasant evening with him and the other leaders of the tribe. A few of them had been wintering along the foot of the Bear Paw Mountains and on the head of Middle Creek. Buffalo had been hard to get in sufficient numbers for their needs. I urged them to go down-river with us, down where they could be sure to live well. But no, they would not do that. Their enemies the Liars (Crees) were down there, and when they fought them, they would be a war party of men, unencumbered by their women and children.

I said that Raven Quiver and I positively knew that only between Big River and Elk River (the Missouri and Yellowstone) were now any buffalo. "*Ha.* Not so," old Three Bears exclaimed. "In the

[2] The meaning of *Apikuni* is much debated. Some interpret it as "Spotted Robe" (formerly even Schultz himself did so), some as "Scabby Robe," with reference to the state of the fur at certain seasons of the year.

long-ago that bad god, Red Old Man, herded all of the buffalo up into the mountains and hid them in a great cave, so that all the people of the earth would starve, would die. But that good god, White Old Man, found them; turned them back out onto the plains. So is it that our enemies, the white man, have now hidden the buffalo, so to kill us off, starve us to death. But Sun pities us. Sun is powerful. He will help us to find them."

That soon came to be the belief of all three Blackfoot tribes. For some years after the buffalo were exterminated, the medicine men kept fervently praying Sun to help them find and free the hidden herds.

We parted from our friends early in the morning; my last words to them were that, with the coming of the fireboats, Raven Quiver and I would return to our Bear River home, there to remain, for there would be no trading for buffalo robes.

A little way below the mouth of Cow Creek, we saw a lone buffalo calf, almost a yearling, standing in the timber, and I shot it. Its fur was so very dark, beaver-fur-like in texture, that I had Hudson help carefully to remove the hide, nubby horns, hooves, and all. It proved to be the very last buffalo that I killed. Months later good Crow Woman carefully tanned it, and still later I presented it to the Smithsonian Institution.

The fifty blankets that we brought down from the Judith did not last three days; trade was good. We were getting many robes from both the Crees and Red Rivers, and from the latter, also, much dried meat and pemmican. As Kipp well said, not for nothing was this, our last winter of trade.

In August, looking for work, there had come to us from the railend on the Yellowstone, on foot and sore from having sat down in a bed of prickly pears, a young man, a giant of a man, who in my youthful days had been my guide in the Adirondack Mountains of New York. Although not needed, Kipp had made him our helper in trade room and warehouse, and the Indians, because of his great size and vigor, had promptly named him *Mansksi Stumik*, "Young Bull." Well, Young Bull was a great ladies' man, and in due time he and pretty young Susie, Tom Burns's wife, became close friends, were much together when Tom was away, trading in camp.

One evening soon after I returned from the Judith, Burns being away, Young Bull went to his cabin to visit with Susie. They had a drink or two, a bite to eat, were sitting cosily before the fire, when, near eleven o'clock, they heard Burns drive his four-horse team and wagon in close to the door. Whispered Susie: "Oh, he's come. He's said he will kill us if he finds us together."

"Well, I'll run," Young Bull proposed.

"No. Then he'll anyhow kill me. You get under the bed."

"Oh, no."

"But, yes! Quick or we die."

Under it he crept and lay still. Hurriedly Susie rumpled the bed-clothes and pillow, snatched off her gown, went to the door, opened it, and said sleepily to Tom, unharnessing his horses. "So. You are come. You wake me up."

"Yes, and you stay up. Get me something to eat. I'm hungry," Tom answered. Presently he came in, looked around, stared at Susie, and growled: "Huh. Thought I'd find Young Bull with you. It's a wonder I didn't."

"You, what for you say that? Me, I'm have nothing to do with him. I ain't seen him," Susie fiercely replied.

Said Tom: "Huh! Woman, no use your lying to me. I know you too well. Some day I'll catch you with him, and then . . . ! Oh, hurry up with that grub. I'm hungry."

Tom ate, smoked. Susie washed the dishes. They went to bed. Under it, Young Bull lay motionless, barely breathing, hour after hour; constantly worrying, wondering what the end of it all would be. He was weaponless. Susie had told him that Tom always went to bed with a six-shooter at his pillow. So, probably, Tom would discover him, kill him.

Well, Tom was a late riser; it was after eight o'clock when he got up, dressed, went off to look for his horses; and watchful, cautious Susie shooed Young Bull from the cabin.

His bed had not been slept in, he had not appeared at breakfast;

we were worrying about him when he came in, sleepy, and shamedly grinning.

"Where you been?" Kipp asked.

Fully, with all detail, he told us of his experience of the night, and how we did laugh.

Well, came spring; came the steamboats puffing upstream; came the fur men, and again John Goewey of Boston was the highest bidder for our robes—2,130 well-tanned buffalo robes, at $7.35 apiece. Charlie Conrad bought our tons of dried meat and pemmican, as well as several thousand hides of elk, deer, and antelope, for —I forget what he paid.

It was several weeks after the fur buyers left that, leaving Long John Forgy to carry on at the post, we all set out for Fort Benton, Kipp and I on the *Helena*, the others with the bull train and four-horse teams on the long trail up there. Nor were we any of us happy. Well we knew that the days of the buffalo were ended.

No More Buffalo

‹‹

INVULNERABLE CALF SHIRT (1882–83)[1]

IT WAS IN JULY, 1882, that we abandoned our trading post at Carroll on the Missouri and returned to our home post, Fort Conrad, at the Fort Benton–Fort Macleod wagon road crossing of the Marias River. The buffalo herds were practically exterminated, and we were sorely grieved over their passing. Forever ended was our exciting, profitable trade with the Indians for their robes and furs.

Our group at Fort Conrad at that time was Joseph Kipp, its owner; his wife; William and Maggie Fitzpatrick; Red Eyes, Takes-Gun-at-Night, and Comes-with-Rattles; Hiram D. Upham with his wife and daughter Rosa; Kipp's Mandan mother, Earth Woman, and her old friend and companion, Crow Woman; Eli Guardipee and wife, Flag Woman, adopted daughter of Crow Woman; my wife, Fine Shield Woman, and I. The men's wives were all Pikunis, better known to whites as Piegans or Blackfeet. However, there was a Canadian tribe of that name, which, though speaking the same language and often intermarrying with the Pikunis, was a distinct tribe of the Blackfoot Confederacy.

Having no more buffalo to hunt, the Pikunis were now encamped around their agency on Badger Creek, fifty miles west of us, and living upon deer, elk, and antelope in their vicinity. A few lodges of them, close friends and relatives, came down to camp near us and hunt. They reported that game was already becoming scarce

[1] First published in *The Great Falls Tribune* (November 11, 1936).

up their way and wondered what the people were to do when it would be killed off.

All the supplies for Fort Macleod were freighted from Fort Benton by bull trains, mule trains, and four-horse teams. In summertime there was much travel on the road, so our store, bar, dining room, and sleeping quarters were well patronized. We had a post office, mail service between Fort Benton and Fort Macleod every two weeks. Alberta was bone dry. Every time the mail went north, by special arrangement, I put two gallons of whisky in kegs in a mail sack, one for Colonel Macleod, one for Captain Windsor. The Northwest Mounted Police patrols could not touch the sacks. The postmaster at the fort quietly sneaked the kegs to the officers. They both made frequent trips to Fort Benton, always stopping overnight with us. They were broad-minded men of culture. It was a pleasure to talk with them. Colonel Macleod was greatly interested in the history of the Province of Alberta, as it was later to be named. One evening he asked Kipp to tell him why he had named the trading post that he had built on Belly River "Fort Standoff."

Then Kipp told the story that I had heard a number of times. "Well, this is how it was," he began. "My partner, Charlie Thomas, and I decided to build a post on Belly River, and trade with the Bloods—trade liquor mostly for their buffalo robes and furs. But in Fort Benton, United States Marshal Charles Hard was watching us closely so that we did not dare load up with wet goods and strike for the north. So at daybreak one morning I walked out from town, and when the stage came along, got in it and went to Helena. There I bought a hundred gallons of high-proof alcohol, twenty cans of it, from Kleinschmidt, who, in the night, hauled it down to the nearest point on the Missouri for me. There, with plenty of rope and dry driftwood, sizable logs, I made a raft, lashed the cans of alcohol upon it, pushed out into the current, and drifted down with it, poling now and then to keep the raft off the shores and sandbars. Two days later I landed at the mouth of Sun River, where Charlie Thomas with four-horse team and wagon was waiting for me. Our two other four-horse teams and wagons, loaded with groceries and various trade goods, and driven by Politte Pepion and Joe Howard, were already en route from Fort Benton to Belly River.

"We loaded the wagon with the alcohol and struck out northward on the many-furrowed Indian trail that closely paralleled the foothills of the mountains. Three days later we topped Milk River Ridge, the divide between Missouri River and Hudson's Bay waters, and, looking back, saw a rider fast overtaking us. I recognized him: he was United States Marshal Hard. How he learned of our plan to circumvent him we never knew. We pushed on down the slope toward St. Mary River. He came alongside, motioned us to stop, and said: 'Well, boys, nice load of alcohol you have there. I arrest you. Turn right around and head for Fort Benton.'

" 'You can't arrest us. We are in Canada,' I answered.

" 'Canada nothing. This is Montana Territory. Just you turn and head back!' he yelled.

"Between Thomas and me, leaning up against the wagon seat, were our Winchester rifles. We snatched them up and I said to Hard: 'This Milk River Ridge back of us is the line. Everybody says it is. Anyhow, we will pretend that it is. Hard, we've just naturally got to stand you off.'

"He hadn't drawn his six-shooter; well he knew that we had the best of him. He stared and stared at us; at last he said: 'When you return to Fort Benton, as you must some day, I'll arrest you all right and send you to the pen for a good long time!' And with that he turned and was gone. We went on to Belly River, built our post, and with good reason named it Fort Standoff. In 1873, when the international line was surveyed, we found that where Hard had overtaken us we were miles south of it. In the spring, when we returned to Fort Benton, Hard did not attempt to arrest us. Judge Sanders, in Helena, had told him that he had no case, that he could not prove we were in Montana, there where he had overtaken us."

"Did you have a good trade at your Fort Standoff?" Captain Windsor asked.

"Pretty fair, considering that there were other traders in the country—Healy and Hamilton, at Fort Whoop-Up, and some camp traders. We got seventeen hundred buffalo robes and some small stuff from the Bloods and North Piegans."

"And then you built Fort Kipp at the mouth of Old Man's River? I have heard that you killed a great Blood chief there, named Calf Shirt. Tell us about it," said Colonel Macleod.

"Thomas and I built that fort in the summer of 1872," Kipp replied and was silent. I well knew that he disliked telling about the killing of Calf Shirt.[2] But our guests were urgent, and he finally began:

"Calf Shirt was a man of terrible temper. Without cause he had killed one of his wives and four men of his own Blood tribe. He had frequently told his wives that he had powerful medicine, that Sun greatly favored him. If he should happen to be killed, he had instructed them, they must sing certain songs, offer certain prayers over his body for three days, and he would return to life, be as well as ever.

"One morning in December, Charlie Thomas, "Diamond R." Brown, Dick Berry, Sol Abbot, Henry Powell, and Jeff Devereaux were playing poker in our kitchen-dining room, and I was alone in the trade room, arranging some goods on the shelves behind the counter. I heard the door open, saw Calf Shirt coming in, apparently sober. I had resumed my work when suddenly he shouted to me: 'Raven Quiver, give me a keg of whisky or I will kill you.'

"I whirled around. He was pointing a big cap-and-ball pistol at me, hammer cocked, cap on the nipple gleaming. I sprang to my right, reaching for a six-shooter on a shelf under the counter. He fired at me, missed, ran.

"I shot at him as he went out and think my bullet struck into his left shoulder. Hearing the shots, the poker players came rushing out, firing at him as he ran for the gate in the stockade. He slowed up, staggered, and fell into a pit that we had dug in getting earth for the roof of the fort. We hauled him out of it, dead, examined him, found sixteen bullet holes in his body. We carried it to the river, dropped it into an air hole in the ice, and it disappeared. Strange enough, it bobbed up in an air hole below, and some women, gath-

[2] See "The Amazing Death of Calf Shirt," by Hugh A. Dempsey, *Montana: The Magazine of Western History*, Vol. III, No. 1 (January, 1953).

ering wood, saw it and ran to tell of their find. Calf Shirt's wives drew his body from the water, carried it to their lodge, asked the various medicine men to help them sing and pray over it for three days and so restore it to life. All refused; they did not want Calf Shirt brought to life, to murder more of his people, they said. The wives, fearing to do otherwise, prayed and sang over the body the prescribed time, then, doubtless with great relief, buried it."[3]

"Well, you saved us the trouble of hanging him when we came to the country," Colonel Macleod said.

PICKETT OBTAINS A WIFE (1883)[1]

AFTER OUR EXCITING YEARS of trading with the Indians for buffalo robes and furs, life at Fort Conrad was very tame for us. Late in that fall of 1882, Joseph Pickett came with his bull train and bullwhackers to winter with us. Except for the bimonthly Fort Benton–Fort Macleod mail stage, travel almost ceased as winter came on. At that time there were few settlers on Marias River: only Mose Soloman, at its junction with the Missouri; I. G. Baker & Company's cattle ranch, Dick Berry, foreman, due north toward Fort Benton; Brian Osborn and his Pikuni wife, seven miles below us; ourselves; Sol Abbot and Henry Powell and their Pikuni families, at Willows Round, twelve miles above us.

One day in December, Osborn came with his wife to trade with us, and Pickett, after seeing the woman, remarked in the presence of his bullwhackers: "How good looking, neat and clean she is. I wish that I could have such a woman."

No more was said about her, but a week or so later, one of the bullwhackers, Nolan by name, rode down to Osborn's place, murdered him, brought his grieving, crying wife up, and said to Pickett: "You said that you wanted a woman like her; well, there she is, herself. I've brought her for you; had to kill her old man to get her."

---

[3] Calf Shirt, as one of the representatives of the Bloods, had signed the "Stevens Treaty" on October 17, 1855, at the mouth of the Judith River. The treaty was ratified by the Senate on April 15, 1856. See Ewers, *The Blackfeet*, 205–25.

[1] Published in *The Great Falls Tribune* (November 11, 1936).

Pickett—all of us—were astounded by the crazy bullwhacker's atrocious deed. We cursed him, told him that we would take him to Fort Benton and turn him over to Sheriff Healy. He stole a saddle and horse from Pickett that night, and, as there was no snow on the ground, it was impossible for us to trail him. We never heard of him thereafter. Kipp's mother, Earth Woman, and Crow Woman took pity on the grieving widow, kept her with them for a month or more, when she took up with Pickett. Some years later, he sold his bull train and with her settled on the Crow Indian reservation. Some of their descendents are prosperous ranchers down there, I am told.

Came the spring of 1883, and again there was considerable travel on the road. In the New-Grass Moon (April) a few lodges of our Pikuni friends and relatives returned to summer beside us and to hunt deer and antelope. They reported that their agent, *Ahsi Tupi* ("Young Person," Major Young) had no food for the tribe, and that they were beginning to starve, having killed off nearly all of the game up there. And, too, their horse herds were becoming infected with a skin disease, something like a smallpox, that took off their hair.

We had a herd of about 150 horses, ranging across the river from the fort. Our Indian friends grazed their small herds in daytime up the Dry Fork of the Marias and, ever fearful of war parties, kept them in our large corral of nights. The Dry Fork joined the river at the lower end of our big bottom just below our fort. One evening in May, Kipp suddenly decided to go to Fort Benton the next morning and sent his young brothers-in-law out to bring in a four-horse team from the herd, so that he could make an early start. They returned at dusk, greatly excited, and reported that a war party had stolen the herd and gone off north with it; their trail was plain in the new grass of the plain. The news excited our friends camped near us: Little Dog, Little Plume, Ancient Man, Tail-Feathers-Coming-Over-the-Hill, Bear Chief, and Kipp's close friend Jack Miller, who was visiting him. They all were brave men, heroes of many battles with enemy tribes. Singing, donning their war clothes, cheered by their singing-praying women, they prepared to ride after the thieves.

Singing a war song, our friends forded the river and were gone into the moonlit night. We worried for them, slept but little, and were up early, looking for their coming. As hour after hour passed without sight of them we fell silent, dared not voice our fears for them. Late in the afternoon, Little Plume's sits-beside-him wife, eldest of three sisters he had married, made a Sun vow: loudly, before us all, she vowed to the Above One that, if He would bring her man safely back to us, she would in the coming Berries-Ripe Moon (July) build a sacred lodge in honor of Him. She had barely finished when we saw our warriors coming, driving our horses swiftly into the ford of the river. And then, singing a victory song, they neared us, Ancient Man waving a bloody human hand tied to the end of a stick, the others displaying enemy scalps and enemy guns. Their women ran to meet and hug them, loudly and repeatedly shouting their names, saying that they were brave, that they had made the enemy to cry.

Ancient Man then tossed the severed Cree hand down upon the ground, and spitefully the women and children got sticks and belabored it, anathematizing it as best they could in their language, which actually was woefully lacking in curse-words; "you female-dog face" was about the strongest of them.

We saw that Tail-Feathers-Coming-Over-the-Hill's head was bandaged and bloody, that Jack Miller's left leg was in like condition and that he was riding one of our horses; and soon we got the story of their night's adventure.

They had sighted the war party, seven of them, soon after topping Rocky Spring Ridge, some thirty miles north of us; the enemy, discovering that they were pursued, had taken shelter in a deep coulee and opened fire when our party had appeared upon its rim, a bullet cutting open Tail-Feathers-Coming-Over-the-Hill's scalp and knocking him senseless from his horse. Jack Miller had been shot in his leg and his horse killed. At that the others of our party had got down from their horses and, rapidly shooting at the Crees plainly visible in the moonlight, in no time had killed them all. They had thought Tail-Feathers-Coming-Over-the-Hill, motionless upon the ground, his head bleeding, to be dead. But he had soon become conscious, and a little later, when he was able to ride, they had set out for home.

I KILL MY FIRST MOUNTAIN GOAT (1883)[1]

SINCE ARRIVING in the country, I had heard much about two large, beautiful lakes, called by the whites Chief Mountain lakes; by the Blackfoot tribes *Púhktomuksi Kimiks*, "Lakes Inside." We did not then know that in 1846, Father Lacombe, S. J., assisted by his faithful guide Hugh Monroe, had set up a cross at the foot of the lower one of the lakes and with prayer had christened them St. Mary lakes.

I remembered hearing John Healy remark that upon the high mountains around them there were plenty of ibexes. That intrigued me. I was anxious to visit the lakes, particularly to learn if the animals described by Healy really could be ibexes, ruminants that, as I had always understood, were found only in the Swiss Alps.

In October of this year of 1883 came my opportunity to do that. One day there came down to the fort our friends Sol Abbot and Henry Powell, and announced that, with Charlie Phemmister, Jim Rutherford, and Oliver Sandoval, employees of Indian agent Major Young, and Charles Carter, a trapper, they were going on a hunting trip to Chief Mountain lakes, and would I join them? Ha! Would I! I put my rifle, shotgun, and bedding into their wagon, and with plenty of provisions we set out up river. We picked up Charles Carter at Abbot's ranch, and on the following day we neared the agency, stopped at the lodge of an Indian friend, and sent him on to notify Phemmister, Rutherford, and Sandoval that we had arrived. (The Indian Agent, Major Young, allowed no whites other than his employees upon the reservation; he gave out that he would arrest any white trespassers, have them tried and fined in the United States court in Helena. His reason for that we were later to learn.)

[1] Published in *The Great Falls Tribune* (November 18, 1936).

Our Indian friend and his family with whom we briefly stopped had only a little flour and some dried service berries in their lodge. He said that game had become so scarce that the hunters were often days in killing a deer or antelope, and worse, many of them had used all of their cartridges and had no furs or hides with which to get more from the agency trader. We gave him ten dollars, and happily smiling, truly grateful, he and his wives hurried up to the trader's store to buy beans, bacon, baking powder, sugar, and tea, provisions that, they said, they had been without since the extermination of the buffalo. In the evening, a number of prominent men of the tribe came in to visit and smoke with us and to tell of their need for food. Their condition worried me. Still, I did not then realize, as I did later, how serious the outlook was for the tribe, else, doubtless, I could have helped save many who were to die from starvation in the next few months.

Early on the following morning, avoiding the agency, we struck the big Indian trail paralleling the mountains, were joined by our three friends with team and wagon, and turned northward into country new to me. It was my first close view of the Rocky Mountains. I could not keep my eyes off them, rising so abruptly, towering so high above the plain. Had they names, I asked. "No, only that farther one in sight ahead, standing out as though in the lead of the others, its east face an almost sheer cliff." That was *Nina Istukwi*, "Chief Mountain" of the Blackfoot tribes, Abbot told me. I thought that never had a mountain been more appropriately named.

At noon we turned down into the beautiful, well-timbered valley of Cut Bank Creek and rested for a time beside the stream. I noted that its deep, clear pools fairly teemed with trout, many of large size. Our friend Oliver Sandoval, or *Imoyinum* ("Looks Furry"), was the son of a noted Spanish employee of the old American Fur Company and a staid, competent Pikuni woman. Of us all, he alone had ever been to Chief Mountain lakes and knew of a possible way for us to get to the lower one of them with wagons. Leaving Cut Bank Creek and following his lead, we crossed the south and then the middle fork of Milk River, the *Kinuk Sisakta* ("Little River"), and then turned into a branch trail running northwest, and up the high, steep ridge dividing the waters of the Missouri and Hudson Bay. Having crossed the Divide, we soon made camp at a large lake on the rim of a valley of Chief Mountain lakes, the *Ahkainus Kwona Ituktai* ("Many Chiefs Gathered River") of the Blackfeet.

The evening was cloudy—a hard, west wind blowing; countless flocks of ducks were hurtling over us. I got my shotgun and some cartridges from the wagon, ran out upon a long, narrow point jutting out into the lake, and began shooting at the flocks. They came and went on the west side of it, and the wind drifted those that I killed to the shore. I was soon back in camp with ten, all of them canvasbacks or redheads, most prized, most delicious of all the varieties of ducks. We quickly dressed them and Carter laid six of them in our big Dutch oven, already heated in the fire, and, against my protest, doused them with several cups of water—I maintaining that ducks should always be roasted, he insisted that they were best when stewed. It was dark when we gathered to eat them. They were tender enough, but to me rather flavorless. Carter said that the soup was grand. I alone refused a cup of it. The meal ended and the dishes washed, we took to our beds. Soon after midnight my companions began complaining of severe stomach pains and went frequently to the brush. Came morning and all were weak and gaunt. An examination of the Dutch oven evidenced that the delicious duck soup that they had eaten, cup after cup of it, had been almost pure grease. Right there and then I gave the lake the name that it bears today: Duck Lake.

We had an early-morning start from the lake and, still following the Indian trail, were soon looking at a scene so tremendous, so beautiful, that I felt I could gaze at it forever. Straight down from us was the lower one of the two lakes; close above it, the other and longer one, from whose shores the mountains rose in grandeur to great heights. It was no wonder that the Blackfeet had named them "Lakes Inside." With all respect for the memory of Father Lacombe, I think that the name he gave them is most inappropriate. It is the hope of many of us—some thousands of Indians and whites—that Mr. E. T. Scoyen, superintendent of Glacier National Park, will soon restore to them their Blackfoot name.[2]

Ours were the first wagons ever upon this branch of the great north-and-south foot of the mountain trail. As we followed it down, we were obliged here and there to cut out quaking aspens and young pines growing in it and heavily to brush several narrow, boggy streamlets in order to cross with the wagons. So going, we came at noon to the foot of the lower lake, turned up along it upon a well-used trail, and made camp on the first of the outjutting points above the outlet. We did no hunting that afternoon but in a few minutes caught, in the first pool of the river, enough trout for our supper and breakfast. To my surprise, there were three varieties of them: Mackinaws, natives, and another that I could not then identify—the Dolly Varden, as I was later to learn.

We regretted that we had not brought saddle horses with which to explore our surroundings and hunt. In lieu of them, on the following morning we crossed the river with team and wagon at a ford a few hundred yards below the foot of the lake. Then we picketed the horses and set out for a long, flat-topped, bare-topped mountain close to the west of the lake, its north end almost a sheer cliff of great height. We took to a steep, well-timbered ridge running up to the mountain and, unused to walking and climbing, soon tired; so much that, upon arriving at the timber line, we had no desire to make the still steeper climb up the shale and rocks to the top of the mountain. Our friend Sandoval said that he had heard the Kutenai Indians tell of a lick close under the north cliff of the mountain that was much used by the various game animals; so, after a good rest, we set out to find it, traveling slowly, cautiously, just within the edge of the timber and scanning constantly the long, steep slope for sight of game. So going until the east end of the cliff was straight above us, we discovered farther on a band of bighorn ewes and young leaving the timber, traveling away from us up the bare slope, beyond range of our rifles. They were not new to me. I had seen hundreds of them on the cliffs of the Missouri River badlands, and had even killed a few. What I was looking for, was most eager to see, were John Healy's "ibexes."

[2] The hope has not yet been realized; they are still labeled Saint Mary lakes on modern maps.

Where the bighorns had left the timber we discovered the lick. It was in a shallow, wide coulee: a bed of oozy, strongly alkaline mud, down which went a trickle of water—it, too, as we proved, bitterly alkaline and sulphurous. The edges of the lick were packed hard by the hooves of its frequenters and covered with their droppings; bighorns, elk, deer, and, we hoped, ibexes had been there. Said Abbot: "All we have to do to get some of 'em is set right here in the edge of the timber, and wait for 'em to come."

The others were for going on past the cliff and around back of the mountain. They left us, and we made ourselves comfortable for, if necessary, a long wait for the game to appear. But the gods were with us. Within an hour some white animals—seven—in single file, came in sight upon the shale east of the cliff, following a trail running quartering down to the lick close before us. "Ha! Ibexes. Headin' straight down toward the lick. Now we were smart to set here, 'stead of trapsin' on, lookin' for 'em," Abbot remarked.

"We will have a good look at them, see what they do, before we shoot," I said.

The trail that they followed turned sharply down to avoid a large boulder resting upon the shale and about a hundred yards from us; as they made the turn we got a clear view of them. Like the buffalo, they had humped backs, low hindquarters, chin whiskers, and long, wavy fringes of hair down to the knees of the forelegs, reminding one of a girl's pantalettes in the wind. But there their resemblance to the buffalo ceased, for their heads were long and narrow, their faces dishlike, of mournful, silly expression, and their round, tapering, sharp-pointed horns curved upward and backward instead of outward—deadly scimitars they would be in a fight.

On the seven came, slowly, steadily, and when at the lick, the nearest of them were not twenty yards from us. But that didn't matter as the wind was right. At once they all drank of the little streamlet running down the center of the lick, then turned out to an area where the white mud was about of the consistency of semi-hard putty, and, to our great surprise, bit out mouthfuls of it that they deliberately chewed and swallowed. Then, as one after another they drew out from the lick and stood, gazing this way, that way, Abbot nudged me; and quietly, screened by the juniper brush in which we sat, we raised our rifles, sighted them, and each fired once, killing each of us one of the seven. The others, instead of running off, merely gave a jump or two and stood vacuously staring at their twitching, dying companions until we arose and started toward them; then with long, swift leaps, they took off up the trail and were soon out of our sight.

Before skinning them, we carefully examined our kills, both mature males that would weigh, each of them, all of 250 pounds. We noted that, for their size, they had tremendous lung power; that they gave off a strong odor of musk; that underneath their long, coarse hair and next to their skin was a short growth of very fine wool; that at the base of their horns were black, rubbery, wartlike growths that fairly reeked of musk. "Well, Abbot," I said as we were sharpening our skinning knives, "I have read descriptions of ibexes, seen pictures of them, so I know that our kills, here, are not of that kind; not at all like them except both kinds have four legs, cloven hooves, and both are ruminants."

"Huh! I can tell you what they are," he said. "They're a kind of goat; built a whole lot like the goats I used to see when I was a youngster, away back in Missouri. True, their horns were kind of crinkly, but they had chin whiskers and hair floating out around their knees, same as these here. Yes, sir, they're a kind of goat."

"Well, we'll call them that. Goats they are from now on," I answered, I little thought that I was to learn, two years later, just what the interesting animals were.

We shouldered the hides and a little of the fat meat of our kills and started back down the mountain the way we had come; however, we were not quite done with goats for the day. When passing the east side of the great cliff, we discovered, not far beyond it, a lone goat walking down the steep slope of the mountain and heading toward the top of a small cliff jutting out from the shale. Having arrived at its outer edge, the goat sat down upon it haunches, its hams, its forepart supported by its perpendicular forelegs; with lowered head it gazed at the scene below, sitting just as dogs like to sit and gaze about them. That a ruminant would assume that posture was almost unbelievable. In skinning our kills we had wondered why the fur on their haunches was flattened, matted, and soiled. That was now explained; to sit upon their haunches was a habit of the goats. In after years I saw many of them resting and keeping watch upon their surroundings in that posture. They were all males. I doubt that the females have that habit.

Abbot and I rested at our wagon for several hours before the others joined us. They arrived loaded with the fat meat of a bighorn ram that Sandoval had killed behind the flat-topped mountain. They said that they had seen a number of elk, a band of goats, and three grizzlies, but had not attempted to kill any of them owing to the difficulty of getting out the meat. We had, that evening, a grand feast of broiled bighorn ribs. Thereafter, for five days we hunted close to our camp and, having killed all the elk and deer we wanted, struck out for home. Owing to our lack of saddle horses we had seen but little of the interesting region and had not even visited the upper lake. I vowed that as soon as possible I would return to explore its valleys and climb its mountains. Well, anyhow, I had given one of its outstanding features a name: Flat Top Mountain.

STARVATION WINTER (1883–84)[1]

DETOURING AROUND THE INDIAN AGENCY on our return home, we again camped with our Pikuni friends, and still more pitiful were the tales they told us of their suffering from want of food; of the decimation of their horse herds from a contagious skin disease. Gaunt, weak, and listless, they were themselves proof of their dire need. I at once gave them all the meat that we had in our wagon— that but a mouthful each for the members of the camp. I advised them to go up to the Lakes Inside country where game was still to be found. Sadly they replied that they had no cartridges and no horses to ride. Crying women came and held their skinny children up before us and asked that, as we loved our own children, in some

[1] Published in *The Great Falls Tribune* (November 18, 1936).

76

way to help their own hungry ones. I answered that I would do all that I possibly could for them.

I had long been a contributor to *Forest and Stream*, best of all outdoor magazines, published in New York, and so had had much correspondence with its owner and editor, George Bird Grinnell. So now, upon arriving home at Fort Conrad, I wrote him about the destitution of the Pikunis and asked what could be done to help them. In due time I received a wire from him, forwarded by mail from Fort Benton, advising that I go up to the reservation at once, make a thorough investigation of the conditions, and send him a full report on it. Twenty-four hours after getting the message, I rode into a camp of the Pikunis a couple of miles above the agency, on Badger Creek, and was welcomed in the lodge of my brother-in-law Boy Chief. In a lodge near it women were wailing for the dead; in answer to my query, Boy Chief said: "They mourn for old Black Antelope. Dead because of his defiance of the gods. Hunger gnawing him, he caught some spotted fish (trout), they, as you know, the property, the food of the terrible Underwater People—food forbidden to our kind. We all begged him not to do it. He would not heed our warnings. Ordered his women to cook them for him. They would not even touch the spotted ones. He cooked them himself, ate them all, four big spotted fish. That was last night. Just before you arrived, he died."

"Too bad. Poor old man. Forever gone from us," I said. Useless for me to say that trout were healthful, nourishing and that in the many streams of the reservation there were enough of them to keep all the tribe from starving. Nor could I advise them to kill and eat their horses, which to them were sacred animals of almost human attributes—animals that they loved almost as much as they did their children. And, different from other tribes, they believed that dogs were sacred animals and therefore forbidden food.

In turn I visited White Calf's and Three Sun's large camps on Two Medicine Lodges River, then Red Paint's camp of about one hundred lodges on Birch Creek. All alike, they were increasingly suffering from want of food—the weaker, tubercular ones already dying. Of big game none remained, either on the plain or in the near-by mountains, and small game such as rabbits, grouse, porcupines, and beavers were becoming very scarce. It was plainly evident that unless food, and great quantities of it, would be brought out to them, the whole tribe would die from starvation before the coming of another summer.

While I was in Red Paint's camp, the Rev. Prando, S. J., arrived for a talk with its leading men and asked me to be his interpreter. Soon we were thirty or forty gathered in Red Paint's large lodge, as one after another they told of their sufferings and asked the priest in some way to try to get food for them. He replied that he fully realized their needs and would do all that he possibly could for them. In the meantime, he said, they should follow his teachings; having led pure lives, when they came to die, their souls or, as I had to interpret it, "shadows" could go away up in the sky, there join World Maker (God) and ever afterward live happily. And then, concluding, he said impressively: "But mind this: if you fail to live good lives, then, when you die, your shadows will go deep down beneath the ground, down to that bad one, Fire Maker, where he will keep you forever burning."

Followed a long silence, broken at last by Red Paint. Said he, impressively: "Black Robe, the whites can do many wonderful things. I doubt not their ability, when they die, to go to their World Maker, far up in the sky. But look at us: have we wings to enable our shadows to fly up into the blue? No. Impossible for us to go up there. Have we claws like the badger to enable us to dig down to Fire Maker, for him to roast us perpetually? No. Black Robe, it is that, when we die, our shadows walk or ride out to the Sand Hills, north of here, there forever to remain. There to hunt shadow buffalo; roast shadow meat over shadow, heatless fires; live in shadow lodges. That, Black Robe, is what awaits us all. And so, I finish." With that, they all arose and one by one, in silence, left the lodge. And sad and worried was the expression on Father Prando's face.

Well, during the more than fifty years since that time, the priests and other missionaries have failed to change in any way the beliefs of the sun-worshiping Blackfeet tribes. Within the past two months[2]

[2] In the summer of 1936.

I have attended the impressive ceremonies of the Tobacco Planters society of the Alberta Blackfeet and the medicine-lodge rites of the Alberta Bloods and the Montana Pikunis. I, for one, am glad that they persist in their ancient faith. Their absolute and enthusiastic belief in it—oh, how different from the apathy of white Christian congregations.

Leaving Birch Creek, I returned to Little Dog's camp on Badger Creek and sent Boy Chief to the agency to tell Rutherford and Phemmister that I wanted to have a talk with them. They came long after dark, and I told them why I was there; asked them if the agent, Major Young, was doing anything toward obtaining food for his starving charges; if he had any on hand to give them.

Said Rutherford: "The old devil, he has plenty of shelled corn, brought upriver from Fort Benton, freighted out from there, but what does he do with it? Every mornin' feeds it to his chickens, the Indians standin' by, awful hungry, and lookin' on."

Said Phemmister: "He knows they're starving, but I don't believe he has written to Washington to get grub for them. What you want to do, to get a line on him, is to talk with his clerks, Ed. Garrett and Charlie Warner."

"I don't know them. Perhaps they won't give me the information I want," I said.

"We'll fix it for you to meet 'em anyhow. Come on," Rutherford offered.

We walked down to the agency. Rutherford unlocked the small gate in the stockade and relocked it after we had passed in. The log buildings formed three sides of the square. The clerks had been in bed. They lit a lamp. I was introduced to them, and when I had told them of my mission there they were plainly wary and frightened. But when I had assured them that I would keep to myself the source of what they could tell me, they talked; freely, bitterly they told of Young's cold-blooded supervision of his charges—he a prominent member of an eastern Methodist church. It was that, for some years, in his annual reports to the Secretary of the Interior, he had stated that he was civilizing the Pikunis; making self-supporting farmers of them. Ha! Civilizing them! Why, they had rarely come to the agency; they had been roaming the plains, living well upon the buffalo, selling buffalo robes for what they needed of white men's goods. Then, suddenly, the buffalo had been exterminated, and Young had had no supplies for the tribe; having reported that they were self-supporting, he dared not ask for help for them and so admit that he was a liar. Yes, and equally as bad as he were his two daughters, also church members. They had confiscated the few blankets remaining to be issued to the Indians and had dyed them, so obliterating the U.S.I.D. (United States Indian Department) with which they had been stamped.

On the following evening I was at home in Fort Conrad writing Grinnell a full report of my investigations on the reservation, urging him to do his utmost in behalf of the starving Pikunis. Mails were slow in those days; it was all of a month before I heard from him; he wrote that he had been in Washington interviewing the powers-that-be, showing them my report, urging that they take quick action on it. President Arthur himself had promised that good supplies of food would be sent to the tribe as soon as possible. So, anxiously, we waited to hear of their arrival. Weeks passed; months; we were learning how slowly the affairs of our government move because of its red tape. More and more families of the starving people came down to camp near us and hunt. Deer and antelope were becoming so few that they could not kill enough of them to supply their needs. We helped them as best we could with staple groceries, at considerable expense. Kipp's frugal, thrifty mother, Earth Woman, and her companion, Crow Woman, had nearly one hundred buffalo robes that they had in one way or another acquired during the last years of the herd. They had Kipp dispose of them in Fort Benton, and the nine hundred dollars worth of groceries that they received from the sale they generously doled out to their hungry Pikuni friends.

Came February, and we learned that, up around the agency, some of the Pikunis were daily dying from starvation. And then it was, when we believed that all were soon to die, that we got most wonderful news from there: Fort Shaw soldiers had arrived with many wagonloads of flour, bacon, beans, and other food for the hungry ones. Beef cattle had been driven in and were being slaughtered for them. One of Our Grandfather's chiefs had come, caused Young Person (Major Young) and his daughters to leave at once, and had put a new agent in his place.

We later made a count of those who had died from starvation that winter: nearly five hundred of the eighteen hundred members of the tribe had passed.[3] So ended the fourth great wrong that the Pikunis had suffered under our government. The others had been: two successive acts of confiscation of their country between the Musselshell and Marias rivers, by orders of Presidents U. S. Grant and Rutherford B. Hayes—both instances in direct violation of the duly ratified treaty which the United States had made with the tribe in 1855; and, earliest of the four, the massacre of 173 men, women, and children of the tribe by Colonel E. M. Baker and his troops on the Marias River on January 23, 1870.

[3] In contrast to these impressions by an eyewitness of many of the events of the Starvation Winter, see Ewers, *The Blackfeet*, 280–96, and Helen B. West, "Starvation Winter of the Blackfeet," *Montana: The Magazine of Modern History*, Vol. IX, No. 1 (1959), 1–19.

Schultz did not have access to Indian Bureau records. He had, however, made a thorough investigation of the plight of the Indians and had discussed it in the Blackfoot language with some of the starving people, including his own relatives by marriage. His account undoubtedly reflects contemporary beliefs and impressions observed at the time and place and was reported in sincerity and good faith.

CHAPTER FOUR

Hunts in the Rockies
with George Bird Grinnell (1884)[1]

IF LIFE AT FORT CONRAD in 1884 was very tame for us men, it was not so for our women. They were more than happy in the quietness and security of it all. For them no more wanderings over enemy-infested plains, no more nights of fear and trembling, listening to the carousing of our drink-crazed customers. In March my wife *Mutsi-Awotan-Ahki* (Fine Shield Woman) gave birth to our son, our only child. I was more than put out when, returning from a trip to Fort Benton, I learned that Father Prando, S. J., had appeared and named him Thomas. Said my wife: "It matters not what a Black Robe does. My uncle, Red Eagle, sacred medicine man, has named our little one from a powerful vision that Sun once gave him: he is Lone Wolf."

Well, that was a good Pikuni name. But I, as I had intended all along, named him Hart Merriam for C. Hart Merriam, noted natural-ist and anthropologist, and a good friend of my boyhood days.

Taking after his mother, artistic embroiderer with beads and colored porcupine quills, our youngster at an early age began con-fiscating my pencils and paper and making drawings of life as he saw it; striving to make better clay images of animals than the Indian children with whom he played. In due time he became a student in the Los Angeles Art School, then in the Chicago Art Institute, and later he was the only student that Thomas Moran, of Grand Canyon fame, ever liked and helped with his wizardry of form

[1] Published in *The Great Falls Tribune* (January 10, 1937).

and color. As Lone Wolf, rather than by his English name, he is well known in the art world for his spirited paintings and bronzes of the life of the old West.

Leaving me in charge of Fort Conrad in that spring of 1884, Kipp and Hiram Upham took over the store of the trader up at the Indian agency and built a store and saloon on Birch creek, just off the reservation, and on the Agency-Choteau-Sun River stage and freight road. Placer gold had been discovered in the Sweetgrass Hills. I had considerable trade from the miners there and from freighters and others plying between Fort Benton and Fort MacLeod, but my heart was not in it. The few days that I had spent at Lakes Inside (St. Mary lakes) in the previous autumn had turned me against a sedentary life. I wanted to be up there again, climbing mountains and exploring valleys as yet untrod by white men, living upon trout, the fat meat of bighorns, deer, and elk. On his occasional visits to me to learn how I was getting on, I would tell Kipp of my longings, but always he would reply: "No, sir; you're not going up there to fool away your time. You've got a woman and a boy to support now; and I need you here. Right here you stay."

Passed the summer. Came winter, and about the only travel on the road was the bimonthly Fort Benton–Fort Macleod mail stage. Again I wrote a number of stories for *Forest and Stream*, had much correspondence with its owner and editor George Bird Grinnell, with the result that, in the spring of 1885, he wrote that he would come out in September and go with me on a trip into the Lakes Inside, the St. Mary lakes country. Kipp was glad to have me go with so important a man, and in due time, getting our friend James Dawson to take my place at Fort Conrad, I moved up to the agency to await the stranger's coming. He arrived on the mail stage—a slender, quiet, fine-appearing man of medium height; in outing clothes that showed much use; his baggage a canvas-covered bedroll, a war sack, a Sharps .45 caliber rifle, and a fly rod. No tenderfoot he, we thought, and so were not surprised when we learned that he owned a fine ranch in Wyoming and that he had been the naturalist with General Custer's Black Hills expedition in 1873.

On the evening of Grinnell's arrival, I had head chief White Calf call a meeting of the prominent men of the Pikunis: Little Dog, Little Plume, Saiyi, Running Crane, and others. They gathered in Little Plume's lodge, and when we entered, I said to them: "I bring to you a true friend of yours. His home is many days' travel to the east; at the edge of the Everywhere Water. When you began to starve, to die, that dreadful winter back, I wrote him about it. What did he do when he had read my letter? He dropped his work, got onto a fire-wagon, went south to Our Grandfather's many-houses town. He went straight to Our Grandfather and told him of your need; told him that you Pikunis would all die unless food, plenty of food, could soon be given you. Said Our Grandfather to him: "How can it be that my Pikuni children are starving, dying, and I not know about it?"

"Answered my friend here: 'Grandfather, it is that your little chief that you have with them, he named Young Person, would not let you know about it because he had many times written you many lies; written you that the Pikunis were following the white man's road, that they had cattle and pigs, grew potatoes and other plants to eat.'

"Said Our Grandfather: 'Too bad. Too bad. Well, they shall not starve any longer than I can get food to them.' And at once he sent for his chief of soldiers, sent for other men, told them what to do. So was it that the soldiers at Point-of-Rocks River (Sun River) brought you food; that Spotted Cap (Charles Conrad) sent you many cattle. So now, my friends, you know that he here beside me and newly come is your real friend and helper."

"Yes! Yes! He is our friend." "Our powerful friend." "He saved us, he is a chief," all cried when I had finished, and one by one came forward and shook hands with Grinnell and earnestly gave him welcome. Then, briefly, he said that he was glad to be there with them, that he hoped to come to them again and again in future summers, that he had other Indian friends, particularly the Pawnees (Wolf People) with whom he had often camped and hunted buffalo.

"*Ha!* The Wolf People! Ever our enemies. You must tell us about them," said Little Plume.

Said Tail-Feathers-Coming-Over-the-Hill: "Later on for that. It is that we now have to name our new friend, make him one of us, a real Pikuni man as, at heart, I know he is."

"Yes, and it must be a powerful name that we give him, a name that will help him to survive all dangers, and attain old age," Saiyi put in. At once the circle gave earnest thought to it. Name after name was proposed and for one reason and another rejected, until, at last, Tail-Feathers-Coming-Over-the-Hill mentioned one that all approved. Whereat he said to Grinnell: "True friend come to us from far, several winters back one of our number died in very old age. He was very wise and of kindly heart, ever helpful to the sick, to helpless widows and fatherless children. Brave he was, a great warrior, victor in many battles with our enemies. He had a very powerful name, a name from a very sacred animal that Sun loves. Without doubt a powerful, sacred name. Helpful friend, come to us from far, we give you that name. You are 'Fisher Hat,' *(Pinutoyi Istsimokan)*."

Exclaimed the others: "We welcome you, Fisher Hat." "We are glad to have you with us this day." Their eyes shining, voices deep and trembly, there could be no doubt of their sincerity. It was really affecting. Grinnell was evidence of it when, haltingly, he told them that he appreciated their good will; that he would ever strive to be worthy of his new name. Then, at length, at their request, he gave them a vivid description of the Pawnees—their country, homes, and occupations, their beliefs and sacred medicines. It was late when we sought our couches.

On the following morning, with my team and wagon, and accompanied by Yellow Fish (Charles Rose) son of a onetime employee of the American Fur Company and a Pikuni woman, we set out for Lakes Inside and that evening camped at the foot of the lower one of them. On the next morning we took to the Indian and game trail running up that east side of the lake and, by much cutting of trees in the aspen groves which it threaded, got our team and wagon out upon the prairie between the two lakes late in the afternoon; then, fording the river, we made camp in the edge of a grove several hundred yards below the foot of the upper lake. We had obtained a good view of it and of the towering mountains rising from its shores, and Grinnell declared that it was more impressive—stupendously, almost unbelievably beautiful—than any view to be seen in the whole length and breadth of the Alps. And as for Yellowstone Park, compared with this part of the Rockies, it was merely flat country!

Early in the morning we were climbing the timbered ridge running up to the east end of the mountain which, in the fall of 1883, I had named Flat Top. It was easy going up to the edge of the timber. From there we had a steep climb up shale and slide rock to the wide, long top of the mountain, upon our way alarming two bands of bighorns that lost no time in running out of sight. We came to rest on the extreme east end of the mountain at the edge of the cliff dropping straight down for some hundreds of feet. On the bare slope running from the foot of it down into the timber was another band of bighorns, ewes and young, quartering down to the lick which our party had discovered in 1883. They drank of its alkaline water, the old ewes ate some of its mud, and then all climbed back up on the slope to rest, some of them pawing out comfortable beds in the shale. Grinnell was interested in a deep, narrow, and timbered valley a couple of miles to the north of us that ended in the big prairie at the foot of the lower lake and had its source in high, steep, here and there cliffed mountains some miles to the west. He said that the long, wide, white banks and fields upon them might prove to be glaciers. Too bad that we had not brought saddle and pack horses, so that we could go up there, camp, and explore the region. I made no reply to that; I was disgusted with myself for not having thought of it. I had planned that we would be simply a hunting party and that from our camp we could easily kill all the game that we would need.

Yellow Fish told us that the Blackfoot tribes had a name for the stream which we saw in the valley; it was *Iksikwoyi Ituktai*, "Swift-Flowing River." Grinnell said that Swift Current River would be more euphonious, and ever since then that has been its name.

As we sat there at the edge of the cliff, Yellow Fish, close at my left, suddenly whispered to me: "Don't move suddenly; slowly, a little turn, and look back; five white big-heads are nearing us." In turn, I translated that to Grinnell, and cautiously we looked back over our shoulders. Sure enough, coming from we knew not where, five big goats in single file were walking slowly toward us. We did not move until they were so near that we could see their eyes; then, as Grinnell slowly and with ready rifle turned to face them, they stopped and stared at us, and again I noted how vacuous, silly was the expression of their faces. Slowly bringing his Sharps rifle to his shoulder, Grinnell took careful aim at the leader, fired; it dropped, the others went bounding off, and we hurried to examine the kill, a big male. Then as we carefully skinned it, Grinnell told us in terms that I could only partly understand, and Yellow Fish not at all, just what the animal was: *Oreamnos Montanus* of the sub-family *Rupicaprinae*—neither a goat nor an antelope but having characteristics of both of them. Others of the group were the *Naemorhedus* of southeastern Asia and the *Budorcas* of Tibet. Said I when he had finished: "Well, for one who has a Yale Ph.D. degree in comparative osteology, you have been quite enlightening in the English that I understand. And, anyhow, we will call the animal a goat."

"At least a pronounceable name for it," he answered.

With its hide and head, we brought to camp a little of the meat of the goat, broiled it, but found it too tough and musky flavored to eat. So, in the morning, we set out to get meat that we could eat; from the foot of the upper lake we began climbing the aspen- and pine-clad slope of the mountain next south of Flat Top; finding some signs of elk, deer, and grizzlies, but seeing none of the animals. At last we came to the upper edge of the timber. From there a wide slope of shale and rocks rose steeply to the foot of the cliffs of the mountain. We climbed halfway up the slope, crossing trail after trail of bighorns and goats, and, coming to one that was particularly smoothed and scattered with droppings of the animals, turned south upon it, Grinnell leading. We had not gone far when, a couple of hundred yards ahead of us, a lone bighorn ram bounced out from a depression in the shale and went leaping swiftly on; at a distance of about three hundred yards he stopped, turned sidewise and stared at us, head proudly up, his perfectly circled horns, like washtubs, carried as though they had no weight at all. No more had it stopped than Grinnell brought his heavy rifle to his shoulder, quickly sighted it, fired, and the ram made one high leap, plowed down into the shale, and was still. Cried Yellow Fish, in Blackfoot, "Oh, *Ho, Hai!* This Fisher Hat, he did not kneel and rest his gun; just stood and aimed it, and with one shot killed the very far-off bighead."

Translating that for Grinnell, I added: "And so, appropriately, this where we are gets a name: it is Singleshot Mountain." That is the name it bears today.

The ram proved to be full grown, and very fat. Its head and horns alone were a heavy burden for one man. With it, and all the meat that we could carry, we turned back down to camp and had a feast of well-broiled ribs.

We found that there was a well-used Indian and game trail running up the west side of the upper lake. It was not used by the Blackfoot tribes, except occasional war parties of them, Yellow Fish told us. It was a trail of other-side-of-the-mountains tribes: Kutenais, Kalispels, Spokanes; and of the North Cutthroats (the Stonies), a mountain tribe of Assiniboines in Alberta. Blackfeet, Bloods, and Pikunis never had been mountain hunters. They had not liked to climb steep mountains for the meat they wanted, when on horseback they could run herds of buffalo and make great killings of them.

On a very warm, windless morning we took up this trail and, having followed it for about five miles, came to a creek that headed up back of Singleshot Mountain and the next one south of it. Saying that he would go well up the creek and try to kill a goat or bighorn, Yellow Fish started up it; Grinnell and I strolled down to the lake, sat on a long point running out in it, admired the view that we had of the mountains to the east and south, and talked of this and that, regretting that we had no saddle horses. Grinnell vowed that he would return a year from then, when, with a complete saddle and pack outfit, we would explore the source of Swift Current River. Passed several hours, and then Yellow Fish, up in the mountains, began shooting. Fourteen shots, as fast as he could work the lever of his Henry rifle; a pause, and then fourteen more shots; another pause, and then, more slowly, still other shots. He was, we thought, making a great killing of bighorns or goats, and we were much worried about it. We did not believe in killing game that was not actually needed for food or for museum placement and study. We returned to camp, and an hour or so later Yellow Fish came plodding in, silent, face drawn and sad, and slumped down upon his bedding.

"Well, what luck?" I asked.

"None. I shot all of my cartridges at a band of white big-heads, killed not one of them," he groaned.

"But you are a good shot; none better. It must be that the sights of your gun are out of place," I offered.

"No. Gun is all right. That every shot I fired failed to kill was a warning to me, a sure warning that some relative, someone dear to me, is dead," dejectedly he answered. And, though hard we tried, we could not turn him from that belief. Such warnings were well known, he said, and he named several hunters who had had that experience: missed, time and time again, game at close range that they had shot at, and, returning home, found that someone dear had died.

Said Grinnell: "Well, friend Yellow Fish, though you had bad luck, your hunt was not all for nothing. That little stream you followed up to where it heads, we name for you. From now on, it is Yellow Fish Creek, and next north of it is Yellow Fish Mountain.

Later, when we arrived at the agency, we learned that, early on the morning of the day of Yellow Fish's unsuccessful hunt, his mother had died. And he said to me: "*Apikuni*, now you know that my warning was true. It is that we Lone People (Indians) receive messages from our gods that the whites are never given by their different kind of gods."

For years the names that we had given to the scene of Yellow Fish's unsuccessful hunt remained. But the map makers of Glacier National Park, United States Geological Survey, in 1912 changed them, to our great disgust, to Whitefish Mountain and Roes Creek.

On that trip in 1885 we named one more outstanding feature of the region; Divide Mountain; the high, sharp-crested peak at the long ridge running eastward to the headwaters of the Mississippi and between the streams flowing to the Missouri and to the Saskatchewan; in other words, the dividing ridge between the waters of the Atlantic and the Arctic oceans. And that name remains.

The longer we remained at the lakes the more we regretted our lack of an outfit for exploring our surroundings of mountains and valleys; how much more interesting than hunting would have been the exploration of a region as yet unknown by white men. But anyhow, our stay of three weeks at the lakes was very pleasant. Of game we killed all that we needed, including a male, a female, and a kid goat that Grinnell would present to the American Museum of Natural History in New York. We caught, too, trout as needed. The pools of the river between the two lakes fairly swarmed with them. Noting that some of very large size would not rise to any kind of flies that he had, Grinnell tried a small spinner, and with the very first cast hooked and, after a long struggle with it, brought to gaff a Dolly Varden trout of about twenty pounds. On the east side of the Rockies, in the United States, the Dolly Varden is native only in St. Mary lakes and River. It is common, however, in all streams flowing into the Arctic Ocean as well as the Pacific from southern California northward.

I felt that in Grinnell, Fisher Hat, the Pikunis and I too had a real friend. I hated to see him go. His last words to me as he boarded the Sun River stage were: "Don't forget that *Forest and Stream* wants all the stories that you can write. *Apikuni*, until next September, au revoir."

CHAPTER FIVE

More Mountain Trails

WE NAME SOME MOUNTAINS (1885–87)[1]

THE WINTER OF 1885–86 was my last one at Fort Conrad. Joseph Kipp sold it to James McDevitt, onetime forceful sheriff of Chouteau County, who intended to become a cattleman there. So I closed the store and post office and moved up on the Blackfoot reservation. I built a home on Two Medicine Lodges River, about five miles north of the agency, and I was ready to continue with George Bird Grinnell our explorations in the section of the Rockies that is now Glacier National Park. He wrote me that he would come out from New York early in September and added that he had learned that a Professor Pumpelly, in the summer of 1883, had crossed the Rockies by way of Cut Bank River pass and had named for himself a glacier that he had discovered there. That was news to me and to all the Indians of the reservation, for we had not seen or heard of the Professor and his party. However, that convinced me that the great white cliff and fields that Grinnell and I had, in the previous autumn, seen on the mountains of the headwaters of St. Mary River and Swift Current River were really glaciers.

In that summer of 1886 three good friends of mine, with their families, came to reside upon the reservation: Hugh Monroe, Rising Wolf, who in 1816, when with the Pikuni tribe of the Blackfoot confederacy, was the first white man to traverse the Foot-of-the-Rockies Indian trail between the headwaters of the Saskatchewan and the Missouri rivers; William Jackson, his grandson, onetime scout for

1 Published in *The Great Falls Tribune* (October 18 and 25, 1936).

General Custer and General Miles, who was with Major Reno on the day of the Custer fight; J. B. (Jack) Monroe, experienced mountain man, hunter, and trapper (not related to Hugh Monroe).

Jack Monroe readily agreed to join our exploring expedition, and when Grinnell arrived early in September we met him at the agency with team and wagon, loaded with a complete camping outfit and the requisite number of saddle horses and pack horses for our purpose. But we were not to make an immediate start for the mountains; the Pikuni chief insisted that their good friend Fisher Hat (Grinnell) visit and council with them. Old Red Eagle, owner of the sacred elk-tongue medicine pipe and bundle, unwrapped it in honor of him, an hours-long ceremony of fervent singing of sacred songs, sacred dancing, and fervent prayers, in which Sun, Moon, and Morning Star were implored to give long and full life to Fisher Hat, true, helpful friend of the Pikunis. The sincerity of the old man and his men and women helpers, their absolute faith in their sky gods, was very affecting, even to us, unbelievers in any faith.

In good time we made camp, as in the previous autumn, close below the foot of Upper St. Mary Lake and on the west side of the river. Two days later, after caching most of our belongings—tent, groceries, and the like—we set out with saddle horses and a couple of pack horses to go up Swift Current River. From its junction with St. Mary River, we followed a good Indian and game trail up its north side, passed several small lakes in its course, and that evening camped on the shore of a beautiful lake at the junction of several of its forks—the Jealous Woman's Lake of the Blackfoot tribes, but now, to our great disgust, named Lake Josephine!

During the summer I had often talked with Hugh Monroe, Rising Wolf, about the St. Mary lakes–Swift Current River country, and he had told me that, years back, with his family he had often camped at the foot of Lower St. Mary Lake; once had wintered there; but had never gone up Swift Current farther than its third lake nor up St. Mary Valley farther than the foot of its upper lake, for always game of all kinds—buffalo, moose, elk, and deer—had been plentiful close to his camp. So when, in the morning, we saddled and packed our horses and set out up the left fork of the river, we felt that we were the first whites ever to traverse it.

Our objective was a long, wide, white slope of snow or ice upon a not far-off mountain. A short ride brought us to a small lake and to a stream of milky water foaming down into it from the white bank above.

"Glacial water! White with the rock grindings of a living, moving glacier!" Grinnell exclaimed.

All three of us excited, we hurriedly unsaddled and unpacked the horses, hobbled them, shouldered our rifles, took up the steep course of the milky torrent, and, a half-hour or so later, came to where it issued from a deep cave in a cliff of clear, green ice, several hundred feet high, and a half-mile or more wide. Impossible to climb it anywhere along its face. Grinnell said that the glacier had once extended all the way down into the valley and pointed to the long moraines, ridges of stones, that it had left there. Its ice was stratified, each stratum a compressed, deep fall of snow of far-back time.

We took up the steep, bare, rock slope bordering the right, the north side of the glacier. There was a deep gap between it and the ice, but we found a narrow in it that we jumped. The ice was everywhere covered with the still-melting snow of the previous winter and strewn with small rocks, tree branches, and twigs deposited by the winds. We saw that there were many crevasses in the ice, going straight down to unknown depth, and, fearing that some of the more narrow ones might still be crusted over with the winter snow, we walked very slowly and cautiously out toward the rounding center of the slope. We had not gone far when a lone bighorn ram suddenly appeared upon its crest and stood rigid, tense, staring at us. It was a long shot, but my faith in Grinnell's marksmanship was justified: With careful aim he fired his heavy Sharps, and down fell the ram and with a few convulsive kicks was still. Said Jack Monroe, as we came to the kill and sharpened our knives to butcher it: "What luck! What good luck! All in one morning, we discover a glacier and kill a fat ram upon it."

"Not luck, but a result of old Red Eagle's prayers for long and successful life for Fisher Hat," said I.

Grinnell, smoking his pipe, happily smiling, said, "Many are the believers in the efficacy of prayer."

We butchered the ram, carefully skinning the head and neck part for future mounting, then set out for the upper end of the glacier, stepping slowly, hesitantly, more than ever fearful of its crevasses. Looking into them, their smooth green ice walls fading into impenetrable darkness far below, we shivered. As at its sides there was a deep gap between the head of the glacier and the slope beyond, owing to heat radiation from the bare rocks, but again we found a narrow place, jumped it, and after a short, steep climb, made the summit of the mountain and found that we were standing upon the Continental Divide. To the west, northwest, and southwest, what a grand, what a breath-taking view we had of tremendous, snow-capped mountains, deep, timbered valleys strewn with lakes; the streams, branches of the Sacred Dancing Lake Creek of the Kutenai Indians, or, as named by the whites, McDonald Creek and McDonald Lake. An hour or more we sat there, taking it all in. Then returning to our kill, we took the head and as much of the meat as we could carry, and in gathering darkness got off the glacier and stumbled down the mountain to the little lake, our meager camp outfit, and thirsty horses. There, after we had built a fire, Grinnell produced a bottle of whisky, poured out three big cups of it, and said: "Let us drink to the very successful day we have had."

"Yes. And we will drink to our discoveries: Grinnell Glacier, and Grinnell Lake," said I.

"Good. That calls for two more drinks," said Jack Monroe, and in due time, after we had feasted upon broiled, fat bighorn ribs, we had them.

On the following morning we brought the rest of the bighorn meat down from the glacier, and in the afternoon moved back down to Jealous Woman's Lake, camping again near its outlet. The steep, wonderfully symmetrical mountain rising from the opposite shore of the lake so impressed me as of outstanding grandeur that then and there I named it Grinnell Mountain. So it was known and spoken of for years until some benighted official of the Geological Survey chose to rename it Stark Peak. Stark? We have never heard of the man.

Came evening, and as we sat before our campfire we heard a horse approaching—a shod horse, as was evidenced by the clinking of its shoes upon the rocky trail—and then came riding to us one whom I well knew: big-hearted, genial Lieutenant Beacom of the Third Infantry at Fort Shaw. Not only a tried warrior was he, but somewhat of a writer and anthropologist as well. Making no mention of my surprise to see him there, I quickly introduced him to Grinnell and Monroe, and, dismounting, he joined us before the fire and volunteered that with a few men of his company he had come from the fort to hunt and fish and was camped close below us, on the river. We had a pleasant evening with him, and he was greatly interested in our discovery of the glacier.

On the following morning, Lieutenant Beacom accompanying us, we set out to explore the headwaters of a creek running south into Swift Current River and joining it a little way below the lake. We found that it headed in two small, troutless lakes on the southwest side of a very high mountain at the head of the ridge dividing Swift Current River and Kennedy Creek. The latter, by the way, had been named by some of our old-timers for John Kennedy, who in 1878 had wintered near the mouth of the creek and traded there with the Kutenai Indians. We saw a number of bighorns and goats on the mountain but did not disturb them. Lieutenant Beacom named the mountain and the creek that we had followed for me, giving them my Pikuni name, *Apikuni* (Far-Off White Robe). The map makers of the Geological Survey misspelled it: they have it "Appekunny." The Pikuni chief, Running Crane, gave it to me. It was the name given him by a Sun priest—so-called medicine man—soon after he was born. Like other young warriors, after he had made a successful raid, killed an enemy, or taken enemy horses, he was given a new name. Some very successful warriors of the Blackfoot tribes had a succession of names during their lifetime.

Upon returning to camp that afternoon, we found that we were practically foodless; during our absence bears had made off with our fresh meat, bacon, and dried fruit, and ripped open our sack of flour. So on the following morning we parted with Lieutenant Beacom and returned to our main camp, close below the foot of Upper St. Mary Lake, where we still had plenty of food. There we remained for a couple of weeks, climbing Singleshot or Flat Top Mountain for what game we needed and fishing occasionally. We then returned to the agency, where Grinnell took stage for the railroad and home, saying that he would again be with us a year from then.

The winter of 1886–87 was a terrible one; we were actually snowed in. With greatest difficulty we on Two Medicine Lodges River made our way to the agency now and then for supplies. By January trader Kipp was out of tobacco and could get no more. But in that respect I was lucky. My wife's uncle, old Red Eagle, had some pounds of it in his sacred elk-tongue pipe bundle and gave me sparingly of it from time to time. Good, plug smoking tobacco. I greatly appreciated the favor. My little son became sick, and his mother got Red Eagle to pray for his recovery—hours-long ceremonial prayers and songs, during which the patient's face and hands were painted red, Sun's own sacred color. And the boy got well, owing, all said, to the Sun priest's prayers.

During the winter a French Canadian at the agency made an eighteen-foot Mackinaw boat for me. Came spring, and I loaded it on a wagon, with wife and son and complete outfit; in good time we made camp in the timber at the foot of Upper St. Mary Lake. When we were on the shore or out in the boat, my wife would often point to the first mountain on the east side of the lake and remark that she thought it the most imposing of them all, rising so steeply and to such great height, right up from the water. Then one day she said: "Up on Swift Current Creek you gave a big ice and a lake Fisher Hat's (Grinnell's) name. That mountain, across, you named because of his killing upon it of a bighead, Singleshot. So now I shall name this mountain that I like best of all. It is *Mekotsipitan Istuki* (Red Eagle Mountain)."

"Why that?" I asked.

"Why not that name? Well you know that by his sacred elk-

96

tongue pipe prayers he made well our sick little one. Yes, and last winter had he not given you of his sacred tobacco now and then you would have gone crazy. Though he worried about it, giving of sacred tobacco for use not sacred, still he gave it to you."

"Right you are. Red Eagle Mountain it is," I answered, and she was pleased.

We were surprised one day by thirty lodges of Kutenai Indians riding in and camping close to us. Some of them, particularly their leaders, Back-Coming-in-Sight, and Bear Hat, spoke Blackfoot well, so we soon got acquainted with and liked them. Mountain people, mountain hunters they. I noticed at once that the legs of the men were heavily muscled and their feet large from constantly climbing for the game they killed. Quite different from the slender-legged men of the Blackfoot tribes, who hunted on horseback or not at all. Again we were surprised when, near sunset, Chief Back-Coming-in-Sight rang a bell and all of his people gathered around him for evening prayers—prayers that the Black Robes had taught them. Said I to my wife: "It must have been that theirs was a poor religion for them to have turned from it to that of the whites."

"Have not turned from their old one. They say that as one belief is good, then two beliefs are even better," she answered.

On the morning after they arrived, many of the Kutenai men set off on foot to hunt, and by evening their camp was red with meat of bighorns, goats, elk, and deer. A few evenings later, one of the younger hunters said that if I cared to accompany him in the morning, he would take me to a place where bighorns were almost always to be found.

Early in the saddle, we struck up into the pines and firs running from the lake up to timber line on Divide Mountain and followed a good trail that I had not known was there. A ride of a couple of miles brought us to a good-sized creek, emptying into the lake about four miles up it. We followed the creek up for about four miles and came to the foot of a lake that I had never seen nor heard of—a beautiful lake about a mile in length, nestling at the south foot of steeply rising Red Eagle Mountain. Leaving the lake, we rode up the slope of the mountain next south of Divide Mountain but had not climbed far—only a half-mile or so—when we got down, tied our horses, and my Kutenai friend, taking the lead, said that we must proceed very silently and cautiously. As we stole on I could see that we were approaching the foot of a steep rock and shale slope running from the mountain cliff far down into the timber. My guide led on more and more slowly; at last signed to me to move up beside him. I found that he was standing at the brink of a wide draw running down into the timber from the foot of the slide rock—a draw of mud and a trickle of water—and in it, drinking and eating the mud, and within close range, were three bighorn rams. "You shoot the lower one of them," the Kutenai whispered. Together we took careful aim, fired; two rams fell, lay kicking, and as the other one ran off up the slide my friend dropped it with a single, well-placed shot. We scrambled down to butcher our kills and I tasted the water in the draw and found it to be very salty; it was no wonder that my friend had said that bighorns were almost always to be found there. Droppings and tracks in the draw, white tangles of hair in the brush above it, were evidence that it was a lick much frequented by goats, elk, and deer, as well as by bighorns.

We had much more meat than our two horses could carry, but it was not to be wasted, the Kutenai saying that he would come on the following day for all that we were obliged to leave. After loading the horses, we laid the remaining quarters of the animals side by side and stuck up over them, he his blanket, I my hat, and so made sure that the human scent of them would frighten off all the various prowlers of the night.

Arriving at camp just before sunset, I was so excited over my discoveries of the day that I had to tell my wife about them before unloading my horses. Said she when I had finished: "That little lake, it will be Red Eagle Lake, and its outlet, Red Eagle Creek."

"Yes," I agreed. And then, pointing, said: "That, on which we made our killing, is Kutenai Mountain, and the salt place on it where the various split hooves go to drink and eat, that is Kutenai Lick." And as we named them, in the long-ago, so are they on the Glacier Park map today.

After camping with us for a couple of weeks, our Kutenai friends moved on to trap and hunt northward and then cross back to their reservation in British Columbia by way of Crowsnest Pass. Somewhat later, after well caching my boat, I moved back to Two Medicine Lodges River and the agency, there to await the coming of Grinnell for another month in the mountains. He arrived early in September, and with him came one of his close friends, George H. Gould, of Santa Barbara, California. With team and wagon, a good camp outfit, groceries, and saddle horses, Jack Monroe and I met them at the agency, and on the following evening we were again in camp just below the foot of Upper St. Mary Lake and on the west side of the river.

George Gould was somewhat of an invalid. Accompanied by Jack Monroe, he hunted and fished near camp, while Grinnell and I ranged farther afield. Again we climbed to the top of Flat Top Mountain; on the shale slope of Singleshot Mountain he killed another fat bighorn, a ram of four years, a welcome addition to our larder. On one unforgettable day we saddled up early and struck out upon the trail running up the west side of the upper lake. The Kutenai Indians had told me that it was one of their own trails, that it ran up to the head of St. Mary River and on through a good pass to west-side Sacred Dancing Creek and Sacred Dancing Lake (McDonald's Lake). A ride of an hour and we crossed the creek that we had named for our friend, *Otokomi*, "Yellow Fish," and a little farther on, at the narrows of the lake, were faced by a high rock ledge up which the trail ran in zigzag ascent. We got off our horses and led them up it—along the edges of little cliffs, across steep rock slides, up two- or three-foot-high steps of rock that they had to jump—and so going, breathless and perspiring, we made the top and paused to rest, agreeing that the trail up the ledge was the most dangerous for horses of any that we had ever known.

Taking to the trail again, we followed it along the slope of the mountain next south of the one that we had named for Yellow Fish. For years afterward it was spoken of as Yellow Fish Mountain, Rose's Mountain, our friend's English name. But on the map of Glacier Park it is now Whitefish Mountain, and his creek is Roes Creek—names without any significance whatever. Charles Rose, now (1936)

99

in his seventy-ninth year, is a respected, influential member of the Pikuni tribe of the Blackfeet. His father, Albert Rose, was for years a trusted employee of the American Fur Company, and as such, one of the builders of Fort Benton. Charles early married *Ahkai Sinahki*, a worthy daughter of Chief Running Crane. Their good son William is anxious to have his father's name restored to the mountain and the creek that Grinnell and I named for him in the long-ago. We are many who hope that the park map makers will make the change.[2]

There was much sign of bighorns and goats in the trail that we were following along the mountainside, but look as we would, not one of the animals could we see. It was well past noon when we arrived at the end of the mountain and, at the brink of a fine stream putting into the lake from the north, got out of the saddle to eat our lunch and rest. There for the first time we obtained a good view of the head of the lake and noted a long white streak in its blue water —the glacial water of the river putting into it. And beyond, at the head of the valley, only a few miles away, were the glaciers—one of them, apparently, several miles wide. Said I, excitedly: "Fisher Hat, there *is* a glacier and a valley for us to explore; we'll get right at it." Grinnell sighed. "Would that we could, but our friend Gould isn't strong enough for the undertaking. We will have to postpone it until next fall."

Long we sat there taking in the beauty, the grandeur of the scene, and so interested in it all that we nearly forgot to eat our sandwiches. At last I got out my telescope and focused it at the upper reaches of the mountain along which we had come, and so discovered, one after another, three bands of goats along it. The first and nearest one, a band of eleven old males, was resting upon the shelf of a cliff —one of them sitting, doglike, upon his haunches and peering at the slope below. The two other bands were females and their young, yearlings and two-year-olds. We saw that it would be impossible to get within range of the first band, so got onto our horses and turned back on the trail to see what we could do with the second band, just going out of sight in a depression in the slope and close to the

---

[2] They have not done so; the maps still bear the names Whitefish Mountain and Roes Creek.

cliffs rising tier on tier to the summit of the mountain. We rode fast until nearly opposite the place where they had disappeared, then left our horses and began the steep climb up the yielding shale. A half-hour or so later, perspiring and all but breathless, we arrived at the foot of the lower one of the cliffs and the trail that the goats had been following. We took to it after a little and, arriving at the rim of the deep depression in the slope, discovered the goats down in it, resting, some of them, others browsing upon the brush and grasses there. Grinnell shot at an old female; she fell, and the others bunched together, stood looking this way, that way, and I had to laugh, so vacuous, silly was the expression of their faces. Twice more the old Sharps rifle boomed; a yearling and then a kid fell; and at that the others took to the cliffs, climbing, jumping up them where it seemed no living animal could secure footing, and soon passed out of sight over the jagged summit of the mountain.

We were long in measuring and skinning the goats, for Grinnell was to give them to the Smithsonian Institution. It was dusk when we got the heads and hides down to the horses and turned campward on the trail; and in the fading light we saw two more bands of goats coming down off the cliffs toward the north end of the mountain. Night had come when we arrived at the narrows, and we dared not attempt to descend the trail down its precipitous, dangerous ledge in the darkness. We unsaddled near the cliff dropping straight down into the lake; hobbled the horses; gathered a big pile of down timber; built a small fire; and stretched out before it for a long and foodless rest, broken now and then by the necessity to replenish the fire, for the night was frosty. Coyotes and owls serenaded us; down at the foot of the cliff a flock of Canada geese softly piped to one another; distant loons now and then gave out their quavering cries. I told of the religion of the Blackfoot tribes; and Grinnell told of the very different beliefs of the tribe that he well knew, the Pawnees, the one tribe north of Mexico that until recently had made annual human sacrifices of captive women to their gods. Also we talked of the plentitude of goats on the mountain back of us and gave it the name that it still bears, Goat Mountain. Came dawn, and as we shivered before our little fire we decided to name the mountains rising so grandly from the shore of the east side of the lake. Said Grinnell: "That one next above Red Eagle Mountain will be Little Chief Mountain; that is the Pawnee name for their friend and my friend, Captain Frank North, leader of the Pawnee scouts in a number of fights with the Sioux." We then agreed that the next one south should be Almost-a-Dog Mountain, for a good Pikuni friend of ours who in his time had been a great warrior and leader of his tribe. And then, because of its fantastic and spired summit, we named the last one of the row Mount Citadel. And so they are named on the maps of today. But, alas! On the maps the stream putting into the lake from the basin between Almost-a-Dog Mountain and Mount Citadel is Virginia Creek, and its falls, Virginia Falls. And we ask: What did Virginia Smith, or Jones, or Spoopendike, or whatever her name, have to do with the exploration of the region, that one of its interesting features should be named for her?

Careful and slow though we were in following the trail down the ledge, my horse stumbled, fell, and badly bruised a leg. Some years later I learned, to my disgust, that the ledge trail had been named the Golden Stairs!

That fall, after seeing Grinnell and Gould off for their homes, Jack Monroe and I, with our wives—my little son had been placed in boarding school—moved out with our belongings and built a fine cabin at our favorite camping place, the edge of the quaking aspen grove on the west side of St. Mary River, a few hundred yards below the foot of Upper St. Mary Lake. It was the first cabin built at the lakes. In November our friends Tail-Feathers-Coming-Over-the-Hill and Ancient Man came out to visit and hunt with us. Every morning, as was their lifelong habit, they got out of their beds, ran to the river, dropped their blankets, and plunged into the icy water for a short bath. It hardened them, they said, and enabled them even in coldest winter weather to butcher the game they killed without so much as frosting their bare fingers. Monroe decided that what was good for them would be good for him, too. But after his third morning bath with them he was stricken with a severe fever, became delirious, and for a time I feared that he would die. He was all of a month in recovering his health. When the lake froze over, and snow upon the ice afforded good footing, we had easy hunting. Hitching a horse to our homemade sled, we would ride up the lake, kill such bighorns as we needed, low down on Red Eagle or Goat Mountain, load them onto the sled, and be early home.

During the winter I continued my contributions to Grinnell's *Forest and Stream* and often heard from him—he writing enthusiastically of our proposed exploration of the head of St. Mary Valley and advising that we must have a large outfit, as he would be accompanied by two friends.

On a day in December, Tail-Feathers-Coming-Over-the-Hill and I were hunting along the foot of Red Eagle Mountain and, having killed a fine bighorn ram and butchered it, we built a fire and sat down before it to have a good smoke. By turns we inhaled whiffs from my friend's long-stemmed black stone pipe loaded with a mixture of good tobacco and fragrant *l'herbe*, he constantly and raptly gazing at the mountains across and up the valley. And at last, pointing, he said: "That mountain there, next above the one you call Goat Mountain, how very high it is, its summit far up into the blue. Of all the mountains that I have ever seen I think it the most beautiful. Were I younger, and were it summertime, how I would like to climb up and lie upon its summit, and fast, and pray Sun for a vision."

I had long admired the mountain, thought it the grandest one in all that region, and had often considered naming it but could think of no name that would be appropriate. But now my friend's remark was helpful; it gave me to see that the name should have some relation to Sun, chief god of the Blackfoot tribes. So, after a little I said to him: "We will name the mountain. Let us call it Going-to-the-Sun Mountain."

"Good. That is a powerful, a sacred name; it could not have a better one," he answered.

Since then, a poet and a writer, visitors in Glacier National Park, have written, the one a long poem, the other a tale, which they solemnly assert give the Blackfoot Indian legend of the naming of the mountain in far-back time!

OLD ACQUAINTANCES MEET (1888)[1]

OUR GOOD FRIEND William Jackson joined Jack Monroe and me in preparing to take Grinnell and his friends into the mountains. With team and wagon, saddle horses and pack horses, camp outfit and supplies, we met them at the agency, September 3, 1888. Grinnell's friends proved to be William H. Seward III, grandson of President Lincoln's Secretary of State, and Henry L. Stimson, who was to be, years later, President Hoover's Secretary of State. Both were keen, young, outdoor men. We arrived at Monroe's and my cabin on St. Mary River on September 5, and on the following morning, with saddle and pack outfit, set out for the head of the valley and made good time until arriving at the creek between Goat Mountain and Going-to-the-Sun Mountain. From there on we had to feel our way. We tried first to go up the floor of the valley, but the down timber and heavy brush obliged us to take to the lower slope of Going-to-the-Sun Mountain and then that of the next one to the southwest which, later, Grinnell named for his assistant editor of *Forest and Stream*, Mount Reynolds. From the far end of its slope we could see that the valley of the river was quite open, so we turned into it, followed it up, and near sunset made camp at a small lake at the south foot of a very steep little mountain, only a mile or so north of the great ice slope that was the main object of our venture. While cutting poles for our lodge we found stumps of some that had been cut all of ten feet above the ground; in a time of very deep snow they had been cut by Indians, as was evidenced by the circular hackings of them. Well, my Kutenai friends had told me that here was a pass in the range that they sometimes used.

That evening, as we sat around the lodge fire resting and smoking, Grinnell said to Jackson: "I seem to know your face. It must be that we have met somewhere before this."

Said Jackson: "*Ha!* I have it! You were the naturalist with General Custer's Black Hills expedition in '74. Well, I was one of his scouts. You and I were together on several little side trips."

"So we were! So we were!" Grinnell exclaimed. And with that

[1] Published in *The Great Falls Tribune* (November 1, 1936).

they recalled interesting incidents of the campaign. Then, at my request, Jackson told of Custer's disastrous campaign of 1876, and his own experiences in it. He related that the scouts had urged Custer not to attack the camp of the hostiles, as they were far too many for him to fight, but he would not heed their warning. "The night before the fight," he said, "We scouts were feeling low, particularly Bloody Knife, a Sioux, who had long been with Custer. He sat before our fire, vacant eyed, face sad, and at last said to us: 'My friends, I have been warned that I shall never see another setting of sun; it is that tomorrow I die.' And with that, drew back from the fire and stretched out beside his few belongings. Came morning. Custer split the command, ordered Major Reno, with part of it, and us scouts to go down the Little Bighorn and attack the upper end of the hostile camp, and he with his companies started to circle and attack its lower end. We started down the valley, scouts in the lead; not an enemy in sight. But soon, out from the timber close ahead of us, singing, shooting, came hundreds of Sioux and Cheyennes, far outnumbering us. I saw Bloody Knife, riding close at my side, go down, he the first one of us to be killed, and brave Charlie Reynolds, our chief of scouts, was the next one killed. Reno saw that there was but one thing to do: retreat to the hills. As his bugler was sounding the call, my horse, shot in his lungs, squealed shrilly and ran, carrying me well into the timber before he fell. I landed at the edge of a thick growth of willows and rose brush and had no more than crept into it than a swarm of the enemy began riding swiftly up past my hiding place and, though some of them saw my dead horse, they never stopped to take the saddle nor the roll of bedding tied to it, so intent were they to keep on and fight the hated soldiers. There I lay all that long hot day, knowing by the firing that Reno was making a stand somewhere up the valley. Came evening, and I saw a soldier moving slowly, aimlessly in the timber. I joined him, a private named Jones; told him that when it was fully dark we would try to join our command. But when in due time we neared the bluff upon which Reno was making his stand, we found that the Indians, great numbers of them, were gathered at a number of small fires in the timber below it. I told Jones that we would turn back.

" 'Back where?' he asked.

" 'You'll see,' I answered, and led him down the valley, looking for dead Indians. Found some, got from them what I wanted: two light-colored blankets—one was white, one red—and two pairs of moccasins. We put on the moccasins; tied our shoes to our belts; wrapped ourselves in the blankets, Indian fashion, and turned back up the valley, Jones all trembly over what we were to attempt. We neared the line of watch fires, walking steadily, easily, hoping to pass them without being noticed.

"But when we were right between two of the fires a man at the one on our left called out: 'You two there, who are you? Where going?'

"I can speak Sioux well, but my heart was hammering and I was trembly as I answered, lightly, carelessly, I hoped: 'Just us. Going up a little way to look where the soldiers are.'

"The man said no more. We kept on; began climbing the timbered slope; presently heard a number of Indians coming straight down toward us. We ran—I to the right, and I knew that Jones had gone in some other direction. I stumbled over a big fallen tree, stretched out close at its side; I heard Indians coming toward me, knew that they had heard us running. Two of them came up against my tree, climbed over it close beyond my head, and I heard one say, as they passed on: 'Couldn't have been deer, not after all the shooting here.' And then the other one: 'None of us would be running in here; they must be soldiers that we have overlooked.'

Soon after they passed, there was some scattered shooting that enabled me accurately to locate Reno's position. I did not move until near morning, then began climbing the slope. I feared that there would be many of the enemy lying up at the edge of the timber, and as I came to it, passed out of it, I expected that every step I took would be my last one.

"But none of the enemy called to me or shot at me, and what was my relief when I heard a sentry shout: 'Hey, you down there, halt!'

" 'Don't shoot. It's me, Jackson, one of your scouts,' I yelled as I ran on up, and was soon within our lines and being questioned by our officers. Jones, about starved, did not join us until the following night, after the hostiles had fled. Well, it is bedtime, so, as the Blackfeet say: *Kyi!* I've finished."[2]

"Oh, no! Tell us more; tell us about Custer," young Stimson pled. But said Grinnell: "We have a hard day before us—a big glacier to visit. I think we should sleep." And sleep we did. However, in evenings thereafter Jackson gave us the whole story of his scout life, beginning in 1873 with General Custer, then with General Miles, and finally with the Royal Northwest Mounted Police during Riel's Rebellion. And very interesting it was. Well, his mother was a daughter of Hugh Monroe, his father, James Jackson, was a brave member of the American Fur Company. So was it that he was born to be a warrior. We all mourned his passing when in 1903 and in his prime he died from tuberculosis.

While breakfasting at sunrise, we counted twenty-seven goats on the mountain rising precipitously from the north shore of the little lake at which we were camped. An hour later we arrived at the foot of the big glacier and the main source of St. Mary River, a number of milky streams flowing from deep caverns in the ice, in places several hundred feet thick. Climbing up onto the glacier, we spent nearly the whole day going over it and estimated its greatest length, east and west, to be three miles, its greatest width, a mile and one-half. That evening we considered naming the glacier.

"Pikuni Glacier," Jackson offered.

"Kutenai Glacier," said I.

"Let us name it Blackfoot Glacier, for that takes in the Pikunis, the Bloods, and the Blackfeet, all three tribes of the confederacy," said Grinnell; and so we named it and the mountain upon which it rests.

On the following morning, refusing any assistance by us, Stimson and Seward set out to hunt goats on the mountain across the lake; we others started for the pass of which the Kutenai Indians had told me. A $\vee$-shaped notch in the summit of the range, a couple of miles southwest of camp, seemed to be, and soon proved to be it; approaching the notch, we found an old trail and along it the old cuttings of

[2] The story is told in greater detail in James W. Schultz, *William Jackson, Indian Scout* (Houghton Mifflin Company, 1926).

the stunted trees that led us directly and easily to it, and presently we were having a grand view of the west side of the range. Upon returning to camp, Grinnell said to us: "Now look: that notch, the summit of the pass, is like the notch in the rear sight of a rifle, and the tip of that west-side mountain just showing beyond it is like a front sight, so let us name this Gunsight Pass, the mountain on its right Mount Gunsight, and this little sheet of water here Gunsight Lake." And as he named them, so are they, too, on the map today.

Upon our way back to camp from the pass, we had heard a lot of shooting up on the mountain that Stimson and Seward had ascended.

"In all, twenty-seven shots," Monroe said.

"Enough shooting to have killed all the goats on the mountain," said Jackson.

"Yes. A real fusillade up there," said I.

"Ha! A good name in remembrance of their hunt up there is Fusillade Mountain," said Grinnell. But when the hunters came in with only the head and hide of one young goat, they were not pleased with the name. However, it has never been changed.[3]

We stopped at Gunsight Lake only four days; then returned to our main camp and supplies at Monroe's and my cabin, just below the upper lake. From there we hunted on Flat Top and Singleshot Mountains for what meat we needed, and fished occasionally. Grinnell and I early one morning saddled our horses and rode up to Red Eagle Lake. From its shore we discovered a number of goats on Red Eagle Mountain and decided that, instead of climbing for them, we would explore the head of the valley. The going was good up the east shore of the lake. At its head we crossed the creek and at once found an old trail running up the valley. My Kutenai friend who had introduced me to Kutenai Lick had told me of it and said that it was another one of his tribe's across-the-mountains trails, but that it had not been used for a very long time. We had but little trouble following it, only occasionally detouring fallen trees. When we were only a little way above the lake, a cow moose and her calf came

[3] For a full account of the naming of the topographical features of Glacier National Park, see James W. Schultz, *Signposts of Adventure, Glacier National Park as the Indians Knew It* (Houghton Mifflin Company, 1926).

from a dense growth of willows, stared at us for all of a minute, then went trotting off. Not for us to shoot the cow, as we had plenty of fat bighorn meat in camp. Farther on, we saw several elk, and there was much sign of them in the trail. About five miles above the lake we began climbing steeply, and so came to the foot of a glacier and, picketing our horses, climbed up onto it. It was, we estimated, not quite so large as Grinnell Glacier. Since it was getting late, we had no time thoroughly to go over it, but we named it for our good, old Sunpriest friend, Red Eagle Glacier.

On our way back we discovered, low down on the south slope of Red Eagle Mountain, a band of goats and, leaving our horses, climbed up toward them, as Grinnell had still a number of requests for them from various museums. We had no difficulty in approaching the band, and he killed two: a mature female and her little one. By the time we got their hides and heads down to our horses it was dark. So again we gathered a lot of down timber for a fire and stopped for the night. Needless to say that we were very hungry when, at about eight o'clock the next morning, we arrived in camp. We stopped there for several weeks, then pulled in to the agency, and our Easterners took the stage for the railroad and home.

Grinnell had for some years, on and off, been with the Pawnee Indians, getting from them their history as they knew it, their religion, and social customs. He told me that in the succeeding summer he would visit the tribe for the last time, to complete a book that he had in mind about them. So I should not expect him to be with me in the succeeding autumn.

CHAPTER SIX

Later Trails and Tragedy

HUNTING BIGHORNS WITH THE BARINGS (1889)[1]

IN AUGUST, 1889, Joseph Kipp and I went to Fort Benton, and upon arriving there genial Charles Conrad of the firm of I. G. Baker & Company said to us: "Glad you have come. I was going to write you. I have a letter from the Baring brothers. They want to have a hunt in the St. Mary lakes country this fall and ask me to engage guides and outfit for them. Well, you are the ones to do that."

"The Baring brothers, who are they?" Kipp asked.

"What, you never heard of them? Why, next to the Bank of England they are the greatest of English bankers, and they have, too, a branch office in New York, managed by the Honorable Cecil Baring. Here, read his letter."

We did so and learned that they would be a party of three, and with them would come Jack Bean of Bozeman, Montana, who in the previous autumn had outfitted and guided them and given them a successful hunt for deer and elk in the Yellowstone country. They now wanted to hunt bighorns and Rocky Mountain goats. The letter was quite explicit in explaining the outfit that would be required; evidently the writer was no tenderfoot. He stated that he did not want saddle horses. He was bringing a large, folding canvas boat, and his plan was to hunt on foot, for the reason that he and the other members of the party were experienced mountain climbers.

Mr. Conrad wrote Mr. Baring that all was arranged for the hunt, and with two four-horse teams and wagons, complete camp outfit

[1] Published in *The Great Falls Tribune* (November 8, 1936).

and supplies, we met the party on September 1. They were Thomas
Baring, head of the firm, a vigorous man of about fifty-five; Colonel
Robert Baring, about sixty, slender and wiry; their nephew Cecil,
about thirty, a fine upstanding man; Jack Bean, about forty-five and
strong. He had been a member of that ill-fated Yellowstone expedition of 1874.

In due time we made camp at the foot of Upper St. Mary Lake,
west side of the outlet, and put up our two tents; our cook, Charlie
Bristol, whom all old-timers will remember, gave us a fine supper,
and in the evening we began to get acquainted with the Englishmen.
I will say right here that finer men I never met. Besides the folding
boat they had brought a forty-five-pound bear trap, both of which
they later gave to me. Then there was a case of champagne, pints,
which only Colonel Baring drank—a bottle in the evening with his
supper. They had, too, six quarts of whisky which had been put
down in their London wine cellar in 1834, and "Governor" Baring,
as the Colonel and Cecil called him, gave out that only on an evening when a kill had been made by one of the party should it be
touched. The weapons of all three of them were double-barreled
Purdy express rifles of .45 caliber. They each had a sleeping bag of
beaver, fur inside, and blankets as well. On that first night they
found the bags too hot, and soon had to crawl out of them.

Came morning, and we had an early breakfast. The Colonel and
the Governor decided to do some fly fishing, and Cecil and I set out
for meat. We took to the long pine ridge running up to the north
of Flat Top Mountain and by ten o'clock were above timber and
slowly climbing the steep shale and rock slope. There was no game
in sight when we arrived on top so, after a good rest, we set out south
along the wide, sometimes flat, sometimes rounded, summit. So
going, we raised seven bighorn rams that had been lying in a depression of the summit; we were almost upon them before they saw
us. They ran, suddenly stopped to look at us, and Cecil fired, dropped
one of them, and how pleased he was; he long examined, admired it
before we got out our knives to butcher it. In due time I made a pack
of its head and long neck skin, he took its hind quarters, and we
started campward. We both had heavy loads; the way was long;

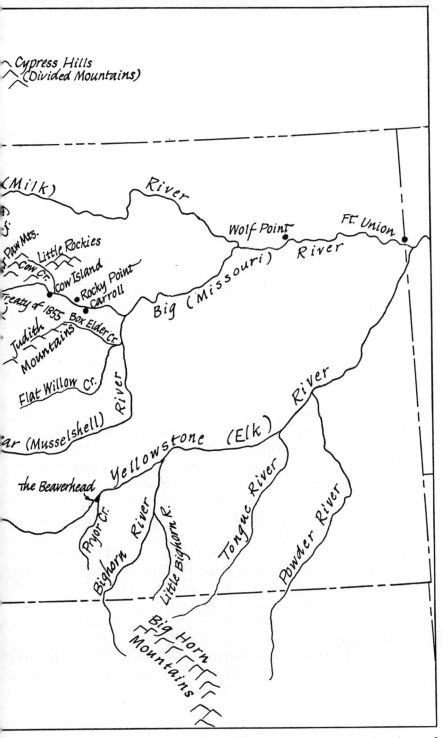

The area ranged by Schultz and his Blackfeet during the time of the buffalo. It is generally bounded by the present state of Montana.

often we were obliged to stop and rest. Evening had come, supper was almost ready when we got in and slumped down before the fire.

The Colonel and the Governor exclaimed over the perfect head of the ram. The Governor hurried to his tent, brought out a bottle of whisky, called upon the cook to produce cups, and partly filled one for each of us. I sniffed mine; what wonderful perfume! I tasted it. In substance it was like very thin syrup, of exquisite flavor. There were about four ounces of it. I gradually drank it all and felt a warm glow from head to toes. I leaned back against a tree and enjoyed the feeling. Presently our cook shouted: "Grub pile! Come an' get it!" I got up on my feet, staggered, fell backward; although not drunk, I was all but paralyzed. I saw Kipp reeling toward the supper layout, saw him drop down upon the tin plates with a loud clatter of them. And with that I slept. Yes, that 1834 whisky was powerful stuff.

At breakfast the next morning we decided to camp well up toward the head of the upper lake, where we would have to do but little climbing for game. We got out my eighteen-foot Mackinaw boat from its hiding place, put the canvas boat together, loaded them with our equipment, and were off. The day was windless; the lake, as smooth as glass. At the Narrows, we saw a band of goats high up on Red Eagle Mountain. The farther we went, the more our party exclaimed upon the grandeur, the impressive beauty of the scene. Said Colonel Robert Baring: "I have been in the Alps of Switzerland, the Himalayas in India, but in neither of those ranges have I seen any setting of lake and mountains that can compare with this before us."

As I had intended before we started, we made camp at the mouth of the creek putting into the lake between Goat Mountain and Going-to-the-Sun Mountain. And when we had set up the tents and were resting, I told of the day when Grinnell and I had come up this far, turned back, killed three goats, and camped all night above the drop in the trail at the Narrows, and so named Goat Mountain.

While I told of that and other of Grinnell's and my experiences in the region, Colonel Baring was putting his fly rod together. I finished, and he stepped over to the shore of the lake where the creek cut in, and we all interestedly looked to see what success he would have. At his very first cast he hooked a good one; expertly played it. Jack

Bean ran to him, offered to take the landing net. The Colonel refused; said that he wanted to handle the trout himself. In due time he scooped it out, a cutthroat of all of six pounds. When asked: "How many of you want trout for supper?" Kipp, Jack Bean, and I said that we preferred the fat meat of the bighorn that we had brought along. Whereat, and no doubt regretfully, the Colonel put away his rod. He was one of the few sportsmen who do not believe in wasting the lives of the creatures of the wild.

Said Charlie Bristol to Kipp and me that evening: "For God's sake get busy; see that they kill something tomorrow. I want another drink of their whisky."

After an early breakfast we set out together, all six of us, crossed the creek, and took to the game trail (the Kutenai trail) running along the lower slope of Going-to-the-Sun Mountain. We had not traveled a mile when we discovered a big male goat on a ledge a couple of hundred yards above the trail. As we were looking at it, the big one moved back and out of sight. Back of the ledge was a high cliff. We waited and waited for the goat to appear at one or the other end of the ledge and at last decided that it had lain down for its morning rest. Said Governor Baring to Jack Bean: "Jack, go up there and raise the lazy beast."

"Sure, I'll do that," Jack replied. Then he scanned the ledge. It would be a difficult climb but it could be done. He laid down his rifle and began climbing the steep slope; he came to the ledge, some thirty feet in height, slowly, arduously ascended it, reached the top, and disappeared. Then, a moment after, he came running out, the big goat after him. He sprang off the ledge, came running, tumbling down it, and the goat stopped at its edge, staring down at him. Governor Baring took quick aim, fired, and the goat also plunged off the ledge, also came rolling, tumbling down, and when Jack got up on his feet, was beside him. And then we laughed. When Jack recovered his breath, he told us that when he topped the ledge the goat was back at the foot of the cliff asleep. But hearing his approach, it wakened, stared for a moment, then sprang up and, fur all fluffed, came leaping toward him. "Gosh! He sure looked fierce. I didn't want them sharp horns of his goring me. You bet I got down off that ledge the best I could," he ended.

The best was none too good. Jack's cheek was gashed, and one wrist was slightly sprained.

As we neared camp Charlie Bristol was stirring a bowl of something for our dinner. He sprang up, saw that we had made a kill, and broadly grinning, waving his long spoon, he danced a hornpipe. Said Governor Baring to him: "Yes, Charlie, get out the cups."

It was a morning or two later that Cecil Baring and I struck up the game trail paralleling the creek at the mouth of which we were camped. On our left—and close—rose cliff after cliff of Going-to-the-Sun Mountain. On our right Goat Mountain sloped sharply up from the creek. A not-steep walk of a mile or so, and we came to a large basin back of the two mountains. A fine glacier on the south side of it proved to be the main source of the creek, and at the head of the basin loomed up the high peak that Grinnell and I had named for a good Pikuni friend, Mount Siyeh (Mad Wolf), now long since dead. He had been a man of fine character, a great warrior, and leader of many successful raids against enemy tribes.

No more had we entered the basin than we discovered a band of female goats and young up on its north slope. Sheltered by the scrub pines and junipers, we thought to have no difficulty in going up close to them, but as we toiled on and were almost near enough to the band for our purpose, the wind suddenly shifted; they got odor of us and went jumping and running up over the crest of the basin and out of sight. We followed; twice during the day we attempted to get near them and failed. The sun was setting when we arrived at the foot of the basin upon our campward way. And then—cheering sight!—we saw a lone, big billy goat on a cliff of Going-to-the-Sun Mountain. We were then in the timber; he had not seen us; he just sat at the edge of the cliff looking down at the foot of it. We climbed up as near as we could, up to the edge of the timber, and from there the goat was a long shot away; anyhow, Cecil opened fire at it with his Purdy express rifle. At the first shot the goat sprang up and stood sideways to us. The second shot seemed to have hit, but the goat started trotting along the narrow cliff, heading to the west. Cecil fired again and again and again; at last the goat came to a stand, and Cecil said to me: "I have fired my last cartridge."

I gave him my rifle, a Winchester of .45 caliber, and one by one he fired all of the cartridges in its magazine, and I had no more. And still the goat stood on the narrow shelf, head to the west, and motionless. As near as we could make out in the gathering dusk, close ahead of the goat the shelf pinched out and was so narrow that it could not turn around and go back. So, cartridgeless, tired and hungry, we dropped back to the trail and thence to camp, there to find that Governor Baring had killed a fine bighorn ram on Goat Mountain. So was it that Cecil and I, too, had an appetizer of the old 1834 whisky before eating the late and bountiful supper awaiting us. And much talk we all had about the goat that we had left on that high, narrow cliff shelf of Going-to-the-Sun Mountain. Would it be there in the morning? We wondered.

I awakened Cecil at dawn. Breakfastless, we sped up the trail, and lo! there was the big billy goat standing motionless on that narrow shelf, just as we had last seen him the night before. We left the trail, climbed up through the timber and partly up the rocky slope below the cliff. Cecil then took careful aim, fired, and the goat slumped off the shelf, came turning end over end down the several hundred feet of the drop, and struck the top of the slope with a tremendous crash. "That ends it. No use to go up there to a shapeless mass of splintered bones and minced flesh," I said. But of course we did go and to our great surprise found the head and horns of the big goat intact. It had struck rump first on the hard, rocky slope, with the result that its hind quarters were as I had described them. So was it that Cecil had a fine goat head which would in time look down from a wall of his home.

That evening just before supper, Governor Baring broached another bottle of the '34 for us, I raised my cup and said: "Let us drink to Baring Creek, Baring Basin, Baring Glacier. And may they so be lettered on the maps of the future."

So are they—two of them, the creek and the basin. And I ask, what right had one Sexton, whoever he is, to have Baring Glacier renamed for him?

Colonel Robert Baring was over sixty years of age, had spent many arduous years in the enervating climate of India, yet still was a vigorous man. So far on this hunt he had made no kill. It was now for me to take him out for a day, Kipp and Jack Bean said. After an early breakfast we got into the canvas boat, and I rowed it diagonally down across the lake, landing at the mouth of a little creek rising in a basin between Red Eagle and Little Chief Mountains. The climb up into it was quite steep but not long, and the footing was good. Upon arriving at the lower end of the basin we at once sighted a band of fifteen or twenty goats at its upper end: females and young, yearlings and two-year-olds. Some of them were lying down, others, grazing; but, unfortunately, they were so located that we could not get within five hundred yards of them unseen. I told the Colonel that there was but one thing to do: sit down right where we were in the scrub pines and wait for them to move elsewhere. We had watched them for about an hour when another band of goats appeared on the crest of the mountain at the extreme head of the basin, and after a pause on the crest, started down the steep, bare slope. Those of the lower band that were lying down at once sprang up, and all stood watching the newcomers. As they came near, the old females began walking stiffly, sideways, shaking their heads, and those of the lower band in like manner advanced. They met, and for five minutes or more we witnessed some very amusing sham battles: wonderfully agile leapings and buttings of the old ones, the young ones looking interestedly on. At times two old ones would stand upon their hind legs, breast to breast, and jab at one another with their sharp horns.

At last they quieted down; for a little they moved restlessly about, nibbling the grass and short brush. Then an old female and her two young started down the slope, and presently all the others were following.

"Colonel, they are coming. I believe they will come straight to us. Be ready," I said.

"What shall I do?" he asked.

For answer, I had him creep out a little way, sit in the shelter of some low junipers, and put his ten cartridges in his hat on the ground at his side. And then I sat close behind him.

Leisurely grazing, the kids jumping and bucking and chasing one another, on came the band, all of forty of them. When about three hundred yards from us they struck the little creek, beginning in a great snowbank high up on the south side of the basin, and there paused to drink. The Colonel raised his rifle, preparing to take aim.

"Wait! Don't shoot now; they may come nearer," I whispered. He nodded assent. And sure enough they presently did resume their way toward us. The leaders were about 150 yards off when the Colonel opened fire, one barrel of his Purdy quickly after the other. No hit. Surprised, the goats simply stood and stared—this way, that way—until the Colonel again fired twice. Then bunching, they started running up the south slope of the basin, and the Colonel kept firing at them as fast as he could reload, still making no hit. He fired his last cartridge at them when they were well up on the steep, bare slope, all of 500 yards away. The ball struck the rocks in front of them with a loud smack and raising of dust spray, and lo! they turned short about and came leaping straight down toward us. "Here, take my rifle, and don't shoot until they are close," I said, and eagerly he grasped my Winchester.

It was, I believe, the intention of the goats to cross the basin and seek safety on the lakeward side of Red Eagle Mountain. Anyhow, that way they were heading and were about to run right into us when the Colonel fired at one of the leaders, an old female, not fifty feet from us, and down she fell. And at once the band turned and streaked off up the basin and over the crest of the mountain.

The Colonel had little to say while I was taking the hide and head of the goat, more than frankly to tell me that he had done some very poor shooting. I countered by relating that, in my first year, first month in the country, I had emptied my Winchester at a band of several hundred antelope, running not a hundred yards from me, without killing or even crippling one of them.

"Well, Colonel, the excitement of the day is over. Ready to go?" I asked. He nodded assent, and I shouldered the hide and head of the goat and led off down the mountain at a pretty swift pace. And little did I think of all that was in store for us before we should reach camp. When halfway down to the lake I stepped upon an old log and, as I sprang off, heard and saw hornets swarming from it. "Look out,

Colonel! Hornets! Keep away," I shouted. Too late. He had come to the log, and the big insects were stinging him—stinging his face and hands. He came on after me as fast as he could run and got free from them; though, as I well knew from more than one experience with hornets, the pain of the many stings was almost unbearable, he did not complain or ever once curse, as I would have done.

We came to the shore of the lake and the boat, and while the sufferer was bathing his stings with the cold water, I scanned the side of Goat Mountain with his field glasses and almost at once discovered four bighorn rams low down upon the north end, straight back from the ledge of the Narrows, where Grinnell and I had once passed a never-to-be-forgotten night. "Bighorns, Colonel! Four of them over there. Do you feel well enough to go for them?" I all but shouted.

"Though I had a thousand wasp stings, still would I go. Hand me the glass; let me see them," he answered. And after a long look: "It does seem that we can easily approach them."

My one worry was that the rams might notice the movement of our boat and at once make for the top of the mountain. However, we were not more than a third of the way across the lake when the high cliff of the Narrows hid us from them. We landed on the first bit of shore south of the cliff, climbed straight up until level with the top of the cliff, then turned off into the timber running from it well up to where we had seen the bighorns. We now had about a halfmile to go, and so anxious was I to learn if the bighorns were still where we had seen them that unconsciously I was all but running. "Oh, slow up, please. I can't keep up with you," the Colonel called to me, and thereafter we proceeded at what to me was a snail's pace. At last we neared the edge of the timber, and eagerly, anxiously, I began looking for the exact place on the rocky slope where the rams had been feeding. At last I located it and my heart went down; the rams were not there. But I said nothing; led on very slowly, watchfully; was about to cross an opening in the timber when I spotted them, some three hundred yards south of their original position. Three were lying down; the fourth was standing, looking off south, head up, his horns perfect circles. What a noble animal it was. I pointed to it and said to the Colonel: "We will get him. Be sure to take a fine sight at him."

"Yes. A fine sight," the Colonel gasped.

I led on, detouring the opening, and then, slowly, foot by foot, approached the upper edge of the timber. When I at last stopped and motioned to the Colonel to shoot, we were within 150 yards of the four, and the ram on watch was turning, looking up at the crest of the mountains. Then presently he turned again, stood broadside to us, looking north. The Colonel slowly raised my Winchester, took long and careful aim, fired. The ram leaped high in the air; fell; kicked convulsively.

"We've got him!" I yelled.

But the Colonel was not at all excited. He merely smiled, said: "Yes, we have him, and a perfect specimen he is."

Well, naturally, one who during long years of army life had been in many battles could not be expected to get excited over the stalking and killing of a bighorn. Nor would it have affected me had I been alone the hunter. My trouble was my anxiety to give Colonel Baring a successful day.

Night had come when, tired and hungry, we drew up to the shore before our camp. Belatedly, the Colonel had his pint of champagne, and I a drink of the '34, the while we told of our successes of the day, and Kipp and Jack Bean skinned and fleshed the heads that we had brought in.

After a month with us our party left for their respective homes, so pleased with their outing that they came again in the following autumn and afterward sent us many English parties to outfit and guide in the region that is now Glacier National Park. Long years afterward, Cecil Baring came with his son Rupert—in 1927 it was—for a last outing. On the death of his elder brother Maurice, he became Lord Cecil Baring; now he is dead, and Lord Rupert Baring writes me that he would love to return to the park.

CONCEPTION OF GLACIER NATIONAL PARK (1885)[1]

HAVING VISITED THE PAWNEES and the Cheyennes, and written his books about them, *Pawnee Hero Tales* and *The Fighting Cheyennes*, George Bird Grinnell continued his annual outings in our part of the country, Jack Monroe, William Jackson, and I always going with him into the mountains. He was one of the three commissioners who in 1896 made the treaty with the Blackfoot (Pikuni) Indians, whereby they sold the mountain part of their reservation to the United States for $1,500,000.

It is interesting, almost unbelievable, the way in which the proposal to sell the strip came about. During George Steel's last term as agent for the tribe, E. C. Garrett, a mystic, a believer in the supernatural, was his clerk. Garrett, returning from a trip to Helena, brought home an ouija board and was greatly excited about it, claiming that it was a medium by which all that one wanted to know would be revealed. To humor him, George Steel and I by turns would sit with him at the board and, manipulating its letters, make it spell out whatever happened to be in our minds. So was it that he and I invented a character, an old miner named Bedrock Jim, and made him, his spirit, say that he had prospected in the St. Mary lakes country, and on a certain stream running into the river had found gold. He said that, when panning the gravel one day, the Indians had killed him. And at last he revealed that his find had been on Swift Current River.

Garrett so fully believed our wild tale that he outfitted an old-timer named Dutch Louis to prospect up there, and, to Steel's and my great surprise, Louis returned several weeks later with some fine specimens of copper ore that he had found in Swift Current Valley. Word of it spread to Fort Benton, to Helena, and elsewhere. A number of prospectors sneaked in there and confirmed the find; said that there would be a second Butte on Swift Current River. Stories of the richness of the deposits appeared in the newspapers. Influential men wrote the Montana representatives in Congress about it; urged that the government buy that part of the reservation. The majority

[1] Published in *The Great Falls Tribune* (November 15, 1936).

of us on the reservation thought that it would be well to sell the strip, provided we could get a good price for it. A minority led by Horace Clark was against selling for any consideration whatever. Joseph Kipp and I talked with the leading men of the tribe about it, with the result that the Commissioner of Indian Affairs was notified that the tribe would talk over the matter with Our Grandfather's (the President's) representatives, provided that Fisher Hat (George Bird Grinnell) would be one of them.

In due time the three commissioners arrived. There followed a week of oratory and dickering. Two of the commissioners thought that $1,000,000 would be plenty for the strip. Grinnell insisted that the price should be $1,500,000 and at last had his way about it. The treaty was drawn up, signed by the Indians and the commissioners, and later ratified by Congress. Whereupon miners flocked into the Swift Current copper district and began extensive work upon the lodes. To the great satisfaction of some of us they proved, after a couple of years of exploitation, to be of no value whatever.

George Bird Grinnell, in his influential weekly journal *Forest and Stream*, had ever strongly advocated the preservation of Yellowstone National Park as originally defined and had successfully fought certain Wyoming interests that would have despoiled it. On his first trip with me into the St. Mary lakes country in 1885, he had remarked how fine it would be if that part of the Rockies could also some day be set aside as a national park and kept intact as a refuge for big game, a pleasure ground for all of the people for all time to come. He wrote for *Century Magazine* an article describing its mountains, glaciers, and its plentitude of game animals, particularly the mountain goat. Also he interested his close friend President Theodore Roosevelt in the proposal and sent his Chicago representative, Emerson Hough, out to see that section of the Rockies and write about it for *Forest and Stream*.

It was on a blustery day in February, 1902, when Joseph Kipp, William Jackson, and I met Hough at Blackfoot station and escorted him down to Kipp's home for the night. Both Jackson and I well knew him, we having been with him in Chicago and at several annual Sportsmen's Exhibitions in Madison Square Garden, New York.

He had come for a strenuous outing in the mountains, and we had thoroughly prepared for it, our outfit comprising the following necessities: a small muslin tent with tin reinforced stovepipe hole in the roof; a folding sheet-iron stove and telescoping stovepipe; coffee pot, two frying pans, knives and forks, several small tin dishes and plates; staple groceries; an ax, a shovel; a canvas sheet; three light, warm sleeping bags; and snowshoes. All made into three pack loads of less than fifty pounds each.

On the following day Hough, Jackson, and I, with our outfit, boarded the caboose of a freight train and near evening got off at Nyack, a station well down on the west side of the range, and passed the night in the section house. The good wife of the section boss giving us an early and hearty breakfast, we put on our snowshoes, shouldered our loads, and started up Nyack Creek. The snow was four or five feet deep, the weather intensely cold, but we were warmly clothed and did not mind it at all. The snow was so heavy, so hard packed, that the going was good. Hough alone carried a rifle.

When no more than a mile from the station we began seeing deer, mostly whitetails, and now and then some elk; twice during the morning we passed yards of moose. But we wanted none of them. Three ruffed grouse that Hough soon killed, neatly necking them, were to be the main part of our supper. When about ten miles up the creek, we made camp close under a high, many-cliffed mountain that was later named for a most noteworthy member of the Pikuni tribe of the Blackfoot Confederacy, Loneman Mountain. In making camp we shoveled a clear place for the tent; put it up, with poles that we cut, on bare ground; set up the stove and cut plenty of wood for it; cut and laid a thick layer of balsam bough tips topped with the canvas sheet on which to put our sleeping bags. And then, warm and comfortable, though our thermometer outside registered minus 33°, we had a hearty supper: fried ruffed grouse, pancakes and syrup, coffee. The dishes washed, we set some dried apples to stew; lighted a candle; sat back on our bedding, smoked, and talked of this and that: Jackson, of his scouting with General Custer and General Miles; Hough, of his camping trips in Yellowstone Park; I, an interested listener of it all. It was late when we got into our warm bags and slept—warmly slept, though the trees about loudly popped in the intense cold of the night.

After an early breakfast, the dishes were washed, and I said: "And now, Mr. Emerson Hough, we will introduce you to Mr. Whiskers-and-Pantalettes, the Rocky Mountain billy goat." And putting on our snowshoes we set out for the base of Loneman Mountain. Soon we neared it and saw a band of females and young, yearling and two-year-old goats browsing along a high, wind-swept ledge, backed by a cliff. Hough got out his field glass and kept it focused upon them for some time. He saw some of them stand upon their hind legs, fore-feet against the cliff, and tear off mouthfuls of the moss clinging to the rock. He remarked upon their whiskers and the long, fluffy hair of their forelegs, reaching to the knees; he said that they were very uncouth animals, lacking entirely the graceful lines of the bighorn and deer. Said I: "If you can see them, frightened, climbing the heights to safety, you will see some graceful work."

No sooner had I spoken than the whole band of them suddenly bunched, went leaping to the right end of the ledge, and began climbing the very steep side of the mountain beyond the cliff—running swiftly along places where, apparently, there was no footing at all; making, even the kids, prodigious leaps from ledge up to ledge; in no time reaching and disappearing over the crest of the mountain. And when they were gone, Hough, lowering his field glass, said: "The most graceful, swift, fearless climbers I ever saw, those goats. I don't believe bighorns would have ventured to make that climb. Why, here and there it seemed that they were climbing on nothing but thin air." We surmised that a cougar had frightened the band.

I spoke of the fear that goats had of predatory animals; told of an incident of the kind that I had once witnessed. On an autumn day several years back Thomas Bird (*Nina Piksi*, "Bird Chief") had set out to hunt up Red Eagle Valley, his four dogs trailing at our heels. Having arrived at the foot of the lake and having seen no game, Bird decided to climb the mountain, Red Eagle, for bighorns or goats; and I set off in the timber on the east side of the lake for whatever I might find—deer, elk, perchance moose. Having no luck,

I turned back a couple of hours later to the shore at the head of the lake; heard Bird's dogs excitedly baying; and saw them, high up on the mountain across, chasing a lone goat down a long slope of it. At the foot of it, the goat never slackened up nor turned; instead, he made a prodigious leap outward and, all sprawled and whirling, struck the foot of the five- or six-hundred-foot drop with a crash like the boom of a cannon. He preferred suicide rather than that the dogs should get him.

Proceeding up the valley, we discovered another band of goats on the next mountain above and saw that they could be easily approached. But they, too, were females and young, and Hough would have none of them. He wanted a big billy, a perfect, mature male specimen for mounting, or none. And so we turned back to camp. On the way we raised a flock of grouse and with a noosed string on the end of a stick, snatched six of them, one after another, from the limbs of a tree. Most appropriately the old-timers named them fool hens.

Luck was against us. We had storms of several days' duration that confined us to the tent; when we did go out, we could find no billy goats—only bands of females and young. It was on our eighth day there that we at last sighted six billies low down on Loneman Mountain; easily approaching them, Hough killed one. On the following day, with its head and skin, we arrived back in Essex, boarded a train and returned to Blackfoot; Hough a day or two later left for Chicago, there to write for *Forest and Stream* the story of his trip and to advocate the making of the region that he had visited a national park.

With his wife and William Hofer, who had been his companion on his Yellowstone Park trips, Hough came in the autumn of 1902 for another outing in our mountains. At the time, William Jackson and Jack Monroe were with Gifford Pinchot and Henry L. Stimson on a hunt, so with Joe Carney and a good outfit I took Hough to Two Medicine lakes, then to Cut Bank Canyon, to St. Mary lakes, and finally up Swift Current River to Grinnell Glacier. Later there appeared more interesting Hough stories in *Forest and Stream*, all in favor of making a national park of the Rockies from the Canadian line south to Marias Pass.

Supplementing the articles in *Forest and Stream* favoring the creation of the park, George Bird Grinnell went frequently to Washington to try to interest Congress in it—particularly the representatives from Montana. And although, as I have said, President Theodore Roosevelt was wholly in favor of it, our lawmakers were not interested. It was not until May 11, 1910, that President Taft signed the bill creating Glacier National Park. So did Grinnell's long years of effort for it bear fruit.

In the meantime, great misfortune became my lot.

TRIALS AND TROUBLES (1903–15)[1]

IN MAY, 1903, my good wife Fine Shield Woman, my close companion for twenty-five years, died from a very painful, incurable disease of the heart, and I became a most lonely man. I was just drifting, caring little what I did when, in June, Ralph Pulitzer of the *New York World* cabled me from Japan, asking if I would take him for an outing in the St. Mary lakes country. I cabled him to come on, and in due time he arrived, and with him came his friend Lieutenant Crimmins and his valet Jim. I was awaiting them with team and wagon, camp outfit, provisions, saddle horses; and my help were Monroe Arnoux and Dan Purdy, guides; Nora and Wyola Aspling, cooks. Arriving at the foot of Lower St. Mary Lake, we camped there for several days, and then with team and wagon and my Mackinaw boat, moved up the lake and camped on its west side, just below the Narrows, there fishing occasionally and having an easy time. Daily, with our field glasses, we would see goats on Yellow Fish Mountain and Goat Mountain, but never any bighorns. Lieutenant Crimmins was no hunter. Pulitzer said that he wanted no goats but would like to kill a bighorn, and finally urged me to take him out for a shot at one.

It was closed season for bighorns. I was a licensed guide. But we

1 Published in *The Great Falls Tribune* (November 15 and 22, 1936).

were in great need of meat. Our killing of one would never be known, I thought. And anyhow, mourning for my wife, I was reckless, did not care what I did. So early one morning Ralph and I crossed the lake in the Mackinaw, landed at the mouth of Red Eagle Creek, followed up its valley to Red Eagle Lake, then climbed Kutenai Mountain, heading for Kutenai Lick. Slowly we approached the draw in which it lay; we cautiously looked down over its rim, and there, not a hundred yards from us, were seven old bighorn rams drinking the salty water, eating the salty mud. Pulitzer aimed his Winchester at one of them and fired; he kept on shooting in spite of my protests and neatly killed four of the seven. Well, they were dead—useless for me to say any more. He got out his camera, took a snapshot of each one as it lay; then we drew the four together, all in a row, he stood close back of them, and I took snapshots of the group with the rest of the films in the camera.

Then there was work for me. I dressed all four of the rams, and with one of the heads and a pack load of meat we returned to camp. On the following day I went back up there with my two helpers, and we got the three other heads; and on the next day, more of the good meat. In camp we carefully cleaned the heads, fleshed the head and neck skins, and when they had dried Pulitzer sent Dan Purdy with them to Fort Macleod, there to send them by Canadian Pacific express to his New York address.

One evening soon after we arrived at St. Mary Lake, I told of a houseboat trip that I had made from Fort Benton down the Missouri to the mouth of Milk River. Ralph Pulitzer was so interested in my description of the wonderful scenery and the plentitude of game along the river that he decided to make the trip, and he had me write Gus Senieur of Fort Benton to build a cabin boat for us without delay. When we broke camp and returned to Blackfoot station, Lieutenant Crimmins left for his home at the Presidio, California; our cooks and Purdy went their various ways; and Pulitzer, his valet, Monroe Arnoux, and I hurried to Fort Benton, only to find that the houseboat was not completed and would not be ready for us for some days.

After a night and a day in the town, Ralph complained of its monotony and asked what kind of a place Great Falls might be.

"A very lively little city," I answered, and we took the morning train for there.

On our way he said: "I have those films of the bighorns in my bag. We will have them developed, get some prints of them."

"Don't do it. Too dangerous. I would not like a photographer to see them," I said.

"There will be no danger at all. I will pay the man well to keep his mouth shut about them," said he.

Having arrived in the Falls, we registered at the Park Hotel, took the films to an upstairs print shop, and proceeded to have a hilarious time. At least Ralph did. I just dragged along with him. The evening ended with a gay foursome at dinner in a restaurant near the Silver Dollar Saloon. Our table was close to its large, plate-glass window; champagne bottles soon decorated it, and we were an interesting spectacle for the many passers-by. My dear friend Doctor Gordon was one of them.

The prints of Ralph and the bighorns proved to be perfect. We sent to Helena for a colored cook named Jim something-or-other; and Arnoux wiring us that the boat was completed, we returned to Fort Benton and were off. The boat was thirty feet long and ten wide, with a cabin twenty feet long containing bunks, table, seats, and other conveniences. Monroe Arnoux had the forward sweep. I manned the rear one and was the steersman. Well I knew the river, its bars and shoals, and, too, I had a War Department map of it. I kept Arnoux informed orally and by signs which way to ply his sweep. Our cookstove, ice box, cooking utensils, etc., were on the afterdeck; cases of canned goods and beer were in the hold under the cabin.

From the mouth of Marias River, down to Judith River, the valley of the Missouri River is a miniature Grand Canyon. Pulitzer was enchanted with the scenery and took many snapshots of it. We safely ran Dauphin Rapids, the worst on the river. A little farther on a sudden, terrific wind of short duration whirled us round and round, carried off our wash tub, and tossed the boat upon a sandy shore. With some difficulty we got back into the channel.

At the mouth of the Judith we spent a couple of hours with dear, gruff, old Bill Norris in his store. Thereafter he had many dry remarks to make about Ralph Pulitzer and his blankety-blank valet. Loading on a couple of cases of Budweiser beer, we resumed our way and in good time arrived at the mouth of Armell Creek and the ranch of an old friend of mine, Joe Carney. We had dinner with him and his sprightly wife; he told of the plentitude of antelope not far up the creek, and Ralph arranged with him to go out for them on the following day. The result was that they brought in a big, fat buck, killed by Ralph. Carney agreeing to prepare its head for mounting and, when dry, to ship it to New York, we stored some of the meat in our icebox and floated on.

I of course had to bring the boat to shore where in the winter of 1880–81 I had helped Joseph Kipp trade for more than four thousand buffalo robes. Not a vestige of Carroll remained; the river had cut into the bottom and swept away our big trading post and cabins, Gus Tyler's post, Tom Burns' cabin, and all the others. Alas! Alas! What good, what exciting times we had there. Almost I wept for those days that were gone—for the good friends there with us, who were now no more.

When we arrived at the mouth of the Musselshell we were again out of meat, so we scattered out to hunt. Pulitzer killed a fat, blacktail buck; with its ribs and loin in the icebox we went on and two days later landed at Round Butte, where a man named Darnell had a ranch. He, his wife, and two fine daughters came down to the boat to meet us, and, to my great surprise, with them was my old friend Dutch Louis, whom I had not seen for some years. Their first kindness to us was to replenish our icebox. We visited them in the evening, and Dutch Louis, telling us that he was fast failing in health, had Ralph and me write out his will, bequeathing his large band of horses to the Darnell girls. Some months later he died there.

During the night I was taken quite sick, and in the morning, remained in my bunk. After an early breakfast Pulitzer and Arnoux rode off with rancher Darnell to hunt. At ten o'clock I heard a boat cross the river; a little later I heard someone jump down upon our afterdeck. I looked out from my bunk and recognized him, and my heart went all fluttery; it was Game Warden Green of Glasgow! And in our icebox was meat of the blacktail! He came into the cabin through the open doorway, greeted me. I told him to make himself at home, and he sat at the table across from me, facing the rear door.

Said I: "No, sit on the other side where I can see you."

He did so, and I yelled to the cook: "Jim, here is Game Warden Green, and thirsty. Bring us some beer."

He brought it, went out. I tasted of my glass of it, tossed it upon the floor, shouted: "Jim, this beer is warm. Go deep in the icebox and get out a cold bottle for Game Warden Green." He brought the fresh bottle, went back again, and soon two loud splashes in the river told me that our deer meat was gone. And was I relieved of my fear!

For a little we talked of this and that. At last Green said: "I understand Ralph Pulitzer is with you. Where is he this morning?"

"Out riding with Darnell. Having a look at the country," I answered, and again went all trembly from fear that Ralph would come in with a deer or an antelope.

Just then Alfred, the valet, came aboard from the shore, in time to hear Green say: "Well, I have to tell you, Schultz, that I'm here to arrest you and him."

"Arrest us—what for?"

"For what you did up at St. Mary lakes. Jack Hall (game warden at Great Falls) saw those pictures of Pulitzer and the four bighorns when the print-shop man was dryin' them on his window sill. You've got the heads right here with you. I'll take 'em for evidence, and you two along with 'em."

"That's all news to me. Jack Hall must have been dreaming," I said.

And then said he: "Of course you would say that. Well, not to waste time, I'll search your outfit right now. Begin with that big trunk that has Pulitzer's name on it."

The trunk was locked. I called Alfred in to open it. Green pawed its contents; grunted; went up onto the roof of the cabin where, under a canvas sheet, were some of our belongings. As he fruitlessly looked at them, I whispered to Alfred: "Run up to the ranch; tell those girls to ride out and warn Ralph that Game Warden Green is here. Tell Dutch Louis to watch for him, prevent him from coming in with a kill." Alfred left at once, and I breathed somewhat easier.

Green came down off the roof to search the hold; regardless of its three or four inches of muddy bilge water, on hands and knees—use-lessly, of course—he examined all that was stored there. He was wet and angry when he returned to the cabin and said to me: "Pretty slick, aren't you. What you done with them heads? Of course you can't tell me. Well, I'll tell you something: Right now, Jack Hall is up to St. Mary lakes, diggin' into what you fellows did there, and later on we'll get you for it. No use now my waiting for Pulitzer. I'm going right back home." Where he got the boat with which he came to us, and what he did with it, I never learned.

When, near evening, Pulitzer returned, we had a good laugh over the Game Warden's discomfiture. We were agreed that the incident was ended; that we would hear no more about it. Never, never, we thought, could the Game Warden secure evidence of the killing of the bighorns.

Arriving at the mouth of Milk River several days later, we gave the cabin boat to a rancher for transporting us and our belongings to Nashua, the nearest railway station. From there Pulitzer, with his valet, set out for San Francisco where, on returning from Japan, he had left his secretary in a hospital. Arnoux and the cook left for their respective homes; and I, lonely and grieving, for New York, just to kill some time.

Upon returning to Montana a month or so later, I left the train at Fort Benton to visit old friends and to my great surprise learned that, during my absence, Ralph Pulitzer had been arrested for the killing of the bighorns and put under heavy bond to appear at Choteau for trial at a later date, and that he was then in Great Falls. I hurried up there to see him but found that he had left for New York. Consulting a lawyer friend, I was told that as a licensed guide I might be tried for conniving at the killing of the game, and if found guilty, would likely get a prison sentence for a year or two. Then Jack Hall arrested me and took me to Choteau for trial.

Came the day and the hour for it. The courtroom was filled with spectators. The case was called. Jack Hall went forward, whispered with the judge, and he announced: "The case is dismissed." Happily I left the room and was walking along the hall when Wallace Taylor, the sheriff, called me into his office and shut the door. "Case dismissed. I'm free," I told him.

"And why? Because they are now digging up what you and Pulitzer did down on the Missouri. You get away from here; go where Jack Hall can never find you," he all but yelled. "Go. Go. And lose no time about it."

I took the first train out and went to Harlem, heading for the ranch of my old friend of the buffalo days, Long John Forgy. Another old friend was the owner of the Harlem Hotel. I told him of my trouble, and he said that if Jack Hall appeared there, he would send his son to tell me of his presence. Forgy and his wife, who was a sister of Louis Riel, made me welcome. I remained with them for some time, until one day my hotel friend's son came swiftly riding to tell me the Jack Hall was in Harlem looking for me.

Forgy hitched up a team and took me to the first sidetrack of the Great Northern east of Harlem. I flagged and stopped train No. 4, told Conductor Smith of my trouble; he hid me in a drawing room and had a dining-car waiter bring me food. He said he thought I would be fairly safe in Minot, North Dakota, and that he would tell the conductors of trains No. 1, 2, 3, and 4 to keep me informed concerning Jack Hall's movements. Minot was a division point; all the conductors stopped at the Parker House, and I should, too.

So I did. Days passed. On a cold, wintry morning, going downstairs for breakfast, I met Smith coming up them. "Hai!" he exclaimed. "I was just going up to your room to tell you that Jack Hall came down with me; he is going to extradite you and take you back to Montana. He's in the office right now."

At the foot of the stairs was a glass-paneled door opening into the office and, straight on, another door facing the street. I stole on down; saw Jack Hall, fur coated, back to me, talking with the clerk. I did not dare go back to my room for my overcoat, gloves, and overshoes. Just as I was, I hurried outside and to ice-covered Mouse River, heading for Canada. There were about six inches of snow on the ground, but the ice was fairly clear. Hungry, thirsty, all day long I traveled up that winding river—hands in pockets when I was not rubbing my all-but-frozen ears. Came night. I saw the lighted windows of a house, went to it, knocked. A bewhiskered, gray-haired man, who from his appearance might have been Uncle Sam himself, opened the door, and I said to him: "How do you do, sir. May I stop with you for the night?"

Long he stared at me and, thinly clad as I was in that winter night, he had reason to think that I might not be a desirable guest. But at last he said: "Well, come in." I entered the warm room and sank wearily into a cushioned chair. His old wife and son of forty years were putting the supper on the table. They told me to sit in. I was too tired to eat, but I drank all the tea that they had. The meal ended, mother and son took the dishes to the kitchen to wash them, and I sat with the old man before the glowing stove in the living room. Presently he said: "Well, young fellow, what the hell's the matter with you anyhow?"

I told him of my trouble—fully told it—and when I had finished, he exclaimed: "Think of that! Chasing a man around for killing a few head of game! Say! I'm an old-time Montanan. I mined in Alder Gulch. My son was born in Virginia City. Man, you can stay right here with me till the drop of a hat."

I remained with those good people until I could no longer bear the monotony of it, and then one day the old man took me in his sleigh to the first sidetrack of the Great Northern, west of Minot. I flagged and stopped train No. 1. Conductor Gleason lost no time in escorting me into a drawing room. On the following day he stopped the train at Willow Creek bridge just east of Blackfoot station and let me off. I ran down to the home of my good friend William Kipp, and there learned that Ralph Pulitzer, not appearing at Choteau on the date set for his trial, had forfeited his bond for $1,500. I sent for my son and arranged with him to join me later on, wherever I might be. Then I flagged another No. 1 train and went on to the coast, to Seattle, and to San Francisco. Three policemen were standing on the wharf as the steamer was made fast to it, and I thought: "At last they get me." My heart beat fast until I had slipped past them.[2]

While in San Francisco, at Grinnell's request, I began writing for *Forest and Stream* the serial that in 1907 became my first book, *My Life as an Indian*. But city life did not agree with me, and I moved to the Pima Indian reservation, Arizona, to live with the agent, Mr. Alexander, and continue writing. There I fell sick, and I wrote the last chapters of the serial in the Sisters' hospital in Phoenix. When my book was published I was assisting Jesse Walter Fewkes of the Smithsonian Institution in the excavation and restoration of Casa Grande ruins, forty miles east of Phoenix. Alternately I lived in Los Angeles and in my shooting lodge, *Apuni Oyis* ("Butterfly Lodge") that I had built in the White Mountains, Arizona, 116 miles from a railroad. For a time I was literary editor of the *Los Angeles Times*.

My son joined me and began his long years in art schools. He became well and favorably known. Some of the owners of his paintings and bronzes are the New York Academy of Design, the Philadelphia Art Museum, the August Hecksher Gallery, now willed to the city of New York, former President Hoover, Mrs. Calvin Coolidge, and other prominent Easterners.

Well, years passed, years of longing to go to Montana, even for a short visit with my old friends, Indian and white. In 1915 I received a letter from Mr. Louis Hill, president of the Great Northern Railway Company, inviting me to summer in Glacier Park and write what I would about it. At once I wrote to Mr. O. S. Warden, asking him to see the state game warden in my behalf. And soon came Mr. Warden's wire: "ALL IS FORGIVEN STOP COME ON."

I was a happy man when, on June 15, I got off the train for the opening day of Glacier Park Hotel. And happily, that summer, I wrote *Blackfeet Tales of Glacier National Park*.

2 The famous "Pulitzer Case" is reported at length by Montana State Game and Fish Warden W. F. Scott, *Second Biennial Report, State Game and Fish Warden of the State of Montana* (1903–1904), 185–91.

CHAPTER SEVEN

Some Wild-Animal Pets

THE BIG BAD WOLF? No indeed! I once had a pet wolf, as good a friend of mine as any dog I ever owned. But before I tell of him I must say that, so far as I can learn, the wolves of North America never attacked human beings. There was good reason for it: game animals and birds were everywhere so plentiful that they had no need to attack their great enemy, man. The Indians have no tales about big, bad wolves. They frighten their children into good behavior by threatening them with the bear. Until the late 1870's wolves fairly swarmed upon the Montana plains; their long-drawn, melancholy howls were ever in our ears. But lone hunters, both Indian and white, when caught out at night and far from home, lay down to sleep without the slightest fear of them.

In 1881, at Joseph Kipp's trading post on the Missouri River, some thirty miles above the mouth of the Musselshell, while out on a hunt with my friend Eagle Head, I once captured a male wolf pup in the underground den which he was occupying with his parents and their other young ones. I gave the pup the Blackfoot name for wolf, *Mahkwoyi,* "Big Mouth," and for safety shut him in our smokehouse, not then in use. But he was so friendly and playful with me that I soon freed him, and he became my close companion, following me wherever I went. And did he know the bell that called us to our meals! When it rang he was the first one into the dining room. And what an appetite he had: two or three pounds of buffalo meat were just a small snack for him. He soon knew his name and would come running from as far as he could hear me yell: *"Mahkwoyi, puk-siput!* ("Big Mouth, come here!").

Speaking Blackfoot only to him, I taught him to heel, to hunt out ahead of me, and to retrieve; and how proud he was, bringing a grouse or a duck that I had shot and dropping it at my feet, then rising, and with paws on my shoulders, licking my face, the while vigorously waving his bushy tail. No deer that we occasionally wounded got away; he quickly overtook and downed it, sometimes killed it before we could come up.

The dogs of the Indians who came to trade with us were mostly afraid of *Mahkwoyi*. It was rarely that he could induce them to play with him. When they did so and in their excitement barked, he could only whine. He did not begin to howl until he was about a year old. Then, one evening, he answered the far-off howling of his kind and, very proud of himself, came running to me for my approval of his feat; he got it, and howled and howled again. When about eight months old he saw his first skunk, ran and seized it, shook it, let it go; the result was that he was drenched with its scent and got sick. Thereafter he gave skunks the right of way; with drooping head and tail tight in, he ashamedly circled past them.

I once came near losing *Mahkwoyi*. My friend Eli Guardipee and I went deer hunting, the wolf at my heels. We ended by being nearly trampled by a herd of buffalo.[1] Afterward, of *Mahkwoyi*, there was not a trace! "Hooked! Pierced! Carried off on some cow's sharp horns," I said, and my heart was low. But as I mourned he came swiftly from we knew not where, to leap up and lick my face, run circles around me, and leap up onto me again; and oh, how glad I was!

A great admirer of *Mahkwoyi* was Captain Williams of the *Red Cloud*, one of the many steamboats plying between Fort Benton and St. Louis. Often he begged me for him; and eventually got him, to my sorrow ever afterward; for he, in turn, gave the wolf to the St. Louis Zoological Park, and there, sickened by confinement, and doubtless longing for me, soon he died.

At our home place, Fort Conrad, on the Marias River, a friend of mine, Tail-Feathers-Coming-Over-the-Hill, once gave me a young

[1] For a more detailed account of this adventure, see chap. 2, III, of this volume.

beaver, offspring of its mother that he had trapped. It was quite young, of about five pounds weight, but old enough to thrive without its mother's milk. My room in the fort had for its floor the hard-packed earth. I sank a washtub in it, filled it with water in which the beaver could drink and swim, and daily brought in a bunch of willows for it to gnaw—the bark of them was its favorite food. *Tsisk-stuki*, "Wood-biter," as the Blackfeet called the beaver, soon became friendly with me, would come waddling when I called to him. And how he loved to have his head and belly scratched! But he was ever silent; so long as I owned him he never made a sound of any kind. When he became quite tame, I carried him to the river often, to let him swim about; and he greatly enjoyed it, always returning to me when I called him.

The inner side of our bunk was nailed to the wall of the room, its outer side supported by two thin cottonwood posts. When we were retiring one night, my wife called my attention to one of the posts; at about its center, the beaver had gnawed it partly through.

"Found it too dry; will not gnaw it any more," I said. But near morning, with a snapping of its wall board, the bunk suddenly tilted down and tossed us out upon the floor, my wife crying: "Enemies have come! Protect me!" I groped about for the candle, lit it; pointed it to the beaver, floating on the surface of his wash-tub pond and staring at us with his beady eyes.

"There's your war party," I answered. He had gnawed the head post of the bunk clear through, and then the other, the weak one, had given way, and the bunk was sloping out and down at an angle of about forty-five degrees. I cased the new posts that I made with lengths of stovepipe.

I lost *Tsisk-stuki* when he was a year old. I had him out for a morning swim in the river when some Indian children came running and yelling along the shore and frightened him. He dived, came to the surface in the swift rapids below, dived again, and that was the last I ever saw of him.

After the buffalo were exterminated and my friend Kipp sold Fort Conrad and his squatter's right to its adjacent bottom land to James McDevitt, we moved up onto the Blackfoot reservation, where he already had a store. There, on Two Medicine Lodges River, I embarked as a cattleman, but close to the west of my ranch loomed up that part of the Rockies that was later to become Glacier National Park. Those towering heights, timbered slopes and valleys, teeming with game, had irresistible appeal to me. I built a cabin close to the foot of Upper St. Mary Lake, procured a boat, and with my wife and one and another of my Indian friends spent much time up there, to the detriment of the cattle business.

One morning in late May, 1889, my friend Bird Chief and I, with rifles and fishing outfit, set off to spend the day on the upper lake. As we were nearing Red Eagle Mountain we discovered a band of goats, nannies and young, yearlings and two-year-olds, feeding at the foot of its steep slope—several of them on the narrow shore of the lake. Some fifty or sixty yards to the north of the band were a big nanny and her little young one. None took any notice of us until we were so near that we could see their eyes; then they suddenly turned about and fled for the top of the mountain with the almost incredible swiftness of their sure-footed kind. And said my friend, excitedly: "*Apikuni!* That lone she one! She left her young one! Hid it! Made it lie down there among those big rocks."

"Are you sure of it?" I asked.

"Sure. Me, my eyes don't lie!"

That excited me. I had seen mother antelope and mother deer, when frightened, somehow make their young lie down, lie still, and run from them; so why not goats, too? I hurriedly rowed the boat to shore, and we sprang out, sped up the slope, soon came upon the little one, lying motionless in a depression in the shale between some boulders. It did not struggle when I took it up; tried to suck my finger when I put it to its mouth. Said Bird Chief: "We have no milk for it; let it go."

"Have plenty for it, as you will see," I answered, and sorely puzzled him. Arrived back at the cabin, I had him run in his horses, one of them a mare with a week-old colt. I held the little goat up to her teats, and it soon took its fill of her rich milk. Thereafter, morning and night, I so fed it, and it soon regarded me, not the mare, as its mother, keeping mostly close beside me. At dawn every morning it would spring up onto my bed and kneeling, butt me with its little head, keep on butting me, urging that I get up and provide its breakfast. Of all the animals that I have known, it was the most agile, playful. One most surprising feat it had. When standing, it would spring high from the ground, and when it came down it would be headed the opposite way from which it had left the ground. Alas! When we had had it for several months, it suddenly sickened and died, and my post-mortem revealed that it had eaten a poisonous kind of weed; its stomach was bloody. I carefully prepared it for mounting, sent it to my friend C. Hart Merriam, and he in turn presented it to the Smithsonian Institution, where now it stands in lifelike pose.

Did you ever hear of a tame skunk? Soon after my late friend Joseph Kipp built Fort Standoff on Belly River in 1871, he caught a young skunk, rammed it down into the leg of a boot, and cut out its scent glands. It grew amazingly fast and large, became very tame, and proved to be a perfect mouser. Kipp's bed was also its bed, and its hunting ground was the warehouse, connecting with the trade room, in which the buffalo robes and other furs bought from the Indians were stored. Now and again it would come sauntering in from the warehouse, to the consternation of Indian customers who were not aware that he was a scentless pet, and they would shout *"Apikaiyi! Nuwah!"* ("A white-stripes! Look out!") and tumble over one another, trying to get out from the room. When the Indians came to trade, their dogs would gather before the fort, uneasily peek into the trade room. Regardless of their number, he would saunter out through the doorway, tail up, and one and all they would run from him, stop and stare, and run again as he approached them. He enjoyed frightening them. He was, indeed, a perfect bluffer, Billy the skunk. Alas! He came to an untimely end. Wandering along the shore of the river, he stepped into a trap that one of the men had set for mink; it had been so set that whatever was caught in it would drown. And so he passed, to Kipp's great regret.

In 1913, I built a shooting lodge in the White Mountains, Arizona, 116 miles south of Holbrook. There one morning in June, 1929, my son Hart discovered an emaciated, very young, male coyote pup nosing around our back porch. It had apparently been separated from its mother for some time. It did not run when he approached it; just lay belly up and trembled and whimpered when he stroked it. A little later, it ravenously ate a pile of pancakes and bacon that we fed it.

Way back in the buffalo days Indians and whites agreed that wolves could be tamed sometimes, but coyotes never. They were, as old Bill Weaver used to say, "plumb wild an' trech'r'us no matter how careful you was in tryin' to gentle 'em." Well, we would undertake to tame this one. That day we named him Smokey, built a shed-like kennel, and fastened him to it with a light, thirty-foot chain.

Smokey ate much more than would a dog of his age and size, and grew amazingly fast. Like a dog, he would bury his excess food in holes that he dug in the ground. He soon would come bounding to the end of the chain to meet us, wagging his bushy tail and leaping up to lick our faces. He whimpered with joy when we petted him and, when freed from his chain, he would run hither and thither and tirelessly play with us. A companion for him was my son's purebred English shepherd Zora, a fine turkey dog and retriever. Early in the autumn we took a long chance with Smokey; we freed him from his chain. But with Zora he remained close at home, having, apparently, no desire to seek his kind, though almost nightly they were yelping down in the valley and up on the near mountain side. The two would occasionally go nosing around the home of the forest ranger, a couple of hundred yards below us, but they never went near the little settlement of Greer, a mile farther up the Little Colorado. But Smokey's days of free wandering were soon to end. The forest ranger brought in a couple of dozen chickens to provide eggs for his large family, and Smokey promptly killed five of them, including a fifteen-dollar, pure Leghorn rooster. Thereafter he was kept his long chain, except when we took him out to hunt or for exercise. And how he did enjoy his outings! Far more swift than Zora, he was everywhere at once—a gray flash exploring every log, every hole that might conceal a squirrel, rabbit, or pack rat. One day he furiously pawed into a hole at the foot of a pine, brought out a skunk and promptly killed it, then rolled and writhed on the pine-needled floor of the forest in vain endeavor to rid himself of the horrible scent with which the skunk had drenched him. That one experience was enough; thereafter he gave skunks a wide berth.

In the following year Smokey became the best hunter and retriever that we ever had. Striking the trail of a flock of wild turkeys, he cautiously sneaked on and dashed in among them so suddenly that they would flutter up into the nearest trees and sit peering down at him, paying no attention to our approach. And shrilly whining, Smokey would alternately look at us and up at the birds, urging that we hurry and shoot them. Dearly he loved the crack of the gun, and when a turkey came hurtling down, he would seize it as it struck the ground and come hurrying to drop it at our feet. Then again whining, looking up at the birds, he would urge us to kill more of them.

The great Apache Forest, in which we were located, abounds in lakes, the breeding place of many kinds of ducks. Strange it is that, in that far-south latitude, numbers of canvasbacks annually breed there. Probably the altitude, 8,000 to 11,000 feet, accounts for it. Smokey had his first duck hunt in the autumn of 1930. Crawling through the rushes bordering a lake, we raised a flock of mallards, fired, and as three of them splashed down into the water, he plunged out after them. He got one by the neck, then swam to another and tried to take it, too, with the result that he lost his grip on the first one. Several times he tried to bring in two at once; then, failing and all but exhausted, he brought in one and rested. But he had had his lesson; after a little he brought in the others separately.

People came from near and far to see Smokey, the tame coyote. He was friendly with all women, but took instant dislike to several men visitors and would not let them come near him. He was very mischievous. Several times, when we were turkey hunting and had stopped to eat and rest, he seized our sack of sandwiches as we drew it from our game bag, ran off a little way, dropped it, and looked back at us; then, as we drew near and were reaching down for it, he was off with it again, only to drop it again and wait for us to come on, which we were just foolish enough to do. Eventually, he would tear the bag open and eat the lunch, then come grinning to us. He took great delight in teasing my wife, particularly when we were turkey hunting. Whenever she started creeping under a wire fence, he would be on the other side, growling, seizing the shoulder of her jacket or her sleeve and shaking it, but always ending by whining and licking her face.

When Smokey was two years old and again when three, and when Zora wanted to have a family of pups, we tried to mate him with her, but it was no go, for the very good reason that coyotes, and wolves, too, mate only in February and the early part of March, while both these attempts were in the summer. Absolutely, Smokey would have nothing to do with her in that way.

One autumn day in 1931, when my son and I were turkey hunting, we raised three coyotes, and Smokey took after them as they ran. We sat down and waited for him to return. Ten minutes passed, twenty minutes, a half-hour; and so worried were we that we actually felt sick, for we dearly loved that coyote, and now he had deserted us to join up with his own kind. We had no more desire to hunt and turned back homeward, plodding along sadly and slowly. But we had not gone far when he dashed swiftly onto our trail and leaped up on us, licked our faces, whining and whining; ran madly around and around us; led off; paused and looked back, as though to say: "Well, come on, let's hunt!" Oh, how relieved we were; how happy. Said my son: "That does prove it; Smokey is fully tame. He loves us, not his wild and wandering kind."

Twice after that, when hunting with Smokey, he took after coyotes that we raised, but he soon came hurrying back to us. We, not they, were his kind of people, he gave us to understand.

Came the summer of 1932, and business matters required our presence in places far from the White Mountains of Arizona. We left Smokey in the care of a good friend who lived near our lodge. Not long afterward we received a terse wire from him: "SMOKEY POISONED LAST NIGHT. HE IS DEAD."

CHAPTER EIGHT

The Making of a Warrior[1]

![decorative border]

It was June, 1881, and dull were the days at Joseph Kipp's lonely trading post at Carroll on the south bank of the Missouri. The Indians had all moved out upon the plain to summer hunt, and empty, monotonous were the hot, slowly passing days to us.

"This is no fun, sitting here day after day, doing nothing, Let me go camp with the Blackfeet for a time," I said to Kipp one day.

"Sure! Go! Have a good time," he answered.

I saddled my buffalo horse, tied on a roll of blankets, and, with Winchester rifle, plenty of cartridges, and some tobacco for presents, set off. Before evening I arrived in the camp of the Blackfeet in a well-timbered bottom of the Musselshell just below the mouth of Crooked Creek. A close friend of mine was Fox Eyes, son of Crazy Dog. They welcomed me, and at once the old man's wife, Badger Woman, and their pretty daughter, Little Bird Woman, prepared a soft buffalo couch for me and gave me to eat. In the evening the head chief of the tribe, Crow Foot, invited me to a feast-and-smoke in his lodge. It was late when I returned to Crazy Dog's lodge and took to my couch.

Wise, frugal, forceful Badger Woman was the head of that little family; Fox Eyes, with his muzzle-loading rifle, its provider; and Crazy Dog, its wasteful burden. An inveterate gambler, on that afternoon, in a hide-the-bone game with some of his cronies, he lost the skins of two beavers that he had caught and then tried to sneak

[1] First published in *The Youth's Companion* (December 8, 1910).

off with two of Fox Eyes' catch. But Badger Woman caught him in the act, snatched the hides from him, and scolded: "You nothing one! You always-losing gambler! Taking of our son's beaver trappings that I am saving until there will be enough of them to buy him a many-shots gun like the one *Apikuni*, here, has. You know how hard it is for him, with his old powder-and-ball gun to provide us with the meat and hides that we need. But still you would steal of his catches to gamble them off! Oh, you shameless, you hard-minded one!" And at that, without a word of reply, Crazy Dog returned to his cronies, lost all of the tobacco that he had, and then came to me begging for more.

"You know how it is," he whispered. "I am so crippled that I cannot hunt. So I gamble. My woman, of course, she scolds me, but I don't mind it. Her heart is good. Well, *Apikuni*, sneak to me some of your tobacco and I will again try to win—plenty win."

Said Fox Eyes to me on the following morning: "*Apikuni*, you know that I have never endured the sacred fast. I have never had time for it; my father crippled, unable to hunt, I have, ever since I grew up, been the sole provider for our lodge. But now the time has come when I must have my fast. So this I ask of you: be you our hunter, provider of meat, while I endure it."

"Yes, I will be your family's hunter; but why are you now so minded to fast sacredly?" I said.

"Because I want to be a real man, a warrior, a member of the Doves, or the Raven Carriers, or some other band of the All Friends warriors society. I have already decided upon my fasting place: a cliff facing Big River and close above the mouth of this South Bear River."

Badger Woman and Little Bird Woman, listening to our talk, became excited and pleased. Said the mother: "Oh, Fox Eyes! Oh, my son! I am so glad that, at last, you are to do this. Too long have you been a lonely, friendless one, unable to join a war party, unable to take part in the dances and the happy feast gatherings of any of the All Friends bands. But now all that is to end. Oh, how proud I shall be of you, someday seeing you returning with a war party, waving enemy scalps, singing the victory song, riding and driving before you enemy horses."

And said Little Bird Woman: "Oh, brother, after your fast, join Seizers; they are the best clothed, best singers and dancers of all of the warrior bands."

"No, you will join the Raven Carriers, they such always-successful warriors. My father, my brother were members of it," the mother said.

There followed some argument between mother and son over which of the medicine men (Sun priests) should be asked to pray for his safety and success in his lone and strenuous fast. The result was that Fox Eyes brought in his horses, roped and led one of them before the lodge of Black Otter, owner of the sacred Thunder Pipe bundle, gave him the horse and said: "*Haiyu!* Oh, powerful, Sun-favored Thunder Pipe man. I am to undergo my lone fast. Help me. Pray for me!"

"Yes. Build a sweat lodge at once and I will join you in it," the old man answered.

Badger Woman, her daughter, and some of their women friends were already building the sweat lodge. In shape it was a semisphere, about ten feet in diameter; its frame, of willows; its covering, an old lodge-skin. In its center a small pit was dug; and lastly, in the near-by fire, some stones were set to heat.

Came presently Black Otter with his sacred pipe, a wooden bowl, and a buffalo tail; and he and Fox Eyes went into the little lodge, undressed, thrust out their clothing, and naked sat. The women passed in the red-hot rocks, and with a stick Fox Eyes rolled them into the pit; lastly, the old man's bowl, filled with water, was passed to him. He dipped the buffalo tail in it, sprinkled the rocks, and, as dense steam began to fill the lodge, he sang the first one of his Thunder Pipe songs and then fervently prayed Sun to protect Fox Eyes, to give him success in the lone fast which he was about to endure. Followed more sprinklings of rocks; more songs; more prayers to Sun, Night Light (the moon), the Seven Persons (constellation of Ursa Major), and Thunderbird. Lastly, with the sacred pipe in hand, Fox Eyes prayed the Above Ones for success in his undertaking, for long life and happiness for his family, and for all of the people of his tribe. We were a crowd of men and women sitting close around the little sweat lodge, listening to it all; the prayers and songs, solemn, fervently impressive, heart stirring, they brought tears to all eyes. Finally the old man and Fox Eyes reached out for their blankets, and, wrapped in them, came out and with heads bowed walked slowly to the river to bathe and dress.

On the following morning, accompanied by his mother, sister, and a half-dozen men relatives for protection, Fox Eyes rode off for his fasting place, and I joined a party of hunters. We were back long before sundown with the choice parts of some buffalo cows we had killed, just in time to see old Black Otter riding the round of the camp, stopping occasionally to sing a sacred song, pray, and call upon the people to pray for the safety and success of Fox Eyes in his lone and strenuous fast.

Three mornings later Badger Woman, Little Bird Woman, and I rode out to visit the faster. At the mouth of Crooked Creek we turned up the valley of the Missouri and then up to the foot of a cliff, where we left our horses, climbed for a time, and turned off upon a narrow shelf of the cliff; presently we came to Fox Eyes in a cavelike depression formed by the overhanging rock. Wrapped in his blanket, he was lying upon a buffalo robe, and at his side were his gun and a red-painted, empty, water bowl. "*Ha!* Here you are: mother, sister, and my good friend *Apikuni*, too," he said.

"Of course," I answered. "I shall come often to see you if I may." We sat down beside him, and his mother emptied a bladder skin of water that she had brought into the wooden bowl; carefully he raised it, took a few slight sips of the water, said that he would like to drink it all.

"You haven't yet had a vision?" his mother asked.

"Last night, the beginning of one," he answered. "I was walking in a valley, in a grassy length of it. A big longtail (cougar) came out from the timber, and I said to it: 'Oh, you powerful, always-successful killer of your food. I am poor. Pity me. Help me; give me of your power; help me to live a long and successful life.' He looked at me, turning his head this way and that way. At last he answered: 'You want me to be your sacred helper. Well, I think that I can . . . .' And then, seeming to see or hear something that frightened him, he went leaping back into the timber, and I awoke and could not sleep again."

"Oh, too bad. Too bad," his mother wailed. "And you so desirous to obtain a helpful vision. And so hungry, thirsty. Oh, I worry about you, here likely to be discovered by some enemy war party that may come along. Well, this day I shall sacrifice to Sun for you. Yes, I shall give him my best, elk-teeth-trimmed gown, pray him to give you quickly a helpful vision and let you safely return to us."

"Yes. Do that. And this I say to you: Do not return here until five nights have passed. Your coming disturbs me. I must be alone, have constant quiet in order to obtain a helpful vision. So now go, and I pray Sun to keep you safe, you three."

"Oh, my son, my son," his mother wailed. "You to lie here five nights without our help? Why, you would die from want of water."

"No. One can live longer than that without food or water. And it may be that I shall obtain my vision this coming night, or tomorrow night. And now go. It is that I must be alone and pray."

Soon after we returned to camp, Badger Woman made a tight roll of her beautiful, valuable, elk-trimmed ceremonial gown, went out and tied it to a limb of a tree. With fervent prayer she gave it to Sun; she sought the great sky god to protect Fox Eyes in his lone fast and to give him a powerful vision. And there the gown would remain, gradually disintegrated by wind and weather. None, not even an enemy war party, would dare to steal a gift to Sun.

Five mornings later I went again with the women to the faster in the niche in the cliff, and was surprised at the change in his appearance in that short time. Emaciated and pale, he lay upon his robe, and feebly he raised a hand to greet us. But he happily smiled and said, almost whispered: "I have been given that which I sought. Take me home.

"Last night, as I slept after long and earnestly praying," he began, "I, my shadow (soul, spirit), left my body and traveled far, crossing a great plain. After a long time I came to the edge of a valley and saw a river in it, and I was glad, for I was very thirsty. Down I ran to it, and to the murmuring of the swift stream. Never had I heard so pleasant a sound; it cheered me, and again I cried out, as I had all the long way across the plain: 'Oh, pity me, Sun, and all you various ones of the shadow world. Be some one of you my sacred helper, that I may survive all dangers and attain old age.'

"I was looking down the river as I prayed. I heard a splash the other way and turning, there, almost beside me, was a certain water animal, sitting at the edge of the water and looking at me. He was so old that his fur was mostly white. 'Oh, young man,' he said to me, 'from afar I heard your cry for help, and so have come to you to be your sacred helper.'

"And then, mother, sister, *Apikuni*, that water animal, he talked with me a long time, telling me what I should do, how sacrifice to him, how call him to my aid when in need. But just what he said, just who he was, that I may not tell you. I wish I could, but you know that no one may reveal what is between him and his sacred helper, lest bad luck come to him."

"Yes, we know that; we will never question you about it, and oh, how glad I am for you. Well we know that all the water animals, even the smallest kinds of them, are Sun favored, and so very powerful. So come, my son, homeward we go," his mother said. His sister gave him her horse and rode double with her mother, and in the late afternoon we were back in camp.

The next evening, well recovered from his fast, for the first time in his life, Fox Eyes gave a feast-and-smoke, and all who were invited came—staid warriors and several sacred-pipe men, believed to be particularly favored by Sun. They drank the soup, ate the rich, broiled buffalo tongues set before them, and during the smoking of the four pipes afterward congratulated Fox Eyes on his endurance and the success of the fast. I was there with them, although I had no right to sit with such dignitaries. But many privileges were accorded the white brother of Fox Eyes.

As my almost-brother filled the pipe for the fourth time, and passed it to the man next on his left to light, he said: "My friends, I now have my sacred helper, but without a shield I cannot go to war. Who will make one for me if I provide the material for it?"

"I will," said Black Otter, oldest of the sacred-pipe men. "And I!

And I!" cried the others, but Black Otter had been first to answer, and it was agreed that he should do it, Fox Eyes saying to him: "I am pleased. I know that you will make me a shield of powerful protection. I give you two of my horses."

To ask that some renowned medicine man (Sun priest) make the shield had been the object of the feast, and all who came knew it. After they had gone Fox Eyes asked me if I would assist him in getting the necessary bull's hide for the shield and the eagle tail feathers for its fringe, and I was all for it. Since a buffalo bull could be killed at any time, we decided to secure the tail feathers first. Now, while it was allowable to kill eagles in any possible way for ordinary purposes, there was but one way to get them for decorating shields, which, to the Blackfeet, were their most cherished, believed-to-be-protective possessions, and that way was, of course, difficult and dangerous.

So was it that, on the following morning, with a couple of buffalo shoulder blades for shovels, and a stout, sharp-pointed length of birch sapling for gouging the earth, Fox Eyes rode to the top of a butte a couple of miles above camp and began to dig a pit in it. It was hard work; we were three mornings in completing it, a pit about five feet long, three feet wide, and four feet deep. We then packed up a lot of willow sticks, laid them crisscross over the pit, and covered them with grass in so natural a manner that the covering had all the appearance of solid ground.

Better than anything else, not excepting even the young of deer or antelope, eagles like the livers of wolves and coyotes. Since it might require several days to kill one of them, we sewed up a wolf-skin, stuffed it with grass in as lifelike a manner as possible, and laid it upon the covering of the pit; last we cut a gash in its side and inserted a large piece of buffalo liver, leaving a part of it protruding. All was in readiness now for catching an eagle when it should come to the bait. Fox Eyes was to sit in the pit waiting and when one came and began eating the liver, he was to reach up, grasp it by its legs, and, drawing it down into the pit, kneel upon it until the life was extinct. This was a hazardous undertaking; there was great risk that the eagle might pluck out the seizer's eyes with its sharp bill or tear his flesh with its poisonous claws.

It was late when we finished our work on the butte and returned to camp. In the evening we sat for a time in Black Otter's lodge, and he sang some sacred songs and prayed Sun to give Fox Eyes success in eagle-catching. On the following morning Badger Woman gave us an early feed of broiled meat and tea, and then Fox Eyes burned some sweetgrass close before his couch, bending over the smoke and grasping handfulls of it with which he rubbed himself. Sweetgrass was a sacred plant; its delicious perfume was greatly prized by Sun; the smoke of it removed all human odor.

Having purified himself, Fox Eyes, as was required of him, said to his mother and sister: "I am going this morning to attempt to catch an eagle, and you women must do all that you can to aid me. Until I return you must remain in the lodge, continuously praying for my success. Also, lest in seizing an eagle he should pierce me with his claws, you must not put any thorny wood on the fire, nor eat thorny berries, and for the same reason you must not use a needle, or awl, or scratch yourself."

With that we saddled the horses that we had picketed the evening before, on our way taking up a human skull which we had found at the edge of a grove and which Fox Eyes was to place in the pit. There was nothing that the Blackfeet dreaded so much as a human skull, but for this very reason it was considered necessary for an eagle catcher to have one in his pit. It was a test of his courage to sit with it during his long times of waiting and watching for an eagle to appear, and there was no possibility of going to sleep and losing his chance to seize one, with such a fearsome object at his side.

When Fox Eyes had settled down in the pit and was comfortable, I carefully replaced the sticks and grass that he had pulled aside in order to enter. Then, saying that I hoped he would have quick success, I mounted my horse and, leading his horse, rode to the top of a butte a half-mile away and sat down in the shade of a pine tree to await the result of our work. The sun was then well up in the blue, and I searched in all directions, but not an eagle was in sight. Not even a hawk. The day was hot. With my back against the tree, I frequently dozed, awoke with a start, and, snatching up my telescope, eagerly leveled it at the covering of the pit. Always I could see the dark blotch of the liver in the stuffed wolf-hide. No eagle had been there. None came that day. Fox Eyes' heart was low when, as sun was setting, we headed back to camp. But there Black Otter restored his courage by saying: "You could not expect to seize an eagle on the first day in your pit, but sooner or later you will get one, for my prayers for your success are powerful."

On the following morning Fox Eyes was again in his pit, and I on watch upon the lone pine butte. Very soon I saw an eagle circling round and round, high above the pit. Suddenly he dived straight down and alighted on the ground fifteen or twenty yards to the east of it. I kept my telescope leveled at him. How big and proud he looked as he stood there plucking at and smoothing his feathers, occasionally cocking his head sideways and looking at the stuffed wolfskin. He seemed to be suspicious of it for he stood there a long time, anxiously watching it. But at last he moved, stalking slowly around the pit. Before he had half circled it, came a raven from I knew not where, at once lit upon the stuffed wolfskin, and began eating the liver. That allayed the eagle's suspicion of it and angered him. With wings half-spread, he swiftly ran to the bait, driving away the raven, and himself began to feast.

"Oh, Fox Eyes," I cried aloud in my excitement, "Seize him! Seize him!"

As if in answer to my entreaty, he did just that. All at once the eagle began to flap its wings and struggle; willow sticks and grass flew in all directions, and then the big bird disappeared. Casing my telescope, I ran to the horses and, after unfastening their picket ropes, was soon riding down my butte and up the other one. As I neared the pit, Fox Eyes climbed out of it and held the eagle up before him for me to see. It was so large that his body was almost hidden by it.

"Oh, *Apikuni!* Isn't it a big one; and how perfect its tail feathers," he cried as I rode up and dismounted beside him. "Oh, Sun! Oh, my powerful water-animal helper," he continued. "You have been good to me; you have powerfully helped me this day."

It was indeed a magnificent bird, a male war eagle,[2] its tail feathers long, smooth, glossy, white with black tips. As we rode homeward with the bird, I was as pleased with the success of the day as he.

"A good beginning," Black Otter said to him. "Catch three more of them, and then I will prepare you for the war trail."

Within ten days' time Fox Eyes had the tail feathers of four eagles, all of them caught at the pit. Wonderfully good luck, all said, for he now had enough of the tail feathers for the fringe of the shield and for a war bonnet, too. We then went out hunting, and with my rifle he killed a buffalo bull, an old, old one, whose once crescent-shaped, smooth, black, sharp horns were now mere rough, pale stubs.

"He has been brave; he has fought many battles and survived them," said my friend, as we were removing the hide from its neck and shoulders. "It is a sign that a shield made of his hide will be my powerful protector, keep me safe in fights with our enemies."

There was evidenced his real faith. To the Blackfeet there was a sign, an omen, for good or for bad in everything, no matter how trivial. We took the piece of thick hide to Badger Woman, and she carefully removed its fur, leaving the glossy, brownish-black surface intact. Then one afternoon it was handed to old Black Otter, and the interesting ceremony of transforming it into a shield took place.

Black Otter was dressed in his war clothes, soft buckskin shirt, leggings, and moccasins, beautifully embroidered with varicolored porcupine-quill designs, and on his head was a horns-and-ermine-skins war bonnet. His hands and face were painted a dull red, the sacred color. By the side of his lodge the piece of bull hide was stretched and pegged to the ground, and, kneeling on it, he began to pray, at the same time starting to cut from the hide a circular piece about four feet in diameter.

"Oh, Sun! Oh, Night Light! Morning Star! Oh, all you Above Ones," he chanted, "Listen and pity us this day. This shield that I am making, give it of your sacred power so that it will keep its owner safe in his encounters with the enemy. Oh, Above Ones! To all of

[2] It was the golden eagle, *aquila chrysaëtos canadensis.*

us, men, women, children, give long good life, good health; help us to overcome our enemies who are ever seeking to destroy us."

Some women were heating a number of stones in a little fire, and near it a small pit had been dug in the ground. The women rolled part of the stones into it, covered them with a thin layer of loose earth. Then Black Otter, with the help of three war-clothed friends, laid the circular piece of hide over the pit and, inserting pegs into slits that had been cut at regular intervals along its edge, fastened it to the ground.

As each man drove in a peg, he counted coup, told of some fight with the enemy in which he had been the victor. Tightly the hide had been fastened down; it began to shrink from the heat under it until it pulled the pegs over. As fast as they loosened, the three men helpers drove them in again; Black Otter carefully supervised the work, often feeling of the hide to make sure that it did not get hot enough to burn, and calling for more hot rocks as they were needed.

In about an hour the hide had shrunk to about half its original diameter, and was at least an inch thick. During that time Black Otter had frequently prayed, and with his helpers had sung a number of sacred songs. Finally Fox Eyes took the hide home and in due time made a beautiful, tail-feathers-trimmed shield of it. Lastly he made a war bonnet of the remaining tail feathers, and was then ready for war. A few days later he did set out with a small party to raid the horse herds of the Assiniboines, and I returned to the trading post. A month or more later Fox Eyes came to visit me, came singing a war song, riding a fine horse and leading another. Tossing its rope to me, he said: "*Apikuni*, I give to you this Cutthroat (Assiniboine) horse. Three of them I took. One Cutthroat I killed and this —see it—many-shots gun I took from him. *Apikuni*, Sun is good to me. My sacred helper, that water animal of my vision, is powerful. *Apikuni*, I am a happy man. I am soon to have a lodge of my own."

"Good! Have three wives, four wives. While you are about it, be a real chief," I said.

CHAPTER NINE

He Sang the Victory Song[1]

❧❧❧❧❧❧❧❧❧❧❧❧❧❧❧❧❧❧❧❧❧❧❧❧❧❧❧❧❧❧❧

IN AUGUST, 1881, slow, idle days dragged on for us at Kipp's trading post. The Indians were still out on the plains, gathering great stores of chokecherries for winter use, hunting only for their daily meat, trading with us not at all.

"I would like to have a few days off to go and camp again with the Blackfeet," I said to Kipp one evening.

"Well, go," he answered shortly.

Early the next morning I saddled my buffalo horse, tied on a slender roll of blankets, and was on my way. In good time I arrived in the Blackfoot camp on Musselshell River, at the mouth of Crooked Creek, where I was welcomed in the lodge of Three Bears, father of my close friend Eagle Head. Like myself, Eagle Head was twenty-two years of age. Presently I was seated on the couch which I was to share with him, while his mother, Spear Woman, and his pretty sister, *Paiót Ahki*, "Flying Woman," were setting food before me: a bowl of soup, a plate of rich, berry pemmican. I ate heartily, cleaned the plate, and drank a second bowl of soup. Then Three Bears lit and passed his huge, black, stone pipe, and we smoked. Later Eagle Head and I went visiting here and there and in the evening looked on at a dance of the Raven Carriers band of the All Friends warriors society. Mature, experienced warriors were the Raven Carriers, and soon to go to war against the Cutthroats.

Spear Woman had decided that her daughter should have a new

[1] Published in *The Open Road for Boys* (September, 1937).

gown of soft-tanned thin antelope skins, and there was much talk about the making of it. There should be, they decided, two suns of red, white, and yellow porcupine quillwork on the breast; a red quill butterfly—symbol of good dreams and good luck—high up on the back; and from the waist down, rows of elk tushes. Six antelope skins were needed for it, the mother said, and it was for Eagle Head and me to furnish them.

So was it that we four rode out from camp early one morning— Eagle Head and I to hunt, mother and daughter to gather choke-cherries. As we turned from the camp, heading up the valley of the Musselshell, Eagle Head broke out with the Defiance Song: "*Ahksi Kiwa! Ahksi Kiwa! Ahksi Kiwa!*" ("I care for nothing! I care for nothing! I care for nothing!").

"Eagle Head," exclaimed Spear Woman, "at once stop singing that bad-luck song else you will get us into trouble! For three days your uncle, Little Otter, sang it before he went out against that bad Cutthroat, White Dog, and he never returned. It is an unlucky song for this family. I forbid you to sing it."

"*Ha!* Just your woman's thought of it. It is a good song; it makes one feel brave," he replied, but sang it no more.

After riding up the valley five or six miles we turned east into a wide brushy coulee. Eagle Head, wearing a cap made of the upper skin and horns of a buck antelope head, was in the lead. As we neared the head of the coulee he motioned for us to stop and went on very slowly, rising often in his stirrups to get a view of the plain. Suddenly he ducked, slid from his horse, and beckoned us to join him. In a moment we were out of our saddles and beside him.

"Step out a little farther, look out through the brush and you will see them, a big band of antelope," he said.

Sure enough, well up on the slope of a ridge about a mile south of us was a band of a hundred or more, all lying down except three or four sentinel bucks keenly watching for the possible coming of enemies, wolves or men. Between them and us stretched a level plain, but close behind the ridge on which they were resting was a long coulee running down to the valley of the river.

Eagle Head spoke swiftly to his mother: "You and sister turn back with us to the mouth of this coulee where we saw the big patch of cherries. Then *Apikuni* and I will go on up the valley behind the ridge until we are opposite the antelope. If they remain where they are now, we shall be able to kill all we want."

That meant that we would make a circle of four or five miles before we would get to the band. Back we all went to the mouth of the coulee, and as Eagle Head and I parted from the women at the edge of the cherry trees he said to them: "There! Pick plenty of fruit; but when you hear us shoot, come hurrying to help butcher our kills."

We left them, eagerly beginning to fill their pouches with the ripe fruit, and rode as fast as we could up the valley. When we came to the mouth of the coulee, Eagle Head turned up to the rim of the plain for another look at the game and reported that the band was still lying down.

We found this coulee to be narrow, winding, and boulder strewn, and it took us some time to work our way up it and past the ridge. At last we left it and rode along until we thought that we were opposite the game; then, dismounting, we picketed our horses and headed for the summit of the ridge. From that high point we looked down the other slope through its growth of sage and found that the antelope were straight below us, but more than three hundred yards away. Save for three sentinel bucks, all were lying down.

Creeping back a little way, Eagle Head signed to me: "They are too far for sure killing. Stay where you are; be ready; I will bring them close to us."

Advancing, he rose until his horned cap showed plainly above the sagebrush. At sight of it the white rump hair of the sentinels bristled. Eagle Head lowered his cap out of sight, then exposed it again three or four times. Apparently the old sentinels thought it was the head of one of their kind, and they resented its presence in the vicinity of their family of does and young. At second sight of the cap, they stepped stiffly forward, shaking their heads, stamping their forefeet, and snorting, causing the whole band to spring up in alarm; and, as the cap bobbed up for the fourth time, the sentinels came charging toward us, followed by the others.

That was what we had hoped to bring about. The leaders of the band were almost upon us when we opened fire, but at our first shots they quartered back down the ridge like the wind and in no time were gone out of range. However, they left eight of their number dead or dying in their wake.

As we put the wounded out of their misery and began plying our knives, Eagle Head remarked that the women had undoubtedly heard our shots and would soon be coming to do their share in skinning the kills. But they did not appear, and Eagle Head said: "That is the way of women. Once they get into a good berry patch they forget all else."

At last we finished the butchering and tied the skins to our saddles. Gathering the meat in one place to be packed to camp on the following day, I tied my handkerchief to a bush beside it to keep the wolves and coyotes away.

It was midafternoon when we mounted our horses and hurried off down the plain to join the women. But when we arrived at the place where we had left them they were not there. Deciding that they must have filled their pouches with berries and gone back to camp, we were about to follow when we discovered their big saddle pouches, half-filled with cherries, lying where their horses had been tied. Their small hand pouches were near by, too, evidently thrown down in haste, for cherries were scattered on the ground.

"What could have happened," Eagle Head exclaimed, "to cause them to leave their pickings so suddenly?"

We saw no signs of anything that could have frightened them, but circling about, we found the trail of their horses headed up the valley away from camp and traveling fast. That alarmed us.

It was easy to follow the horses' hoofprints in the broad, dusty game trail, which soon led us to the river and across it into a body of timber. There we found something more to confuse us, for a herd of buffalo had swept up through the bottom, obliterating the horses' tracks. Whence had come the buffalo? We had not seen them. And what had caused them to run up the valley? Evidently they had been frightened into flight after the women had gone up through the grove. We rode this way and that, searching the various trails for some explanation, Eagle Head calling loudly upon his gods for help.

"Oh, Sun! All you Above Ones! Help us to find my mother, my sister, and save them from whatever danger they are in," he repeatedly cried.

It was I, riding out to the edge of the grove, who found the reason for the flight of the women. In a game trail I discovered the footprints of a number of horses on top of those of the buffalo. Calling Eagle Head, I showed them to him.

"*Ha!* A war party! We must hurry! Come on!"

A mile or so farther on there was a sharp bend in the valley to the west, where the buffalo herd had left it, going due south up a depression in the plain. The horse tracks continued in one of the game trails.

We were speeding through a large grove when suddenly Flying Woman sprang out from a growth of willows bordering the trail, shrieking to us to stop. Her eyes were big with fear, and when Eagle Head sprang from his horse and embraced her, she was trembling and so hysterical that it was hard to understand what she said.

"They are an enemy war party—eight riders—we saw them coming —had a good start on them—they scared some buffalo that followed us—then turned off—my horse too slow—Mother made me get off, hide here—she rode on with it—said she could go faster than enemies —would reach you first."

"You stay here until we come for you," Eagle Head told her as he remounted his horse. "But if we don't return before night, head for camp, and be sure to keep in the thick timber as much as possible."

"Yes, brother," she replied, then added as we were starting on: "They ride our people's horses. White Antelope's old black and white pinto is one of them; Heavy Runner's yellow and white, another."

That meant that we had some chance of overtaking them. They had, no doubt, raided the outside herds of our camp, and in their haste had taken slow travois and pack horses.

Perspiration washed furrows in Eagle Head's painted cheeks, and his eyes were wild; he was half out of his mind in his anxiety for his mother. I, too, was worried for her and for ourselves. Speeding up our horses, we tried to make up the several precious minutes we had lost talking with Flying Woman. The trail of the war party was not hard to follow, and at last on the farther side of a ford we learned that we were not far behind them, for the stony shore was still wet with water that had dripped from their horses.

"Take courage! Take courage!" Eagle Head called to me. "We are overtaking them!"

"I do take courage," I answered stoutly, at the same time feeling very uneasy about the outcome of our chase—we but two against eight men.

The sun was low when, hot on their trail, we left the valley and turned west on the plain. There they were a half-mile or so away, chasing the woman, who was about that distance ahead of them and still leading her daughter's horse. She was gradually circling, with the intention of heading back downriver, but she was losing ground, for her pursuers were cutting across the circle. We cut, too.

Our horses were winded, but so were those of the enemy, and ours were speedier. Slowly we gained on them. The fleeing woman, looking back, saw that her pursuers were creeping up on her. Suddenly she stopped, turned her mount, sprang onto the one she had been leading, and sped on. While making the change, brief though it was, the enemy had come within shooting range of her, but they did not open fire; it was evident that their object was to capture her. So intent upon it were they that they had not discovered Eagle Head and me pursuing and gaining on them.

We were within three hundred yards of the party when one of them, looking back, discovered us. At once we opened fire on them, shooting as fast as we could take sight and work the levers of our Winchesters, they shooting at us in return. Almost at once one of them pitched head foremost on the ground, and a horse dropped, its rider landing upright on his feet. Then with an almost human shriek of agony, Eagle Head's horse fell, lay still, pinning the young Indian's right foot and ankle to the ground.

"I will free you," I shouted, springing from my horse.

"No. Keep on shooting. I can free myself," he yelled.

One of the riders kept on in pursuit of Spear Woman, while the others began circling around and around us, shooting as they rode.

The man whose horse had been killed was not in sight. I felt sure that he was crawling through the sagebrush to get a close shot at us. Surely this hidden, crawling one was our greatest danger. Between shots at the circling riders, I scanned the sagebrush for some betraying movement of his presence.

Though taking careful sight at the circling riders, we were making no kills of horses or men. The enemy's bullets thudded into the brush and ground around us, some of them all too close. A bullet brained my horse. As it fell, I sprang and crouched at its side for some protection from the man off there in the sagebrush, without doubt crawling slowly, steadily toward us. I shivered.

Eagle Head's voice was firm as he urged: "Keep courage! Keep courage! Shoot with careful aim to kill."

I did not answer, but kept shooting at the nearest rider, a big man no more than 250 yards away. Intermittently he sang as he fired his single-shot rifle at us, reloaded, and fired again without haste. He seemed to be saying: "You are to die!"

Eagle Head, as he afterward told me, was shooting exclusively at him. One or the other of us shot his horse, breaking a foreleg. It stumbled, tried to go on three legs, gave up. The Indian sprang off, dove into the sagebrush, also to crawl in closer. I felt that our end was near. It was a sickening thought.

Between shots I looked off at Spear Woman and her pursuer; he was gradually gaining on her; would surely overtake and seize her, make her his slave. Terrible, oh, terrible would be her fate!

I fired two more shots at one of the circling riders and missed. No slight sign could I see of our crawling enemies. In their own good time they would get us. Desperately I slipped my four last cartridges into the magazine of my rifle, thinking to myself that I would never get a chance to use them all. With careful aim I fired at the circling Indians; missed again. Levering another cartridge into the barrel of my rifle, I looked off at Spear Woman and her pursuer, and could hardly believe my eyes.

"Eagle Head! Eagle Head!" I shouted. "See them! We survive!"

A little way beyond Spear Woman forty or fifty riders had come up out of a coulee and were galloping toward her, waving their hands and shouting. At sight of them her pursuer turned abruptly and headed for his companions, who stopped circling us and drew together, yelling excitedly.

"Our fighting men! We survive!" Eagle Head shouted joyously.

The two horseless Indians sprang up behind two of their party and all were off, madly quirting their beasts and heading for a coulee away to the south. Eagle Head and I fired our remaining cartridges at them, but neither of us made a kill. And then our warriors were speeding past us, yelling happily, noticeably gaining on our fleeing enemies.

At last came Spear Woman. Springing from her horse, crying and laughing both, she hugged and kissed Eagle Head, turned and did the same to me, saying again and again: "Oh, how powerful, how good is Sun! He brought our warriors to our rescue; he saved us!"

Eagle Head ran and seized the horse of the man we had killed. It was strange, I thought, that one or the other of our horseless enemies had not tried to take it for his getaway.

Said Spear Woman, "Oh, my saved ones! Didn't you make any kills?"

"One," Eagle Head replied. "I killed him. Now I count coup upon him!" And with that he ran and scalped the man, a Cutthroat, and took his belongings, a Springfield carbine, belt of cartridges, knife, and war bonnet in a parfleche case.

Spear Woman happily looked on, singing and exclaiming again and again: "My son Eagle Head, he killed this enemy. Brave is my son Eagle Head!"

So happy were they over the kill that I refrained from saying that it might have been my bullet that tumbled the man from his horse.

Our enemies and their pursuers had gone out of sight beyond a low ridge of the plain, but now, as we heard distant rapid shooting mother and son fervently prayed the Above Ones, Sun, Moon, and Morning Star, to keep our warriors safe and help them to kill off the enemy.

Anxiously we awaited their return, and presently they appeared topping the ridge, singing the victory song, waving scalps, leading the horses that the Cutthroats had stolen from our herds during the night. All seven of the Indians were dead out there on the plain, and not one of our rescuers had been killed.

So was it that I had a horse to ride homeward, in place of my fast buffalo runner that had been shot. We found Flying Woman right where we had left her, and gave her back her own horse to ride.

That evening our lodge was crowded with visitors to hear us tell of our day's experiences. At last, when all had gone and we were about to take our rest, Spear Woman said to Eagle Head: "My son, it was your singing of the Defiance Song that nearly caused the end for us today. Now you know that you should never sing it, the terrible, terrible bad-luck song."

"Yes, I sang it," he replied, "and what happened? Why, we killed eight Cutthroats, took eight guns and many other things. Mother, can't you see that it is the best of good-luck songs?"

And to that Spear Woman had no answer.

CHAPTER TEN

A Day's Hunt with Eagle Head

◄◄◄◄◄◄◄◄◄◄◄◄◄◄◄◄◄◄◄◄◄◄◄◄◄◄◄◄◄◄◄◄◄◄◄◄◄◄◄

SOON AFTER SUNRISE of a day of June, 1881, my friend Eagle Head and I brought our horses to a stand in the edge of some stunted pines, tied them, and signed back to Archie Amiotte, trailing us with team and wagon, to halt. We then moved on a few steps through the pines to the brink of the valley of Big Crooked Creek and looked into it, hoping to see a herd of buffalo, but only a lone old bull was there, straight down from us. Patches of his thick, winter coat, faded to a lusterless, dingy yellow, still clung to his new, short growth of dark fur, which, coming so late in the spring, was a sure sign of old age and waning vigor. His once beautifully curved, sharp black horns were now merely whitish, short stubs, His beard, even, was ragged and unkempt. A younger generation of bulls had driven him from the herds of which he had long been a leader.

We had come out to get some meat for Joseph Kipp's trading post at Carroll. Well, we would get it. Off to the south and the east of us were several herds of buffalo and bands of antelope grazing on the rolling plain. As we were trying to determine which one of the herds would be easiest, surest for us to approach closely, a distant, thunderlike rumbling attracted our attention; it came from somewhere up the valley, several stretches of which we could not see. "*Ha!* Buffalo coming! Frightened!" Eagle Head exclaimed.

"Yes, and they will start all the other herds to running," I said.

But they were not buffalo. Around a sharp bend of the valley just west of us a band of forty or fifty wild horses appeared and came on down it at great speed. A big, proud bay stallion led them, and he was a beast to stir one's heart as he passed, his heavy, long mane and tail streaming straight back, his shapely feet hitting the turf with a springy lightness that a fox might have envied.

Occasionally he turned his head to look back; it was plain that he was holding himself in to suit the pace of his following, mares, colts, yearlings, and two-year-olds. Soon they passed down around a bend of the valley. They had not been an unusual sight—wild horses were then fairly plentiful on the plain between the Missouri and the Yellowstone—but the beauty and grace and strength of the leader of this band was something not to be forgotten. "Oh, oh! If he were only mine!" Eagle Head fairly groaned.

But that was out of the question. Our horses had not sufficient wind and speed to overtake him, and if they had, and we succeeded in roping him, he would undoubtedly put up such a fight that we would be glad to let him go.

We remained seated in the pines, hoping to discover what had frightened the horses. The lone old bull had paid little heed to them; he had only raised his head for a moment and looked at them. Then he lowered it again and stood motionless and humped up, a most melancholy object.

The horses had barely disappeared around the bend when a big gray wolf—attracted no doubt by the sound of their passing—came to the rim of the valley straight across from us and looked all up and down it. Eagle Head said that he had recognized the thudding of the horses' hoofs on the hard ground—so different from the rattling of buffalo hoofs—and his mouth was watering; better than a buffalo calf, better than elk or deer or antelope was the meat of a colt to him, and he wanted some.

But the herd had passed and he was disappointed. He stared down at the old bull, turned and walked away from the valley rim, turned again and came back to it, squatted upon his haunches, pointing his nose to the sky, and gave four long, loud, and melancholy howls. From the southwest came the answer of one of his kind. He howled again, and from the south and the west came other long, loud, answering howls. I know of nothing so sad as the howling of wolves; they chillingly voice deep, hopeless despair.

"He is calling his relatives. I think he intends to feast upon the old bull," Eagle Head said.

The wolf looked this way, that way, whence the answering howls had come, at intervals howling again and again, but without replies. Presently, however, a wolf appeared, coming from the south. The two met, sniffed at one another, wagging their tails; then side by side stood looking down at the bull, the caller-wolf howling again. The bull paid no attention to it, did not even look up at the howler. Slowly, stiffly he lowered himself to the ground and began chewing his cud.

There was more wagging of tails, more questioning sniffing of one another, as, one by one, five more wolves came in answer to the calls; once two of them playfully put on a sham fight, standing upon their hind legs and, breast to breast, snapping each at the other's neck. "*Ha!* Although the moon is still far off for wolves to mate, they are fighting!" Eagle Head exclaimed.

"Fighting wolves hold their tails stiffly up. These two are wagging their tails; they are playing," I said.

"*Ha!* True. True. So they are," he agreed.

By this time they had milled around so much that we could no longer distinguish the one who had called them together, but it was probably he who now led off over the rim of the plain and down the slope of the valley, the others closely following. The old bull got wind of them when they struck the floor of the valley, and with surprising agility he got up onto his feet and faced them. Trotting, they completely circled him, at a distance of about fifty yards, then stopped, facing him, looking this way, that way, and sniffing the air for scent of anything inimical to their plan. But they did not suspicion our presence; the wind was in our favor.

Eagle Head always maintained that it was the caller, the leader of the wolf band, that planned and ordered the attack upon the bull. Certain it was that together, suddenly, they leaped forward, two to feint attack upon his head, the others to run swiftly to and fro behind him, getting ever closer to his heels, their purpose to hamstring him. He seemed to know their plan—perhaps he had been attacked by wolves before—he sought to protect his rear, and to do that tried to face all ways at once. Old though he was and huge, between anger and fear he developed a surprising agility. To run from them was impossible; the battle had to be fought there on the spot. He lunged now at this wolf, again at that one, wheeling all the time; in fact, he spun round and round like a huge, erratic top. We could hear his snorts of rage. "It is not fair. I am going to save him!" I exclaimed, raising my rifle; but Eagle Head stayed my aim.

"It is his time to die," said he.

"But he wants to live as much as we do."

"Yes, he does, but it is not for us to interfere. Old Man—World Maker—created buffalo for food for men and wolves. Should you save this old and worn-out bull from them, they would only travel on and pull down the next one—and it, perhaps, a young cow that we may need some day."

There was good sound sense in that argument, and I lowered my rifle. The bull was whirling around swiftly, kicking vigorously and deftly, once planting a hoof in the side of a wolf with such force as to send it high in the air.

But in a few minutes the bull showed signs of weakening, and no wonder; the tremendous strain of his defense was too severe for his old and stiffened joints. He kicked less frequently; the wolves dashed in closer and closer. In passing, one of them snapped its jaws on a hind leg, just above the gambrel joint, where the great tendon—the hamstring—is most exposed. Lightninglike it was, but that one snap severed the cord and the bull lurched backward and sideways, and nearly fell. As he struggled to right himself, all of the wolves vied with one another to get at the tendon of the other hind leg, tore it in two, and the rear part of the big body sagged to the ground. Then for a moment the bull held his foreparts erect, his great shaggy head elevated at a most unwonted angle, and what a pitiable sight he was! But the strain was too great; little by little his forelegs gave way altogether, and suddenly his whole body was prone on the ground.

The wolves were watching, waiting for this, and made a simultaneous dash for the bull's flank—not for his throat, as it is erroneously said to be their method of finishing a victim. It was their intention to take their meal from the living flesh.

But that was more than I could stand. I broke from cover and ran down the hill. The wolves stared at me a moment and then, pausing frequently, trotted off down the valley. I could have shot one or two of them but forebore, as their summer coat was valueless. I hurried to the bull and put him out of his misery with a bullet through the brain.

Eagle Head followed me down with the horses, and as I mounted mine and we rode on, he remarked that the whites were queer people.

"You are hard to understand," said he. "To see you drive the wolves away and end their work with a bullet, one would think that you have the heart of a woman."

The wolves were watching us. As we topped the rim of the valley they began running back up it to feast upon their kill.

Rejoining our teamster, we found him in a sullen mood. "What you been doing out there so long?" he growled.

"We were watching some wolves kill an old bull," I answered.

"Huh! That's just like you. Foolin' away your time, my time. Do you suppose I want to sit here all day?" And then pointing: "Just see the buffalo off there, and off there! Come, get busy."

"We are going to," I answered. "We will run that herd off there to the west, grazing toward the creek. You drive down into the valley and up it to the second bend, then stop there until you hear us shoot."

Eagle Head and I rode back into the valley and up it, to keep well ahead of the team. We had gone about a mile when, rounding a sharp bend, we saw, not far ahead, a big mother wolf sitting on a mound of yellow earth on the north slope of the valley and some pups playing around her. But we had only a brief glimpse of them: warned by their mother of danger, they scampered into a hole at the upper side of the mound, and she ran up to the top of the slope and stood staring down at us.

"I want one of those pups to raise; to be ever close to me; to hunt for me. Will you help me dig it out?" I said to Eagle Head.

"Ask me that after we have made our run and had our fill of broiled liver," he replied.

A little farther on we climbed to the south rim of the plain for another look at the herd of buffalo; they were about a mile from us and a half-mile from the valley, grazing slowly in to water.

Riding leisurely back down the slope and on up the valley, we twice more climbed to the rim of the plain to see how the herd was progressing and at last dismounted in some willows by the creek, right where the herd would come to water. When its leaders appeared we would get into our saddles, be ready to speed out and into it when it was close. Time passed. Again and again we exclaimed upon the slowness of their coming. At last we heard a sudden thundering of hoofs, and with it came the herd, compactly, a brown torrent of heaving, shaggy heads and humps pouring swiftly over the rim of the plain and down the slope of the valley.

"When I go to water I run," I sang as I sprang up onto my horse.

"Cease singing that sacred song of the buffalo bull, else you will bring us bad luck. You know that only our medicine men may sing it!" Eagle Head yelled to me.

The buffalo were coming so swiftly, so compactly, that it would be suicide for us to ride into them; our horses would be gored, we would be overthrown, trampled to death in the twinkling of an eye. So we fled across the creek, through the willows bordering it, and came to a stand. The leaders of the herd endeavored to stop at the creek, but the irresistible pressure of the dense mass of thirsty animals in their rear forced them across the stream, through the willows, and almost upon us. Since cows with calves were poor at that time of year, we each shot a yearling, and at the report of our rifles the whole herd affrightedly whirled around, crashed back through the willows, and turned down the valley, we after them, in among them; and what excitement—yes, and dangerous sport—it was! There was always the chance that one's horse would stumble and fall, or be gored by the sharp horns of an angry cow. That would be the end for the rider; he would be cut to pieces by the hoofs of the dense crowd of buffalo coming on in his rear.

I headed my excited, eager, well-trained horse after a two-year-old bull, broad and rounded of rump and therefore fat. With ears turned back and champing his teeth as though he were going to bite him, the horse brought me up alongside the bull and I put a bullet into his lungs. At once blood gushed from his nose, so that was the end for him. One after another, three more I killed; a yearling and a two-year-old heifer, a big dry cow. And I wanted to keep on and kill and kill, but would not as it would be but a waste of life, so I fought my excited horse to a standstill. I saw Eagle Head still keeping on, shooting occasionally. But soon he gave up the run, turned back, and I rode on to meet him.

He came singing, waving his rifle; he halted and said: "What happiness, this running and killing of buffalo. I killed eight. How many, you?"

"Five. We have killed too many; the meat of four will be a big load for our wagon. The rest will be wasted. I take shame for us," I said.

"Not so. We should have killed more. I forgot to tell you that I told some of our people camped back of your trade-house to trail us and we would give them of our kills. They will be here. We should have killed more."

This made me feel better. As we were butchering one of my kills, our teamster came and got busy, and a little later a number of Eagle Head's Blackfoot friends and relatives arrived, men and women with pack horses and travois horses, and fell to work—happily chatting, singing as they plied their knives. They were all old men and women, some of them widows, and sincere in their praise of us for giving them of our kills.

Over a fire of dry willows we broiled some liver, ate our fill of it, and with our wagonload of meat struck out down the valley. Rounding a bend close above the wolf den, we saw that both the father and mother were there with the pups, but upon sighting us the old ones sent the pups scampering down into the den and then trotted off to a safe distance to watch us uneasily. With the shovel that Archie always had in the wagon we commenced digging into the den. The large hole sloped down at an angle of about forty-five degrees, and soon we discovered that it had small side chambers. We were about to pass one of them, partly filled with loose earth, when I saw the tip of a fuzzy tail sticking out from it. Reaching in,

I got my hand under the pup's belly, lifted it out, and held to its nose one of the several pieces of meat that I had ready. Eagerly the pup seized it, gulped it down, and wagging its tail, sniffed for more. It was of the sex that I wanted, a male.

"Enough!" I said. "Let us go."

I had Eagle Head lead my horse, and rode home in the wagon with Archie, holding the pup in my lap. It showed no fear and, filled with meat, was lazily contented, sleeping most of the way in. I had myself a fine new pet.[1]

[1] For the full story of this pup, see "Some Wild-Animal Pets," chap. 7 of this volume.

CHAPTER ELEVEN

Fire at Fort Benton Courthouse

GONE WERE THE BUFFALO. No longer came the Indians to camp near our post at Fort Conrad and to trade with us their fine robes and other products of their exciting hunts. Now the only break in the monotony was the bimonthly arrival of the Fort Benton–Fort Macleod mail stage, Jack Lee the driver. This was an event, for it brought the news of the outside world as well as the mail to our post office.

Yes, life at Fort Conrad was tame. So when, one spring, our womenfolks said they wanted to go to Fort Benton to buy some dress goods, Kipp and I were only too glad to take them, in the hope that we too might have some fun in the metropolis. We hitched four horses to a light wagon, the women piled in, and we were off. We nooned with "Froggy" at the Pend d'Oreille and stopped for the night with Captain Nelse (Narcise Valleau) at his Teton River ranch. A great joker, sometimes too practically so, was Captain Nelse. He it was who, when a Helena big gun was orating at a political meeting in Fort Benton, suddenly arose, stretched, yawned, and said: "Well, as that's so, I'm goin' to have a drink. Who'll join me?" A moment later the politician was staring at an empty hall.

At noon next day we looked down upon Fort Benton from the rim of the hill, and lo! Oh, happy sight, four steamboats were tied to the levee. Said Kipp to me: "We'll probably see some lively doings in the old town tonight."

Down in the bottom, at the outskirts of the town, many bull trains

were parked, waiting to load freight for Helena, Bozeman, Fort
Macleod, and other points. Tom Clary and Bob Ford hailed us as
we passed their outfits. Keno Bill's woman, Yellow Bird, was re-
lated to our women, so we left them at his house, put our horses in
Jim McDevitt's stable, and made for Bill's saloon and bottles of
Budweiser beer.

Bill's news was that one of the steamboats at the levee was the
Black Hills—biggest boat that ever came up the river—and we ought
to see her. So we did. To our crude ideas of elegance she was a floating palace. The other boats, the *Helena*, the *Benton*, and the *Josephine*, were dwarfs compared with her.

We went to I. G. Baker & Company's store and had a powwow
with *Sisukikaiyi Istsimokan* ("Spotted Cap,"—our good friend,
Charlie Conrad). Then our women came in to trade and we had to
interpret for them. My woman, Fine Shield Woman, wanted a trunk,
a big one, with a tray and prettily papered inside.

"But you have plenty of parfleches for the storing of our things,
so why that?" I asked.

"We no longer follow the buffalo; they are gone. We now live
the life of the whites. So it is that I want a trunk. Yes, and a hat such
as white women wear."

Both she bought, and other women's things, and was happy
until, before a mirror in Bill's house, she put on the hat. "Oh, how
horrible am I under it," she cried. "I see now that our kind cannot
wear the like. At once I will trade it for another pair of shoes."

Came night, and Kipp and I wandered from saloon to saloon, taking an occasional drink, here dropping and there winning a few dollars at the faro tables; meeting many friends, at last two close friends
from Choteau, Jack Miller and old man *Kaiyo*. Both were onetime
employees of the old and retired American Fur Company. I loved
their tales of the activities of the old adobe fort under its builder,
Alexander Culbertson, and its later factor, James Dawson.

The saloons were doing big business, with rollicking, spendthrift
crowds of men—bullwhackers, mule skinners, traders and trappers,
and clerks and crews of steamboats. It was in George Bourrasa's
saloon that we four fell in with the clerk of the *Josephine*, a man Kipp

and I well knew, and when he proposed that we go to Eva's place and drink some beer, we were in the right mood to follow him.

Eva was handsome, a really beautiful woman, and successful in her occupation. Her house was amply large for the dozen girls that she kept. Pleasantly she welcomed us, ushered us into the big sitting room, in which the girls were chatting, laughing, drinking with a lot of men, some of them of our acquaintance. Kipp at once stood treat, a Negress bringing in the round of beer for all and collecting $5.00 for it. The clerk of the *Black Hills* went to the piano and sang a couple of songs to his own accompaniment and sang them well. We had some dancing, interspersed with rounds of drinks—Jack Miller and then I treating in our turns. It was old man *Kaiyo's* first visit in a red-light house. That he was embarrassed by the far from demure manners of the girls was plainly evident, and when one of them plumped herself down upon his lap, he seemed to shrink to a mere shadow of himself.

"Well, my young man, are you going to treat?" the girl asked.

Not understanding English, he looked to me for help. "She wants you to buy the drinks," I explained.

"Oh, yes. Tell her to go. Quickly go and get them." And when she had gone: "Without shame, these no-good white women. Never, never again will I enter this house."

Eva's room was next back from the one in which we sat, and there she kept pretty well to herself. It was well known that she was the faithful and jealous mistress of a certain high official of the county. He came in at about eleven o'clock, nodded curtly to one and another of us, and, not seeing Eva, went quickly on into her room, instantly closing the door. By that time we were, some of us, feeling our drinks and somewhat hilarious. But soon, above the din of our noisy doings, we heard loud and angry talking in that adjoining room; and even as we listened, that high official came running from it and making for the front door, Eva shooting at him—Bang! Bang! Bang! The girls squawked and the men yelled, running this way, that way. Too many of us blocked the doorway so that the fleer from Eva's wrath went through a front window, sash and all. At that, Eva drew back and closed her door from us; and said the clerk of the

Black Hills: "Well, that is that. We'll have a round of drinks on Eva because she missed him. Where is she, that there Negro waitress?"

It was just then that we heard, through the sashless window, men running and shouting in the street. One of our circle, leaning out, inquired the cause for it, then turned and shouted to us: "The courthouse is afire! They want help! Come on!"

Fumbling for his hat in the dim hall, Kipp put on the first one that he touched, a wide-brimmed beflowered woman's hat, and ran; we all followed—men and girls—as best we could.

The courthouse was blazing. Red flames were bursting from several of its rear windows as we joined the crowd before it. Came running a file of men drawing the fire engine, another crew hauling the hose cart. Tom Todd, fireman hatted, stood upon the engine shouting orders. One end of a hose was attached to the engine; the suction end reeled out to I know not what water hole. As the nozzled hose was snaked onto the building, a dozen men grasped each long handrail of the engine and the pumping began—clink, clack, clink, clack. Up and down, clink, clack, clink, clack, and a stream of water about the size and force of that of an ordinary garden hose was sprayed on the fire. Tom Cummings and John Wrenn, holding the brass nozzle of the hose, shouted back that they wanted a heavier stream of water, and Tom Todd, still up on the engine, yelled to the pumpers: "Harder! Faster, fellows! Now! Go to it!"

But that was strenuous, tiring work, that pumping, and others soon took their places—one of them Kipp, still wearing the woman's hat; and how the crowd did laugh at sight of the red-flowered contraption swaying as he pumped. Particularly, I noticed Charlie Conrad and John Power pointing to it and almost overcome with mirth. And then, when the scantily clad owner of the hat sprang in and snatched it from his head, the whole crowd roared.

All soon realized that the courthouse was doomed, that our puny efforts could not save it, and so we dispersed and let it burn. Kipp and I and our two friends, with others, repaired to Keno Bill's saloon to quench our thirst. Said one, as we were lined before the bar: "Strange, how the courthouse got afire. Surely its stoves are not kept going these hot days."

"Huh. Nothin' strange about it," Bill replied. "Some records in it just nat'rally had to be destroyed to keep certain fellers I know out of a heap of trouble."

Said Kipp to me: "Well, *Apikuni*, that's that. We sure have had a right enjoyable time tonight. I think we better go see how our womenfolks are getting along. We don't want them worrying about us, you know."

Part II: *Stories of Their Adventures Related to* Apikuni *by Indian Friends*

((>

CHAPTER TWELVE

The Theft of the Sacred Otter Bow-Case (Told by Bird Chief—James Bird)[1]

THE SUMMER OF 1846 was about gone when our little war party returned from the far south—the Always-Summer-Land—with the big band of horses that we had taken from the Mexicans. My brother-in-law, Mad Wolf, brought the sacred white-otter bow-case of his dead brother, Bear Head. I shall never forget that day of our return, our triumphant entry into the great camp of the Pikunis, for, seeing that Mad Wolf had recovered the sacred bow-case, the people went wild with joy, believing as they did that Sun valued a white otter more than any other sacred animal, even a white buffalo, and would therefore particularly favor the owner of the sacred bow-case and the whole tribe as well.

Briefly, the history of the sacred bow-case was that Bear Head and a Cree medicine man named Skunk Cap had one day discovered a white otter, rarest of all albino animals, and had simultaneously shot at it, Bear Head being the one to kill it. But Skunk Cap had angrily claimed that it was his shot that had killed the animal and in various and mean ways had tried to get possession of it. Bear Head, making of its white-furred, softly tanned pelt a beautiful bow-case, had publicly vowed that he would in due time sacrifice it to Sun, hang it to the center post of a sacred lodge that, in the Berries-Ripe Moon of every summer, the tribe built in honor of the great sky god.

[1] Onetime engagé of the Hudson's Bay Company, died on the Blackfoot Indian Reservation, Montana, in 1902, in his eighty-ninth year.
Condensed from *Boy's Life* (July, August, and September, 1935).

Not long after making the vow, Bear Head, his brother Mad Wolf, and Skunk Cap joined a war party going to the far south to raid the horse herds of the Mexicans. In a fight that the party had down there with the Many Bracelets people (the Navajos), Bear Head was mortally wounded. Before he died, his grieving brother promised him that he would bury him with all of his possessions and, in the following summer, come back for the sacred bow-case and himself sacrifice it to Sun for the good of the tribe. So poor Bear Head died, and with some difficulty the party got his body and belongings up into a house of the ancient and vanished Cliff Dwellers and came home with the horses that they had taken from the Mexicans. Soon thereafter Skunk Cap left the Pikunis to go we knew not where.

Came spring again, the spring of 1846, and from some friendly Gros Ventres visiting in our camp we learned that Skunk Cap had wintered with their tribe and had recently gone on to the Cutthroats (Assiniboines) to organize a war party of them to raid the Mexicans —the Gros Ventres being against going that far on raids.

Cried Mad Wolf upon hearing this: "Ha! Raid the Mexicans, that cowardly Skunk Cap. No! He is southward going to steal my brave, dead brother's sacred otter bow-case. We must be off at once, get there first, or he will do it." And that got our medicine man and wise warrior, *Pinukwiim*, to organize a war party to hurry south to prevent the theft. This was a war party that I was glad to join for I wanted to see the far-south country and its strange tribes.

Some fights we had down there, some men we lost, and at last made camp one evening at the mouth of the canyon in which poor Bear Head's body lay. Not for anything, not for one hundred head of horses would any of our companions have gone up to that place of the dead, so, just before dawn, Mad Wolf and I set out to get the sacred bow-case, should it still be there.

It was very dark in the narrow, high-walled canyon. We stole up it until opposite the great cave and its many ancient houses, and waited until dawn to see our way up into it. Then, climbing the narrow and dangerous trail, we heard the echoing thuds of falling rocks and sensed that there was someone in the cave. So there was. Skunk

Cap. Skunk Cap alone, tossing back the rocks with which Mad Wolf had filled the doorway of the house in which his brother's body lay.

With quick and silent run, Mad Wolf seized the thief's gun, leaning against the wall of the house, and sickening was his fright, his pleading when he turned and saw us. And then he turned and ran, and Mad Wolf quickly fired and killed him, killed him even as he whined to us that he was the last of the Cutthroat party.

Said Mad Wolf as we entered the dusky house and saw the shrouded form upon the floor, the sacred bow-case upon the tripod above it: "Brother, I am here at last. Brother, I have come for you . . . ." What more he said I did not hear for I somehow sickened and turned and hurried out. Then soon he came with the sacred bow-case, and we filled the narrow doorway with the rocks and rejoined the party. A moon later we were back in our far-north lodges and enjoying a well-earned rest.

Came spring, the spring of 1847, and we set out from Musselshell River where we had wintered for Fort Lewis, there to trade our buffalo robes and furs for goods of the white men. So going, we camped, late of an afternoon, on Judith River, and Mad Wolf invited me to a feast in the lodge of his father, Lame Bull, with whom he lived. A number of guests came in, and when the pipe was going the round of us, talk was of the remarkably successful winter we had had—mild weather, practically no sickness, plenty of buffalo and fur animals close to camp.

Said Lame Bull, pointing to the sacred bow-case tied to a lodge pole at the head of Mad Wolf's couch: "My friends, it is because of that sacred thing, my son's recovery of it, that Sun has been so good to us. Why, he will always love and care for us, his Pikuni children, for not far off now is the Berries-Ripe Moon when we build the great lodge for him, and my son will hang to its center post the sacred bow-case, it at last to be the great sky god's very own." To that all gave hearty assent, and the pipe smoked out, we arose and went our homeward ways.

Early next morning shouts of men and shrieks of women awakened me, and, hurrying out and joining a crowd before Lame Bull's lodge, I learned that, in the night, Mad Wolf's sacred otter bow-case had been stolen. None in the lodge had heard anyone enter or leave it. What enemy could have so quietly taken it? What enemy could have known just where it was in Lame Bull's ravens-painted lodge—so heavily painted with ravens that it was very dark inside at night? Apparently no war party had entered camp, for all of the fast, trained, and valuable buffalo horses that, for better safety, had been tied before the lodges of their owners for the night, were still there, and a hurried inspection of the herds grazing about in the long bottom proved that not a single horse of them was missing.

As I returned to my lodge to wash and dress and eat, the strange quietness of the camp struck me. For once there was no early-morning chatting and singing of the women as they went about their work; even the children, usually so noisy at their play, were quiet. The loss of the sacred bow-case was a terrible blow to all.

Mad Wolf, unkempt, drawn faced, came in to sit with me. Said he: "Bird Chief, who do you think stole my sacred bow-case?"

"Must have been someone of an enemy war party," I answered.

"No. No enemy war party was here, else some of our buffalo horses would be missing. But well you know that I have enemies right here in our camp. Two of them: Short Bow and Fox Head. One or the other of them stole it."

It was true that the two had long been at odds with Mad Wolf. They did not speak to him, nor he to them, when they met. In a fight between some of the Pikunis and a war party of Snakes, Fox Head had claimed, and still claimed, that he killed one of the enemy who had actually fallen to Mad Wolf. And in a night raid upon the Crow camp Short Bow had insisted that he had taken a certain horse that, as others of the party agreed, had actually been led out by Mad Wolf. But for all that I could not believe that either of them had stolen the sacred bow-case.

"It is not reasonable that they would take it for it could do them no good. They could not keep it nor give it to Sun," I said. And my wife put in: "Mad Wolf, dear brother, they would not dare incur Sun's anger by stealing that which you have vowed to give him."

"The crazy-heads care not for Sun. They will do anything to

cause me trouble. One or the other or both of them stole my sacred bow-case and hid it," he growled, and with that left us.

At a secret council of chiefs and medicine men in head chief Lone Walker's lodge, Lame Bull told of his son's suspicion of the two, with the result that the whole tribe of us was ordered out to look for the bow-case. All up and down the long bottom, all through the cottonwood groves and along the berry-bushed slopes of the valley, two thousand men, women, and children searched for it, and without result. Then Mad Wolf was summoned before a second council of the wise ones and asked to agree that whoever could find the sacred bow-case should have the honor of giving it to Sun at the appointed time.

"What, let Fox Head or Short Bow produce my sacred bow-case and later on give it to Sun! Oh, no! No! No! he cried.

Long they pleaded with him—Lame Bull even tearfully. They said that the welfare, the future of the tribe for all time to come depended upon the recovery of the bow-case, long since promised to Sun. At last he gave in. But nothing came of a second thorough search for it, which, we later learned, had not been joined by Short Bow and Fox Head. Said Mad Wolf when our old-man informer had gone: "So that's how it is. They dare not bring my sacred bow-case from where they hid it for fear that I would kill them."

From Judith River on to Fort Lewis the Pikunis were a dejected, silent people. I wondered if they would ever get over the loss of the sacred bow-case. Day and night they were in constant fear of their sky god's displeasure. We arrived at the fort to find the shelves of the trade room bare of goods, so no trading in of our robes and furs until the keelboats would arrive from Fort Union at the mouth of the Yellowstone with fresh supplies. We went into camp just below the fort, and long and gloomy was our wait. It was the time of year when war party after war party of the Pikunis annually set out to raid enemy tribes; but now, fearful of Sun's displeasure, believing that he would not aid them, none would go. So, no more happy feast-gatherings; no more dancing; no more story-telling, jesting around our evening lodge fires.

On a day in June the first keelboat of the season arrived. Antoine Bissette was its captain, and with him was his Pikuni wife Mink Woman, who in the previous fall had gone downriver with him to winter at Fort Union. From her we got astonishing news: because of three Cree half-blood trappers, visitors in our camp, a Cutthroat named Bull-Turns-Around, he whose medicine was a lodge painted with a big buffalo bull, had stolen Mad Wolf's sacred bow-case and vowed ever to keep it, as that would cause the Pikunis continually to have bad luck.

Arriving at Fort Union, the three had told of their stop with us and of seeing the sacred bow-case owned by one Mad Wolf who lived in a ravens-painted lodge, he whose war party in the far-south land had wiped out Skunk Cap and his war party of Cutthroats—true enough, except that one of them, Bull Turns-Around, had managed to survive the dangers down there and return to his people. When new grass began to show green, he left in quest of the bow-case, and, as the boat was leaving the mouth of the Yellowstone, had returned with the sacred thing upon his shoulder, loudly singing as he met his tribe.

Breathlessly the crowd of us listened to the woman and when she had finished plied her with questions until, at last, Lone Walker shouted: "Enough, my children. Go your ways for we old ones must council about this, decide upon a way to recover the sacred bow-case."

But Mad Wolf, quickly stepping up to him, said: "Chief, I shall not council with you about it. The sacred bow-case is mine, my very own; so it is for me in my own way to go to recover it.

Said Lone Walker after some thought: "Right you are. It is your very own. Once you recovered it and I believe that you will do it again. Go, my brave one, and we will constantly pray Above One for your safety and success."

Late that evening Mad Wolf came into my lodge and said to me: "Well, eight friends have promised to go with me after my sacred bow-case, so, with you, we will be ten to go."

Somewhat reluctantly I answered: "*Ah*."

Early next morning as Mad Wolf was eating with me, came in a youth and said to him: "I have this for you from Fox Head and Short Bow. Said they: 'When your sacred bow-case was stolen, you promised that whoever could recover it should have it to give to Sun. So is it that we go to take it from the Cutthroat thief.' "

"No. They shall not go. It is for me to get it. Hurry back, you, and tell them so," Mad Wolf roared.

"Cannot tell them. They left last night, and with them fifteen of their friends," whimpered the youth, and fled.

"Gone. Sneaked away to go down there and make trouble for us," Mad Wolf groaned. And then to me: "Bird Chief, we must be quickly off, get to the Cutthroats' camp ahead of them."

But Lame Bull would not allow us to leave until he had gathered us in a sweat lodge and prayed long and earnestly for our safety and success in our dangerous undertaking. That our rivals, the Fox Head–Short Bow party, had hurried off without the sacred bath meant bad luck for them, our wise ones said. As it was, we set out at noon. Rightly we should have waited until night to leave, for well we knew that large war parties from enemy tribes were roaming the country, and to be discovered by one of them might mean our end.

Mink Woman had told us that, when finished trading at downriver Big House, the Cutthroats would summer hunt along the lower reaches of Milk River. So, after five days of travel down the valley of the Missouri, at the mouth of Cow Creek we turned off northeastward to pass the east end of the Wolf Mountains, strike Milk River, and follow it down until we should sight the enemy camp.

The afternoon was hot and we were tired, for we had been traveling day and night with but short intervals of rest—constantly urged on by Mad Wolf, fearful that the rival party might still be ahead of us. We were now in very dangerous country, for the Wolf Mountains were favorite lookout points for enemy war parties seeking camps of our Blackfoot tribes to raid them. As we neared the east end of the mountains (now named the Little Rockies), the plain ahead was black spotted with herds of buffalo. Bad for us as we would unavoidably frighten some of them, start them to running, and so be discovered by any enemies that might be looking down from the heights beyond.

The risk was so great that Morning Eagle, eldest of our party, and then several others asked Mad Wolf to call a halt until night. But no. We must take the risk, he answered, get ahead of Fox Head and Short Bow and recover the sacred bow-case. Soon afterward a big herd of the buffalo got wind of us and ran thundering off south for several miles before recovering from their fright. Then at sunset, as we neared Wolf Creek (now called Rock Creek), we frightened another herd.

Said Morning Eagle as we watched their flight: "My medicine tells me that we are nearing trouble. I advise you all to call upon Him Above for help." None made reply to that. Worriedly we kept on —some, as I saw, with lips working in silent prayer.

Night had come and the moon was rising when, following a broad and dusty buffalo trail, we turned down the slope of Wolf Creek Valley, hurried to get water. Laying down our weapons, we knelt upon the shore, were beginning to drink, when suddenly guns boomed and men shouted in the brush across from us. Morning Eagle, close at my side, dropped face down into the creek, and as the rest of us snatched our guns from the ground and sprang up, a bullet seared the skin of the left side of my neck.

We could not see the enemy, doubtless reloading their guns. Said Mad Wolf: "Turn back into the timber. Hurry." Said Little Plume: "They shall not scalp Morning Eagle. Help me lift him." We carried him and his gun well into the grove, made sure that he was dead. There followed a long silence. We could hear no movement of the enemy. Said one of our number: "I would like to know who they are, and how many."

"Cutthroats. That I know from their shouting though I can't speak their language," I answered.

Said another: "He warned us of near danger and now he is dead, our good friend here. That your fault, Mad Wolf. You would make us travel in daytime, frightening buffalo herds for our enemies to see."

"I meant it for the best. To recover my sacred bow-case, give it to Sun, gladly would I sacrifice my own life," he answered. And just then some whitetail deer came leaping past, plain warning that our enemies had crossed the creek below and were sneaking up to attack us again.

Nothing to do but abandon poor Morning Eagle's body. We stole off up the grove, carefully feeling our way that we step on no dry sticks to break and tell of our going. So at last, making sure that we were not being trailed, we turned into the creek, drank, crossed over, climbed the east slope of the valley to the edge of the plain, and there stopped to rest and talk over the misfortune that had befallen us. But soon we heard, down whence we had come, the shrill nickering of a horse, and then of another one.

"*Ha!* A sitting-on-top war party," said Mad Wolf (*i-ke-tópi*, meaning "riding"). "Perhaps we can go down there and take their horses."

We were soon to learn that that would be impossible. Out from the timber came a large band of horses—a lone rider in the lead, at least thirty riders in the rear urging them on. Up the slope they came to pass not far to our left. We flattened ourselves in the grass and short sage, watched them come on. They topped the slope so near us that we could hear them grunting, "*Hu-hu! Hu-hu!*" as they smacked the slower ones of the band with their rope ends. It was a band of a hundred head or more. We counted the riders: thirty-two. Out upon the plain they swept, eastward going, our direction, too. As we got up to follow, said Little Plume: "Maybe those, their stealing, are Pikuni horses."

"Probably are. They came from the west, only our tribe in that direction," said another.

"Matters not their horse-stealing if we can only take my sacred bow-case from them," Mad Wolf said.

That night we passed the east end of the Wolf Mountains and struck down a fork of Sage Creek (now Beaver Creek), a tributary of Milk River, or, as we called it, Little River. With the coming of day, we were right on the trail of the Cutthroats' war party. Hungry and tired, we killed an elk, broiled and ate our fill of it, slept for an all too short time, pushed on down the valley.

In midafternoon we were startled by hearing someone shout,

"*Hai!* Pikuni men. *Hai!* My relatives, wait for me." And from the timber on our left came running to us Black Weasel, a member of our rival party, and gasped: "Mad Wolf. Oh, my friends, how glad I was when I saw you coming, saw who you were. I have had a terrible time . . . ."

"Now, now, calm yourself. Sit down, get your breath and tell us about it," Mad Wolf scolded.

Down he plumped and after a little said: "Below here this morning Fox Head said that we could rest. We were asleep in the timber when along came a war party of Cutthroats with many Pikuni horses, among them *Pinukwiim's* black-and-white-spotted fast buffalo horse. Mad Wolf, one of the Cutthroats, tall, big, had your sacred otter bow-case at his shoulder. They got down from their horses a little way above us, began taking off their clothes making ready to bathe. Short Bow said that when they had all passed through the brush to the creek, he would run and take the sacred bow-case. Fox Head told him he must not attempt it, too dangerous. But when they went to the creek, he ran to get it, and we all ran the other way, down through the willows into a big grove. I fell, struck my knee against a rock. Pain was terrible, could run no more. The others kept on. I limped across the creek, hid in some rose brush. The Cutthroats were yelling; two shots were fired. That the end of Short Bow, I thought.

"It seemed a long time that I lay there. At last I heard the Cutthroats singing, driving their stealing of Pikuni horses down the valley, not looking for my companions else they would not be singing. When they were gone I rubbed my knee, felt better. Someone, maybe He Above, seemed to be telling me that Short Bow had been killed, telling me, too, that I should not try to overtake the others. So I turned back for home. How glad I was when I saw you all coming. Mad Wolf, Chief, have pity. Let me go on with you."

Mad Wolf, after scolding him for joining the other party, allowed him to go with us. An hour or so later we found Short Bow, scalped and mutilated, killed before he could reach the pine-grown slope of the valley for which he had evidently headed. I proposed that we bury the body but the others were strongly against it. We had been unable to bury Morning Eagle, dead because of this one's fault, so let the buzzards have their way with the remains, they said.

Knowing now that our rival party was surely ahead of us, Mad Wolf kept us going at swifter pace, and with less rest than ever. At dawn the following morning we struck Milk River and turned down its wide and partly timbered valley. The next morning just before daybreak, utterly worn out, we took shelter in a heavy growth of chokecherry brush at the top of the south slope of the valley, and Mad Wolf named me to stand watch with him—we to sleep later on.

We afterward often said that Sun himself made us turn up to that berry brush for our resting place; had we gone on, we would, undoubtedly, all of us have been killed. A few minutes after we had comfortably seated ourselves in the lower side of the brush to begin our watch, a hundred or more riders appeared rounding a sharp bend of the valley a half-mile below. Men riders, hunters, coming to run a large herd of buffalo that, upon the plain across from us, was slowly grazing in to drink at the river. And following the hunters came their women to help them butcher their kills and pack home the meat and hides. Yes, we surely would have met them had we kept on down the valley.

When directly opposite us, they halted in a small grove of cottonwoods. The buffalo, arriving at the rim of the plain, ceased grazing and came leaping down the slope eager to get to water. As they began passing the grove, the hunters charged out among them, shooting, singing, yelling; and all went swiftly up the long bottom, all save the stricken cows and young bulls and heifers, falling, dotting the ground in their wake. Our awakened companions joining us, we all stared resentfully at the scene for, as Mad Wolf said, this was Pikuni country and these Pikuni buffalo that the Cutthroats were killing. And how many they were—all of two hundred in the short run that they made. Their women joining them, all went to work on the kills, and several hours later they went back down the valley, their horses loaded with all that they could carry of red meat and brown hides.

Well, we had learned that the camp of the Cutthroats was close below. Said Mad Wolf: "Now at last, this coming night, we make our dangerous attempt to recover my sacred bow-case. Pray, all of you, as you never prayed before. Pray Sun to prevent Fox Head and his followers from interfering in our attempt. Oh, strongly pray Him Above to give us complete success."

"*Ah*, pray we will," all answered and did pray long and fervently and lay down and slept.

When night came we were rounding the sharp bend of the valley below when, a mile or so farther on, the angry barking of dogs, in answer to the howling of wolves, warned us that we were nearing the Cutthroats' camp. And presently, looking out from the edge of a grove, we saw it there before us in a long, grassy bottom, midway between the timber-fringed river and the slope up to the plain, its big circle of lodges in the moonlight dimly glowing with the fires within them. We could hear the people talking, singing, drumming happily over their successful buffalo run, see them visiting from lodge to lodge. We sat down, to make no further move until they slept, and said Mad Wolf: "In a buffalo-painted lodge, somewhere in that circle of them, is my sacred otter bow-case. We must, oh, we must get off with it this night."

"How are we to do it?" I asked.

"Listen, closely listen to this, my plan to get it," he answered. "We locate the buffalo-painted lodge. Then we go into the camp, take, each of us, one of the fast buffalo horses there tied, and meet a little way out from the painted lodge. Then, while you all hold my horse ready for me, I will go into the lodge, kill that stealer of my sacred bow-case, run to you with it, and we will be off. There. What think you of it?"

"Too much for you, alone, to undertake," Little Plume replied. "That thief, that Bull-Turns-Around, may be awake and fight you as you enter, so I will go with you, do my best to kill him while you are doing what you have to do."

Said Mad Wolf, and feelingly: "That will be very helpful. I do not like to ask it of any of you. Brave Little Plume. Generous Little Plume . . . ."

There followed a long silence—each of us busy with his own thoughts; I dreading what was before us. I did not want to go into the camp to sneak out a horse for well I knew the danger of it.

190

Anxiously we waited for the camp to quiet down. But presently, in the center of the great camp circle, a fire began to glow, then another and another until four of them were brightly blazing. And in the light of them, to the throbbing of many drums and fierce singing, men began to dance while, apparently, the whole tribe looked on. Well, that would soon end we thought. But it didn't. It went on and on. Was it that the Cutthroats had, like us, a number of secret, warrior societies, and had chosen this night to dance, each of them in turn? Anxiously we watched our clock, the Seven Persons (Ursa Major). Slowly they turned, telling us of the passing of the night, at last of the nearing of the new day, and still the drumming, singing, dancing of the warriors continued. Reluctantly we stole up into a patch of cherry brush at the rim of the plain, there to wait for another night to do our work. But first we drank and drank at the river and ate of the dry, crisp roasted meat that we carried for just such an emergency.

Came morning, and with my telescope I sought to find the buffalo-painted lodge in the big camp a half-mile away. I soon located it in the north side of the circle of them—a big, black painting of a buffalo plainly in sight on the south side of a big, new, white lodge of buffalo leather. I could even make out the red life line running from its mouth back to a red-painted heart in its body. By turns during the day we kept watch upon the lodge with the telescope, and so saw Bull-Turns-Around, himself, coming and going from it. Tall, very tall, he was, and of heavy build. Looking at him, Mad Wolf prayed: "Oh, Sun, help us. Help us that, this coming night, we put an end to him, that stealer of my sacred bow-case."

It was a long, hot, and anxious day that we passed up in that patch of cherry brush. Mad Wolf, at times, fearful that Fox Head and his followers were to cause us trouble, tried to dispel our gloom by saying: "Now why so poor faced? Take courage, all of you. I know that we shall recover my sacred otter bow-case this very night and with it homeward go."

It was near midnight when we descended the slope, came to a stand close north of the sleeping camp, and Mad Wolf gave us last instructions: "Little Plume, Bird Chief, you two will go with me.

You others enter the camp farther on to take the horses we will need. Here, right here where we stand, will be our meeting place if all goes well. Then here you all will wait with the horses while we return to the camp to do you-know-what. And listen. Should anything happen that we have to run, our meeting place will be upriver where, this morning, we drank. So. We go."

Mad Wolf leading, I close following Little Plume, we three approached the camp. So slowly did we move that we were long in nearing the buffalo-painted lodge. We stopped a little way from it, and Mad Wolf was signing to us that we would take three of the horses picketed before lodges to the right of it, when guns suddenly began booming in the timber bordering the river and near the opposite side of the camp. We dropped flat in the grass. At once men began running from their lodges, shouting to one another as, weapons in hand, they sped toward the timber to fight whoever their enemies might be.

Though watching for him, we did not see Bull-Turns-Around come from his lodge. What we did see was a man off to our left running toward the lodge, and then we recognized him, Fox Head. Fox Head himself. We sprang up, took after him, Mad Wolf in the lead, seized him at the entrance of the lodge, fearlessly shouting: "Go back. Not for you my sacred bow-case." But for answer, Fox Head broke loose, dived into the lodge, we close behind him. In there, as in other lodges, women and children were chattering, shrieking with fear, for shooting and shouting continued at the river.

But the man of this lodge, this Bull-Turns-Around, had not gone there and, angrily yelling, he crushed Fox Head's skull with a blow of his war club. He would have killed Mad Wolf had he not parried the stroke with the barrel of his gun. Then, before Bull-Turns-Around could strike again, Little Plume stabbed him deep in his breast, and even as he fell Mad Wolf was cutting his sacred bow-case from the lodgepole to which it was tied and saying to us: "I have it. We must go, and go fast."

"Not until I have this," Little Plume answered, stooping over that Bull-Turns-Around and taking his scalp, there right before his women and children, now silent, paralyzed with fear. Then, as we ran from the lodge, a woman coming from one near by saw us and loudly shouted for help.

We sped up the valley as fast as we could go, the shouts of men taking after us loud in our ears. But we had a good lead on them; gaining the timber, we hurried to our agreed-upon meeting place and there found our companions awaiting our coming. And seeing what we had with us, Mad Wolf's sacred bow-case and Bull-Turns-Around's scalp, they went all but crazy over our success.

We were sure that the Cutthroats would not venture into the timber after us, so we drank and, crossing the river, continued on up into the timber on that side of it until morning when we hid in another patch of berry brush up at the edge of the plain. We talked over our exciting experience of the night and by turns slept and kept watch for the enemy. But none appeared that day or later. We thought then that Fox Head had set his party to make pretense of attacking the Cutthroats so to give him good opportunity to make off with the sacred bow-case.

Upon arriving in the Pikuni camp ten days later, we learned that such had been his plan, with the result that the Cutthroats had killed three of his men while they were retreating across the river. So there was mourning for him and the three, and for Short Bow and Morning Eagle—six dead in the quest of the sacred bow-case.

We gave the scalp of Bull-Turns-Around to their relatives. They blackened their faces, hands, and feet, and with it danced here and there in the camp the sad scalp dance, slow bending of knees in time with the slow, wailing, scalp-dance song. But the mourning was drowned by the rejoicing of the people over the recovery of the sacred otter bow-case.

Sun's sacred lodge was soon to be built. Mad Wolf would give the sacred bow-case to Him, hang it to the center post. Without doubt, the Pikunis would prosper as never before. "Oh, Sun. To our brave Mad Wolf, give him long life and happiness," was their fervent prayer.

CHAPTER THIRTEEN

Three Bears' Combat for a Wife[1]
(Told by Hugh Monroe, Indian by Adoption)

IT WAS IN THE SPRING OF 1858, years after I had left the Hudson's Bay Company to become a free trapper and roam with my wife's people, the Pikunis, that I first met Three Bears. I was sitting with Beaver Child (Alexander Culbertson, factor of the American Fur Company at Fort Benton) when Baptiste Rondin came hurrying into the comfortable office and said: "Beaver Child, chief, he is one lone man across the river; wavin' his robe; signin' he wants to come over. I'm look at him with my spyglass. Front, top hair all roached up; looks like he is one Crow."

"Can't be a Crow, alone in this Pikuni country. But whoever he is, go and bring him over," Culbertson replied.

"But I'm no want to go. Maybe a big war party of Crows hidin' there in the brush. That be the end for me," Rondin whined.

"Never mind. I'll go," I said, and was soon turning the boat to land, stern first. He was a tall, well-built young man awaiting me.

[1] Published in *The American Boy* (April, 1941) and in *Cavalier* (February, 1958), under the title "The Duel." Hugh Monroe, who in 1816 was in the employ of the Hudson's Bay Company and accompanying the Pikuni tribe of the Blackfoot Indian Confederacy, was the first white man to traverse the country between the Saskatchewan and the Missouri rivers. I have told the story of his first two years with the Pikunis, as he related it to me, in my books, *Rising Wolf the White Blackfoot* and *Red Crow's Brother* (Houghton Mifflin Company, 1919 and 1927), and more briefly in *Friends of My Life as An Indian*, 40–75, and *Signposts of Adventure* (Houghton Mifflin, 1923 and 1926), 47–51. All visitors to Glacier National Park are familiar with his wonderful monument, Rising Wolf Mountain, which we named for perhaps the first white man who ever saw it, Hugh Monroe, called by his adopted people *Mahkwí Ípwoatsin*, Rising Wolf.

He had a fine, firm face and big, honest, eager eyes. He wore a plain buckskin shirt and leggings, quilled moccasins of Crow design, bow-and-arrows case at his shoulder. His hair was neatly combed in Crow fashion. Surely a Crow, I thought. But as the stern of the boat grated upon the shore, he surprised me by saying in perfect Pikuni-Blackfoot: "Oh, white man! Generous white man! I am a Pikuni man. I seek my Pikuni people. Can you tell me where they are?"

"They will arrive here today to camp and trade. I live with them. I came on ahead, my woman and I, last night. Get in. We will cross," I answered.

He shoved the boat out, springing in, and said, "Oh, Sun is good to me; he has helped me to survive the many dangers so that today I shall meet my own people."

"Who are you?" I asked.

"I am Three Bears," he proudly answered. "White man, perhaps you knew my father, Running Wolf, killed by the Crows when I was a young one of five winters; and if you knew him, you knew my mother, Red Bird Woman, a Crow slave since that time, and now—*haiya!*—but recently dead!"

"Let me think . . . . Yes, I do remember them. We were camped on Bear River. They were of a small party that went off to hunt. We never saw, never heard of them again," I answered.

"Are any of their close relatives—my close relatives—still living?"

"Yes. Your father's brother, Black Eagle; your mother's brother, Little Otter; several women."

"Oh, good! Good!" he cried. "My mother often told me of them." And then, pointing: "They must be my people, there coming down off the plain."

It was the long caravan of the Pikunis, chiefs in the lead, heading for the fort. There were two thousand men, women, and children riders; several thousand pack horses; more thousands of loose horses; countless wolflike dogs. We landed, hurried to the entrance of the fort where Beaver Child, in brass-buttoned, blue-cloth uniform, sword at his side, waited with his many *engagés* to greet the on-coming chiefs. The cannon in the east bastion boomed a welcome to them; they answered by firing many guns. All in their war clothes, singing a peace song, they neared us, and Three Bears, close at my side, breathed hard as he stared at them with eager eyes.

"Oh, white man! I feel queer, poor, inside me. You tell them who I am," he gasped. "Yes. Wait," I answered.

The chiefs, noting his roached-up hair, glared at him as they came on and got off their horses; kept looking back at him as they moved on to be welcomed by Beaver Child. Biding my time, I grasped the young man's arm, led him forward, and said to them: "Chiefs, this is Three Bears, son of Running Wolf and Red Bird Woman. From the Crows he has just now come."

For a little, puzzled, thinking back, they stared at him; then loudly, happily exclaiming, they came hurrying to welcome him, excitedly hugging him, questioning him, claiming him as their own. Word of his arrival reached the people making camp just below the fort, and came running his relatives and almost smothered him with their embraces. Each uncle, each aunt, wanted him for his, for her, very own, to make a son of him, and they quarreled, were very bitter to one another until Chief Big Lake turned to them and said: "Now, now, be not fire-heads. You all know that Black Eagle, his father's own brother, has best right to him."

None could deny that, and after a little Three Bears, all but overcome by their friendliness, managed to say: "At last to be here with you all, oh, what happiness for me. I want to be close to you, my relatives."

That evening Big Lake called a meeting of the chiefs in his lodge to hear Three Bears tell of his years with the Crows, and I was present. Sadly, so low voiced that we could barely hear him, he began his tale but soon became loud and fierce as he told of the wrongs that he had suffered from some of them.

"My mother often told me that I was five winters old and the only little one of the party of seven men and five women who went out from Bear River to hunt that day," he began. "With my mother and the other women I watched the men run a big herd of buffalo and kill many. We then rode on to help them butcher their kills. All were at work—my father and mother were at work on a cow when suddenly many enemies came riding out from a coulee and shooting at us, and my father yelled: 'They are Crows. Get down behind this cow. Crouch low.' He then stood over us, shooting, reloading his gun, yelling to his friends: 'Keep up your courage. Protect your women.' But not for long. He fell, shot dead. My mother cried to me: 'They have killed him; are killing all the others.' She snatched me up and ran. A big Crow seized her, looked closely at her and me and signed: 'You are beautiful. You shall be my woman. Your son shall be my son. I will raise him up to kill many Pikunis.' He then took my father's weapons, signed to my mother: 'You and your son get upon your horses and go with me. If you refuse, I will kill your son, tie you to your horse, make you go with me.' Signed my mother to him: 'Crow man, because I love my son, want him to live, I will do as you say. But this I tell you: You and your kind are to cry for what you have done to us this day.'

"So. Southward we rode with that Crow war party. Across Big River (the Missouri), across Elk River (the Yellowstone), and far up Bighorn River we came to the Crow camp. There our captor, Lone Butte, took us into his lodge, to his wife, Curlew Woman, and his son of ten winters, Long Elk. Lone Butte and his wife were kind to us. All the Crows were kind to us—all except that Long Elk. From the first he hated me. Persecuted me in every way he could; kept saying to me: 'My father killed your father. Your mother is my father's slave. You are a nothing-boy. Your kind of people are cowards; we Crows always make them cry.'"

"*Ha!* The Crows! The dog-face Crows! Why, our long-ago fathers drove them south across Elk River, and ever since we have held them there," roared Chief Big Lake.

"The older we grew, the more Long Elk abused me," Three Bears continued. "I wanted to kill him; begged my mother to let me kill him. But she said no. For if I did that his father would kill me, and without me she could not live. We must be patient, bear our wrongs, she said, until I grew up, became big and strong. We would then on some dark night quietly leave camp, return to our people. Last winter we decided that when summer came we would escape. But in the beginning of the New-Grass Moon (April), as we were all preparing to move camp, a horse that she was loading kicked my mother, kicked her back, terribly crippling her. Lone Butte and his wife were kind; in every possible way they helped me care for her. When we moved camp we laid her in a robe-lined travois, and in the lodge Curlew Woman was ever at her side to wait on her. Then one day, when running buffalo, Lone Butte's horse stumbled, fell with him, and the big herd trampled him to death. Two days later, after painful suffering, my mother died, and Curlew Woman and others helped me put her robe-wrapped body in a tree. Why did I not kill Long Elk then and leave? Because some time before he had gone with a war party to raid Spotted Horses People (Cheyennes). Well, I would wait for him to return, in the night kill him, and go. Days passed. He did not come. More and more I grieved for my mother. It was unbearable, living there without her. I longed to return to you, my Pikuni people, as, when she was dying, I promised her I would do. More days passed, and still Long Elk did not return. It was a long way to the country of the Spotted Horses People. It might be that he, his party, might never return. I could no longer bear my loneliness there without my mother. I had to come to you, my relatives. But after a time with you I shall go back to kill that Long Elk if he be still alive."

Cried one of his aunts: "Oh, no! No! You are too young to go. You would be killed."

Said Black Eagle: "Almost-son, you are not to go back to that Crow camp until you have learned, fully learned the ways of the war trail, as I shall teach them to you."

Somehow Three Bears took great liking for me, and I, for him. So was it that, one day, he said to me: "You know how it is: we men are very close-mouthed about women. But I must tell you about one, for you are different. I know that you will not laugh at me."

"Tell it. I will not laugh," I answered.

"It is that I go back to the Crow camp not only to kill that Long Elk but also to try to get a girl he wants. A girl who loves me and hates him."

"It would be difficult to do both in the short time you would have," I said.

"Yes, that is the trouble. But I must somehow try to do it," he went on. "This girl, Mink Woman, and I are of the same winters. She is tall, slender, and round. Has beautiful face; big, kind eyes; hair braids almost touching the ground as she walks. Her father, Old Bull, when she was little, had a vision. His sacred helper came to him as he slept and said: 'Keep your daughter ever close to you as she grows up, do not let her marry, for I have a certain use for her.'

"Old Bull obeyed his vision. Refused to give the girl to any one of the many who wanted to marry her. Long Elk offered him twenty horses for her, but the father refused. Then Long Elk, watching for the chance, said to the girl one day as she was going for water: 'Run off with me. We will go to our relatives, the Minnetarees, and live with them.'

"Answered the girl: 'Run off with you? Long Elk, I hate you. Go away. Never speak to me again.'

"Said he to that: 'I care not what you say. Not far off the time when I shall seize you, carry you off.'

"Mink Woman ran to her father about it, and he was very angry at Long Elk; so were many of the people. She was a sacred woman. All men must keep away from her, they said.

"Always, when by ourselves we met, Mink Woman smiled, and her eyes were kind as she looked at me. I loved her, but she, so sacred, could not love me, I thought. So was I surprised and, oh, how happy and how worried when, meeting her one day, she said to me: 'Three Bears, why don't you ask me to run off with you? Go with you to your Pikuni people?'

"She so surprised me that, for a little, I could not answer. And then I said: 'Tell me truly. Do you love me? Will you go with me?'

" 'I have always loved you, just you, no other,' she said, and then no more, for just then came her mother to overtake her on the water trail. I hurried to my mother about it, and said she: 'A good girl, that Old Bull's daughter. When we go, she goes with us. She will be a good wife to you. And how that will make to burn that Long Elk's insides.'

"Well, now that I was going, could wait no longer for Long Elk to return, I would take Mink Woman with me, I decided. We had talked about it, and she had said that she would be ready in any night that I would come and awaken her. All that day I tried to have secret talk with her, and she tried for it, too, but always people were near. She started to go alone for water, but her mother shouted: 'Come back. Wait. I shall go with you.' Later, she took a rope, walked off as though going for wood, and her mother ran and seized her, yelling, 'Have you become crazy that you want to go off alone for this and for that? Come back, sit down. Never shall it be said that my daughter is bad.'

"Anyhow, I knew where Mink Woman slept; her couch was the second one from the doorway on the south side of the lodge. I had twice been in it and seen her sitting there. Night came. Long I sat waiting for what I was to do, sitting close to the two horses that I had saddled for us to ride. At last the fire in her lodge died out, but still I waited until I felt sure that all within it slept. Then I crept to her side of the lodge; noiselessly pulled out two lodge-skin pins; reached in under the loosened lodge-skin; softly, lightly felt for her; touched her rounded, robe-covered hip. It would not do to prod her there, else, startled, frightened, she would cry out. I felt for her farther up; touched her hair; found her face and put my hand firmly upon her mouth to hold her quiet and whisper that I had come for her. *Ha!* It was not hers but her mother's mouth that I held, and jerking away she yelled: 'Enemies are here! One seized me! Help! Help me!' Rising Wolf, is it that you are laughing at me?"

"No. No. Something in my teeth; feeling for it," I answered, hiding my grin.

"It was not something for laughter," he continued. "The other wives cried out, and Old Bull yelled: 'It is that Pikuni youth after our daughter. I will kill him!'

"As I sprang up and ran, the awakened people in the other lodges began yelling. The men ran out from them with ready guns, one of them shouting: 'Enemies have come! Here are two saddled horses that they have tied.'

"As I ran for the near timber instead of for the horses, several shots were fired at me, but I got safely into it and kept on in it all the rest of the night. And so going, traveling by night and in the daytime lying hidden, at last I came to you all. But this I tell you—to you alone: I shall soon go back, do my utmost to kill my enemy and get my girl."

"No. You must do as your uncle said, "I began, but he cut me off: "*Ha!* Wait and wait, and in the meantime that Long Elk somehow takes my girl? No! And, Rising Wolf, this that I have told you is for yourself, alone."

I put a finger to my lips.

Our trade at the fort ended, with plentiful supplies of powder and balls, tobacco, and other goods, we moved northwest to Two Medicine Lodges River to summer hunt. One morning soon after we arrived there young Three Bears was missing, as I was appraised by the loud talk of his uncles and the crying of his aunts. No horse was missing; he had left on foot, so it would be useless to try to find him, bring him back, Black Eagle said. Nightly one of his aunts added a stick to the little pile of them that marked the days of his absence, and when they numbered thirty he was believed to be dead. Then a few days later, riding a big, strong horse and leading another equally good one, he quietly returned. Aunts cried over him, uncles hugged him, and could hardly wait until he had been fed to hear him tell what he had done. His tale to them was short; only that he had taken Long Elk's two buffalo horses, tied before his lodge, but had failed to get at his enemy, as he had been discovered in the camp and had escaped from some who pursued him only because the night was rainy and dark. But, a little later, his tale to me was much more than that.

"Well, Rising Wolf, my heart is low, very low," he began. "Night after night as I traveled south, I thought only of what would be best for me to do in the Crow camp. Should I, this time, try only to kill my enemy, and later try to get my girl, or should I try first to take her and later go again to try to kill him? I thought that the Crows would be somewhere up Bighorn River, but upon crossing Elk River I found the fresh trail of them, followed it, and sighted their camp just below Beaverhead Island. It was then that, at last, I decided just what I would do: I would take Long Elk's buffalo horses that always, of nights, he kept tied before his lodge, and lead them to the edge of the timber, tie them, and go back for the girl. Should I get her quietly out to the horses, I would have her wait for me there while I turned back in and killed Long Elk, and then we would be off.

"All day long I lay in the edge of the timber, watching the camp. Came night, and I moved up close to it. In Long Elk's lodge he and some of his friends were having a good time: singing, dancing. I could go to the doorway of the lodge, shoot him, run off. I was tempted to do it. But then I would not get the girl. No, she first, then he. At last the camp became quiet, the lodges dark. Long Elk's buffalo runners, as I had expected, were tied before his lodge. Well I knew them, the black-and-white-spotted one that he had stolen from the South Entrails People (Arapahos) and the big gray that had belonged to his father. Slowly, quietly I loosened their ropes, led them to the timber, tied them there, and turned back to Old Bull's lodge to get my girl. This time I would make no mistake; I would know her by her very long hair braids; her mother's braids were thin and short. Again I pulled two lodge-skin pins at the edge of the head of her couch, slowly, noiselessly, snakily got head and shoulder in past the lodge-skin and very lightly felt for her, touched a thick, long hair braid; then put my left hand on her mouth and whispered in her ear: 'It is me, Three Bears. Come, we go.'

"She put her mouth to my ear and whispered: 'Be careful. My mother sleeps beside me.' Then she began very slowly to turn, to roll toward me. I drew back, she followed, came halfway out from under the lodge-skin, and I grasped her arms, was pulling her, raising her, when her awakened mother seized her legs and yelled for help. Hard, hard though I pulled, I could not free her from her mother's grip, nor pull them both out from under. Cried my girl: 'Three Bears! Go! Go!' Her father roared: 'Pikuni thief, I will kill you this time!' Jumping out from the doorway of the lodge, he fired at me as I ran. Men were coming from other lodges and he yelled to them: 'He is that Three Bears. Come on, we must kill him.'

"I ran not toward the two horses that I had taken but away from them, to the brush of the valley's slope; when in it, I turned right from the way I had been heading and dropped flat. *Ha!* My pursuers kept on up the slope, some passing so near that I could hear their loud breathing. When they had gone I half-circled the camp, got safely to the horses, mounted one, and leading the other, soon swam the river and headed for here. Came morning, and from the top of a pine-grown hill I saw Crow riders down on the plain, going in all directions looking for me; saw them, discouraged, turn and head back for their camp. So, Rising Wolf, you know how I again failed to get my girl."

Said I: "Well, now you know how it is, Mink Woman's mother always sleeping with her, constantly watching her, you better be looking for some other girl."

"No. I want Mink Woman, no other one. Somehow, in some way, in time I shall have her. Yes, and the scalp of that Long Elk, too," he shortly replied.

"Well, the Crows will be watching for you to return; best that you go not back to their camp for some time," I advised, and to that he gave grave assent.

About a month after Three Bears' return, we left Two Medicine Lodges River and camped in the Sacred Rock bottom of Bear (Marias) River. There one night—about midnight it was, and the moon was shining—Black Eagle awoke, had to go out. His two buffalo horses and Three Bears' two were picketed before the lodge. Thrusting aside the door curtain and stepping out, Black Eagle yelled to his sits-beside-him wife: "Woman! My gun! Quickly bring it!" Three Bears came hurrying out with it and his own gun, too. Already the intruder had left the camp circle. He gained the near timber before they could clear the intervening lodge and fire at him, and from its shelter he yelled to them, something strange and loud, and Three Bears cried: "*Haiya!* He is my enemy, Long Elk!"

Many of us men were running to the two, asking what had happened. We were soon searching the grove for the Crow. In it, and in other groves above and below, we searched for him all the rest of the night, failed to find him, and Three Bears' heart was low. As we were returning to camp, I asked him what it was that the Crow had shouted.

"Oh, just something to me," he mumbled.

"Come now, what did he say?" I demanded.

"Well, this he said: 'Slave woman's son, next time I come I shall not fail to take back my buffalo horses that you stole and kill you. And this I tell you: Mink Woman, mine she is to be.' " And after a little: "Well, me for the Crow camp again, and soon."

"Now more than ever they will be watching for you to come. Don't go for another moon or two," I advised.

"You are right, always right. I heed your words. But oh, how hard for me will be that waiting," he sadly answered.

Came Falling-Leaves Moon (September), and we moved to Fort Benton, traded for good supplies of powder and balls and other necessities, and went on across Big River. Camped for a time on Arrow Creek; then on Yellow (Judith) River; finally moved to South Bear (Musselshell) River, there to winter. Sun had set when we struck its valley, turned up it to find a good camping place, and suddenly our scouts came hurrying back to us and said that just up around the near bend was a big camp of people, by appearance of their lodges, Crows. That terribly frightened our women; they begged that we turn right back whence we had come. No, said our chiefs. We would give the Crows no chance to attack us as we were long strung out upon the trail; we would camp right where we were. Never, never should it be said of us that, right in our own country, we had fled from the Crows.

While we men stood ready to fight, the women set up the lodges, got in wood and water, but would not start their fires until Chief Big Lake shouted to them: "You women, to have our lodges dark would give the Crows to believe that we fear them. So build your fires at once and keep them burning. Take courage, you women, we will protect you, keep you safe."

Impossible for them not to fear. They fumbled, trembled at their work. The children were so frightened that they did not cry. When the lodges were all set up we drove our horses within the circle of them, held them there, and then, let come whatever might come, we were ready for it. As soon as it was dark, Big Lake sent scouts out to learn what the Crows were doing. Returning, they said that, like us, their lodge fires were burning, and they, too, were holding their horses close within their camp.

Said an old man, Weasel Head: "I don't understand how they dare come up here in our country to camp and hunt."

"They probably thought that we would not come down here to winter," said another.

Came Big Lake's sits-beside-him wife and other women and begged him not to attack the Crows, not to fight if he could possibly help it. Said he: "This we will do. If we have no trouble during the night, in the morning we will, a few of us, approach their camp, signing for them to come out and meet and talk with us. Should they do so, we will give them the chance to go, unharmed, back whence they came."

We men sat on watch all night, ready to fight, but the Crows did not appear. With the dawn our scouts reported that their scouts were watching our camp.

Three Bears and I were two of the ten men whom Big Lake named to go with him for a talk with the enemy. Sun was well up when we rounded the bend of the valley, slowly approached the big camp, close ahead. Big Lake, in the lead, signed for peace, then signed for a talk. A crowd of the Crows was gathered, watching our approach. When about two hundred yards from them we stopped, and at once ten of them came toward us, and Three Bears excitedly whispered to me: "That outside one on the left, Long Elk, himself!" I stared at him, for a man so tall, so big but not fat, I had never seen. Huge was his nose; small, his eyes; his heavy, otter-fur-wrapped hair braids hung down to his heels. He stared, angrily stared at Three Bears, and Three Bears, teeth gritting, stared at him. In line the ten of them came, stopped three or four yards from us, and Big Lake signed to them: "We have come to talk with you."

"Yes. Good that we talk together," signs-answered one who proved to be their chief, Kills Many.

Then Big Lake: "Sign talk is good, but mouth talk is better. Three Bears, here, will interpret for us. So, let us sit."

The other agreeing to that, down we all sat, and Big Lake, continuing through Three Bears, asked: "You Crows, why are you here in our country, killing our buffalo, our elk and antelope and deer?"

Kills Many: "Buffalo. They wander far south, far north, far east, far west. They belong to all of the different peoples. We Crows follow them, kill them to supply our needs."

Big Lake: "You have no right to camp and hunt in this, the country of us Pikunis, and our brothers, the Blackfeet, and the Many Chiefs (the Bloods)."

Kills Many: "We do not admit that this is your country. It is our country."

Big Lake: "Three summers back, where Yellow (Judith) River flows into Big (Missouri) River, we made an agreement, a writing with men Your and Our Grandfather sent out to us.[2] They agreed and so wrote it on their big, white, square leaves that all of the plains and mountains from the country of the Red Coats south to South Bear (Musselshell) River was the country of our three tribes. They put their names to it. We put our names to it. You Crows were there. You heard all of the talk. You did not object, you did not even speak, yet now you say that this is your country."

Kills Many: "We were alone there. Against your three tribes it would have been useless for us to speak."

Big Lake: "You fully know that this is our country, that you have no right here. But our women are begging us to pity your women and children and not fight you."

Quickly Three Bears turned that into Crow and then excitedly said to Big Lake: "Chief, one of those there sitting is my enemy, Long Elk. I want to fight him; I must fight him, kill him." And as he said that he also signed it so that the Crows could understand. And at once

---

[2] The "Stevens" treaty with the Blackfoot tribes at the junction of the Missouri and Judith rivers, October, 1855, was later ratified by Congress. It stipulated that the three tribes were sole owners of all the country from the Canadian line south to Musselshell River, and from the Rocky Mountains between those two boundaries to a north-and-south line cutting the junction of the Missouri and Milk rivers. However, President Grant, by executive order, took from the Indians, without their knowledge or consent, all of the country between the Missouri and the Yellowstone. And later, President Hayes, in a like manner, sequestered their lands between the Missouri and Marias rivers. The "Stevens" treaty, be it remembered, had provided also that the region between the Yellowstone and the Musselshell should be a common hunting ground where all parties to the treaty should enjoy full and equal hunting rights for ninety-nine years.

Long Elk signed and said, too: "Kills Many, I am going to fight that Three Bears, the slave woman's son. I am going to kill him!"

Signed Big Lake to Kills Many: "I think that your angry young man and my angry one should fight one another."

"Yes."

"And this I propose," Big Lake continued. "If my young one kills your young one, then you all must break camp and go back across Elk River into your own country. But if your young man kills our young man, then you all may camp and hunt in our country until summer comes."

"Good. As you say, so shall it be," signed Kills Many.

Well, Long Elk and Three Bears wanted the fight to be right then and there, but Big Lake and Kills Many would not have it that way. As just such between-tribes combats had been fought before, so must this one be fought. After much talk it was agreed that it should take place at midday, on horseback, the weapons only lances and shields; the place: the open bottom midway between the two camps.

We returned to camp, Three Bears worrying because he had neither shield nor lance. But these were soon furnished, and Black Eagle dressed him in his own war clothes and war bonnet of eagle tail feathers.

Midday came, and on foot we all set out for the fighting place—we men escorted Three Bears, riding the pinto horse that he had taken from Long Elk, our women and children, frightened, silent, closely following. The Crows had already come down around the bend of the valley and were sitting in a row in the short-grassed bottom. In like formation, when about a hundred yards from them, we all sat down, and Three Bears, close in front of Big Lake, got down from his horse, for Long Elk had not yet come. No more had he sprung from it than from the opposite line a woman started running toward him, a man and then a woman taking after her; all the Crows jumped up, shouting, shrieking. Tossing the rope of his horse to us, Three Bears ran to meet her, his sweetheart, Mink Woman, of course. Grasping her arm, he threatened her pursuers; they stopped, turned back, and he hurried her in to us—Black Eagle's women running to get her to sit with them. At once the Crows became quiet, all but the two who had pursued her. Yelling, menacing Three Bears, pointing to him, they showered him with Crow curses. It was then that Long Elk, escorted by three men afoot, came around the bend on a big bay horse, and he, too, was in war clothes and carrying a shield and lance. Mink Woman's father and mother ran to meet him, tell him of her flight to Three Bears. For a moment he paused, listened to them, then came riding swiftly toward Three Bears—now upon his horse—and shouting, as we afterward learned: "Slave woman's son, now I kill you, take Mink Woman to be mine."

So big, so powerful appearing, was Long Elk upon his big horse that it seemed he must at once overcome and kill much smaller, lighter Three Bears on his smaller horse, riding straight to meet his charge. But though Long Elk tried hard to make his horse crush down the other one, he could not do it; just before they were to meet it swerved sharply off, and the lance thrusts of the riders were without effect.

When they regained control of their excited horses, Long Elk was at the east end of the lane between us and the Crows, and Three Bears was at its other end. Silently, scarcely breathing, we all waited for what next they would do. That silence was oppressive, menacing. I whispered to Black Eagle: "When one or the other of the two fighters fall, big trouble comes." He did not answer.

Again and again the two rode at one another and without result, for they could not make their horses pass each other closely enough for their lance thrusts to take effect. So, after their third charge Three Bears sprang from his horse and shouted and signed to Long Elk: "Get down! We will fight afoot!"

But would Long Elk do that? No! He rode straight at Three Bears, there on foot and waiting, and loudly our people shouted: "Oh, the Crow coward! The dog-faced coward! He will kill our brave one!"

When almost upon Three Bears, Long Elk made a down thrust at him with his lance, but Three Bears dodged it and hurled his own spear at him as he was passing. It struck into his back; went deeply in, and he slumped from his horse, lay quivering. Then as Three Bears ran to him, knife in hand, and gave him a finishing stab, our people, crazily happy, sprang up and sang and danced and shouted again and again: "Three Bears, ha! Three Bears, ho! Brave, a real man, is Three Bears." And the Crows, angrily they yelled; some of their crazier warriors tried to run out at Three Bears, and Kills Many and other chiefs held them back.

Three Bears did not scalp Long Elk. Raising one of his long, heavy, otter-fur-wrapped hair braids, he cut off the end of it, held it out to the gaze of the Crows, and hurled it down upon the ground, as much as to say that his enemy was not worth scalping. He then caught his horse and came in to us. In the silence that followed, Big Lake stepped forward and signed to Kills Many and his Crows: "We pity you. We leave you here. This time you may camp in our country, kill all you need of our buffalo. But when you return to your country, come not back again across Elk River."

The Crows buried Long Elk, placed his robe-wrapped body on a scaffold that they made, and then broke camp and moved farther up the river. That night and thereafter we kept strong watch upon our horse herds, but they did not attempt to steal them. Our scouts kept constant watch upon them until, about a month later, they re-crossed Elk River.

About the happiest couple in our camp were Three Bears and his pretty Mink Woman.

CHAPTER FOURTEEN

The White Quiver Saga
(Told by White Quiver)

WHEN IN HIS PRIME my long-ago friend *Ksiks Unopachis*—(White Quiver) was a noted warrior of the Pikunis, largest, most powerful one of the three Blackfoot Indian tribes. He was born about 1850 and died on the Blackfoot Reservation, Montana, in 1931. He was very quiet and reserved, seldom joining the gatherings of his story-telling, laughing, joking, fellow tribesmen around their evening lodge fires. It was during the annual Medicine Lodge ceremonies of the tribe, when one by one the warriors counted their coups that he particularly shone, holding his audience all but breathless as he told of his raids, his killing of enemies, and his taking of enemy horses.

On a night early in September, 1885, a war party of Crows made off with a band of horses owned by some of the Pikunis who were camped on Badger Creek, not far above their agency. A year previous to this, following instructions from Washington, the agents of the various Northwest Indian tribes had notified their charges that they must absolutely cease going on raids against their enemies. But now, having himself lost several of his horses in the raid of the night, White Quiver declared that he cared not for the orders of *Kaahks Anon* (Our Grandfather, the President). He was going to take revenge upon the Crows. Several of the Pikuni warriors wanted to go with him, but as always he refused their company. He had always been a lone raider and always would be. His sacred, powerful, secret helper, a certain animal that had appeared and counseled with him in his long-ago fasting vision (dream) had told him that to be successful, to survive the wiles, the bullets, and the arrows of his enemies, he should always go alone against them.

There follows his tale of his last and greatest adventure, as he often told it in the long-ago:

It was Running Wolf who came hurrying into my lodge that morning and said that a war party had made off with some of our horses during the night. They had taken his swift black-and-white-spotted horses that he had tied before the doorway of his lodge. I went out with him, with the others who were camped above us, and we found that forty-one of our horses had been stolen. We found, too, the defiance of us by the stealers: their coupstick set upright in the ground behind Running Wolf's lodge, the piece of deer leather tied to it, painted with a black bird. *Ha!* The war party were Crows!

Returning to my lodge, I told my women to put into my war sack several pairs of moccasins, some pemmican, my little sacks of sacred paint, and to build a sweat lodge. Late in the day Red Eagle, powerful sacred man, owner of the Sun-favored Thunder Pipe, went into the sweat lodge with me, and, thrusting out our blankets, we sat naked within it. The women rolled in the rocks that they had heated red; we poked them into the little center pit we had dug, and, dipping a buffalo tail in a bowl of water, Red Eagle sprinkled them with it. As steam filled the lodge, and we perspired, he prayed Sun, Moon, and Morning Star to keep me safe from all dangers along the way that I was to go and to give me success in my raid upon the Crows. I prayed too, and we smoked as we sang Sun's songs and the songs of the Thunder Pipe. It was dusk when we reached outside for our blankets, and, wrapped in them, ran to the creek and plunged into its cold water; then we went home to dress.

Sad-faced and silent, my women set hot food before me. "Don't you dare cry, for that would bring me bad luck," I told them. "Be cheerful; laugh; sing; count the days of my absence as you pray for me, and that will bring good luck to all of us." Came in Red Eagle and others for a short visit and smoke with me—one advising that I ride his fast horse, so that I could quickly go to the far Crow country. I replied that riding to war was too dangerous. A horse, though well hidden in the timber during the day, was likely to be discovered by enemies, who would then look for its rider. Well, my visitors soon left. I slung to my sides my war sack and sacred, slender-cased, war bonnet, took my rifle, and started off upon the long, southward trail that I was to follow—my women, as I had ordered, singing the Wolf Song, good-luck song for the hunter, the warrior, as I left them.

Day was near when I arrived at *Osaks Ituktai* (Backfat Creek, Dupuyer Creek) and went into hiding in its brush for the day. Three mornings later I came to where Bear River joins Big River (Marias and Missouri rivers), and there, needing meat, I killed a deer. In the evening I built a small raft to keep my belongings dry, and, swimming and pushing it, crossed to Big River's south shore. I was then two nights in making Yellow (Judith) River, right where we Pikunis had camped and hunted four winters back. And sad were my thoughts; then there had been plenty of buffalo on the plains, plenty of deer and elk in the mountains. How happy we all had been there until some white soldiers arrived and said that they were come to move us back to our own country, to our agency on Badger Creek. Our chiefs told the soldier chief that we were, right there, in our own country; that twenty-five winters back, at the mouth of Yellow River, we had made a treaty with some of Our Grandfather's men, and they had put into writing the fact that from Elk (Yellowstone) River north to the Red Coats' country and from the summit of the Backbone (Rocky Mountains) between them and east to the mouth of Little (Milk) River was the country of us Blackfoot tribes. But the soldier chief said that our chiefs were wrong; that, many winters back, Our Grandfather had ordered that all of the country from Elk River north to Bear River was the country of the whites, and that we would have to pack up at once and return to our agency. So that we had to do, because we could not fight the many white soldiers who would attack us, kill off our women and children if we refused to go. So was it that we never again had buffalo; so was it that, for lack of them, many of our people died. And now there were no more buffalo; the whites had killed them all off. Close above where I lay hidden in the Yellow River brush were some white men's houses, and where once our buffalo had grazed, now grazed his white horns (cattle). Is it any wonder that I felt sad?

Two mornings on from Yellow River, I arrived at the foot of Black Mountain, that lone, bare, black lift of rock at the head of It-Crushed-Them-Creek (Armell Creek) and climbed it for my rest and sleep. It had ever been a lookout place of war parties. Upon its summit was a circle of rocks, piled breast-high by some long-ago war party for shelter from the winds. I got into it, sat, and, happening to look down, found an arrow point of shiny black stone, there lost or given to the gods, perhaps, by some warrior of the very long-ago. I put it in my pouch. My finding of it, I thought, was a sign of good luck ahead for me. Once before I had rested in this rocks circle with a war party led by Heavy Runner—I his servant, learning the ways of the warrior. Then north to Big River, west to Yellow River, east to Other-Side Bear River (the Musselshell), and beyond them as far as we could see were countless herds of buffalo and antelope. And now what did I see as I looked down on It-Crushed-Them Creek? White men's houses; white horns and sheep grazing where once our own food animals had grazed. I must not think of all the wrongs we had suffered from the whites, I thought. It is now for me to do successfully this that I have set out to do. I prayed to the Above Ones, to my own secret helper, and slept.

On the following morning, just before Sun appeared, I went into hiding in the timber of Other-Side Bear River, right where, five winters back, thirty lodges of us Pikunis had camped and hunted buffalo. We had come there from the big camp of our people at Raven Quiver's (Joseph Kipp's) trading post on Yellow River. Soon having all of the meat and hides that our pack horses could carry, we set out to return there and that evening camped on It-Crushed-Them Creek. On the following day, when we were nearing Yellow River, Cold Maker brought upon us a terrible storm, and before we could arrive there two of our women and a boy froze to death. I was thinking about it as I lay down to rest. I slept and had a vision: Appeared my sacred-animal helper and said to me: "This was a bad-luck camping place for your people; some of them died upon their way back from here. It may cause bad luck to you." *Ha!* Right then I awoke, but what I had been told was enough. I moved on up the valley and lay down in some berry brush upon its west rim. And none too soon. When climbing up there I had frightened a small herd of white horns, and they had run off up the valley. And now came three white men riding down it to learn what it was that had caused them to run. Well I knew what they would have tried to do had they come upon me in the open. They disappeared in the bend of the valley below but after a time came back up, riding in the timber bordering the river, still looking for the cause of their white horns' alarm. And then I saw them no more.

On my third night after leaving Other-Side Bear River, I traveled as fast as I could go, hoping to reach Elk River and hide in its timber before daybreak, for the Crows might be camped right where I would strike it. As the sky in the east began to whiten, I walked still faster; ran at times. But day came, and the breaks of the river were still well ahead of me; Sun would be up in the blue before I could get down into its valley. I had been running but stopped to get my wind, consider what to do. To lie on the plain all day, and without water, would be painful; even then I was very thirsty. I said to my-self, I must go on to water. I must risk being discovered by some enemy, early traveling out on the plain. So I went on—walking fast, then more and more slowly as I had stronger and stronger feeling that I should not try to get to the river. It was my sacred helper, I believed, warning me of danger. But I was so thirsty; would be still more thirsty. I stopped; my dry throat urged me to keep on. But my secret warning of danger was compelling. Though I all but choke from want of water, I will not go on, I at last decided, and sat down in some sagebrush, filled and lighted my pipe; with prayer, wafted smoke up toward the Above Ones and down toward Mother Earth. *Ha!* I had not quite finished the smoke when two riders came out upon the plain from the river breaks, and I saw that they were Indians. They rode eastward, now at a trot, again at a walk, often turning in to look at the heads of the coulees. This was Crow country; doubtless they were Crows, looking for their horses that had strayed off in the night. After a time one of them, well in the lead, signed to the other one: "Come on! Come on!" and together they rode swiftly down off the plain out of my sight, having probably found their horses. Then how sure I was that the Above Ones and my secret helper, sacred animal of my vision, were powerfully aiding me; would surely help me to do this that I had set out to do. Hunger, thirst were nothing. I prayed to my powerful helpers, I sang the Wolf Song, lay down, and slept at times during the day.

I was sitting up when Sun was going down beyond the western mountains, going on to his far-off island home in the Everywhere Water. I was so thirsty that my throat and lips were swollen. The plain, so far as I could see it, was bare of any kind of life, but I was taking no chances of being discovered by Crows or whites. I waited until it was fully dark, then set out for the river. I struck the rim of the plain where, in the morning, the two riders had appeared; looking down into the valley, there, as I expected it would be, I saw the Crow camp. There were more than a hundred lodges, all glowing red with their evening fires; and faintly came to me the drumming and singing of happy people. I stole down into the valley. The camp was in a wide, long bottom of grassland and well out from the timber bordering the river. There were many horses grazing in it. I did not want any of them; my takings would be the powerful, fast, valuable horses that were nightly tied before the lodges of their owners. I passed the camp so closely west of it that I could plainly hear the people talking and little children squalling. On weak, trembly legs I pushed on through the timber and at the shore of the river, knelt, and drank and drank of its cold, soothing water. Then I sat back and for the first time ate of the pemmican in my war sack; not much, for I was saving it for just such times as this—times when, close to my enemies, I could neither kill a meat animal nor build a fire.

The water and the food gave me back my strength. I cautiously moved out to the edge of the timber to look at the camp; I would wait for the lodge fires to die out, the people to sleep, and then go in for the horses. Straight out from me, midway between the camp and the timber, some men built a large fire and began dancing in the light of it. I could plainly see them, their beautiful war clothes, their longtail war bonnets. Very graceful was their dancing and fierce their singing, in time with their four drummers-and-singers, old men, close to the fire sitting. Now and then when they rested, one after another would get up and tell of his killings of enemies and takings of enemy horses. How I wished that I could understand their talk! Then, presently, one of them, a tall, big-bodied man, telling of his raids, sign-talked, too, and I plainly saw him sign: "Five summers back, three of us, Striped Eagle, Long Bear, and I, set out to kill enemies. On foot, northward we traveled. This side of where Big River and Yellow River come together, out on the plain, we saw three riders. They rode down into Yellow River Valley and we heard shooting. We walked back into the valley. Walked down through the timber, looking for them. We saw them—a deer skinning. We approached them. I leading. I killed two. Striped Eagle killed one. We took their guns; their horses. They were Pikuni men . . . ."

Ha! My cousin, Fox Head, was one of those three he told of killing; they went out hunting, never returned, we never knew what had been their end. But now, knowing it, I burned with anger. I had loved my cousin. "Though I die for it, I will kill that man, his killer," I said to myself, and carefully aiming my rifle at him, fired. He threw out his arms, fell; those there with him began loud yelling. I sprang up and ran back into the timber, then up the valley in it, slowing to a careful noiseless walk. Out in the camp men were still shouting, some women were crying. That crying made me happy. I had killed the man who caused my cousin's women to cry.

I knew that for the night I was safe enough in the timber. In the morning I would be well hidden when the Crows began searching all up and down the valley for the killer of their coup-counting warrior. But where to hide? I did not want to go far for, come night again, I was going into that camp for horses. I turned in to the river; drank; lay down on the shore, slept a little now and then. When the first faint light of day came, I looked for a good hiding place and found it: a big pile of driftwood at the end of a long, sandy point running out into the river. I took off my moccasins and leggings, waded out. The pile was higher than my head. I got into it; found a comfortable place to sit, and under it, a way to crawl and safely hide at the very bottom of the pile. I made a screen of drift brush through which to look, ate a few mouthfuls of pemmican, filled and lit and smoked my pipe, felt so happy that it was hard to keep from singing a victory song. I was so near the Crow camp that I could hear now and then, though faintly, the barking of the dogs.

Sun was but a little way up in the blue when I saw a rider coming up the shore of the river and heard others coming up in the timber, now and then calling to one another. The shore rider came on bent over, looking for footprints or any other sign of the killer of the night. Well, he wouldn't find any of mine. With some fine brush that I gathered I had swept out my footprints as I made them in crossing the sandy shore to the water. So was it that, when the rider came to my point, he crossed the base of it without even looking out at the driftwood in which I sat watching him. Soon he passed around a bend of the river above and was gone. Below me the river ran straight a long way without a bend; so I saw women of the camp come out to it for water; men drive their bands of horses out to drink. Children, too, came out and played for long upon the shore. I felt safe there in the drift pile. I got down into the bottom of it and slept upon the dry sand.

Sun was passing down behind the mountains when I awoke and crawled up to my sitting place in the driftwood. Some of the Crows were driving their horses to drink and catching their best ones to tie before their lodges for the night. I prayed the Above Ones to help me safely get off with some of them. As soon as it was dark I left the drift pile, ate a very little of my pemmican, drank, and walked slowly down through the timber to the place in its edge where I had sat the night before. But now the people in the camp were not as they had been then. They were not singing, drumming, dancing, nor even laughing. Their quiet talking was like the far-off buzzing of bees. They were sad because of the one of them I had killed. He must have been a chief, I thought.

The stars were shining in the clear sky, but Night-Light (Moon) did not appear. Impatiently I waited for the lodge fires to cease burning, for the people to sleep. Often I looked up at the Seven Persons (Ursa Major). They had moved around nearly to their middle-of-the-night position when, again praying the Above Ones for help,

I got up and stole toward the camp. Nearing its upper end, I moved more and more slowly—a step or two at a time. A horse was standing before the doorway of the uppermost one of the lodges. It was not frightened, did not move as I approached it. One of the sleepers in the lodge was snoring. Untying the short picket rope of the horse, I led him off very slowly, so slowly that his hoofs made no sound upon the thickly grassed ground. Going to the edge of the timber, I tied him there and went back for another one. But that time I got two. Then I hesitated. Should I or should I not go back to the camp once more? The horses that I had were good ones; perhaps I should be satisfied with my taking and go. But it would be as easy to make off with four as it would with three; and I had strong feeling that the Above Ones and my secret helper would keep me safe. Back I went and led out another horse, a big, fat, well-built stallion that I at once named *Sikopi* ("Black-and-White-Spotted") because of his color. I rope-bridled him, got onto him, and leading the three others, rode slowly up onto the plain. There turning the three loose, I drove them fast, heading for home.

The Crows, no doubt, rode far and wide in search of the stealer of their four horses, but they failed to find me. I had but one bad time on my long, back trail and that was my own fault. I had stopped for the day at Yellow River, and with the horses well hidden in a dense, high, growth of willows, I had a good rest and sleep; toward evening, over a small fire, I broiled and ate plenty of the meat of a deer that I had killed that morning just before entering the timber. But I was too eager to go on, to get home with my fine taking of Crow horses. Though I better knew than to do it, though I well knew that I should remain right where I was until real night came, I started on just as Sun was going down to his western home. And no more had I gotten out upon the plain than two white men who were driving a band of white horns toward the river, saw me, came riding and yelling after me. I rode fast, too, as fast as I could drive my three loose horses. Then soon they began shooting at me with their short-guns (six-shooters), and I saw that they could overtake me. Well, I had to stop them or be killed, so I stopped, got down from my horse and began shooting with my rifle—not right at them, but close to them. *Ha!* At once they knew that I had the best of them with my long-barreled rifle, and as I fired a fourth time they turned and fled.

Near morning of my tenth night of travel from Elk River, I came to our Pikuni camp, strung out along Badger Creek above our agency. My women were to stop with my cousin, Little Dog, and his family during my absence, so I happily went into his lodge, almost shouting: "Wake up, my cousin! Wake up, my women! I am here! I have been successful: I killed a Crow! I return with four Crow horses!"

My women sprang up and hugged me, shouting: "Our man has returned! Our man has killed an enemy! Our man has taken four enemy horses! Our man, White Quiver, he is brave!"

But Little Dog did not speak until the women had quieted, and then he said to me: "News of what you have done arrived ahead of you. The Crow agent wrote our agent that a Crow had been killed and four Crow horses had been stolen, perhaps by the Pikunis. If that proved to be true, he asked our agent to seize and hold the horses, and he would send for them. So is it that our seizers (Indian police) are looking for your return, to take the horses, should you have them.

Hearing that, oh, how angry I was! "Are we their slaves, that the whites can do this to us?" I cried. "That we fight our enemies, raid their horse herds, is of no concern whatever to the whites."

"It is as it is. You well know that we have to obey the order of the whites; we are too few to fight them. There is but one thing for you to do if you would profit from your long, hard raid: Take your four horses to the north-land and trade them to our Blood or Blackfeet relatives. And go now, at once, before our seizers begin their daily rounds."

"Yes! Go! Go at once lest our agent have you seized and put into his iron-barred-windows house," my women wailed.

"Give me food and I will go. Never shall the Crows get back these horses that I took from them," I said.

Hurriedly I ate the food that my crying women set before me, and tired, sad and angry both, was off again and facing a fierce wind- and snow-storm that Cold Maker had brought from his Always Winter Land. It was not midday when, despite the storm, I topped the ridge just beyond Little River (Milk River), along which were strung the piles of stones that mark the south edge of the Red Coats' land. I felt relief when the stone piles were behind me: I was now free from pursuit by our seizers. Steadily I kept on, riding my powerful *Sikopi,* driving my three others as fast as I could make them travel. Night had not come when I neared the big house (fort) of Bull's Head (Colonel Macleod) and his Red Coats, and the white men's houses below it. One of the little houses was the home of my friend *Kaiyó Kos* (Jerry Potts, a Blackfoot half-blood, a noted character of the buffalo days). I decided to stop with him for the night, learn where our Blood relatives were camped, and go on to them in the morning.

Tying my horses before the house, I went in and was made welcome by his mother. Bear Child, she said, was interpreter for Bull's Head, and was with him in his big house, but would come home at night. His mother set plenty of food before me. I ate, rested, smoked. Then I went out to picket my horses for the night, but they were gone! I could hardly believe my eyes! How strange that they could be stolen right there in the many-houses (town) of the Red Coats! As I stood there worrying, looking here, there, trying to decide what to do, came Bear Child himself, all but shouting as he neared me: "White Quiver! Was it you who tied four horses here before my house?"

"Yes! And they are gone! Stolen!" I yelled.

Hugging me, his cheek against my cheek, he said: "No, not stolen. The Red Coats have them. You took them from the Crows, did you not?"

"Yes. And killed a Crow, too. But the Red Coats, they have no right to seize my takings from our enemies."

Said my friend: "It is that Bull's Head received a writing from the Crow agent. A writing describing four horses that had been stolen, probably by a war party of our tribes, and asking Bull's Head to seize and hold them for him if they appeared in this Red Coats' country."

"Oh, Bear Child!" I said. "Surely it is nothing to Bull's Head what we in the Big Knives' country do. Come, let us go to him, and you interpret for me. I am sure that he will give me back the horses when I explain my taking of them."

"Well, we can try that, but not tonight, for Bull's Head is having a feast and dance in his house. So, tomorrow," he answered.

That evening, of course, I had to tell Bear Child and his mother all about my raid upon the Crows in their Elk River country, but I was not happy in doing it. And I slept but little, worrying about the horses; oh, I just could not bear losing them, particularly *Sikopi*, he so powerful, so gentle, so eager to go wherever I would guide him.

In the morning, on our way to talk with Bull's Head, I saw my horses; with many others they were in a very long, four-sided corral in front of his Big House, and two Red Coats, one at each end of it, were watching that no one take them. We went into the big house. Bull's Head was sitting, smoking. He got up, smiled friendlily, strongly shook hands with me, and I knew that he liked me. At once, Bear Child interpreting for me, I told him why I had come; asked him to give me back my horses.

Said he in reply: "White Quiver, my friend, if I could have my way about it, you would have those horses right now. But I can't have my way. It is this: The big chief of the Red Coats, my chief, made an agreement with the big chief of the Big Knives. It is, they say, that Indian tribes shall no longer raid one another. To that end, they have agreed to seize and return to their owners all the horses that they steal from one another. So, don't blame me for holding your horses. I have to do as my chief orders me to do. See, this is a writing that I got from the agent of the Crows five days ago. He says that a Crow was killed and four Crow horses were stolen, it is thought, by a war party from one or another of the Blackfoot tribes. The horses are: one black-and-white-spotted stallion, one yellow mare, one brown horse with white spot on forehead, and one gray horse with short tail. And he also says: 'Should these horses appear in your country, please have your Red Coats seize them, and hold safely until I can send for them.'"

With that he finished, and I just stood, seeing nothing, and so disappointed that I was sick in my stomach. Then looking at me with kind eyes, he said: "White Quiver, I have great sympathy for you and your kind. I know how much you enjoy raiding your enemies, but it has to end. White men's writings travel much faster than the fastest riders can go. From now on any enemy horses that you may get upon your raids will be taken from you by the white seizers as soon as you arrive home with them."

I had no reply to make to that. I turned, went out the door, on past the big corral and the Red Coats there guarding the horses within it. Back to Bear Child's house I slowly walked, and within it sat and grieved and grieved, his mother sympathizing with me. Came night, and Bear Child returned and tried to cheer me, in vain. Then, as we were going to our couches, he asked: "Tell me, friend, what is it that you now intend to do?"

"My thoughts are all mixed. I have no plan for anything," I answered.

But in the night, after much prayer and after a vision that I was given by the Above Ones, I decided upon a way to get back my horses. Came morning, and I said to Bear Child: "I want you to interpret for me once more, and I want you to get Bull's Head to send you on some errand that will keep you away from here tonight. For tonight I shall get back my horses and you are not to be blamed for it."

"But you can't get them; the Red Coats watch them all night," he said.

"You do what I ask; you will be surprised," I said, and he gave in.

Again we went in to Bull's Head, sitting, smoking in his room, and I said to him: "Bull's Head, give me your hand." He held it out; I took it, pressed its palm, closed the fingers on it, and still holding it, said: "My horses; they are in your hand, but between the fingers there are places that can be opened. Bull's Head, this is to tell you that tonight I shall get back my horses." And with that I gave him his hand.

He laughed. "White Quiver, what a joker you are."

"Maybe not," I answered, hurried from the room and back down to Bear Child's house, and told his mother what I planned to do.

"Oh, but it is too dangerous; the Red Coats will probably kill you," she cried. And after a little: "Well, as you are strong-minded to do it

I will help you all I can, pray with you for your success, give you the buffalo robe and rope that you need." Then soon came Bear Child, riding a Red Coats' horse, and entering, said that he had prevailed upon Bull's Head to send him on an errand to the North Pikunis and that he would be all night with them. And after short, serious talk with me, he left.

Came night, and long Bear Child's mother and I prayed and sang Sun's sacred songs for my success. I then cut the buffalo robe into two pieces, and with them, the rope, and last helpful words from that kind woman, I left the house. The night was very cold; the snow, ankle deep; the sky was clear, the stars brightly shining. I stole as near to the corral as was safe for me and sat down. Four Red Coats were guarding it, one at each of its corners. Every little while they would all change corners, passing one another at the center of their sides of it. They kept doing it; and when they stood at their corners they often stamped their feet and slapped their bodies, for it was very, very cold. I had on buffalo-robe moccasins; a capote over my two shirts; two pairs of leggings; buffalo-robe gloves and cap. I was comfortable. I sat at the edge of a coulee that ran down not far from the north and long side of the corral; its bars were in the center of its east side. I began to fear for the success of my plan. I prayed the Above Ones for help as I never had prayed before. I could see that the Red Coats were getting colder and colder. At last, one of the two at the upper end of the corral ran down into the coulee, built a fire, and stood warming first one foot, then the other, and warming his hands. After a little, he went back to his corner, and the Red Coat at the other, north corner of it hurried to the fire and got warm; then, by turns the other two Red Coats went to the fire and got warm. And at last, after further pacing of the sides of the corral, they all gathered at the fire, which they had kept replenishing, and began smoking their pipes. My chance had come; from where they stood in the coulee they could not see the corral! I hurried into it. My four horses stood together, apart from the many others, all strangers to them. I roped *Sikopi*, started with him toward the corral bars, and the three others closely followed. There were three bars. I let the lower one down noiselessly, placed a piece of buffalo robe on it to prevent the next bar tunking upon it, and let it down; and used the other piece of robe to deaden the sound of the third bar. I then led *Sikopi* out, the others still following, rope-bridled and mounted him, and started off slowly so that the Red Coats would not hear; but at once I had to ride fast, for all the horses in the corral had started for the entrance and were now coming fast, with thunderous noise. My three horses kept close to *Sikopi's* tail; the herd of others began to scatter out; the Red Coats could not see where I was heading. Oh, how happy I was! I wanted to sing!

No Red Coats pursued me. Near the middle of the next day I passed out of their country and was safe there where they could not follow me. I stopped for the night on Little River; killed four grouse and had a feast. On the following night I arrived at Badger Creek; went into Little Dog's lodge. When he and my women had greeted me, I said to him: "The Red Coats took my horses from me, but I got them back. Now you and Running Crane and White Calf, you three chiefs, I give you each a horse, and you have got to help me: You have to order our agent's seizers never to let him know of these Crow horses."

"I will go to White Calf and Running Crane in the morning: give each one his horse. Rest; don't worry; you will not lose your *Sikopi*," he answered.

But I did worry, watching for approaching seizers until the following evening, when, returning, Little Dog said to me: "So far as your takings of Crow horses are concerned, the seizers have gone blind. Gladly they said that they would never see them."

CHAPTER FIFTEEN

Cut-Nose[1] (Told by *Apikuni*, but Actually Related to Him by Bear Head)

Amunis Ahki ("OTTER WOMAN"), daughter of Eagle Plume, was the most beautiful girl of the Pikunis. She was fairly tall, exquisitely formed, of perfect features; her hair in two neat braids hung far below her waist. She was her mother's able assistant in all the lodge work and was given to sitting with her elders more than mingling with those of her own age; she loved to listen to the tales of the medicine men and the sacred Sun-lodge women—tales of the gods and their wondrous deeds. Seven times her mother had been leader of the women who annually built the great tribal offering to Sun, the medicine lodge, as we old-time traders called it. It was the girl's great ambition to be herself one of those sacred and honored women.

Only married and widowed women of absolutely blameless characters could vow to Sun that they would build him a great lodge. But now, in her eighteenth summer, Otter Woman was promised to young Black Elk. He was off with a war party to raid the horse herds of the Crows; upon his return, the two were to live in a lodge that their mothers had made, for which they had gathered the furnishings. Then when Black Elk should go again to war, or if he should fall sick, it would be her privilege to vow to Sun that, if he would keep her man safe in his encounters with the enemy or, on the other hand, cure him of his illness, she would build a sacred lodge in his honor.

1 Published as "A Blackfoot Tragedy" in the *Los Angeles Times Magazine* (March 27, 1932).

Many a youth, many a man of the tribe had sent friends to Eagle Plume to recount their brave deeds, enumerate their riches, and then offer many horses for his handsome daughter. But the chief was different from most fathers; to each emissary he replied that it was for the girl herself to decide whom she would marry. And of them all she had chosen Black Elk—not for his wealth, as he had but few horses; nor for his bravery, as he had never been in a fight with the enemy. She had said "Yes" to him because of his known kindness of heart, his unremitting care for his mother and her younger children, and because she had always loved him, though silently and from afar.

And now Black Elk had been gone forty-one days. Soon now he would be returning, coming with enemy horses, enemy weapons, enemy scalps, now a real warrior, to claim her for his woman. Daily that powerful Sun priest Three Bears had ridden the round of the great camp, shaking his rattle, singing the song for the absent, naming each member of the war party and calling upon the people to pray for their safety in the enemy country and their quick return with much enemy property. How proud she was when she heard the old priest name her man-to-be—four times shout out his name and call upon the people to pray for him. How long and earnestly she prayed for him—not only then, but frequently during the day—and promised Sun rich offerings for his safe return.

At this time—it was the summer of 1879—the great camp of the tribe was pitched on Arrow Creek, a stream rising in the Belt Mountains and joining the Missouri River about a hundred miles below Fort Benton. I was there, a guest in the lodge of my friend Bear Head, and having a grand time running herds of buffalo with him and other keen horsemen of the tribe; hunting grizzly bears, deer, elk, antelope, bighorns; and of evenings sitting with the old men and listening to their tales of war—dramatic recitals of their myths and legends and the wondrous power of their sky gods. And listening to the talk of Bear Head's women and their friends, I learned much of the gossip of the camp—among other things, of the approaching marriage of young Black Elk and the daughter of Eagle Plume, whose lodge was close on the left of ours in the great camp circle.

On several occasions I saw the girl standing with hands raised to the sky, praying for the safe return of her sweetheart as old Three Bears rode by shaking his rattle and calling upon all to pray for the absent ones. Beautiful, lissome she was. Her kindly, serious eyes, her every action bespoke the fact that here was a real woman.

Close back of camp, on the north side of the creek, was a high sandstone cliff; there lone old men were wont to sit, alert for signs of any approaching enemy, looking sadly down upon the activities of the great camp, off to the billowing plain, scene of many a successful hunt, of exciting adventure when they had been young and full of life. Early one morning, as Bear Head and I were going to the creek to bathe, there were three of the oldsters perched upon the cliff. Pointing to them, he said: "*Apikuni*, don't you dread the time when we, too, will be sitters upon cliffs, just feeble cliff-sitters, nothing more?"

"Let's not think of it," I answered.

We did not bathe that morning, for as we neared the creek the old men upon the cliff sprang up and stood alertly staring at the plain to the south, hands shading their eyes from the early sun; waved their wraps and shouted to attract our attention; and then in the sign language: "Pikunis coming; driving many horses; they are near." Wherat Bear Head and I ran back to camp, an excited camp, everyone staring at the south rim of the plain, excitedly talking; children bawling, dogs barking, horses prancing at the ends of their picket ropes. And presently appeared a big band of horses hurtling down the slope, the war party close following. They had stopped somewhere not far out and painted themselves and their mounts; put on their fringed and beaded and quilled war clothes and bonnets of eagle feathers. On they came, brandishing their weapons, holding aloft some scalps, singing fiercely the Victory Song. What a sight, a stirring sight, they were!

The women and children ran out across the flat to greet their returning husbands, fathers, brothers, sweethearts; surrounded and escorted them in, shouting their names, praising them for their bravery and success in despoiling the hated Crows. Meanwhile, the men in camp, standing before their lodges and enjoying the lively scene, were counting the riders, and suddenly Bear Head nudged me and said: "*Apikuni*, it is not to be all happiness; they were forty-one when they left us, and now they number but forty. Hear you not the sad crying?"

And then we saw that Otter Woman was one of the stricken; her mother was bringing her in, supporting her wavering steps, and she was crying: "Black Elk! Black Elk! Black Elk! *Haiya, haiya!* My sweetheart Black Elk! He is dead, he is dead. *Haiya! Haiya!*

The two went into their lodge. We saw Black Elk's mother, sister, an aunt, and cousin going slowly back to their lodge, all of them mourning for their loved one. A little later, Bear Head invited one of the party to come in and smoke with us, and he told us how the youth had been killed: The party had night-raided a camp of Crows, well up the Bighorn River, and taken off with more than a hundred horses. But before reaching the Yellowstone they had been obliged to stop and fight a party of about fifty Crows too closely pursuing them. They had driven them back, killing five, but Black Elk had been too brave, too crazily brave; he had kept on after all of his companions had given up the pursuit, and so had been shot down. But, resuming the chase, they had prevented the Crows' counting coup upon him; they had given the youth decent burial on a bank of the Yellowstone and brought back his horse and various belongings to turn over to his father.

So passed young Black Elk. His sorrowing sweetheart, his mother, and female relatives gashed the calves of their legs, unbraided their hair, fasted, and daily went out a little way from camp and mourned pitifully and long, until they became hoarse and could no more than croak his name.

Gradually the mourning became less intense; finally, ceased. And again youths of the great camp, dressed all in their best and painted and armed came and stood silently, stiffly before Otter Woman's lodge, and for hours at a time—that the usual way of Blackfoot courting of a girl; and how foolish, how simperingly silly were their faces when passing children and even their elders asked them what they were doing there. Hoped each of them to get a smile, a nod of assent from the worshiped one, but she went to and fro about her work as though they were not present. And then, one by one, they sent friends to her father to speak for them; but always the answer was: "My daughter bids me say to you that she will never marry. You should know as well as I do that she is not of two tongues."

So at last all courting of Otter Woman ceased. And then one day she asked her father to organize a party to make a raid on the Crows and allow her to accompany him as his pipe carrier, his servant; for she wanted to learn the ways of war and in time become a leader of war parties, as that ancestor of theirs, that virgin warrior, Running Eagle, had led parties in the long ago.

"Yes, successfully for a time, until she was shot down in a night raid upon a camp of the River People," said Eagle Plume.

"*Ha!* But what a happy way to die. Father, it is that I want to avenge fully the passing of the one I love, the only one I ever could love. I want to fight and fight and fight the Crows; make them pay dearly for what they have done to me."

"Oh, no! No!" her mother cried. "Daughter, you were not born for the war trail; your ways are the ways of real women; you love the lodge and all the lodge work. She was a man in a woman's body, that Running Eagle; when of but few winters, she demanded of her father a real bow and arrows. She hunted with him; killed buffalo, deer, elk, even real bears."

To Otter Woman, it was as though her mother had not spoken; she kept her eyes on Eagle Plume, and after long thought he replied: "This that you ask of me is very serious. I will pray the Above Ones to give me a revealing vision; it is for them to point out to me what answer to make to your request."

Time passed and Eagle Plume seemed to be unable to get the dream that he wanted; then one day he came hurrying into his lodge and said to the girl: "Daughter, the Above Ones, as you know, have given me no vision about that which you asked of me, and now I know their reason for denying it to me: I have just now been visiting with Talks-with-the-Buffalo. He has asked me to give you to him."

Otter Woman laughed. And then: "That man! Of your own age: of two wives and many children! He must be crazy. What did he say when you told him that I shall never marry?"

"I did not tell him that. You know, daughter, that he is my more-than-friend, my more-than-brother; that in our fight with the Assiniboines, in the Bear Paw Mountains, he saved me from them though himself badly wounded."

"What? You told him then, that man of many wives, and old, of heart so cold that he never laughs, that he could have me?"

"No, daughter, I did not give you to him; I said that I would ask you to become his woman."

"Knowing well that I will not do it. Surely you were not afraid to tell your more-than-friend that I am not for him?"

"Daughter, it is that every woman of our tribe should marry, have children. All too few are our men. They fall in battle with our many enemies; they are continually being crippled, killed in the chase. Now you, desiring revenge upon the Crows, you can do far more by raising children, brave, strong youths to fight them, than you can by going yourself against them. Daughter, as you love me, as you love your mother, I call upon you to marry Talks-with-the-Buffalo, saver of my life. It is your plain duty to have children by him, brave sons to grow up and fight our many enemies."

The girl made no reply to that. She went out and across the camp to the lodge of her dead sweetheart's mother, Mink Woman, and remained with her a long time. Bear Head and I were sitting with Eagle Plume, smoking with him, when she came home; he had been telling us of Talks-with-the-Buffalo's sudden request for her, his hope that she would go to him. Very solemn, downcast, she was as she sat down beside her mother, leaned against her and said: "Father, I have been with Mink Woman; she thinks, as you do, I should marry, have sons to grow up and avenge the death of him we loved. So is it that I will marry your more-than-friend." And with that she began to cry. Bear Head and I got up and quietly left the lodge.

With her various belongings, the girl moved into her new home that evening, and presently we learned that she was not happy there; *Otahki*, the younger of the two sisters Talks-with-the-Buffalo had married, was very jealous of the new wife and was slyly doing all that she could to make trouble for her in her new life. Even, at times, she boldly lied about her, told their man that, when the two went to get wood for the lodge fire, she herself did the heavy work, the other merely idling about and taking up a few dry branches now and then. To all of which Otter Woman would never make denial, and Talks-with-the-Buffalo would look at her, at each of them in turn, and grimly smile.

Otter Woman often came to visit her father and mother and tell them, incidentally, of fresh meanness that the jealous one had put upon her. And at last Eagle Plume, angry and hurt, said to her: "Daughter, I see that I made a mistake in urging you to marry my more-than-friend. I am disappointed in him. As he will not protect you from that lying woman it is for me to do so; go at once, and take up your belongings, and return home."

"No, father, no," she replied. "You showed me my duty to our tribe. I shall remain with the man to whom you gave me, no matter how much his second wife lies about me."

But as Bear Head said afterward, little did Otter Woman, or any of us, realize how mean was that jealous woman's heart.

Came from the north, from the camp of our brother tribe, the Bloods, four young men to visit friends in our camp, and one of them was Low Horn, he who was nicknamed "Handsome Man." And rightly: he was unquestionably the handsomest of all the men of the three tribes of the Blackfeet. So handsome, so graceful in all that he did, so perfect of figure and face that I shall not attempt to describe him. A bachelor and a lady killer he was, too, desired by all the maidens and doubtless by many a married woman. Some men were so jealous of him that when he staged one of his spectacular dances around the circle of the camp, they ordered their women into their lodges, there to remain until he had passed. Yes, Handsome Man was a dandy, a "fop," as we would say. He had no war record other than having been on one successful raid upon the horse herds of the Crees. Was he, as some maintained, a coward, deserving to be forced to wear a woman's gown, instead of shirt and leggings and breechcloth?

On a hot summer morning, soon after he arrived, word went the round of the camp that Handsome Man was going to dance. Under a shelter of poles and brush, close to their lodge, sat Talks-with-the-

Buffalo and his women, and as I was passing he invited me to sit and smoke with him. I casually noticed that his sits-beside-him-wife, as the Blackfeet call a man's first wife, was idle; the two others were busily quilling the uppers of a pair of moccasins for their man, quilling in ancient designs and gorgeous hues.

"Would that I could have a pair of moccasins as beautiful as those are to be," I said.

"Get married, then, and have all the pretty moccasins that you can wear," Otter Woman replied.

"Easy to do were I as good looking as he there coming," I said, pointing to Handsome Man, flanked by his singing, drumming friends and just then starting to dance along the inner line of the lodges of the big camp circle.

On they came, Handsome Man slightly in the lead, dressed in a suit of beautifully fringed and quilled war clothes, face and hands and moccasins red painted, brandishing a war club banded with snow-white eagle plumes. Lithely, gracefully, he danced, in perfect time with the thrilling singing and drumming of his followers. Said Talks-with-the-Buffalo, lips contemptuously curling: "But why war club, weapon that he has never used and never will use upon the enemy?"

"But he is still so young; give him time, my man; give him time to use it, as I am sure he will," the sits-beside-him wife replied.

"*Ha!* Wouldn't use it were he to live ten hundred years," he growled and spat upon the ground.

For all its apparent ease, Handsome Man's war dance was strenuous work, particularly on a day so hot; finally tiring, perspiration streaking his painted face, Handsome Man motioned his followers to be silent, and came to a stand close in front of our shelter. And just then Otter Woman held out a questioning hand to her jealous enemy, *Otahki*, and said, "Give me Handsome Man." And then; "Oh, what a mistake! I meant my awl; my awl that you borrowed."

But before she could finish, *Otahki* was already all but shouting to Talks-with-the-Buffalo: "My man! Did you hear her, your new wife? She told me, 'Give me Handsome Man.'"

Talks-with-the-Buffalo frowned, stared at Otter Woman. She

returned his gaze, frankly, unflinchingly, and said, "I don't know why I named the dancer for he is nothing to me, nothing at all; no more than the passing wind."

"What a lie! She loves him so much that she can't think of anything else, even to remember that it was her awl that she wanted."

And Handsome Man and his followers heard; they had heard it all, so close were they to our shelter. The followers were embarrassed; their heads drooped; they looked at the ground, anywhere but toward us. But Handsome Man was pleased; boldly, smilingly, he looked at Otter Woman; glanced at angry Talks-with-the-Buffalo and again at Otter Woman. Happily, smugly, he looked at her, sure that, despite her denial of him, she, the most beautiful woman of the camp, was still another victim of his charms. Warily he glanced again at her grimly scowling man; again he smiled at her, and, signing to his followers to resume their drumming, went singing and dancing from us with renewed vigor and grace. Of us all, *Otahki* alone watched his sprightly going. Otter Woman raised her drooping head, tearfully, pleadingly looked at Talks-with-the-Buffalo, and began: "My man . . . ."

He shrugged his shoulders, looked away from her. As though half-dazed, she fumblingly gathered up her quilling materials and went slowly into their lodge. *Otahki* laughed. Her sister *Paiota* frowned at her and said: "Be still, you!"

Silently I handed the smoked-out pipe to my friend and joined Bear Head and his women, sitting under their sun shelter. They had sensed something unpleasant whence I had come, and I told them what had happened. Poor Otter Woman. Never could she be at peace there in that family, they said, for *Otahki* was of very mean heart, very jealous of her, and would do all that she possibly could to make Talks-with-the-Buffalo cast her off.

I had at that time a fly rod, one that I had brought from the States and dearly cherished, for it was, so far as I knew, the only fly rod in all Montana Territory. At sundown that evening I went fishing, accompanied by Bear Head. Not that he fished, or even ate fish, for they were the food of the dread Underwater People and therefore taboo by all of the Blackfoot tribes. But he keenly enjoyed watching me handle the fragile tackle and happily shouted at the sudden leap of a big trout to seize the fly, and its furious and sometimes successful struggle to free itself.

On this evening we struck the stream a few hundred yards above camp and turned down it. And I had no luck, whipping pool after pool and getting not a single rise, though we could see many large trout in their clear depths. But at last, when it was really dusk, I hooked a big one, and after many rushes and leaps it gave up the struggle and I got it out upon the shore. It was enough, more than enough, for my breakfast, so I unjointed and cased the rod, and we went on down the shore to strike the camp water trail and so avoid tearing our way through the thick and thorny brush. Our moccasined feet were noiseless upon the sandy shore; we had rounded a sharp bend and turned into the well-worn trail when from a dense growth of willows two others came into it. In the deeper darkness of the timber they were so near that we recognized them: Handsome Man and *Otahki!* Each had an arm about the other's waist. They had, of course, made sure that there was no one at the stream; sought only to avoid anyone coming out from camp; so, great was their surprise at seeing us almost upon them. It was *Otahki* who first saw us, and with gasping "*Nayeyah!*" she broke from him and ran for camp, he plunging back into the willows whence they had come.

Bear Head and I went on, came to a stand upon reaching the open, but could not distinguish *Otahki* among the many going to and fro in the big camp; she had doubtless already gone into her lodge. We wondered how she had managed to slip out by herself to meet Handsome Man, and probably not for the first time. For only very old women and women already branded for infidelity went alone beyond the circle of the camp, even for wood or water.

Said Bear Head: "That *Otahki!* I have always suspected that, given the opportunity, she would be that kind of woman.

"What are you going to do about it, tell Talks-with-the-Buffalo what we have seen?"

"No. We men are not tale bearers—gossips. She will soon be discovered in her badness and be made to suffer the punishment that she deserves."

The following day broke so hot and windless that, right after our morning meal, we all gathered in the slightly cooler shade of our sun shelter. So was it that we saw *Otahki* emerge from her lodge and after a moment move slowly out into the camp circle, pausing now and then to speak with some of those she met. Bear Head gave me a nod and a look of understanding when she appeared, and we kept our eyes upon her; and so, as it proved, did his two wives, for suddenly the elder of them exclaimed: "Bear Head! Look at *Otahki*, across there; close in front of Three Bulls' lodge, standing and talking with Handsome Man. What a bad one she is."

"Pretending to be so good! What can they be talking about? I am minded to run and call Otter Woman out, so that she can get Talks-with-the-Buffalo out to see them there," said the younger wife.

"You two, you are not to speak of it to anyone. It matters not to us what that woman does," Bear Head emphatically told them.

"But it does concern us. You know how mean she is to Otter Woman; we should do all that we can to help her, she our close friend," pleaded the older wife.

"You two, you heard me," Bear Head crossly replied. And just then *Otahki* and Handsome Man parted, she strolling down to the lower end of camp and thence back to her lodge, and he entered Three Bulls' lodge, in which he was a guest.

Later in the day, when for a moment we chanced to be alone, Bear Head said to me: "Those two, this morning; no doubt they arranged for another love meeting in the brush."

Otahki and Otter Woman, always together as was proper, were the water carriers for Talks-with-the-Buffalo's lodge. On this evening, near sunset it was, as the two were going for a supply to last the night, *Otahki* suddenly exclaimed: "Oh, I forgot that I need water for myself; for washing my other gown. I will go back for another bucket and meet you at the creek."

Otter Woman went on across camp and into the trail running through the timber to the creek and, when about halfway to the stream, heard a quick step close in her rear. It couldn't be *Otahki* back so soon, she thought, and then, before she could turn to look, Handsome Man was upon her; clasping her tightly to him; pinioning her arms to her sides and saying, "You are here, my sweetheart. I am glad; glad. Come, hurry. Our horses are out here a little way; a good one for you."

"Let me go, you dog-face, you nothing-man," she cried, struggling to free herself.

"Why talk that way? This is no time to talk. Come on," he urged.

Harder than ever she tried to get out from his encircling arms; to bite him. Little by little he was forcing her backward from the trail; suddenly her foot struck a fallen sapling and she went down upon her back, he with her; and then he was trying to raise her up onto her feet. She felt for her sheath knife with her now free hand; grasped its handle but could not draw it. He was saying to her: "Why pretend, my sweetheart? Come, we must hurry to the horses."

"You dog-face! Are you crazy? Go with you? Never! Let me go. Let me go," she cried.

And then they heard one all but shout: "Badger Woman! Look at them. Look at her, that Otter Woman; she who always pretends to be so good."

At that, Handsome Man sprang off into the brush, and, free of him, Otter Woman got up and faced *Otahki* and that one with her, solemn-faced Badger Woman, sits-beside-him-wife of Red Bird's Tail. And laughing, dancing, pointing, *Otahki* again said to Badger Woman: "Oh, what a two-tongue she is! It was only this morning that she said that Handsome Man was nothing to her; no more than the passing wind. Well, Talks-with-the-Buffalo shall know of it at once. I am going, going, going to tell him, at once, to tell him what we found here."

Away she went, lightly running, swinging her empty pail. And said Otter Woman to the other: "I hope that you don't think that I am a bad one, a liar. I had never spoken with that dog-face. He surprised me, seized me; wanted me to run off with him. I was trying to get at my knife to stab him when you two came."

Old Badger Woman made no reply to that; she only stood and stared at the young one, sorrowfully stared at her, then turned and went back upon the trail, shaking her head, muttering to herself.

Hardly knowing what she was doing, Otter Woman recovered

her bucket, filled it at the creek, and trembling turned back toward camp. She dreaded returning to her lodge and facing Talks-with-the-Buffalo. She was minded to go straight to her father and mother, seek their protection. But no. She was innocent; never in her whole life had she done anything that was not right; all knew that she was a good, virtuous woman. She would tell her man that the Blood, the dog-face that he was, had made a surprise attack upon her, and he could not help believing that she spoke the truth. "Oh, Sun; all you Above Ones: Pity me; help me," she silently prayed, and thrust aside the door curtain and went in.

But only *Paiota* and *Otahki* were within; and the latter meanly smiling, said to her: "You are wondering where is our man? Well, he took up his gun and went out to kill your sweetheart, Hand-some Man."

"You bad woman, you know that he is no sweetheart of mine. Oh, what a terrible tongue you are!" Otter Woman replied.

"I know, and so does Badger Woman, what we saw out there near the creek. *Ha!* when our man returns he will make you cry; and then out you go, you and all that you have here."

Said Otter Woman then to the elder wife: "Surely you don't believe that the dog-face Blood is anything to me?"

"Girl, all I know about is what I hear. I am sorry, but truly it all looks bad for you," *Paiota* replied.

None of this came to us until later; but about this time we in Bear Head's lodge became aware of excitement on the other side of camp, and presently Bear Head went out to learn what was going on there. So was it that, after a while, we learned that Talks-with-the-Buffalo was seeking Handsome Man; wanting to kill him. But the latter had disappeared, gone off with two horses, one of them owned by a Blood friend, and taken without his knowledge or consent. Upon learning that, Talks-with-the-Buffalo had come home, saddled his fastest buffalo horse, and set out in pursuit of him. And then, of course, and soon, we learned, the whole camp learned what it was all about, *Otahki* being only too eager to tell of her and Badger Woman's discovery in the timber.

The tale of it came to Eagle Plume's lodge, and he and his woman hurried to their daughter and urged her to return to them; they were not going to allow her to be disfigured because of *Otahki's* lies. And that one they denounced with all the epithets of the Blackfoot language. But Otter Woman would not listen to their pleadings. She had done no wrong; she had prayed the Above Ones for help; they were with her, they would not allow her to suffer for something that she had not done. To leave her man's lodge now would be to admit that she was guilty.

It was near midnight when Eagle Plume and his woman went back to their lodge, without their daughter. And when, a little later, we took to our couches, Talks-with-the-Buffalo had not returned.

But he came back sometime in the night, so Bear Head's elder wife said when she had built our morning fire and awakened us. And she had it from *Paiota* that he had not overtaken Handsome Man.

As Bear Head and I were returning from our early plunge in the creek, he said to me: "In Talks-with-the-Buffalo's lodge, this morning, there will be a big talk about Otter Woman. If he fails to invite us, we must anyhow attend it."

"Will you tell the gathering what we saw out here, two nights back?" I asked.

"I don't know. I don't know what I shall do about it." And then, when we were almost to the doorway of our lodge, he brought me to a stand and added: "The strength of our tribe is in our women. The good ones should be praised, favored in every way; the bad ones should be punished."

It was about ten o'clock when Talks-with-the-Buffalo stood before his lodge and shouted invitations to this and that prominent man of the camp to come to his lodge for a talk. Bear Head and I were not named. We saw the great ones go in one by one: White Calf, the head chief; Running Crane; Three Suns; Fast Buffalo Horse; Little Dog; and other clan chiefs and medicine men to the number of twelve. Then we slipped in after them and seated ourselves just to the right of the doorway. Came in then still another uninvited one, Otter Woman's father, Eagle Plume, and sat down on my right. His face was grim. And last of all came Badger Woman and her man and sat just within the doorway.

Grim, too, was Talks-with-the-Buffalo, upon his couch at the rear of the lodge. *Paiota*, solemn of face, sat with him as was her right. Upon her own couch, to the left of the fireplace, was *Otahki*, erect, bright eyed, eager for the talk to begin. Upon a third couch, between that of *Otahki* and the doorway, sat Otter Woman; bowed over; motionless; blanket over her head and partly concealing her face. The invited ones were all of them on the right side of the lodge, their seats spreadings of soft buffalo robes, White Calf nearest of them to their host.

None spoke. The silence became oppressive. White Calf broke it: "Yes?" he asked.

"Ah, yes," Talks-with-the-Buffalo replied, and then: "My friends, you have heard recent talk about one of my women, Otter Woman, there sitting. I now want you to hear just what her accuser says of her, and then help me decide what shall be done about it."

"*Ah. Ah*," several of the gathering acquiesced, and he sternly said to the accuser: "*Otahki!* Talk!"

"*Ah!* I will! she eagerly replied. And then: "Chiefs, and you, sacred men, listen: From the time when Otter Woman came here to live with us, I suspected that she was bad, and then I made certain that she was. It was when Handsome Man came dancing to where we sat. I had borrowed her awl, and wanting it, she held out her hand and said to me: 'Give me Handsome Man.' It was him she was thinking about, not her work. It was him she wanted, not our own man, so good and kind to her. Given the opportunity, I knew she would be his sweetheart. So was it that I decided to watch her closely.

"Last evening, as on every evening, she and I went to get water for the night. I forgot that I needed some for myself, and when we were halfway to the creek I remembered and went back for another bucket. Again on my way to the creek, I asked Badger Woman to go with me, and she did. As we were going along we heard talking, saw a movement of some brush near the trail; we went nearer and saw a man and a woman upon the ground. The man saw us, got up and ran away. He was Handsome Man. And then we saw that the other was Otter Woman. I had been right. She was a bad woman. I ran and told our man about it. There. I have told you the truth. That is all."

Another long silence. Broken by White Calf: "Badger Woman, what have you to tell us about this?"

The old woman did not reply, nor look up. She stared at the fire-place, stonily, as though she had not heard the chief. And after a little he said, impatiently: "Come now, you heard me. Talk!"

Then as it became evident that she did not intend to reply, old Red Bird's Tail gave her a vicious nudge and hissed: "Talk, woman! Answer him, if you don't want me to make you cry."

"Don't strike me, you mean old man," she said to him, and then to White Calf, to us all: "Oh, how I hate tale-bearing. Hate it! Hate it! But if you must know: yes, we came upon the two, out there in the timber. But I don't believe that Otter Woman is that Blood man's sweetheart; she appeared to be angry; as though she had been fighting him."

"So I was. I was trying to get out my knife and stab him," Otter Woman cried.

"*Ha!* If he wasn't her sweetheart, if she hated him, why didn't she cry out, shout for help, as any frightened woman would have done?" *Otahki* loudly queried. And I saw that that impressed the chiefs, several of them nodding to one another, and Little Dog exclaiming: "*Ah*, Proof enough that she was there to meet the worthless Handsome Man."

It was then that we heard a commotion in the crowd that had gathered before the lodge; subdued talk and exclamations of surprise; and bounced in and stood glaring at us, Otter Woman's mother. And all there looked up at her as though they could not believe their eyes, their mouths wide open in astonishment; for never before in the history of the tribe had a woman intentionally come into the presence of her son-in-law. It was something that was just not done; son-in-law and mother-in-law used every precaution to avoid even seeing one another at a distance.

Said this one now: "Yes, I know what you all think of me, but I don't care." She ran on and knelt beside her daughter, clasped her in her arms, and continued: "You, Little Dog, I heard what you said. Yes, and I know what you all think. But I am here to tell you that you are wrong; that my daughter has ever despised that Handsome

Man. You shall not, shall not punish her, mutilate her for something that she has not done!"

With that, she clasped Otter Woman closer to her and sat glaring at drooped over Talks-with-the-Buffalo and at the row of chiefs; and they were mute, not yet having recovered from their astonishment at her presence here.

Bear Head gave a little cough. Whispered to me: "I am going to tell them what we know of this."

"Yes," I sighed, and he began.

"Talks-with-the-Buffalo; chiefs; and you, oh, Sun's men: *Apikuni*, here at my side, and I were not invited to this talk, but we anyhow came, and for a purpose—for the good of our tribe. You remember what happened to us some summers back, when a certain woman, vowing that she was pure, a faithful wife, took part in building our great offering to Sun, Sun's lodge, and afterward proved to have been a bad woman. Because of her lying vow her man died; our war parties were defeated; many of our hunters crippled, some killed in their endeavors to keep their loved ones supplied with food. Well, it is to prevent another such misfortune that *Apikuni* and I are here. My friends, not Otter Woman, but her accuser, that woman there, is the unfaithful wife, the secret sweetheart of that one we call Handsome Man."

As Bear Head finished, he was rigidly pointing to *Otahki*. And suddenly she drooped; shrank back from the edge of her couch and faltered: "Oh, no. No. You lie."

"Oh, yes, you bad one. And know this: *Apikuni* and I are the two who discovered you and Handsome Man hugging one another there on the trail," he replied.

"You saw them doing that? When? Tell us about it," Talks-with-the-Buffalo demanded.

"Oh, no. No," *Otahki* wailed; and drawing her blanket over her head, sank still lower upon her couch and trembled with fear of what was to come.

Bear Head was not five minutes in telling of our discovery of the two in the timber and of *Otahki's* meeting with her lover in camp on the following day. He finished, and Talks-with-the-Buffalo said to him: "Bear Head, it was good of you and *Apikuni* to come and tell us all this. But for you we would doubtless have punished the wrong woman. It is terrible, how very bad some women are. Very, very terrible. And there is something more that I want to know about this bad one of mine." And then he roared, "You *Otahki!* Sit up! Remove your blanket!"

"Oh, no. No," she pleaded, then shrieked as he sprang to her, tore off her blanket, and jounced her to a sitting position upon her couch. Returning then to his place, he said to her: "The truth, now, or I will cut out your tongue: As are a man and wife to one another, so were you with that Blood man, out there in the timber?"

Her "Yes" was so low that we barely heard it.

"And then you lied to him; you told him that Otter Woman loved him, wanted to run off with him to his Blood tribe."

Again a faltering, frightened "Yes."

"You didn't care how bad, how mean you were if only you could get Otter Woman into trouble, cause her to be despised by all. Well, we have now six such women in our camp, and you shall be a seventh one."

"Oh, no! No! No! Oh, Talks-with-the-Buffalo, oh, my man, pity me, pity me," she shrieked. And her sister *Paiota* said to him: "She is so young. Oh, only send her off, and let that be the end of it."

"You, *Paiota*, close firmly your mouth," he replied. And then to the row of us: "My friends, little did I think that I would ever be shamed as this woman has shamed me. You agree, do you not, that she should be made to suffer the punishment that our tribe has ever inflicted upon women of her kind?"

"*Ah! Ah! Ah!*" they emphatically replied.

"*Ah.* It is decided. Little Dog, Running Crane, and you, Fast Buffalo Horse, do you three seize her, firmly hold her."

"Oh, no! No! No!" the woman shrieked, springing from her couch and making for the doorway. But the three had her before she could reach it; they drew her back across the lodge and held her before her man; by arms and head firmly held her; and he, pinching her nose with thumb and finger, with one quick stroke of his knife, cut it off, and contemptuously tossed it into the fireplace. By that time I was going, and feeling a little sick. I had not wanted to see that cruel cutting, but I did. I got out into the open and saw the crowd that had gathered before the lodge scattering, each his own way and silently.

So was it that *Otahki* became one of that despised little group of cut-nosed women of the tribe—women with whom the good women would not associate; women who were refused the comfort of entering Sun's lodge and making offerings to Those Above. Daily from lodge to lodge they begged for work and food and the privilege of sleeping near the doorway. None liked to look at them, so closely did their faces resemble the face of a human skull.

No wonder that the women of the Blackfoot tribes were, with few exceptions, extremely virtuous!

CHAPTER SIXTEEN

Puhpoom[1]
(Told by Raven Quiver–Joseph Kipp)

ICCICCICCICCICCICCICCICCICCICCICCICCICCICCICCICCICCICCICCICCICCICCICC

FROM ONE OF MY OLD NOTEBOOKS: "Fort Conrad, December 20, 1883. Last night *Mastúnopachis* ("Raven Quiver," Joseph Kipp) told us another one of his long-ago, exciting adventures: his recovery of a fast buffalo horse that a Pikuni Indian had stolen from George Steel."

Here is Kipp's story:

When Matt Carroll and George Steel bought Fort Benton from the American Fur Company in 1864, they took me on as one of their clerks, though I was then only seventeen. At the time George Steel, or *Sistsikum-aiokat* ("Sleeping Thunder"), as the Blackfeet called him, owned a very fast buffalo horse named Puhpoom that he greatly prized. He thought so much of it that he appointed me to take especially good care of it.

I loved that black horse Puhpoom. Large and powerful he was, and of fiery eye and willful temper; yet to me he was always gentle, whinnying when I went to feed him, nosing me and nipping my arms and shoulders when I was cleaning his shining coat, and always standing still for me to mount him for his daily exercise. I loved to see Sleeping Thunder start out on him for a buffalo run. How grand, how brave they were—the horse prancing, shaking his beautiful head and jerking on the bit, eager to be off; the man, keen-eyed, long-haired, and of fine figure, sitting the saddle as if he had grown there!

[1] First published in *The Youth's Companion* (July 3, 1923).

And how elegant was his dress, a long coat of fine blue cloth and brass buttons, trousers to match, and brightly polished boots.

Sometimes Sleeping Thunder allowed me to go out with him for a buffalo run, and at such times I rode his second-best horse, a rather small but very swift and enduring sorrel. Came the spring of 1865, and we went out quite often for a run, each carrying a weapon new in the country, a Henry repeating rifle. Baptiste Champine or Joseph Trombley always followed us with team and wagon to help butcher our kills and bring in the meat.

To see Sleeping Thunder and that black horse approach and run a herd of buffalo was a sight worth while. We would keep out of sight of a herd as much as possible until we were near to it, Puhpoom dancing along sideways and trying to get the bit in his teeth in his eagerness to rush right in among the animals. When we reached the last point of concealment, in a coulee or near the brow of a ridge, Sleeping Thunder would suddenly give the horse his way, and with quick, long leaps it would go with almost the speed of an antelope, its ears flat back, and its eyes all alight with red fire. Right into the thick of the herd it would lope, scattering the frightened, fleeing animals; and such was its training that the rider had only to head it toward a certain one of them and point with his gun, and it would run up alongside, always on its right, and swerve out a little after the gun was fired. Then Sleeping Thunder would indicate the next one he wanted, and Puhpoom would quickly take him on to it. So they would go, on and on, often for more than a mile, and leave in their wake a string of dead and dying cows. Seldom did Sleeping Thunder kill less than eight cows on a run; and once, running a herd in the level fort bottom, he killed sixteen, every one of them a selected, fat cow!

The longer I cared for that horse the more I loved it. Several times a day, when free to do so, I would go to the stable and comb and brush it and talk to it and see that its manger was full of the greenest of hay.

The stable was on the north side of the fort. A small door in the adobe wall of the stockade gave admittance to it and to the high corral enclosing it. There was a gate in the corral, and it, as well as the little door, was padlocked every night. That was my duty, and I never failed to do it. Mine also, the duty to feed and water Puhpoom every morning as soon as I got my clothes on.

Winter came on; and now that the fur of the buffalo was at its best, full grown, thick, and dark, Sleeping Thunder rode Puhpoom out to the chase more often than ever. All was well. Came Christmas Eve. On the morrow we were to have, employees and all, the great feast of the year—a feast to be topped off with that greatest of all delicacies, real plum pudding. Sleeping Thunder's wife and my mother had been making them for days—a pudding for every family in the fort.

"Mother, dear mother, make me a little one, all for myself," I asked of her, and she said that she would.

"This is the Big Medicine Day," I said to myself when I got up the next morning. "Christmas Day; Plum-Pudding Day!" I hurried on my clothes. I built the fires in kitchen, living room, and office, hurried out to the stable. Puhpoom was not in his stall. "He has loosened his rope; is in with some other horse," I said and ran the whole length of the stable only to find that he was nowhere in sight. And then I noticed that the corral gate was open; its heavy chain, dangling from it; the padlock, broken, was lying on the ground. In the dust were the moccasin prints of a man and the tracks of a horse going out.

I ran back into the fort, up the stairs and into Sleeping Thunder's bedroom, shouting to him: "Puhpoom is gone! Someone has stolen him!"

Sleeping Thunder rose on one elbow and looked at me with half-open eyes. "What do you mean?" he asked. "Stolen Puhpoom—they couldn't do that, you know!"

"But they have! Someone has taken him!" I yelled, and told him about the open gate, the broken padlock, the horse tracks and man tracks in the dust.

Sleeping Thunder sprang out of bed quickly and, reaching for his clothes, shouted: "Run! Rouse the fort. Tell Baptiste Champine to come to me at once."

Most of the employees were already up, and I soon had them gathered with Champine—he was the fort's hunter—in the office. Sleeping Thunder came in half-dressed. "Baptiste, someone has stolen Puhpoom," he said, so excited that he breathed heavily and the words almost choked him. "Now hurry. Take your men and get after the thief. I'll give two hundred dollars to whoever recovers the horse."

We were out of the room and running for the stable almost before he finished speaking. Breakfast? We hadn't time for it. We saddled quicker than we had ever done before, and took to the trail of the thief. There was no snow in the bottom, but here and there in the ground the tracks of the horse showed dimly. They led us straight down the bottom and up on the hard, gravelly ridge, but there we lost them. In that direction, at the mouth of Marias River, the Gros Ventres were encamped; evidently someone from there had taken the horse. We were about to go on when Baptiste, off to our left, called to us: "I have the trail. Come on."

He did have it. The thief had turned and had ridden north toward Teton River. Step by step we followed the tracks across the ridge and down to the rim of the valley. In it, along both sides of the timbered stream was the camp of the North Blackfeet, three hundred and more lodges. That branch of the great confederacy of tribes was not friendly to us. True, many of the hunters and their women came daily to the fort to trade with us, but they came with anger in their hearts and cursed us while exchanging the buffalo robes and furs for our guns and ammunition and various goods. It was that one of their war parties had recently met some white trappers at the Three Forks of the Missouri and in a fight with them had lost five men, and now the whole tribe was in a rage. The Big Knives had spilled Blackfoot blood, and Big Knives' blood must in turn be spilled.

There on the top of the slope we held a short council. Some were for going down into the camp and looking for the buffalo horse; others frankly acknowledged that they were afraid to go. Baptiste settled the matter by saying that we should all return to the fort and Sleeping Thunder. So back we went.

"*Ha!* Hum! So that's where Puhpoom is, in the Blackfoot camp!"

Sleeping Thunder exclaimed when Baptiste told him the result of our search. And then he was silent a long time, twisting about nervously in his big armchair; we stood quietly before him.

"Well, my men, you may go to your quarters," he said at last. It is Christmas Day, you know. I hope you will all have a good dinner and enjoy yourselves."

The men thanked him and went out. I remained. "Sleeping Thunder, let me try to get Puhpoom back," I pleaded.

"No," he answered very shortly. "I am responsible to your father, away down there in St. Louis, for your safety. What would he say to me if I should allow you to take such a risk and you were to be killed? And besides—you have a big place in my heart. I love you too well to allow you to take any chances of being killed. You may go now. I'll try to think of some way to recover Puhpoom."

I went to my mother's room—she was with Sleeping Thunder's woman, they cooking the big dinner—and lay down. I felt sick. Heartsick. I loved Puhpoom, and he was gone. I would never see him again. At last I fell asleep.

My mother awakened me for the big meal, and I took my place at the table. Sleeping Thunder put a roast boss rib and some rice upon my plate and I tried to eat. I took a few mouthfuls and gave up. I couldn't even eat the dish of plum pudding that my mother set before me, so sick was I over the loss of Puhpoom.

Several days passed in which a few families came from the Blackfoot camp to trade. They did not speak about Puhpoom, nor did we. On the third day came in witty, sharp-tongued Three Bears, the Blackfoot camp crier, and orated before us all: "Our Eagle Ribs, *ha!* What a powerful hunter he is! Maybe you Big Knives haven't heard that he recently obtained a fast buffalo horse, a big, powerful, black, fast buffalo horse. Well, yesterday he ran a buffalo herd on that horse and killed nine fat cows. Yes, he is the fastest, best-trained buffalo horse that any of us ever saw. Eagle Ribs says that he would not part with him for all of the trade goods in this many-houses place."

None of us spoke when Three Bears had given us his news. We were all looking at Sleeping Thunder, standing back of the trade counter, grimly scowling. Laughing shrilly, Three Bears turned and went out of the door. Then Baptiste Champine stepped up to Sleeping Thunder and said: "Chief, what do you say to our going over to camp and taking your Puhpoom away from that thieving Eagle Ribs?"

"No. It can't be done without a killing; you would probably all be killed. And even if you weren't, that would end our trade with the tribe; they would go north to the Hudson's Bay Company with their robes. All about it is, I lose Puhpoom."

Now came a time of misery for me and for Sleeping Thunder, too, as every few days Three Bears would come over from the Teton and, strutting around in the fort, boast of Eagle Rib's successful buffalo runs on Puhpoom. Again I asked Sleeping Thunder to allow me to try to recover the horse, and again he said that he would not let me take the risk.

Soon came a clear, still evening. I went early to bed, and after all the inmates of the fort had gone to their quarters I sneaked out to the stable, saddled the little sorrel horse, and was soon heading for the Blackfoot camp. When near it, I tied the horse in the brush and, wrapped in a blanket in Indian fashion, so partly concealing my face, I began wandering among the lodges. In a few of them the people were still chatting, smoking, singing, telling stories; and some were still going to visit here and there. I was terribly scared of them; if anyone should stop me, the chances were that I could never get out of the camp alive. I gripped my six-shooter under my blanket and cocked the hammer, ready to fire if I must and to run for my horse. Once a passing man did speak to me. "Where are you going?" he asked.

I gave him, hoarsely, a flippant answer: *"Kahkok saiskinip"* ("You are not to know"). He laughed and kept under his way.

Well, although I wandered all through the great camp and examined every one of the buffalo horses tied before the lodges of their owners, I could not find Puhpoom; and well I knew that Eagle Ribs had not turned him loose with his herd; he had either hidden him away from camp or had ridden him to visit some brother tribe, the Pikunis or Kainahs. Daybreak was now not far off, so I hurried back to my sorrel horse and rode home, terribly disappointed at the failure of my search but determined to search again on the following night. I got back to the fort and into bed just in time to escape being seen by some of the early risers.

I was very sleepy all that day. At sundown I ate a hearty meal and went to bed, intending to sleep a short time and then start out again in quest of Puhpoom. When I awoke the fire in the hearth was out, so I knew that the night was half-gone. Nevertheless I got up, hurriedly dressed, and was soon riding the sorrel back to the Teton. Again I tied my horse below the camp, and this time sneaked straight up to Eagle Rib's lodge—not to be mistaken, for it was painted with the animals of his medicine, four otters. My heart went low when I saw that Puhpoom was not tied before it. However, I had learned during the day that Eagle Ribs was at home, so it was certain that he had the horse hidden somewhere out from camp.

Returning to the sorrel, I got into the saddle and rode through the timber below the camp, then the timber above it, and without result. And in the east the sky was whitening with the first light of day. Eagle Rib's lodge was in that part of the camp on the north side of the river, and straight back of it a deep, wide, partly timbered coulee ran well up into the plain. Day was so near that I felt I should not go up it. But I was desperate, and regardless of the risk, I went. I passed several bands of horses, some grazing, some resting. And then, in a small, grassy park between two stands of timber—oh, I could hardly believe my eyes—there was Puhpoom, picketed in the center of it! He whinnied—and how good the sound of it was in my ears. Riding close, I jumped down and took his rope from the picket pin. He trotted to me and I put my arms around his neck and hugged him. Then back up on the sorrel and leading him, and he so willing, I turned down the coulee on a swift lope. Ha! Just as I got to the mouth of it I nearly ran into an early horse herder, a gun in his hands, a coiled rope on his arm. He aimed his old weapon at me, fired, missed, then began yelling: "Eagle Ribs! Eagle Ribs. Here is Raven Quiver running off with Puhpoom!"

I sped through the north-side camp and crossed the iced river before any of the aroused people could get out to shoot at me. But now I had to cut through the camp on the south side of it, and several men, naked except for their breechcloths, were running out from their lodges, guns in hand, to intercept me. As I approached the nearest of the lodges, its door curtain was suddenly flipped aside and old Three Bears poked out his head, and open mouthed, big eyed, stared at me.

"Tell Eagle Ribs to come tonight, and get Puhpoom," I yelled to him.

Then two men fired at me, missed, and I was clear of the camp. But as I topped the rim of the valley I looked back, saw some riders starting from both camps after me. I didn't have to urge on the sorrel and Puhpoom; they were heading for home, for their warm stable and good green hay; they fairly flew. My pursuers followed me only to the top of the ridge between the two rivers and there came to a stand, giving up the chase. A little later I came to the big gate of the fort, yelled for admittance, and the watchman let me in. As I got out of the saddle, Sleeping Thunder came running down his stairway and straight to Puhpoom.

"Oh, boy!" he said to me. "You got him back! You got him back! Your mother has been crying; we were all terribly worried, wondering what had become of you. But you got Puhpoom back to me. The two hundred dollars are yours. Come on to the office and tell me all about it."

That very afternoon Three Bears again came to the fort, and we twitted him so about my recovery of Puhpoom that he didn't remain long. As he was leaving, Sleeping Thunder said to him: "You tell Eagle Ribs that, from now on, two men will sleep in the stable. So, if he tries again to steal Puhpoom, he will surely be killed."

Needless to say that Eagle Ribs heeded the warning.

CHAPTER SEVENTEEN

Battle on Sun River[1]
(Told by Three Suns)

IN THE AUTUMN OF 1833 the Pikunis killed a large war party of Crow Indians on Point-of-Rocks River, or, as the fur traders later named it, Sun River. The story of the killing and of all that led up to it was often and best told by Three Suns, a noted Pikuni chief and warrior, who died in his camp on Two Medicine Lodges River, Blackfoot Indian reservation, Montana, in 1896, more than sixty years after the battle. Follows his story as he used to tell it, as nearly as we can remember it after all these years:

The valleys of Point-of-Rocks River, Milk (Teton) River, and Big (Missouri) River were favorite wintering places of our people in the long-ago. They afforded good shelter and wood for our lodges; and buffalo, elk, deer, antelope, and beavers were very plentiful. When I was in my eighth summer, our Pikuni tribe, after trading our furs to the whites on North Big River (the Saskatchewan), moved down there to winter and as usual split into various camps for easier hunting and trapping.

So was it that my father Bear Chief located his camp of about forty lodges on Milk (Teton) River close north of Red Old Man's Butte (now Priest's Butte). Calf Looking with his many lodges located on Point-of-Rocks River right where, later on, the whites' road (Fort Benton to Helena) crossed the stream. Chief Big Lake with his very many lodges moved on to Big River and camped where, long after-

[1] Published in *The Great Falls Tribune* (September 5 and 12, 1937).

ward, some Black Robes lived. Old Mission, not far below there, was Heavy Shield's camp, and Big Skunk set up his camp of many lodges on Point-of-Rocks River, close to where it flows into Big River.

Came Falling-Leaves Moon and a number of the men of my father's camp and Calf Looking's camp set out to raid the horses of the Flatheads (Kalispel tribe), going by way of the pass at the head of Two Medicine Lodges River. There were four who went from Calf Looking's camp and one of them was Big Snake, he who had the longest hair of all of our people, men and women. It was gray, and its braids were so long that they hung down almost to the ground as he walked. To the right front braid was always tied a white shell in which were seven holes, they representing the Seven Persons (Ursa Major), to whom he prayed. In a sun-given vision that he had experienced they had appeared to him and said they would be his sacred, powerful helpers.

It was in the Falling-Leaves moon when the war party set out to raid the Flatheads, and winter had come when the members of it from my father's camp returned—came charging, singing in with many horses that they had taken from the Flatheads and proudly waving some Flathead scalps. And at once they inquired for the four other members of their party: Big Snake, Yellow Weasel, Cut Finger, and New Robe. Had we seen them or heard of their return? Learning that we knew nothing of them, they went on to say that, soon after they had crossed the Backbone (the Rockies), Big Snake and his three friends had left them; had turned north to raid the Kutenai people, and they wondered what had been their success.

Early morning after the return of the war party, my father told me to round up our horses and catch two of them, his fast buffalo horse, Short Tail, and my favorite horse, Striped Face, for he was going hunting and I was to accompany him and help him butcher his kills.

I soon had the horses tied before our lodge. My mother set food before us. We ate plenty, saddled, and were off, riding southward out upon the plain, expecting soon to sight a herd of buffalo. But none were in sight when we topped the rim of the plain, and we rode on and on, my father repeatedly saying: "Now, this is strange! But three days ago everywhere out here were herds of buffalo grazing, resting, and now there are none. Nor have our hunters been out this way. Why, then, did the herds leave so suddenly? I don't like it. I believe that it is a warning that danger of some kind threatens us."

"Then let us go back, go home, or hunt north of our camp," I proposed.

"No. We will keep on. Watch carefully ahead for the danger, whatever it may prove to be," my father answered.

We rode on and on, still without sighting a buffalo herd nor even any old, straggling bulls. So going, we came to a large, grassy lake, upon which many flocks of swans, geese, and ducks were resting, feeding, loudly honking and quacking—a flock now and then rising and going on southward toward the Always-Summer-Land.

Said my father: "Those water birds are better off than we are. They can go where Cold Maker cannot follow them, and we have to endure his snow and cold."

"But why can't we all go, too, down into that Always-Summer-Land?" I asked.

"Good reason why we can't: so many tribes of enemies down there that they would kill us off."

No sooner had he answered my question when, topping a little ridge just beyond the south end of the lake, we discovered not far ahead a party of men on foot—a war party of some kind, without doubt. And seeing us, one of them stepped aside from the others and signed to us: "Come on. Join us. Smoke with us. Our hearts are good. We will be at peace with you."

"Oh, don't go. They are our enemies. They will kill us," I cried to my father.

Again the man signed to us, this time saying: "Come on. Join us. Smoke with us. We are Crows. We will be friends together."

Said my father to me: "My son, though they are Crows, our worst enemies, I cannot be a coward. I have to accept their offer, go smoke with them. So come on."

Oh, how frightened I was as we neared those many Crows—fifty-three of them—all well armed, staring solemnly at us. Signed their leader as we came to them and got down from our horses: "It is good that you have come to smoke with us Crows. Now, tell us, who are you?"

Signed my father, "We are Pikunis." Then said to me, as it is bad luck for men to speak their own names: "Son, tell them who I am."

Tremblingly I complied. "He is my father. His name, it is Bear Chief. He is a Pikuni chief," I signed.

"Good," the Crow leader signed. And then: "You are Bear Chief, Pikuni chief. I am Painted Shield, Crow chief. So now we will sit and smoke together and have a good talk."

With that he pointed to the near top of a small ridge that the wind had blown bare of snow. We went there, sat down in a circle, and Painted Shield had one of the men fill and light a big pipe to be smoked in turn by all. As it came to my father I felt better and said to him: "You smoke the peace pipe with them, so is it that we are safe. They will not harm us in any way."

"With any other enemy war party that would be true. But the Crows are different. They are liars. A peace smoke means nothing to them. Son, I have to be very wise else this will be the end for us," my father answered, and again I was full of fear.

As the pipe went the round of our circle, was smoked out, refilled, and started on another round of us, my father and the Crow chief sign-talked to one another. Painted Shield said that he was leading his party to cross the Backbone and raid the horse herds of the west-side people; my father, in turn, said that we were on our way from our camp on Milk River to visit in the camp of the Pikuni chief, Calf Looking, on Point-of-Rocks River. Hearing him say that, how surprised I felt. Almost I cried out to him about it but held back in time, well knowing that whatever he said or did he would have good reason for it.

And then, at last, my father signed to Painted Shield: "My friend, see, Cold Maker is coming down from the north with more cold wind and snow. Best that you and your friends go with me to Calf Looking's camp and rest. Eat plenty, sleep in the warm lodges, and so in the morning be strong to go on your way."

All of the Crows looked to the north. True, Cold Maker was coming, hidden in a black cloud low down upon the plain. Signed Painted

Shield: "Bear Chief, it is true; Cold Maker is coming. We will be glad to go with you to the camp of your friends for the night. So let us go at once. You and your son lead the way. Walk your horses, even trot them. We will keep up with you."

We had traveled but a little way when Cold Maker overtook us with his fierce, cold wind and snow so blinding that we could only dimly see each other. But my father was sure of his course, and as we neared Point-of-Rocks River, Cold Maker was suddenly gone on with his storm and Sun was setting in clear, blue sky. As he passed out of sight behind the Backbone, we came to the rim of Point-of-Rocks River and looked down upon the camp of Calf Looking. But instead of the forty lodges of his band we could see only ten, and my father groaned: *"Haiya, haiya!* Oh, how unfortunate for us. So few of them there! Oh, Sun. Pity us. Help us in some way to survive the danger of these many Crows."

Then Painted Shield was signing to him: "Those down there are the lodges of your kind, your friends?"

Smiling, pretending to be happy, my father answered: "Yes, those down there are my relatives. Come, we will join them. Good are their hearts. Soon you will be resting before their lodge fires, eating plenty, smoking." And with that he led us on, loudly singing our song of peace and friendship. All of the people of the lodges ran to stand with Calf Looking and his women before his lodge and stare at us, the men with weapons ready for instant use. And oh, how big, how frightened were the women's and children's eyes.

Calf Looking, laying aside his gun, advanced to meet us, and my father signed and also said to him: "Calf Looking, this is Painted Shield and his war party of Crows. I invited them to stop with you all for the night."

"Good! Good!" he signed to Painted Shield. "Crow chief, we are glad that you have come. You all will rest and smoke and eat with us. My lodge will not hold you all, so, Painted Shield, divide your men, half of them to stop in that lodge next to mine, the lodge of my brother, Running Rabbit."

"I will do as you say. Generous you are," Painted Shield sign-answered and, turning to his men, named those of them to go into

Running Rabbit's lodge. Then soon the rest of us were sitting in Calf Looking's lodge, and his wives were hurrying to prepare food for us. He was filling his big pipe, then passing it to Painted Shield to light. As it went from hand to hand along the row of the Crows, and they began talking to one another, my father said to Calf Looking: "Why are you so few? Where are the others of your band?"

"Three days back they moved up to Shield-Floated-Away River (Dearborn River), there to hunt bighorns."

"Oh that I could have known it so that I could have taken these Crows to my camp instead of to yours. They so many, we so few. I feel that this night may mean the end of all of us."

"But out there where you met them they smoked with you, did they not? And here they are smoking with us. You are needlessly worried for us. Smokers of a peace pipe do not harm the givers of it."

"Were they Flatheads, Kutenais, or other enemies, that would be true. But Crows, our very worst enemies, are different. Well you know what liars they are . . . ."

"But still they would not turn on us after smoking with us. So stop worrying. I am sure that, come morning, these Crows will peacefully go upon their way," Calf Looking ended.

My father just sat quietly, staring at the fire, eating but little when the food was passed to us, taking no part in the sign-talking of the Crows and Calf Looking and several of the men of the camp who had come in to visit and smoke. One of them was Little Otter, whose lodge was the fourth one above us.

Night had come when we finished eating, and Calf Looking again filled his big pipe and passed it for the circle of the gathering to smoke. Then, as Painted Shield was sign-telling of a raid he and some of his friends had made upon a camp of Parted Hairs (Sioux), we were startled by sudden shrieking of women, Little Otter's wives. One of them shouted: "Little Otter, come! Hurry! Your dog, Short Tail, has brought in a fresh scalp . . . ."

Then another wife: "Little Otter! It is the long, shell-tied-to-it hair braid of Big Snake. These Crows surely killed him, hid his scalp here in the snow."

At that, we Pikunis stared questioningly at one another, and, as

257

Little Otter arose and hurried from us, the Crow chief signed to Calf Looking: "Those women yelling, frightened. What troubles them?"

"It is nothing. Just that a dog bit one of Little Otter's women," he answered.

Said my father to Calf Looking: "We have but one chance. Someone must hurry to Big Lake for help, get him and his many braves here before day comes."

Said White Wolf: "I will send my son, Bird Rattle, on my fastest horse."

"Do that, but don't jump up and hurry out. We are being watched. Soon I will give you cause to go."

True, the Crows were worried. They sat stiffly up, watching my father, Calf Looking, and White Wolf as they talked, and now and then they spoke to one another, their voices low.

Calf Looking began thrusting his hand in his tobacco sack, then into one at the head of his couch. He frowned, grunted, and said and signed to White Wolf: "My north white men's rope tobacco is all gone. You have plenty of it. Bring some for our Crow friends and us to smoke."

"*Ah! Ah!*" White Wolf replied and, rising, carefully wrapped his buffalo robe around him and went out.

Calf Looking smiled, briefly hummed a peace song, appeared to be happy and carefree, and, turning to face Painted Shield, signed to him: "Chief, tell us of your travels, where your people were camped when you left them, and by what way you came up into the country of the Pikunis."

Signed Painted Shield: "Where Big Horn River joins Elk River (Yellowstone) we left our people. That was fourteen nights ago. We crossed Elk River there, crossed Big River where your Bear River (Marias) runs into it, followed up your Milk (Teton) River for a long way, and then struck across the plain. We were going to cross the big mountains at the head of your Two Medicine Lodges River. We have come far. We are tired. It is good that we eat, rest, and smoke with you tonight and so be strong to go on our way tomorrow."

Said my father to Calf Looking: "The liar. They were not headed to cross the mountains. They have been up there. Somewhere up there they killed our good friend, Big Snake, and doubtless his three companions also." And then he signed to Painted Shield: "We are glad that you and your friends are here resting with us. Tomorrow you all will be strong enough to go on across the big mountains."

White Wolf then returned. As he came in through the doorway, one of Calf Looking's wives excitedly cried to him: "White Wolf, did you manage to send your son for help for us?"

My father began sign-telling the Crows about a war party that he led to raid the horse herds of the Blue Paint People (Nez Percés) far beyond the Backbone country. I got up, wrapped my robe close about me, and went outside. Tied in front of the doorways were fast buffalo horses of the men who owned them. How I did want to straddle one and ride away! But no, I could not leave my father, be a coward. Whatever was to be his fate must be mine. I thought that the Crows intended to kill us all. All around camp the horses of Calf Looking and his men were grazing, hundreds of them. Of course the Crows were thinking how horses-rich they were going to be; how proud, as they would drive them into the camp of their people, down across the Elk River; how happy they would be, how happy their people, as they rode in, waving the scalps and the guns they had taken from us, and shouting that they had killed off a whole camp of the Pikunis. I could not believe that our messenger would bring Big Lake and his warriors in time to save us.

Perhaps it was not Big Snake's scalp braid that the Crows had hidden, that the dog had found. I wanted to see it. I didn't want to see it. The thought of looking at it made me feel sick. But I must see it. I must be sure that it was or was not the scalp braid of that great Thunder Pipe man. As I thrust aside the door curtain of Little Otter's lodge, his women gave little cries of fear. I said: "Women, are you sure that it is the head hair braid of Big Snake?"

"Looks just like it," Badger Woman answered.

"We are sure of it," said Spear Woman, Little Otter's sits-beside-him-wife.

"But you may be mistaken," I said.

"You shall see it. You, Badger Woman, show it to him."

"Oh, no," the other answered shivering. "I can't touch it." Then to me and pointing: "It is there under that calf robe. You, yourself, look at it."

I moved to the place between two couches, knelt, thrust my hand under the robe and touched something cold and sticky. It was the half-dried scalp part of the braid. I drew it out, stood up, held it before me, shoulder high. The long, gray, shell-tied-to-it braid, its end wrapped in otter fur, touched the ground. The shell was pierced with seven holes. Without doubt it was the right-side-of-the-head braid of Big Snake. I put it back under the robe and turned to go, but Spear Woman stopped me.

"Boy, go tell our man to come to us, with his gun remain with us, protect us as best he can," she pleaded.

And then Badger Woman: "And on your way, turn into the lodge of Sun Weasel and ask him powerfully to pray the Above Ones to save us from the Crows."

I stepped into Sun Weasel's lodge, owner of the elk-tongue sacred pipe. He was not there. His sits-beside-him-wife, Antelope Woman, was the leader of the powerful Gathered Women (*Mahtokiks*) secret society. She had on her sacred headdress of owl feathers and was praying Sun to save us. The two other wives were joining in her prayers, their cheeks wet with tears. Their children were silent, sitting big eyed, frightened. I gave Badger Woman's message and Antelope Woman said to me: "I am praying. You are from Calf Looking's lodge. Quickly return there and tell our man that we want him to come to us, to stay here with us."

My father and I had hobbled our horses. As I neared Calf Looking's lodge, I came to them, standing, head down, hungry, unable to paw the snow to get at the grass with their fettered feet. I removed their hobbles and said to them: "Go free; eat; it is not likely that we will ever ride you again."

When I entered the lodge the Crows sharply eyed me, several of them muttering something. I gave Little Otter and Sun Weasel their women's messages, but did not move. It was hard for my father and Calf Looking and the others to keep up pleasant, interesting sign-talk with the Crows. My father told of his war trails, of strange adventures with animals, and had the Crow chief tell of his experiences. But it was plain to see that they, too, were very tired of it.

At last Calf Looking went outside and, returning, said: "The Seven Persons have turned around to their middle-of-the-night position. I know that you Crows are tired. So this I propose. My women and I will move to Sun Weasel's lodge so then you many Crows can all lie down here and comfortably sleep. We will early return to feast you, smoke with you before you leave to go on across the great Backbone."

Signed the Crow chief to that: "That you say is good. You are generous. When morning comes, we will be glad to eat and smoke with you before we leave."

"Then we go," signed Calf Looking and told his women to gather and take out their buffalo robes and blankets. With that we Pikunis all moved out, stood before Sun Weasel's lodge, undecided about what to do. Said White Wolf: "Perhaps we should have our women and children take to the timber, travel up it as far as they can go, and we men remain here to do the best we can when the Crows attack."

Said my father: "No, that will not do. The Crows are watching us. Were the women and children to sneak out into the timber, they would attack us at once. They want to rest as long as they can. Without doubt they have decided to attack us when day comes and they can see to shoot straight. So I propose that you all go to your own lodges, let your fires die down, give the Crows to think that we do not suspect anything. Nor will they kill us if our messenger brings Big Lake and his fighters here before day comes. For that, pray, all of you. Pray hard."

He finished, and one of Calf Looking's women began to cry, calling out, "Oh, no! Do not keep us here. Let us women and children go to the timber . . . ."

Calf Looking put a hand over her mouth, kept it there, told her to be still, then said to my father: "Bear Chief, wise you are. We will do as you say. So now, friends, all of you to your lodges. Keep your women and children quiet and yourselves be constantly ready for whatever is to happen."

With that the men went to their lodges, my father and I with Calf Looking and his women into Sun Weasel's lodge. At once the women began to tell of their fears; the children, to whimper. Sun Weasel scolded them, made them be quiet. He, my father, Calf Looking, and I sat closely side by side before the dying fire. Occasionally those three whispered to one another, one and the other of them rising and going slightly to pull aside the door curtain and look up at the Seven Persons as they turned with the passing of the night. Never can I forget the fear I felt that night.

At last my father whispered to us: "Day is now not far off. Be ready. Be brave, all of you, for whatever we have to face."

Not long after that we heard, somewhere to the south of us, the faint boom of a gun. Hissed my father: "They come, Big Lake and his brave ones. But why, oh why, did they shoot?"

Even as he spoke we could hear faintly the thudding of many feet, and then from the doorway he said: "Going, the Crows. Running. Going down into the timber."

"Yes. And are going to find a good spot to make a strong fight against us," said Sun Weasel.

At that we followed him outside and just in time to see the last of the Crows running down into the timber bordering the river. "They heard it, that gun," said my father.

From all the lodges came the women, children, and the men to join us. All excitedly talking, all hopeful, almost sure that we were to live. Then soon we heard the thunder of many hooves. It grew louder, still louder. And then we were running to meet Big Lake and his braves, more than two hundred of them, as they came riding swiftly into camp.

My father was shouting: "Big Lake! Big Lake! Hear me! Hear me!"

And when the big crowd of them came to a stand, Big Lake shouted: "You calling me. Who are you?"

And then my father, for once speaking his own name, so excited was he: "It is I, your friend, Bear Chief. The Crows heard your gun and have gone. Why, oh, why did you shoot?"

"That young Spotted Elk, his horse fell with him. His gun went off. The Crows, which way did they go? We must hurry after them."

"Into the timber. Down the valley. But Big Lake, you must not take after them now. Wait until day comes. Then we will all take after them, kill them all off."

"Right you are. That we will do. And while we wait, get busy, you men and women of these lodges, and give us to eat and smoke."

All of them excited, happy, singing, talking, they crowded into the lodges, closely surrounding the fires. So many of them that the women could do no cooking. But it did not matter. They smoked, kept on talking and laughing and singing, the while Big Lake, Calf Looking, Sun Weasel, and my father, in Sun Weasel's lodge, made their plan to take after and kill the Crows. Nor would they hurry about it. They insisted that the men all eat and smoke and let their horses have some rest before starting out on the trail of the enemy.

So it was that the sun was well up in the blue when we all left the camp. Big Lake appointed two men, White Wolf and Cut Finger, to be scouts, to follow the trail of the Crows in the timber; we others were to ride outside it and do as they would occasionally tell us.

We soon learned that the Crows had kept on and on, apparently finding no place they liked in which to make a stand against us. So it was that, near midday, not our two scouts, but we, riding on the east rim of the valley, discovered the Crows, saw them disappearing under a high cut bank on our side of the river and not far ahead of us.

We raced to that cut bank and got down from our horses. Yes, there were the Crows, straight under us and cowering under some scattered small trees and a few clumps of willows.

Then my father and Big Lake shouted, "Now, you brave ones, shoot them. Take good aim. Shoot to kill."

And in a very short time it was ended. Fifty-three Crows, all of them killed, and not even one of us Pikunis wounded. Oh, how happy we then were. My father well said: "How completely we have avenged the Crows' killing of Big Snake and his three friends."

CHAPTER EIGHTEEN

Three Suns' War Record
(Told by Three Suns)

EVENTS IN THE LIFE of *Ninókskatosi*—("Three Suns," otherwise known as "Big Nose"), last war chief of the Pikuni Indians, were portrayed by him on an elk skin. This elk skin was given by Big Nose to Captain L. W. Cooke (later Brigadier General, U.S.A.), Third United States Infantry, while he was acting Indian agent for the Blackfoot, Blood, and Pikuni Indians in 1893–94. The following notes, interpretative of the various pictographs on the skin, were made by Captain Cooke from verbal descriptions given by Big Nose himself. At that time Big Nose was about seventy years old.

SCENE I (1870):

Represents the capture of eight Pondera (Pend d'Oreille) Indians by the South Piegans, with whom they were at war. A large village of the Piegans were in camp in the Cypress Hills near old Fort Walsh, Northwest Territory. The Piegans succeeded in surrounding their foes and were about to kill them when Big Nose interceded in their behalf, thus saving their lives and permitting them to return to the Flathead country from whence they came. It seems that at some previous time Big Nose had received a large silver medal from the United States government in Washington; he was told at the time that he must not kill or permit his people to kill anyone and that he and his people must make peace with all tribes as well as with the whites, hence his efforts to save the lives of this party.

SCENE 2 (1867):

Piegan camp near the Cypress Hills, Northwest Territory. Five Sioux Indians were discovered attempting to steal horses. Big Nose with a party of thirty Piegans attacked them, killing five of the party, with the loss of one Piegan. Big Nose killed the first one. One Sioux escaped. (Apparently there must have been at least six Sioux.)

SCENE 3 (1860):

A fight with the Crows on the "swift stream" which empties into the Yellowstone just west of where Fort Keogh is situated. The Piegans, led by Big Nose, numbered forty-two, and the Crows, twelve. The Piegans charged and the Crows ran into the brush. Their leader, however, stood his ground. Big Nose threw down his gun and closed in on the Crow, grappling with him. Another Piegan shot the Crow in the stomach; the Crow then drew a knife, but before he could use it the man who had already wounded him cut his arm and caused him to drop the knife. Big Nose then stabbed the Crow to death. For this deed Big Nose was given the name of "Crow Chief."

SCENE 4 (1861):

Near White Sulphur Springs, Montana. A surprise by the Ponderas. The Indian shown falling was the brother of Big Nose. The Piegan party numbered eleven, and the Pondera, sixty. The former retreated to the brush. The brother recovered, and one Pondera was killed.

SCENE 5 (1855):

Sweetgrass Hills, the east butte. At this time the Piegans and the Ponderas were at peace, and sixty lodges of the Piegans and ten lodges of the Ponderas were camped together. Late at night, when soundly sleeping, Big Nose heard a gun fired and then another. They all sprang to arms and when they emerged from their lodges, they discovered that they were surrounded by about four hundred Sioux. So close had been the fire that the Piegan horses corralled inside the circle of lodges were nearly all killed. Those not killed made their escape, except for the sorrel pinto horse ridden by Big Nose. The Sioux by this time had possession of half of the Piegan lodges. Big Nose on his pinto, which was wounded in the neck and then exchanged for the yellow horse, held his people together in the other half of the village, fighting till morning. The yellow figure was a Sioux, wounded by a Pondera, and he ran off followed by Big Nose, who pursued and stabbed him to death. The Sioux then withdrew with a loss of sixteen killed; the Ponderas and Piegans lost eleven.

SCENE 6 (1855):

In the Cypress Hills, Northwest Territory. Two hundred lodges of Piegans were in camp. Two Sioux stole some of their horses. Big Nose and a few others gave chase. The horses of the Sioux gave out and they tried to escape on foot. Big Nose overtook the one shown in the scene, killing him with his knife.

SCENE 7 (1860):

In the Judith Basin in Montana. Big Nose crawled up on a Pondera lodge under cover of night, taking the horse shown picketed there. In the meantime the owner opened fire, shooting Big Nose through the coat. There were thirteen Piegans in the party and sixty lodges of Ponderas. The Piegans were a hundred miles from their own people. The horse shown was the only one taken, owing to the early discovery of the raiders by the Ponderas.

SCENE 8:

Medicine pipes captured in battle.

SCENE 9 (1855):

Near the Cypress Hills, Northwest Territory. Eight Sioux attempted to steal horses from the Piegans. There were about four hundred lodges of Bloods and Piegans in camp. The Sioux stole six horses, were pursued, overtaken, and all killed but one. Big Nose held the horse and exchanged shots with the Sioux leader, whom he killed.

SCENE 10 (1859):

Prickly Pear Valley, near where Helena, Montana, now stands. Big Nose and party, twenty-one in number, left their camp where the old Blackfoot agency stood, on Badger Creek (fifteen miles from the new agency at Browning, on the Great Northern Railroad). Reaching the Prickly Pear, they found a camp of sixty lodges. Big Nose and another crawled up. Big Nose cut a fast horse loose from a lodge to which it was tied; his companion was killed in attempting a similar feat at another lodge. (It was the custom to secure their best horses—war ponies—by passing the lariat through the door of the lodge and fastening it to a lodgepole inside.) Six horses were obtained, and the raiders all escaped except the one noted above.

SCENE 11 (1847):

West butte of the Sweetgrass Hills, Montana. Three hundred lodges of Piegans were in camp there. Fifty-three Crees made a night attack upon the Piegans, who were asleep when fired upon. Piegans fought little during the night, but when daylight came a general charge was made upon the Crees. Big Nose mounted and charged among the Crees. His horse was shot in the head. After he was dismounted Big Nose killed one Cree with his gun and two with his knife. All the Crees were finally killed; the Piegans lost thirteen killed and five wounded. The lower part of the scene also shows Big Nose, after being dismounted, in combat with a Cree. The latter hit Big Nose on the head with a flintlock gun, and a Piegan then shot the Cree from the rear.

SCENE 12 (1881):

Judith Basin, Montana. Forty lodges of Piegans were camped there. Three Sioux attempted to steal horses. They were discovered before they could carry out their design. All three were killed by Under Bull and Young Bear Chief. Big Nose took, as shown in the drawing, the gun from one of them. He charged on the Indian whose gun would not fire.

SCENE 13 (1875):

Cypress Hills, Northwest Territory. Two hundred lodges of Piegans were camped there. Four Sioux were discovered in a thicket, were surrounded, and would have been killed but for Big Nose. He took to the brush, but his squaw *Ksískstukyake* ("Bear Woman") caught hold of him and tried to pull him away. He put her to one side and went into the thicket, crawling slowly toward the Sioux until he could see them behind a breastwork they had made in a circular opening in the thicket. Three were armed with Winchester rifles, two belts of cartridges, with their knives lying in front of them. The fourth had an old flintlock gun. Big Nose parleyed with the Sioux, telling them the Great Father wanted all the Indians to make peace. He displayed the medal already referred to and a pipe he had with him, asking them to smoke, to come with him, and he would feed them and send them safely home. They threatened to kill him, even poking their guns in his face; he paid no attention to this but continued to ask them to smoke. After making signs that they would not be hurt, he could see that their leader was weakening. Big Nose then sprang inside the breastwork and grabbed him; Big Nose's squaw grabbed another and then they all came out, the Piegans not injuring them. They then turned the Sioux over to the commanding officer at Fort Walsh, Northwest Territory.

He first sent word by an Indian, now called "Jack the Ripper," to the commanding officer that they had the Sioux prisoners, but he would not believe it until Jack made oath of it. The commanding officer then sent seven soldiers and one officer and four extra horses to get them. When the officer came he was still incredulous; but when shown the pit, which was deep, and the protection afforded by the heavy fringe of thorn bush, he was amazed at the conduct of Big Nose, and made notes and a sketch of the place.

SCENE 14:

Four bows and quivers, tomahawk, powder horn and bullet pouch. These were coups and were taken by Big Nose in his different battles.

SCENE 15 (1863):

North Cypress Hills, on the Elbow River, Northwest Territory. A large war party of Piegans were on the march when they came upon four Sioux, in thick timber, who had dug a pit in which they were well protected. The Piegans surrounded and fought them all one day, losing four killed and seventeen wounded. The tree shown as leaning over the Sioux was a large one up which Big Nose finally climbed, his squaw trying to pull him back. Armed with a double-barreled shotgun loaded with bullets, he killed all four Sioux; although they had been many times shot at, they had earlier been saved by the large limbs of the tree.

SCENE 16 (1854):

In the Snake country. A party of 124 Piegans encountered a lodge of Snake Indians—father, mother, and two grown sons. The gun shown was owned by one of the sons. The three men were killed, the woman being spared. The Piegans then returned to their own country without further incident of note; this took thirty-six days, as they were not mounted.

SCENE 17 (1858):

On the Milk River, in Montana, where Chinook is now situated. The Piegan camp there consisted of five hundred lodges. Nearly as many Assiniboines and Crows were camped about twenty miles away. Fighting began about midway between the camps at about nine in the morning, ending in defeat of the Crows and Assiniboines, who had seven killed and ten wounded, the Piegans losing one killed. The two horses shown were captured, one being wounded in the neck. The rider of the black horse, when dismounted by the wounding of the horse, escaped into the brush. Big Nose ran up, and the horse got away. Sitting Woman, a noted Crow chief, rode the black horse and disgraced himself by hiding in the brush. During the next charge Big Nose captured the other horse. The sorrel horse, being very fat, broke down and was captured, his rider getting on behind another Indian, thus making his escape.

SCENE 18 (1856):

At a point where Great Falls, Montana, now stands on the Missouri River where it comes out of the mountains. A war party traveling at the time discovered a band of elk and thought to kill some meat. The elk ran into a large clump of timber, Big Nose following. While trying to sneak up on the elk, a bear surprised him by charging. The bear was almost upon him when the fatal shot was fired.

SCENE 19 (1845):

On the Missouri River, south of where Helena, Montana, now stands. A war party of Piegans were going into the Snake country, twelve in number. Traveling along, they saw elk in the edge of the timber. Big Nose, being a good shot, went after them to get some meat. The brush was thick, and the bear was almost upon Big Nose when it stopped. He shot the bear, being so close the animal was powder burned.

SCENE 20:

Scalps taken by Big Nose. Some, however, were killed by others —the first to take has the honor.

SCENE 21:

Four Indians killed not shown in other scenes: two Sioux, one Snake, and one Pondera.

SCENE 22:

Battles. Big Nose had been in thirty-six battles, not all shown. He had killed eleven (?) Indians in all, being himself wounded nine times—six by gunshot, and three times by being struck over the head with a gun.

CHAPTER NINETEEN

Gros Ventre Slaughter[1]
(Told by Big Brave)

━━

SAID MY OLD FRIEND Big Brave to me on a recent evening: "*Apikuni*, how terrible that was, how many men, women, and children were killed after we of the Blackfoot tribes ended our long friendship with the Entrails People (Gros Ventres), warred against them, and all because of a crazy mistake. Why, we became the Entrails People's friends, protectors, long before the white men came into our country to trade with us. The Entrails People came to our very-long-ago fathers, came crying, and our fathers said to them, in the sign language, of course: 'Who are you? Whence come you? What troubles you?'

" 'We are the Entrails People,' they replied. 'We come from far-downriver country. There the Cutthroats (Assiniboines) became too many for us to fight; we had to flee from them because they were killing us off. We ask you to pity us; let us live in your great plains-and-mountain country.'

"Replied our long-ago fathers: 'Entrails People, we welcome you into our country. Wander in it as you will. Live upon our buffalo. Your enemies are our enemies, and we will join you in fighting them.'

"So it was that we and the Entrails People became close friends in the long ago. Oh, how very saddening it is that we did not always remain so; then how many many lives of the four tribes of us would have been saved. Now, tell me, how long ago was it that the first white men came up into our country and met us?"

1 Published in *The Great Fall Tribune* (May 19, 1940).

As nearly as I could put it into Blackfoot, I gave him the following, from my readings of the journals of the early fur traders in the Northwest. It was that for some summers previous to 1754 the Hudson's Bay Company, from its westernmost post, York Factory, on Hudson Bay, annually sent some mixed-blood Chippewa Indians with canoeloads of goods up the Saskatchewan River to trade with the Blackfoot tribes. Then in that year, 1754, a trusted employee, Anthony Henday, was given charge of the trade-goods flotilla, and told to urge the Blackfeet thereafter to come to York Factory to trade their catches of beavers and other furs. Henday and his canoe-men met the Gros Ventres at a point some thirty miles north of the present city of Calgary, and to his surprise he found that they were an equestrian people, owning great numbers of horses. To his proposal that they go to York Factory to trade they replied that it was too far away and in timbered, buffaloless country; therefore, both they and their horses would die along the way.

Dissatisfied with the result of Henday's mission, the company in the spring of 1772 sent another employee, Andrew Cocking, in charge of the trade-goods canoes, and he was told to do his utmost to persuade the Blackfeet to trade at York Factory. But in that, like Henday, he failed, as he also met the Gros Ventres. He did, however, give some interesting information about the Blackfeet in his journal: that they were skilled horsemen, killers of great numbers of buffalo in drives that they made, and that they made and used vessels of pottery for cooking and other purposes.

That much I told my friend Big Brave. I did not add that later traders mentioned what they believed to be a fourth tribe of the Blackfeet, giving them the name of Falls Indians, because they lived mostly at or near the falls of the Saskatchewan. Still later, French *engagés*, because of the sign for them—locked hands curving downward and outward from the pit of the stomach—named the Gros Ventres "Big Bellies", which is the name the whites have for them today. But when I told of the Blackfeet as pottery makers, my old friend exclaimed about it and asked: "Do you think that the white trader wrote the truth about it, or did he lie?"

"Without doubt, the truth," I answered.

"Again tell me the number of winters since the white traders were with our long-ago people and saw those dishes."

"It was 175 winters back that he saw the dishes and wrote about them."

"And now our people have no knowledge of it. Why, even my grandfathers and grandmothers did not know that our people once made earth dishes, else I would have heard them tell of it.[2] *Ha!* But see: There is a song that our women sing to their little ones that may be about those dishes. Listen. This is it:

> *Ponokahyo, aksa kitahwatop?*
> (Elk, what do you eat?)
>
> *Kahsimi ni tahwatop.*
> (Sage I eat.)
>
> *Ponokahyo, aksa kitsi taiswitan?*
> (Elk, what dish do you use?)
>
> *Okwitok sota nitsi taiswitan.*
> (Stone dish I do use.)"

He finished, gave me a questioning look, and I said: "They made the dishes of sticky clay, then burned them so that they became very hard, like stone."

"*Ha!* Then the song is surely about those dishes, and we of today do not know it, do not know that our long-ago people made them. We are poor minded; we lose, we forget our past. You whites, how wise you are. You write about the things that you do, you see, and the knowledge of it is always with you. Well, tell me how long ago it was that that first white trader came to our people."

"*Ha!* It was 183 winters back, and the Entrails People had come to us for protection before that time. Well, I am of eighty-four winters. I was in my tenth winter when our long friendship with the Entrails People ended."

[2] It seems strange that Big Brave would not have known of the Blackfoot traditions of pottery-making. Wissler, Kidd, and Ewers all obtained such traditions among the older people. (See John C. Ewers, "The Case for Blackfoot Pottery," *American Anthropologist*, Vol. XLVII, No. 2 (April-June, 1945), 289-99.

(In that I knew he was right, for I had learned from the late Joseph Kipp, George Steel, and others that the break between the Blackfoot tribes and the Gros Ventres occurred in the summer of 1863.)

"Well, as I said, it was because of a crazy misunderstanding that our close friendship with the Entrails People ended," my old friend continued. The rest of his tale follows:

Came the New-Grass Moon of summer, and our brother tribes, the Blackfeet and the Bloods, moved north to trade their furs to the whites on North Big River (Saskatchewan). We Pikunis and the Entrails People traded at Many-Houses (Fort Benton); and then the Entrails People moved north and camped on Bear River (Marias), and we Pikunis traveled up Milk River (Teton) and camped on it near Red Old Man's Butte (Priest's Butte).

Came from their other-side-of-the-mountain, timbered country, a war party of Kalispels, to raid the horse herds of any camp of us plains people that they could find. Traveling down Bear River and discovering the camp of the Entrails People in the timbered bottom, they lay hidden until dark, then took a large number of their horses and started homeward with them, heading to recross the mountains through Easy Pass (Cadotte Pass). A few of the horses that they had taken were poor and tired, and as they were crossing Milk River, in the night it was, they dropped them, as it happened, close to the camp of us Pikunis. So was it that those tired ones joined a band of our horses that were grazing up on the plain straight out from our camp.

Came morning, and our men hurried out to round up their horses, drive them to water, and saddle those that they were to use. Three young men went onto the plain for their herds and were surprised to find some strange horses with one of the herds; they were the ones that the Kalispels had let drop out from their stealings. As the young herders were staring at them, wondering whose they were, how they happened to be there, came a party of Entrails men, riding swiftly on the trail of the Kalispels; and, seeing some of their horses there in the herd that the young men were rounding up, they believed that a party of us Pikunis had stolen them. So they killed two of the young herders. The third one, escaping from them, hurried into camp, shouting that a war party of Entrails People had killed two of his friends. Butterfly was then our head chief. He thought that the young man was crazy. Our close friends, the Entrails People, would never attack us, he said.

"But I recognized two of the killers. I know not their names, but I have often seen them in their camp, and visiting in our camp," the young man cried.

Yelled Butterfly: "Well, whoever they are, we have to take after them. Hurry, you fighters, saddle your horses, take up your guns and we go."

Those who had already brought in their horses were soon ready to go, and off they rode, a hundred and more of them, Butterfly in the lead, and they were not long in overtaking some of the Entrails party, for their horses were tired. They killed five of them, the rest leaving their horses and escaping in heavy timber. They examined their kills; found that they really were Entrails People; even knew the names of two of them, and Butterfly sadly said: "So ends our long friendship with the Entrails People. From now on they are as much our enemies as are the tribes of the Parted Hairs (Sioux). Too bad! Too bad!"

On that day and for long afterward our Pikuni camp was sad. We mourned the passing of our two young men, and some of our women even cried over the ending of their close friendship with women of the Entrails People. Yes, for a long time there was no happy singing, drumming, story-telling around our evening lodge fires. At that time a great warrior was Red Plume, chief of our Raven Carriers society. Said he one day, as its members were gathered in his lodge: "Well, as the Entrails People are now our enemies, we must make them to cry. Two nights hence I am starting to raid their camps on Bear River. Go with me, those of you who are minded."

They were about a hundred who set out with him, and they went afoot, vowing that they would return riding horses of the Entrails People. They did not find the camp of the enemy on Bear Creek. As was later proven, they had left the stream, never to return to it. From that time on they camped and hunted in and around the Wolf Mountains (Little Rockies), Lower Little (Milk) River, and from there south of Big (Missouri) River to Elk (Yellowstone) River."

Following the trail of the Entrails People from Bear River, Red Plume and his party discovered them camped just north of Hairy Cap (east butte of the Little Rockies), and that night they killed a number of them and took more than three hundred of their horses. From that time on war parties of our Blackfoot tribes frequently raided the Entrails People, and they in turn sometimes raided our camps and horse herds but did us little harm. Not long after we fell out with them they made a peace smoke with the Crows, who were also our bitter enemies.

Came the third summer of our hatred of the Entrails People (1866); Butterfly had died, and in his place, Many Horses became head chief of us Pikunis. The head chief of the Entrails People was Sitting Woman—a strange name for a man. Well, in the Green-Grass Moon of that summer, Many Horses counciled with our medicine men and foremost warriors, and they decided that we should make our great, every-summer offering to Sun[3] this time at Divided Mountains (Cypress Hills, Alberta).

Little did we think when we set out for the Divided Hills, in the Berries-Ripe Moon (July) of the summer, that we were there to have a great and successful fight with the Entrails People, and many of their new friends, the Crows. It was not until many winters later, when the white soldiers made us cease fighting one another, that we made peace with those tribes and got their account of the fight.

Arrived at the Divided Hills, we made camp along the edge of a large grove on Seven Persons Creek (Maple Creek), so named because, long before then, a war party of our tribe had killed seven Liars (Crees) there. Well, a war party of Entrails People saw us traveling toward the Divided Hills and hurried back to their camp and told of it.

Then said their chief, Sitting Woman: "The Pikunis love that part of their country. Without doubt they are going there now to build

---

[3] The early fur traders named this annual, days-long, sacred ceremony of the Blackfoot tribes "Medicine Lodge; Sun's Lodge." The Blackfoot name for it is *Okan* ("His Vision"). It is their belief that their dreams, to them visions, are their actual experiences as they sleep.

their great offering to Sun. So is it that we, with our Crow friends here camped with us, will go up there and kill them all off. Yes, and we will have our women go with us, so that they can load our pack horses and travois with all of the valuable belongings of the Pikunis that we can take."

So, Entrails People and Crows, men, women, and children, all of them, set out to put an end to us Pikunis, and upon arriving at the Divided Hills, after consulting with the Crow chief, Sitting Woman sent a few of his men on ahead to look for our camp. Very early that morning, nearly all of our horses had been brought in, watered, and were grazing and resting in our camp and in the near-by long, wide grove of cottonwoods. Advancing cautiously, Sitting Woman's scouts discovered six of our lodges at the lower end of our camp; they could not see the others because of the long grove screening them. As they looked, they saw a boy leave one of the six lodges and head for a band of horses that were grazing on the slope of the valley; stealing up to him, they killed him with bow and arrow, and so silently. Then they turned back to report to Sitting Woman.

"What?" cried he. "Only six lodges? Are you sure there are not more, the many lodges of the Pikunis?"

"Absolutely, there are but six lodges, and we killed a boy that went out from them to get his horses. Come, you yourself, and you will see that we are right," one of the scouts answered, and he started on with them. In due time he saw, as they had said, that there were but six of the Pikuni lodges.

"It must be," he told them, "that the big camp of our enemies is much farther on. Go back, one of you, and tell our people and the Crows to come on. We will kill off these Pikunis here and then cautiously go on, surprise attack the rest of their kind, and put an end to them."

But in the meantime the father of the boy that the scouts had killed, worrying about his long absence, came out looking for him, found him killed, and hurried back to camp with the body, shouting, "Enemies are here; they have killed my son." And just then one named Running Wolf, who had gone out early to look at the valley and hills, came running in and said that many enemies were coming—

apparently a whole tribe of them. Whereat all of our warriors, young and old, hurried to saddle their horses and get ready to fight. I saddled one of my horses; slung my bow-and-arrows case to my side, told my father that I was going to charge out with him.

"No. You are too young for that. Remain right here with your mothers and little sisters and brothers, and if the enemy comes, protect them as best you can," he answered.

Shouted Many Horses: "Now, my brave fighters, we will all ride to the upper end of the grove and there charge out at the enemy as they come near us."[4]

Off they went, and after a little I started to follow them. "Come back. Come back," my mother shouted at me. "You are to stay with us. Your father told you so."

"I will go only a little way until I can see the enemy, and will hurry back to you," I answered, and kept on. We arrived in the upper end of the grove just as the enemy had come down off the plain into the valley, and, oh, they were many! Many! So many that I had sudden, great fear of them. They will surely kill us all, I thought. On they came until we could see that following the men were their women and children with their pack horses, travois horses, bands of horses.

I heard Many Horses laugh his queer, screeching laugh and then say, "So, my brave ones, so sure are they of wiping us out that they have brought their families along. *Ha!* We are going to be rich. My children, when I raise our war cry, ride out at them, ride fast, and shoot to kill, kill, kill!"

On they came, those many enemy warriors, wearing their war clothes, their war bonnets, their feathered shields; their shining guns in hand, and, oh, how powerfully, how strong-mindedly they sat upon their prancing horses. And how unsuspecting of the hundreds of us, staring out at them from the shelter of the grove. On they came, those proud Entrails and Crow warriors, and I began to tremble from fear of them. Would Many Horses never give us the cry to charge out at them? Well, when it came, I would turn and ride the other

---

[4] John C. Ewers gives a somewhat different version of the battle. According to Ewers (*The Blackfeet*, 243), Many Horses did not lead the Blackfeet in their great victory over the Gros Ventres but was killed while buffalo hunting by the enemy before the battle began.

way, on and on, anywhere to be safe, I thought. He waited until the enemy leaders had come so near that we could almost see their eyes; and when he gave the shrill cry and his hundreds of warriors yelled it and charged out from the grove, I was somehow crazily with them and yelling, too.

Ha! At sight of us, what did those Entrails and Crow warriors do? Did they raise their guns and come hurrying to meet us? No! At once they turned and fled, they and then their families, and we after them, in among them, shooting, shooting, shooting them down. There was so much to see at once: enemies falling, our warriors strewing the ground with them; women and children squalling, riding back as fast as they could go; pack horses and travois horses running in all directions and spilling their loads. I drew an arrow from my case, fitted it to my bow, began overtaking an enemy with intent to kill him; but when, with good aim, I drew back the bowstring with all my strength, it broke apart and I all but fell from my horse. He was an old, gray-haired one, that enemy, and he carried a gun, a short-barreled flintlock gun as I could plainly see.

The bravest thing that a warrior can do is to seize an enemy's gun, or bow, strike him with it, then kill him. I rode up close beside this old man, snatched his gun from him, and then he looked at me so pitifully, saying, in my own language, "Oh, pity me. Do not kill me," that I only tapped his shoulder with the gun and let him go. For that, afterward, I got great praise and great scolding from my father. "You were very brave to seize the enemy's gun, you so young, but you should then have killed him," he said. "If you continue pitying your enemies, you can never, never become a real warrior."

As I said, the Entrails People and the Crows were riding back as fast as they could go, our warriors overtaking and killing them. We could have killed them all but for the eagerness of our warriors to scalp and to take the weapons of their kills, so to prove their bravery. And, too, they were, many of them, horse hungry, especially our poor ones, so, instead of keeping on and making their kills, they would turn off and round up bands of the enemy horses and claim them as their own. As at last our pursuit and killing of the enemy was ending, I came upon my father's close friend *Ikinaiyi* ("Top

Knot") chasing a woman. He overtook her, pulled her from her horse, got down off his horse, and signed to her: "You are now my woman. Do not ever try to leave me. If you do I will kill you." Oh, but she was beautiful, that woman, of perhaps thirty winters. Surprisingly, she signed to *Ikinaiyi:* "I hated my Crow man. He stole me from my people. Do not worry. I will never try to leave you.' "

"*Apikuni*, friend," continued Big Brave, "you well knew her, she whom we named Crow Woman."

"Yes, well I knew her. She and her close friend, Earth Woman, were my almost-mothers," I sadly answered.

Then he went on:

Well, our chase and killing of the enemy ended, and the valley was strewn with their belongings; lodges and lodgepoles, lodge furnishings, buffalo robes and furs, clothing, parfleches of food. Came from our camp the women to gather up all these valuable things, and how they did sing and chatter and quarrel as they were doing it. Came, too, our old men, and several of them cut a large number of short willow sticks and began counting the enemy dead. They painted red the end of a stick for every body that they came to, and when they had finished, counted the sticks.

"*Ha!* My brave children, in all you have killed 363 of the enemy," one of them shouted to us and began singing, and we all sang with him. Oh, what a happy, happy day that was for us all.

My old friend ended his tale and signed to me to fill a pipe.

And now about Crow Woman, as the Pikunis named her. After Kipp's Mandan mother, Earth Woman, secured her release from her captor,[5] she was a member of the Kipp family until she died in 1906.

[5] For the full story of Crow Woman, see Chapter 2 of this volume. In this earlier chapter, Crow Woman was captured by Spotted Elk; here, he is Top Knot; in Schultz's *My Life As an Indian*, p. 77, the Blood who captured and married her is named Deaf Man; but in his *Bird Woman* (Houghton Mifflin Company, 1918), p. 4, the captor is called Lone Otter. The discrepancies are more apparent than real, owing to the different names held by one and the same Indian at different times in his career.

Gros Ventre Slaughter

And when I, a youth of eighteen, came west and was welcomed by Joseph Kipp, Earth Woman and Crow Woman truly mothered me for many years. Oh, what grand women they were!

CHAPTER TWENTY

The Baker Massacre
(Told by Bear Head, a Survivor)

IT WAS FIFTY-SIX YEARS AGO, in November, 1879, that I first met *Kai Otokan* ("Bear Head"), a young and forceful member of the Pikuni tribe of the Blackfoot Confederacy; and we soon became close and lifelong friends. And now in our old age he still comes daily to visit and smoke with me, or I go to sit with him in his lonely, widower's cabin at the Blackfoot Agency.

"*Apikuni*, how fast we old ones are dying off. Of those of us who survived the massacre of a great camp of our tribe by the white soldiers, sixty-five winters ago, only four are now alive: my cousin, he named Comes-with-Rattles, and I; Heard-by-Both-Sides Woman and Good-Bear Woman. Well, I am going to tell you again of that terrible wrong that we suffered, and I want you to write it for the whites to read; for the whites of this time to learn what their fathers did to us."

The "terrible wrong" was, of course, the massacre of nearly all of a large camp of the Pikunis on Marias River, Montana, by Major Eugene M. Baker and a troop of cavalry and mounted infantry from Fort Shaw in January, 1870.

"Yes, I will write it," I answered, "but the whites will want to know something about you, about your life before that time of the great killing of your people. So begin with your earliest remembrances."

Thereafter, for several evenings, he talked and I wrote, and so I present his tale, as nearly as I have been able to translate it into English:

I was born seventy-nine winters ago on Yellow (Judith) River. My father, Bear Head, was a tall, handsome man and a great warrior. My mother, Fair Singing Woman, was beautiful. Though quite young, she had even then become a sacred woman, one of the women who, every summer, build a great lodge to give to Sun. Dearly my father and mother loved me, and I loved them. As soon as I could walk, my mother furnished me with soft, beaded, deer leather clothes for summer, furs for winter. And my father gave me little bows and arrows and taught me to ride gentle horses; gave me six horses when I was in my sixth winter. Four of them were mares, so I was soon having quite a band of horses of my own. I loved to play with the boys, and I loved to sit before the evening lodge fires listening to the warriors and hunters telling of their brave deeds—the old men telling of the power and goodness of Sun and all the other gods.

Came my eighth summer, and my father, getting ready to go with a party against some of our enemies, said that I must go, too. My mother objected; cried; said that I was too young to go to war, that it would be too dangerous for her little one. Said my father to her: "Last night, as I slept, Sun gave me a vision. We were a war party. Our young one was traveling at my side. We discovered enemies, fought, and killed them. The meaning of that is plain. It is that your young First Rider goes with me, with our party, and that he will survive the dangers that we encounter. And well you know that I was of his age when I first took to the war trail. So must he now go. I shall make of him a real warrior."

First Rider—that was the name given me when I was born; given me by an old medicine man because of one of his visions, in which he saw a member of a war party be first to take an enemy horse and ride it off.

Well, my mother knew that my father would have his way about me, so she made no more objection to my going but got together the things that I would need, extra pairs of moccasins, a rope, awl, and sinew thread; and crying, she said to me: "You have to go. I shall pray, constantly pray the Above Ones to give you safe return to me."

I was eager to go. I wanted to become a great warrior, kill many enemies, take many enemy horses, and so be honored, made a chief by my people. At that time we were camped on Big (Missouri) River, a short distance below the mouth of Bear (Marias) River. My father was to be the leader of the war party. Other prominent members of it were Tail-Feathers-Coming-Over-the-Hill, Buffalo-Painted-Lodge, False-Heavy-Runner, and Owl Child. In all we were seventy to go. Came the day for us to prepare for our departure. Sacred-pipe men prepared sweat lodges for us. How proud I was when, with my father and others, I entered the one owned by Red Eagle, whose sacred bundle was that of the Thunder Pipe. We thrust our wraps outside and sat in a circle, naked. Women passed in stones that they had heated red hot. We rolled them into a pit in the center of the lodge, and with a buffalo-tail asperger Red Eagle sprinkled them with water from a red wooden bowl. As dense steam arose and filled the lodge, he began his sacred songs, in which we joined. He prayed Sun, Morning Star, and other Above Ones to keep us safe upon our dangerous trail and give us complete success against our enemies. He passed his sacred pipe, and by turns we each drew a few whiffs of smoke from it and prayed Sun to help us get the particular things that we wanted. This one desired enemy horses; that one, enemy scalps; and so on. Myself, I prayed Sun to help me take an enemy gun. The ceremony ended, Red Eagle said to us: "Go, my brave ones, and Sun be with you. Myself, I will daily ride through camp during your absence, shouting your names, calling upon all the people to pray for your success and your safe return."

With that, we reached outside for our wraps, then ran to the river, plunged in, and after a short bath hurried to our lodges to dress and go. Came night, and singing a war song, we struck out northward with only four horses, I riding one of them, the others carrying some of our belongings. My weapon was a powder-and-balls, five-chambered pistol that my father had bought from the Many-Houses (Fort Benton) trader named "Sleeping Thunder" (George Steel). I was afraid of it, for once when I had fired it all five of its loads had exploded, burning my hand. As we traveled, I prayed Sun to help me take an enemy gun. Between prayers I asked myself: "How can you, a boy of only eight winters, take a gun from an enemy?" And always I answered: "Sun is with you. He will help you do it."

I had never traveled in the night, so feared the darkness, the possibility that we might run right into an enemy war party. Herds of buffalo, running from our approach, caused my heart to beat fast. Wolves, near and far, were continuously howling; coyotes, yelping. But they were harmless. I loved to hear them. I was glad when came the first, dim, white light of the new day, and we turned down into a grove of cottonwoods in a coulee to hide and rest until night should come again. One of our party killed a buffalo cow, and we quickly broiled and ate our fill of its meat. My father named two men to sit up on the edge of the plain and watch for enemies until midday, and told two others to watch for the rest of the day. And then we all lay down and slept.

So going, night after night, and without trouble of any kind, we passed the west end of the Bear Paw Mountains, near *Ahya Kimikwi* (Divided Mountains, the Cypress Hills, Alberta). At daybreak of a morning, we saw that we were near them, and at the same time discovered two riders on the plain, not far north of us, and coming our way. We got down into a coulee before they could see us and spread up and down it, watching them come on, and quite widely apart. One of them was heading straight toward the place where my father and I and a few others lay concealed. When he came near enough, at a word from my father, we all fired at him, and down he went; his horse, too; and we ran forward, my father in the lead. The man was badly wounded, dying. My father handed me the long stem of his pipe, told me to strike the man with it, count coup on him. I stepped to his side; his face, mouth, shot and bloody, sickened me; and I drew back. "Hit him! Hit him!" my father yelled at me. "Hit him, or I will make you to cry." So, at last, I struck the top of his head with the pipe stem, and with that my father and others shot him again and he died. My father again yelled at me: "Now, First Rider, out with your knife and scalp him." And as I hesitated, "At once scalp him, else you will no longer be son of mine."

Oh, how I hated to do that; but groaning, almost crying, I did it, taking a piece of his head skin from which dropped one of his long hair braids; and then my father had me take the dead one's gun and other things, he and the others there with us shouting: "Young First

Rider, little First Rider; he takes an enemy gun; he takes an enemy scalp."

Then how pleased, how proud I was of myself. And I thought, powerful is Sun. Good to me is Sun. I prayed him for a gun, and I have it.

While this was going on some of our party farther up the coulee had killed the other rider. Both were Atsinas (Entrails men, Gros Ventres), a tribe with which we had long been at war.

We now all got together again, and my father said: "Without doubt these two Atsinas we have killed were early hunters from their camp. More will be coming from it. It is best that we go to a good place to conceal ourselves for the day."

We found not far back on our trail a well-timbered coulee, and there had a good rest, our lookouts seeing none of the enemy during the day. Came evening, and my father decided that we would remain right where we were until near morning, then go on very cautiously, looking for more of the enemy to kill. So we lay down to get more sleep, my father at one side of a big rock, Heavy Runner at his other side. Sometime past the middle of the night my father awoke us all by suddenly calling out: "Heavy Runner! Awake! I have had a vision. I must tell you of it."

"Tell it," Heavy Runner grunted, and my father continued: "This I visioned: This big rock here, it nudged me and said, 'Your enemies are camped not far north from here. Be wise. Seek them very cautiously and you will have good luck.'"

"Ha! A good vision; a good warning. We will carefully heed it," said Heavy Runner.

Said one lying close to me, "First Rider, your father, Sun powerfully favors him. A good vision, this that Sun gave him. I can hardly wait for the good that is to be ours." We all were so excited about it that from then on we slept but little.

When the Seven Persons (constellation of Ursa Major) warned us that day was not far off, we again set out northward, passed the place where we had killed the two riders; and then, nearer the Divided Mountains, as day came, we stopped in a brushy coulee, and my father sent Heavy Runner up onto the ridge, close ahead of us, to look for enemies.

As he neared the top of the ridge, Heavy Runner climbed very slowly. At last he got onto hands and knees, crept to the top, looked over it for some time, then crept back down a little way, and stood up and signed to us: "Four men with one horse, coming." *Ha!* Good news. At once we began singing that war song, "Enemies are coming. We shall kill them."

Heavy Runner crept back to the top of the ridge, and my father sent Buffalo Child to scout farther west on the ridge. Heavy Runner soon signed to us: "Another enemy has appeared. He is coming straight toward me." And then Buffalo Child signed: "The four men with one horse, they are heading to strike the coulee close above the point running to it from this ridge."

At that my father named some of us to remain right where we were and led the rest up the coulee; I, of course, kept close to my father. As we moved on Buffalo Child came down off the ridge, joined us, and said that we must hurry up to where the four enemies would strike the coulee. We did hurry and when past the point my father had us scatter out along the coulee, lie at the top of its slope, and cautiously look off upon the plain. We soon sighted the four enemies, one of them on the horse.

They were coming at a fast walk, guns ready to fire, looking for deer or antelope, as no buffalo were anywhere in sight. Presently they stopped, appeared to be arguing about something, and after a little one of them struck off by himself, heading to strike the coulee farther west than would the three. Meantime, Heavy Runner had come down off the ridge and joined those whom he had left below; the lone enemy first discovered was nearing them.

I was terribly excited as I watched the three enemies coming nearer and nearer to us. My father had ordered us not to fire at them until he gave the word for it. But Owl Child, always very strong willed, suddenly shot and killed one of the three, and then we all fired and killed the other two.

The fourth one of these enemies, farther to the west and still some distance from the coulee when he heard us shoot, saw his friends fall, at once turned and ran, and Berry Child took after him, was fast gaining upon him when suddenly he stopped, turned, fired, and Berry Child fell dead. He had ever been Buffalo Child's closest of friends, his almost-brother, so now Buffalo Child shouted to us: "It is for me to avenge my close friend's death. He is mine, mine alone, that Entrails man." And was going even as he shouted that. Excitedly, breathlessly, we watched him gaining upon the fleeing man, he trying to reload his gun as he ran. That very difficult to do. At last Buffalo Child got so close to him that they were almost together, but still he did not shoot.

"*Ha!* He is going to strike him!" Owl Child yelled. Then he shouted, as though Buffalo Child could hear: "Buffalo Child! Be successful! Strike him! Strike him!"

To strike an enemy, however slightly, and before fighting him, killing him—that, you know, is the very bravest thing a warrior can do. Oh, how pleased we were when now we saw Buffalo Child strike the fleeing one's shoulder with his gun barrel. The man had not succeeded in reloading his gun. Stopping short and turning, he raised it as a club, but even as he swung it Buffalo Child shot him; and how we did yell as we saw him fall, he the last one of the four. And meantime those of our party below had killed the lone rider that Heavy Runner had discovered.

But we had lost good, brave Berry Child. His almost-brother wept when we brought his body into the coulee and buried it, covered it with rocks and brush, and we all felt very sad. We moved away from the grave, and my father sent two scouts to the top of the ridge to watch for more of the enemy. None appeared during the day. Said my father, when evening came: "The Entrails People, missing the seven of them we have killed, will be constantly watching for their killers, for us to appear. We are too few to fight the many of them, so we now turn back for home."

That we did, arriving there in good time and sighting no enemies along the way. My mother both cried and laughed when I appeared before her with my gun and shouting to her so that all could hear: "I struck a living enemy, an Entrails man, and see: I took his gun, his scalp."

I swelled with pride of myself; stalked about the camp with my gun, envied by boys of my own age and boys much older; and admired, made much of by the girls. The gun was a North Traders (Hudson's Bay Company) cap-lock, smooth bore, without rear sights; a nothing-gun, some of the boys said, but to me a most valuable weapon. I had plenty of powder, balls, and caps for it, so often shot it at birds, stones, and knots of trees until, at short distance, not more than a hundred steps, I could mostly hit the mark. It was in Falling-Leaves Moon of that summer that a boy said to me: "Yes, you have a gun, but what good is it to you? You can't kill anything with it."

The next morning, after I had helped my father round up our horses and drive them to water, and after he had gone back into the lodge, I rode up the valley looking for something worth while to kill. Rode a long way until, at last, I saw a herd of buffalo coming down off the plain to drink at the river. I sprang from my horse, tethered him, ran on up in the timber, and when the herd began passing close in front of me I aimed carefully at a big cow, at a point just back of her foreshoulder and low down, and fired. Boom! At once the whole herd swerved, ran crashing up through the willows, my cow with the rest. I had missed. So near to me and I had missed. I hated myself; almost cried as I took to the trail of the herd; then, laughing and yelling, ran, for there upon the trampled and crushed willows was my cow, blood bubbling from her mouth and nose, and breathing her last.

Then what to do? She lay upon her belly, and I had not strength to turn her up to remove her insides. I cut out her tongue, skinned, laid bare her fat hump; cut off a foreleg at the knee, and with it for a club, struck and struck the hump until its feather (dorsal) ribs snapped, broke where they rose from the backbone. Easily then I cut off the whole hump, tied it and the tongue to my saddle, and rode back down the valley. It was past midday when I struck camp, and instead of going to my lodge rode round and round in its great circle for all to see, particularly the boys, that I was a real hunter, had made a killing.

At last, as I neared my lodge, this one and that one yelled: "There he is, the missing one. He has returned."

289

Came rushing out my father and mother shouting: "You bad boy; where have you been? We have looked all over for you . . . ." Then stopped, stared, and laughed as they saw the tongue and the feather ribs tied to my saddle. And cried my father: "Why, he has been hunting. He has actually made a killing, this strong-minded one of ours. Who was with you? Who took off those feather ribs for you?"

"I was alone. I cut and clubbed them off with my knife and the cow's leg," I explained. And the people gathered around, clapped hands to mouths in surprise, one old man saying: "And he so young, so little and weak. How strange."

"Not strange at all. My son, of course he would be that way," my father proudly answered.

After that no boys made fun of me and my gun.

In the following summer, my ninth one, when we were camped on Little (Milk) River, close north of the Bear Paw Mountains, we learned that there was a large camp of the Lying People (Cree tribe) camping on North Big (Saskatchewan) River right in our country and killing our buffalo. Of all our enemies they were the worst— always coming into our country to hunt our buffalo, we always fighting them, driving them back to their north, swampy country. It was Rising Wolf (Hugh Monroe), that brave, wandering, beaver trapper, married to one of our women, who told us about them.

"The Liars, they have come again to steal our food," our people cried.

"We will make them to cry," my father shouted, and called upon our brave ones to go against them. Said that I should join the party. We were not many, there on Little River; the greater part of our tribe were camping and hunting on Big (Missouri) River. But seventy-seven of the men in our camp hurried to him, said that they were eager to go with him against the Liars.

So again I sat in a sacred sweat lodge with my father and other warriors, listening to Red Eagle's powerful prayers for our success against the Liars and our safe return. In turn I lifted his sacred Thunder Pipe aloft and myself prayed Sun for help in all of my undertakings.

My father, listening, said to me when I finished: "You omitted something; you did not pray Sun to help you obtain any particular success against the enemy. Pray again."

So again I raised the sacred pipe to the sky and pleaded: "Oh, Sun! Help me to take Liars' horses and safely return with them."

Hearing me, those powerful men of our circle smiled, one saying: "Asking for help in capturing enemy horses; and he so young."

"But Sun heeds the prayers of the very young, as well as those of us old ones," old Red Eagle said.

"True, how true," others cried, and I felt all puffed up with courage; was eager to go.

Night came and we set out northward, all of us on good horses. Three nights later, just before dawn, we arrived in the Divided Mountains (Cypress Hills) and stopped in the pines on a north slope of a ridge, expecting to rest there during the day. But when Sun came up we discovered out on the plain a party of men on foot and coming toward us, coming from the valley of a little creek where the smoke of many lodges was rising. My father examined the party with his far-seeing instrument, told us they were Liars. It was that, since our friend Rising Wolf had seen the tribe of them on North Big River, they had moved still farther south in our country—right into our Divided Mountains where not only buffalo but elk, deer, and antelope were very plentiful. This party of them coming up a coulee was right then approaching a herd of buffalo grazing on the plain not far out from us.

Said my father: "What do they think we are? Just nothing-people that they can come down here and steal all that they can use of our meat, our furs? Get ready, my friends. Put on your war bonnets, make ready your guns, and we will ride out there and make those dog-face thieves to cry."

Each member of our party had his war bonnet along; and some, their war clothes also. We carried them in smooth, painted, parfleche cases tied to our saddles. I even had a horns-and-ermine fur bonnet that my father had made for me. I prayed to Sun for help, prayed him to keep me safe from the enemy guns, as I put it on. When nearly ready to go, we saw a lone rider come out from the camp in the valley and head toward the party on foot. He was coming slowly, allowing his horse to walk.

By the time we had finished dressing ourselves and mounted our horses, the enemy hunters had left the coulee and, screened by a sharp little ridge in the plain, were approaching the herd of buffalo. We all lined up in the lower edge of the pines and at a shout from my father raised a shrill war song and charged out upon the plain. Seeing and hearing us, the buffalo went leaping and thundering westward against the wind, and the party of hunters got closely together and, with guns and bows and arrows ready, awaited our coming. Well they knew that they could not escape from us by running for their camp. Well they knew that their end was near.

Still singing our war song, we rode swiftly to pass to the right of them, we shooting at them with our many-shots guns and seeing some fall; they returned our fire with their bows and arrows and the poor guns that they had. I shot at one who was fast shooting arrows at us; shot again, saw him fall. Then, before I could shoot again, False-Fast-Runner and his horse, close in front of me, were suddenly killed, and as they went down my horse stumbled against them, plunged down to his knees, and almost I went on over his head. But for quickly grasping the back of my saddle with my left hand I would have gone off. I was terribly frightened. Bravely my horse lunged and lunged until he got back on his feet and carried me on, and then we were all of us well past the enemy and, headed by my father, turning to charge past them again. And loudly we yelled as we saw that they were many who were down, dead, or wounded. Twice more we charged past them, shooting more down until at last but five were standing and able to fight. Said my father, as again we turned: "Now, my brave ones, once more we charge; be careful, aim to kill, so that we this time put an end to them all."

This time, well spread out, we rode straight at them, shooting over our horses' heads. Almost at once four of the five went down. The fifth one, singing, stood for a little with his gun at his hip, singing to us to come on. For all of our shooting, we were failing to hit him; it was as though he might be a man of sacred power, protected by his gods. At last, when we were almost upon him, he raised his gun, after long aim fired it, and killed my father's close friend, Big Elk.

And then my father raised high his gun, brought it powerfully down upon the Liar's head, and that was the end for him.

As I started to get down from my horse and help finish off the few wounded, still-living Liars, I felt an itching in my side, and putting down my hand, clutched the feathered end of an arrow sticking into the roll of the blanket around my waist; found that it had pierced my shirt and cut a short streak in my skin. I called to my father and he came running, drew the arrow on through my shirt and out. Called upon others near to come see my wound; said that Sun had turned the arrow from piercing my insides.

And said one, Little Plume: "His war bonnet, when it was finished, old Red Eagle prayed Sun to give it power to protect your young son. It is no wonder that the arrow did not pierce him."

I had gone all trembly when I discovered how narrow had been my escape from being killed. But now as my father and Little Plume said, Sun had protected me; my war bonnet had power to protect me. So I ceased trembling, remained upon my horse, and looked around at the dead Liars; there were thirty-three of them. They seemed to have had no pride of themselves. Their leather clothing was old and soiled; their hair, uncombed, unbraided; their moccasins were soft soled; their guns, mostly old North Traders muzzle loaders; some were even without guns and using bows and arrows. But though poorly off for weapons, how persistent they were in coming to camp in our country and to steal our game. And now these, here, had killed False-Fast-Runner and Big Elk. So was it we were sad and silent as we took their bodies back into the pines for burial.

Said my father as we covered them: "Our poor, poor friends. What could they have done, what mistake could they have made, that they had not the Above Ones' protection?"

For a time we sat and looked off toward the valley in which the Liars were camped. None came in sight; smoke was no longer rising from their lodges. Said one sitting near me: "That lone rider we saw, we should not have charged out from here until he joined the hunters, for we could then have killed him, too. When he saw us, how quickly he rode back."

My father had out his far-seeing instrument, was looking through it at the valley at the place where we had seen the rising smoke, and after a little he said to us: "Many, many Liars out there, in the brush on the rim of the valley; mourning for their dead; looking for sight of us."

Said Many-Tail-Feathers: "We will tonight make them to cry still more."

"No. I feel that the passing of our good friends, False-Fast-Runner and Big Elk, is warning to us not to attack the camp of the Liars," said my father. "There are very many; too many; some of us would be killed. We have terribly punished them. They wait only for us to leave, to bury their thirty-three dead and then return to their north country."

That did not please Many-Tail-Feathers and a few others like him, crazily brave. They urged, come night, we at least should go to the rim of the valley, shoot down into the lodges of the Liars, and then leave. But my father would not agree to it. We remained right where we were during the rest of the day and as Sun was setting turned back for home, and in good time safely arrived there.

In my tenth and eleventh summers I went with my father's war parties against several enemy tribes, and we always had good success; I myself took three horses in a night raid that we made upon a camp of Crows.

Besides my mother, my father had three other wives, my almost-mothers, and they had four daughters, my almost-sisters, the eldest one of them married to a man of terrible temper, one named Owl Child. In my twelfth summer, my father gathered a large war party to go against the Cutthroats (Assiniboines), and this time left me to care for our family during his absence. Owl Child was one of those who went with him. Near the mouth of Little (Milk) River the party discovered a camp of the enemy, successfully fought them, and then Owl Child claimed to have killed a Cutthroat who without doubt had been killed by my father. They quarreled about it, and Owl Child, crazily angry, killed my father. When the party returned, bringing us the terrible news of his death, Owl Child was not with them. He had gone to his own relatives in Mountain Chief's camp. The head chief of our camp of the Pikunis was Bear Chief, better known as Heavy Runner. Our tribe was so very large that, in order to hunt successfully, we were generally divided into a number of camps.

So now it was for me, only twelve summers old, to provide food for my mourning mothers and sisters and care for our band of horses, nearly a hundred head. We had a large, well-furnished lodge; my mothers and sisters were good workers. But my father's powerful many-shots gun had been buried with him. It was hard for me with my old cap-lock gun to kill enough buffalo for our food and other needs. But my mother encouraged me, saying that I must do my utmost to get well-furred buffalo cow hides for them to tan into soft robes, so that, come spring, I could trade them for a many-shots gun.

In the first moon of winter (November), when the new fur of the buffalo became full grown and dark, I hunted almost continuously, one or two of my family always accompanying me to help butcher my kills. All through the winter, even in the coldest weather, we kept at it, older hunters saying that they were astonished at my perseverance, and I so young. Always in our lodge robes were being tanned and fat meat was being dried or made into pemmican for our summer use. Came the New-Grass Moon (April) of summer, and we all moved in to Many-Houses (Fort Benton) and made camp. Next morning we loaded our fifty-five soft-tanned, head-and-tail buffalo cow robes on some horses, unloaded in front of Spotted Cap's (Charles Conrad's) trade house. Spotted Cap, followed by his three hands-out-goods men, came out to meet us, help us unload our many packs of robes and carry them inside. We loved Spotted Cap. He was married to Sings-in-the-Middle Woman, she a member of our brother tribe, the Bloods. He spoke our language, was very kind and generous. Already he had heard that I had taken my dead father's name, so said to me as he grasped my hand: "Bear Head, how happened it? Whose are they, these many robes?"

"My killings, my mothers' tannings. Spotted Cap, I want a many-shots gun and three hundred greased shooters for it," I answered. (The bullets of the .44 caliber, rim-fire cartridges for the Henry repeating rifle were heavily coated with hard grease, hence the Pikuni name for them.)

He put his arm on my shoulder, hugged me, and said: "Bear Head, though you had not one robe, I would give you a many-shots gun and plenty of greased shooters. Why? Because I loved your father. He was a real man. And I love you; pity you so young, and so many mothers and sisters to care for."

It made me to have wet eyes, that he said to me. My mothers and sisters were crying. Loudly they wept, moaning: "Our brave man, our brave father; he is gone. Gone to the Sand Hills. *Haiya! Haiya!*" It was some time before we could begin to trade.

"A many-shots gun. Here it is, Bear Head," said Spotted Cap as he handed me a shiny new one. "And here are the greased shooters for it." And he laid six boxes of them on the counter.

I gave him ten robes for the gun and the greased shooters. My mother and sisters then traded the rest of the robes for the various goods they wanted: blankets, cloth for gowns, other women's things; sugar, tea, an ax, and knives. Because of our hard winter's work, all of our needs were supplied. We felt rich as we returned to camp.

When all the families of our Heavy Runner band had finished trading, we moved up to Two Medicine Lake, there to cut new lodgepoles, make new lodge-skins, and summer hunt for meat and what few hides were needed. It was easy for me now with my many-shots gun to keep my lodge supplied with meat and the various kinds of hides for the women to tan for our clothing and for other uses.

No sooner had we camped at the lake than my mother told me that she wanted four bighorn hides for a new gown. The next morning I rode to the upper edge of the timber on the mountain close west of the lake, tied my horse, looked up at the bare slopes and cliffs rising from the timber to the summit. Quite near me were eleven male bighorns lying upon a slope of small rocks, chewing and chewing the grasses with which they had filled their first stomachs. I shot at one and it began rolling down the steep slope. The others sprang up and ran for the top of the mountain. I shot and shot at them until there were no more greased shooters in my gun and killed four more. *Ha!* Five bighorns I had killed in no time. Had I been using my old powder-and-balls-and-cap gun I would have killed one, and the others would have run away before I could reload it. How happy I was that I owned the many-shots gun. I sang as I rode home with the five hides and some of the meat. Arriving there, I told of my five kills, and several needy ones rode up the mountain to get the carcasses and the good fat meat that I had left upon the high slope.

Some days later I rode out again for meat for my family, this time in the valley below the lake. Presently I saw three elk go down a grassy slope and enter a big stand of pines and cottonwoods bordering the river. I got off my horse, picketed him, and, following a game trail, went slowly into the timber after them. There was such a thick growth of willows and rose brush in it that I could see but a little way in any direction except straight ahead along the trail. I was turning a bend in it when I heard a pattering of feet, and suddenly two small young bears, playfully running and biting at one another, ran into me, and getting my odor, ran on loudly squalling.

Then, angrily roaring, came their mother, a big real-bear (grizzly) rounding the bend of the trail and straight toward me. Twice I shot at her, knew I hit her each time, but she kept leaping on; with two or three more leaps she would be upon me, kill me. Aiming at her big, wide mouth, I fired another shot. The bullet went through her mouth, her throat, and, as I afterward found, broke her backbone. She fell, slid almost to my feet, and, quivering a little, died.

I found that I was trembling, so weak that I had to sit down. I said to myself: "My last shot. If it had missed her mouth, my body would now be lying there, torn all apart."

That morning when I got up, I had prayed Sun to pity me, to help me survive all dangers that might beset me, and to give me success in all of my undertakings. I now knew that Sun had helped me. That swiftly coming, leaping bear, never could I have shot her in her mouth had He not helped me do it. Raising my hands to the sky, "Sun," I vowed, "the hide of this real-bear, softly tanned, I shall give to you in the coming Berries-Ripe Moon."

A crowd of people gathered around me when I came to the doorway of my lodge and drew the big hide down off my saddle. My mother and my almost-mothers came running out, and my mother cried: "Oh, my son. You should not have done this. So dangerous are real-bears; it might have killed you." "I had to kill it or be killed," I answered, and told all about it and of my Sun vow.

Said my mother when I had finished: "Never was a real-bear better tanned than this one will be, for you to sacrifice to Sun."

In the Berries Ripe Moon (July) as agreed upon, all the bands of our tribe gathered at Four Persons' Butte (Milk-Teton River) for our sacred-vow women to build, as they did every summer, a sacred lodge for Sun. There with Mountain Chief's band was Owl Child, whom we had not seen since he killed my father.

My mother, first to see him, came hurrying back into our lodge and said: "That dog-face, that bad Owl Child is across the circle. All dressed up and proudly walking around." And with that she cried; my almost-mothers and my almost-sisters cried; and I took up my many-shots gun and said that I would go and kill him. Mothers and sisters, they seized me; took my gun from me; said that I should not attempt it for I might be killed, I their only support, and then what would become of them?

"But when I grow up, I surely will put an end to him, my father's killer," I said, and meant it.

On that first day of our getting together to build the lodge for Sun, it was told all through our great camp that Owl Child had been struck and knocked down by Four Bears, a white man married to *Kahkokimah Ahki* (Cutting-off-Head Woman) of our tribe, and that Owl Child was now saying that he would soon go back up to Wolf-Also-Jumped Creek to kill the man. Four Bears had made love to his (Owl Child's) wife, tried to get her to leave him; then had beaten him when he was unarmed. For that, Four Bears must die.

Four Bears (Malcolm Clark) had been a West Point cadet. Dismissed from the Academy for gross infractions of its rules, he had entered the service of the American Fur Company on the Upper Missouri River, remaining with it until it went out of business in 1864. He had then taken to ranching on Wolf Creek, near where the Fort Benton–Helena wagon road crossed the stream. He is said to have been a man of violent temper and ruthless disposition.

My mother was one of the sacred-vow women who built the great lodge for Sun that summer. When it was completed the people came with their most loved belongings to sacrifice them to Him Above. Praying him for his pity, his help, asking him to give them long and full life, they made their offerings, and the Sun priest tied them to the center post of the great lodge. Myself, I gave my real-bear skin. My mother had softly tanned it, and on its flesh side I had painted a picture of myself shooting the real-bear as it came leaping toward me. As I entered the sacred lodge and handed the robe to Red Eagle for him to attach to the center post, I felt grateful to Sun for all that he had done for me. Earnestly I prayed him for long and full life for my family, for all the Pikunis, and for myself.

The sacred ceremonies ended, again the bands of our tribe separated, going one way and another to pass the summer. Our Heavy Runner band departed to cross Big (Missouri) River and camp and hunt here and there along Yellow (Judith) River.

All of our bands kept in frequent communication with one another and so in time we got some bad news. It was that Mountain Chief's band had gone to Many-Houses (Fort Benton) to trade, and there some drunken white men—Grouse, Night Watcher (Henry Kennerly), Real White Man (Peter Lukins), and others—had, without cause for it, hanged Heavy-Charging-in-the-Brush and had shot and killed Bear Child and Rock-Old-Man, three prominent members of the band. That made us feel very sad, very angry. We decided to trade no more at Many-Houses.

It was not long after the murder of our three men at Many-Houses that visitors brought us more news: Owl Child, leading a few of his friends, had gone up to Wolf-Also-Jumped Creek and had himself killed Four Bears. I was present when Heavy Runner and other leading ones of our band got together to talk about it. They agreed that Owl Child had been justified in killing him. Much as I hated Owl Child for killing my father, I had to admit that he had had good right to kill this fire-hearted, quarrelsome, white man. Four Bears had tried to steal his woman; and failing in that, had struck him, beaten him. In no other way could Owl Child have wiped out that terrible disgrace. Well, that was naught to me. I was not forgetting my vow: the time was coming when I would make Owl Child cry for what he had done to me and mine.

In Falling-Leaves Moon (September) we moved back across Big River, and were camped on Two Medicine Lodges River when winter came. All the other bands of our tribe were east of us, here and there along Bear (Marias) River. A white man called "Big Nose" (Hiram Baker), who had come with a wagonload of cartridges and other things to trade for our buffalo robes and furs, told that the whites were more and more angry about the killing of Four Bears, and were trying to get their seizers (soldiers) to make a big killing of our tribe and so avenge his death. However, the seizer chiefs (army officers) seemed not to listen to their demand. Our chiefs talked over that news and thought little of it. As Heavy Runner said, the killing of Four Bears did not concern us. If the whites wanted to get revenge for it, they should kill Owl Child.

As the winter wore on the buffalo herds drifted farther and farther away from the mountains, and we had to follow them or starve. We moved down to the mouth of Two Medicine Lodges River; then in Middle-Winter Moon (January), moved down on Bear River and camped in a bottom that Mountain Chief's band had just left, they going a little way farther down the river. It was an unhappy time: the whites had given us of their terrible white-scabs disease (smallpox), and some of our band were dying. And the buffalo herds remained so far out from the river that we had to go for a two or three days' hunt in order to get meat for our helpless ones. One evening I arranged to go on a hunt with a number of our band. We were to travel light, take only two lodges to accommodate us all; my mother and one of my sisters were to go with me to help with my kills. Came morning and I set out for my horses; could not find them on the plain. Sought them in the timbered bottoms of the valley; did not come upon them until late in the day. The hunting party had long since gone. I told my mother that we would join the next party of hunters to go out. We still had dried meat to last us for some days.

On the following morning I found my horses in the timber well above camp and was nearing it with them when, suddenly, I ran into a multitude of white men: seizers. I was so astonished, so frightened, that I could not move. One of the seizers came and grasped my arm; spoke; tapped his lips with his fingers: I was not to speak, shout. He was a chief, this seizer, had strips of yellow metal on his shoulders, had a big knife, a five-shots pistol. He made me advance with him; all of the seizers were advancing. We came to the edge of the camp; close before us were the lodges. Off to our right were many more seizers looking down upon them. It was a cold day. The people were all in their lodges, many still in their beds. None knew that the seizers had come.

A seizer chief up on the bank shouted something, and at once all of the seizers began shooting into the lodges. Chief Heavy Runner ran from his lodge toward the seizers on the bank. He was shouting to them and waving a paper writing that our agent had given him, a writing saying that he was a good and peaceful man, a friend of the whites. He had run but a few steps when he fell, his body pierced with bullets. Inside the lodges men were yelling; terribly frightened women and children, screaming—screaming from wounds, from pain as they died. I saw a few men and women, escaping from their lodges, shot down as they ran. Most terrible to hear of all was the crying of little babies at their mothers' breasts. The seizers all advanced upon the lodges, my seizer still firmly holding my arm. They shot at the tops of the lodges; cut the bindings of the poles so the whole lodge would collapse upon the fire and begin to burn—burn and smother those within. I saw my lodge so go down and burn. Within it my mother, my almost-mothers, my almost-sisters. Oh, how pitiful were their screamings as they died, and I there, powerless to help them!

Soon all was silent in the camp, and the seizers advanced, began tearing down the lodges that still stood, shooting those within them who were still alive, and then trying to burn all that they tore down, burn the dead under the heaps of poles, lodge-skins, and lodge furnishings; but they did not burn well.

At last my seizer released my arm and went about with his men looking at the smoking piles, talking, pointing, laughing, all of them. And finally the seizers rounded up all of our horses, drove them up the valley a little way, and made camp.

I sat before the ruin of my lodge and felt sick. I wished that the seizers had killed me, too. In the center of the fallen lodge, where the poles had fallen upon the fire, it had burned a little, then died out. I could not pull up the lodge-skin and look under it. I could not bear to see my mother, my almost-mothers, my almost-sisters lying there, shot or smothered to death. When I went for my horses, I had not carried my many-shots gun. It was there in the ruin of the lodge. Well, there it would remain.

From the timber, from the brush around about, a few old men, a few women and children came stealing out and joined me. Sadly we stared at our ruined camp; spoke but little; wept. Wailed wrinkled old Black Antelope: "Why, oh, why had it to be that all of our warriors, our hunters, had to go out for buffalo at this time. But for that, some of the white seizers would also be lying here in death."

"One was killed. I saw him fall," I said.

"*Ah*. Only one seizer. And how many of us. Mostly women and children; newborn babies. Oh, how cruel, how terribly cruel are the white men," old Curlew Woman wailed.

"Killed us off without reason for it; we who have done nothing against the whites," said old Three Bears, and again we wept.

As we sat there, three men arrived from Mountain Chief's camp below. They stared and stared at our fallen, half-burned lodges, at our dead, lying here and there, and could hardly believe what they saw. They rode over to us, asked what had happened, and when we had told them of the white seizers' sudden attack upon us, it was long before they could speak. And then they said that we were to live with them; they would take good care of us poor, bereaved ones.

Said old Three Bears: "We had warning of this. That white trader, Big Nose, told us that the whites were going to revenge the killing of Four Bears by Owl Child. But why didn't they seek him, kill him, instead of slaughtering us here, we always friendly with the whites?"

That Owl Child—he had killed my father, and now he was the cause of my mother's and all my womenfolks' lying dead under their half-burned lodges. Well, as soon as possible, I would kill him, I vowed.

That night the white seizers did not closely watch the hundreds of horses that they had taken from us. We managed to get back about half of the great herd and drive them down to Mountain Chief's camp. During the day our buffalo hunters returned. With many horses loaded with meat and hides, they came singing, laughing, down into the valley, only to find their dear ones dead under their ruined lodges. The white killers had gone, turned back whence they came. As best we could we buried our dead—a terrible, grieving task it was—and counted them: fifteen men, ninety women, fifty children. Forty-four lodges and lodge furnishings destroyed, and hundreds of our horses stolen. *Haiya! Haiya!*

And to this day I deeply regret that I had no opportunity to fulfill my vow: even then Owl Child had the terrible white-scabs disease, and a few days later he died.

Bear Head finished his tale and I was silent, and very, very sad. The murder of the three Pikunis, Heavy-Charging-in-the-Brush, Bear Child, and Rock-Old-Man, by the three white men at Fort Benton had caused no particular comment. But the killing of Malcolm Clark (Four Bears) was different. The newspapers and the residents of the territory were loud in denunciation of the outrage; as it was, no settler, no traveler, was safe from the Indians, they said. The commanding officers at Fort Shaw and Fort Ellis as well as the Secretary of War were called upon to punish severely the Indians, to make the country safe for the whites, above all to make reprisal on Mountain Chief's band, of which Owl Child was a member.

So was it that Major Eugene M. Baker of Fort Ellis was chosen to lead an expedition against the band. Early in January, 1870, he left Fort Ellis with four companies of the Second Cavalry. Arriving at Fort Shaw, he arranged to have fifty-five mounted men of the Thirteenth Infantry under Captain Higbee join his command; and Joseph Kipp, a Fort Shaw scout, was sent out to locate the band. He found it in a bottom of Marias River Valley due north of Goosebill Butte and, returning to the fort, so reported. On the following morning the expedition set out northward and that evening camped on Teton River, close under Priest's Butte. Two mornings later, looking down upon the camp on Marias River, scout Kipp at once said to Colonel Baker: "Colonel, that is not Mountain Chief's camp. It is the camp of Black Eagle and Heavy Runner. I know it by its differently painted lodges."

And he was right. Since he had been there a few days previously, Mountain Chief's band had moved down the river about ten miles, and this band had come down and occupied the deserted campground.

Said Colonel Baker: "That makes no difference, one band or another of them; they are all Piegans and we will attack them." And then to one of his men: "Sergeant, stand behind this scout, and if he yells or makes a move, shoot him." And finally: "All ready men. Fire!"

I obtained later some more information about the massacre:

HISTORICAL SOCIETY OF MONTANA [seal]

DAVID HILGER, LIBRARIAN
ROOM 106, CAPITAL

HELENA, JAN. 16, 1936

James Willard Schultz
Indian Field Service
Browning, Montana
DEAR MR. SCHULTZ:

Answering your letter of Jan. 14 the information requested on the Baker Massacre is as follows:

Col. Philip R. De Trobriand was in command at Fort Shaw at the time, Major Eugene M. Baker was in command of the expedition and was chosen by General Sheridan because of his experience in the Indian warfare in Oregon. These are Sheridan's orders verbatim, "If the lives and property of citizens of Montana can best be protected by striking Mountain Chief's band, I want them struck. Tell Baker to strike them hard." Baker marched from Fort Ellis with four companies of the 2nd cavalry and was joined at Fort Shaw by 55 mounted men of the 13th infantry under Capt. Higbee. Joe Cobell and Joe Kipp were scouts with the soldiers on the expedition. On the morning of Jan. 23, 1870 they came upon the band of Piegans under Bear Chief and Big Horn on the Marias, 37 lodges. The camp was still asleep and many of the people were ill with smallpox. Baker's orders were "Open Fire; continue as long as there is any resistance." The official report from De Trobriand was 120 men killed, 53 women and children, 44 lodges destroyed and 300 horses captured. The report from Vincent Collyer of the Board of Indian Commissioners was 173 killed: 15 fighting men (between 12 and 37 years of age) 90 women and 50 children under 12 years of age. This information came from Lieut. Pease, agent for the Blackfeet. One cavalry man was killed.

Am interested in the account of the killing of Malcolm Clarke and it is probably the true version. Am always glad to be of service to you at any time.

Very truly yours,
[signed]
(MRS.) ANNE MCDONNELL
Asst. Lib.

CHAPTER TWENTY-ONE

Plenty of Buffalo Meat
(Told by Many-Tail-Feathers)

I◁•I◁•I◁•I◁•I◁•I◁•I◁•I◁•I◁•I◁•I◁•I◁•I◁•I◁•I◁•I◁•I◁•I◁•I◁•I◁•I◁•I◁•I◁•I◁•I◁•I◁•I◁•I◁•I◁•I◁•

To DECOY AND SUDDENLY PUT TO DEATH a herd of buffalo, that is just what the prehistoric, nomadic, Indian tribes of our northwestern and Canada's western plains did whenever meat and hides were needed. And they continued that activity into historic time, even up to a period definitely determined to have been somewhere around 1843–46. The Blackfoot, Crow, Assiniboine, Gros Ventre, and Kalispel Indian tribes all did it; but I shall tell only of the four Blackfoot tribes' way of it, as I have been an active member of them for sixty-three years and have heard their stories of it all many, many times. The Blackfoot belief that dreams are actual experiences of their shadows (souls) while their bodies sleep, and that Sun is the supreme god of earth and sky, enters into it all.

To begin with, there are four tribes of the Blackfoot Indian Confederacy: the Blackfoot, Blood, and North Piegan tribes of Alberta, and the Pikuni tribe of the Blackfoot Reservation, Montana. Of all the story tellers (historians) of the four tribes, I considered Many-Tail-Feathers of the Montana tribe best of all. He died in 1925 in his ninetieth year, and it was his father, also named Many-Tail-Feathers, who, because of his powerful dream, put an end to the decoying and slaughtering of buffalo herds by the four tribes. And so to my old friend's tale of it all, as follows:

In that very-far-back time our ancestors were but one large tribe, the Blackfeet. It was not easy for the hunters to obtain meat and hides for their families, so the tribe frequently moved camp. But even at that they would be in the new location only a few days when the buffalo and antelope, the deer and elk and moose, would retreat, and the hunters with their pack dogs were obliged to go farther from camp in order to obtain food for their women and children.

Came a winter when the tribe was camped on North Big (Saskatchewan) River, not far out from the Backbone (Rocky Mountains). The snow became more and more deep; the buffalo and antelope and other game disappeared, and the people began to starve. Daily, nightly the people prayed for help. They sacrificed more and more of their choicest belongings to Sun, tied them to the branches of the trees as they begged Him to bring the buffalo herds back; but He heard them not. Hungry, weak, a woman was out in the timber gathering wood for her lodge fire when she heard a strange singing— someone singing a song so strange, so powerful that it made her hold her breath as she listened. She looked for the singer but could see no one. At last she realized that the song was coming from a big, old tree. She went to it, looked into a hole in it, and saw a round gathering of buffalo fur. At once the singing ceased and from the fur came a man's voice saying: "Woman, I am a buffalo stone; a giver of good luck; take me to your home, to your man, and I will teach him and his friends my songs; powerful songs that will bring the buffalo that you starving people need."

The woman was terribly frightened, but hunger made her take out the ball of fur. With trembling hands she opened it and the stone was there in its center, a brown stone about as long as a finger, and of much the shape of a buffalo—head, body, and four legs. The woman hurried with it to her man, told him what it had said. He called in many of his friends and, when they were seated, at his request the buffalo stone began singing. Carefully they listened, repeatedly sang, learned perfectly the songs. As the buffalo stone told them to do, they kept on singing all through the night; constantly singing and praying for buffalo, plenty of buffalo for their hungry women and children.

When daybreak was near, came a fierce wind and snowstorm from the north, and with it, snow-blinded, a herd of buffalo right into the camp. Hurrying out from their lodges with ready bows and arrows and even spears, the men killed many of them, while the women and children shrieked with fear. Well they might, for the snow-blinded animals ran about, right into several of the lodges, trampling and injuring the occupants, knocking over the lodges, poles and all. So was it that the people again had plenty of meat and hides; and he who owned the buffalo stone became a chief. However, after that one night of causing the buffalo to come, the buffalo stone never talked or sang again. In time, the people found and kept many buffalo stones and prayed to them, for it was well proven that they were givers of good luck, though not always to be relied upon to bring buffalo when wanted.

It was some time after that first finding of a buffalo stone that a man who had one attached to his necklace went out to hunt. It was in midsummer; and the biting, stinging flies were plentiful in the windless, timbered valley. The hunter went down the valley a long way seeing no meat animals of any kind, and the flies became more and more troublesome. To get rid of them he decided to go up onto the plain where a wind was blowing and turn homeward along the rim.

Nearing the top of the valley slope, he proceeded more and more slowly and at last looked out upon the plain. Not far away was a herd of buffalo, a few of them standing on watch for danger, the rest lying down. He had come up in sight of them so slowly that the watchers had not noticed him. He was wearing a thin buffalo-leather wrap. Though not so annoyingly as they had done in the valley, flies were still biting him, and to be rid of them he spread out his wrap and flapped it several times. At once the buffalo on watch turned and stared at him. After a little he spread out his wrap with both hands and flapped it as though it were his wings; at that all of the resting buffalo sprang up and stared at him, tossing their heads, stamping the ground with their forefeet. Never had they seen anything like that; they wondered what it could be. Slowly a few of the herd advanced a little way, stopped; but now the others were coming on, crowding the leaders forward. Again he did his winglike flapping of the wrap, and at that the whole herd began running swiftly toward him. Terribly frightened, dreading that he would be trampled to death, he sped down the slope a little way and took shelter against the lower side of a rock that was none too large, hearing the oncoming of the herd louder and louder in his ears. Nor did they stop to look for him where he had stood. Like a swift river of brown water down the slope they came, raising a cloud of dust with their earth-spurning hooves, even brushing against the rock which sheltered him, and then going on. Nor did they stop until they came to the shore of the river in the valley far below. Then standing up, wiping the fright-sweat from his face, the man scolded: "I am a crazy coward. I have no right to carry a bow and arrows, a weapon of any kind. Why, as they passed me here, safe in the shelter of this rock, I could have killed two or three fat ones of the herd."

Hungry, more and more angry at himself for not making use of his bow and arrows there in the shelter of the rock, the man trudged slowly homeward; sat down in his lodge, refused the food that his women offered him, angrily saying to them, "I am a crazy coward. I have no right to eat your food."

"But it is your food, your meat; you killed it, brought it to us," his sits-beside-him-wife said. He did not answer.

Came evening and the man stepped out from his lodge, shouted invitations to certain ones of his friends to come and smoke with him. When they were comfortably seated and the pipe was going the round of their circle, he told them of his experience with the buffalo, and of his cowardice, his failure to attempt to kill some of them that so closely passed him, safe there in the shelter of the rock.

Said one of his friends when he had finished: "How strange that was. Of course we have always decoyed antelope, enticed them close in and killed them, but I never thought that buffalo could be decoyed by any strange thing that they saw."

Another friend: "Doubtless that buffalo stone you wear brought the herd running toward you."

Still another: "Now that we know that buffalo can be decoyed by something strange to them, perhaps we can devise some way to make a success of it, make great killings of them." And to that all gave quick assent.

309

So was it that our far-back fathers began trying to decoy success-fully and kill a buffalo herd. We know not now in what ways they made their no-doubt-many attempts to do it, but at last they devised a sure way to accomplish their purpose. At the foot of a cliff some-where in North Big (Saskatchewan) River Valley they built a very large enclosure of such material as the tribe could gather: dead and fallen tree trunks and branches, rocks and brush; the cliff itself formed the inner side of it. Then from the top of the cliff, directly above the enclosure, they set out two ever-diverging lines of rock-and-brush piles that extended far out upon the plain. This con-trivance they named, simply, *piskan* ("corral, fence").

When all was finished, the chiefs, counseling together with pray-ers and songs to Sun, appointed a man who had a buffalo-stone ritual to be the decoyer *(áhwa waki)*. Then every evening in the lodge of the decoyer a gathering of Sun-favored men went through the buf-falo-stone rite, earnestly praying Sun to bring a herd of buffalo to a position from which they could be decoyed. Also, several hundred men and women were named to be the frighteners *(áwpwo taks)*, they to hurry out and lie at the rock piles whenever called upon.

Kyi! It was not long until a herd was seen to be grazing out beyond the widely separated ends of the lines of rock piles, just beyond the little ridge on the plain that would prevent their seeing the fright-eners hurrying out to the rock piles or the decoyer running to the ridge. He slowly climbed it, so slowly that the buffalo did not notice him when he gained its crest. His wrap was a buffalo robe, fur side out; he grasped its outer edges, flapped it as a bird flaps its wings, and cried: "Whoo hoo! Whoo hoo! Whoo hoo!" At once every animal of the herd stopped grazing and stared at him; continued to stare as he repeated his flappings and whoo-hooing again and again.

At last, bending over as much as he could and still keep upon his feet, he ran along the top of the ridge a little way, then turned down the side of it out of their sight; soon he returned to the crest, did more wing-flapping, whoo-hooing; again disappeared; again returned to the crest and saw that a few of the cows were trotting toward him—they always more alert, inquisitive than the bulls. As, well-humped-over, whoo-hooing, he again started to run along the crest, the cows broke into a swift lope and so did the whole herd after them.

At that he dropped his robe and ran down off the ridge, straight toward the center of the space between the ends of the two lines of rock piles. On and on he ran, the buffalo after him, gaining upon him. They passed within the ends of the rock-pile lines, and the frighteners began rising upon either side of them and in their rear, shouting, waving their wraps, so frightening them that they did not notice the decoyer as he turned aside and dropped down at a rock pile. On and on the whole herd loped, straight toward the cliff. When the leaders came to it they could not stop nor turn aside. They were forced off it and, as though blind, all the others followed them, a waterfall-like stream of them whirling over and over and dropping into the great *piskan* at the foot of the cliff. Many were killed by the fall. Those still alive were soon finished by the many hunters there in wait.

Ha! How happy the men and women were as they sprang into the *piskan* and with their flint knives and stone axes and hammers began butchering the animals—a whole herd of buffalo decoyed and killed with ease; enough meat for the whole tribe for many days. It is no wonder that the hunters sang and sang and gave praise to Sun for his helpfulness. No longer in hot summer days, through deep winter snow, would they have to travel far and wearily in quest of meat for themselves, their women, and their little ones. And as for their decoyer, all agreed that he had become a sacred man, one to be honored, cared for in every way.

With ever-plentiful supplies of meat and hides obtained with their *piskans,* our far-back people had easy living; in time they became so many that for various reasons they had to separate. So was it that they became three tribes: the Siksikas (Blackfeet), the Kainahs (Bloods), and the Pikunis (Piegans). From North Big (Saskatchewan) River south to Elk (Yellowstone) River and from the Backbone (Rocky Mountains) far out eastward on the plains, they traveled and camped, fought off enemy tribes, made of that their own vast country. So was it that, at last, they had *piskans* along every one of its many streams and constantly depended upon them for their living.

Then, we know not how long ago it was, a war party of the Pikunis, traveling into the far south, the Always-Summer-Land, made a very strange discovery, so very strange that they could hardly believe what they saw: enemies of some kind were riding animals (horses) as big as elk and leading others packed with their belongings. Said the leader of the party: "Elk-dogs! That is what those strange animals are. My friends, we must have some of them."

Came night. Waiting until the enemies were asleep, the Pikuni war party went to their camp, took many of the strange, useful animals, and in time got safely back to their far-north people with them. At once war parties of all three of the tribes began going to Always-Summer-Land to obtain some of the elk-dogs. They took them from different Indian tribes and from a different kind of white men living there. Also, from some of those men that they killed they got strange weapons: very long big-knives (swords); long, iron, pointed spears; and iron shirts (shirts of mail). No doubt you remember that our friend Curly Bear, who died not long ago, had one of them that was taken by one of his far-back ancestors, and that it was buried with him. Well, the time came when our three tribes had so many elk-dogs that they no longer went into the Always-Summer-Land for more of them.

Our far-back fathers soon found that nothing was so exciting, so satisfying as the running of a herd of buffalo with a fast, well-trained elk-dog. With a good bow, a quiver of arrows, and such a horse, a hunter could often select and kill ten or twelve fat cows in a single run. So was it that *piskans* were not used so much for obtaining plentiful supplies of meat and hides. Still, used they were, for, as some of the wise, old, Sun's men said, it was not right to let old and sacred customs die.

A favorite *piskan* of our Pikuni tribe was the one on the south side of Milk (Teton) River and just below Old Man Lying Butte (on Teton River, nine miles above Choteau, Montana, U.S. Highway 89). When I was in my eighth summer (approximately 1843), we Pikunis moved from Two Medicine Lodges River to camp, for my father, Many-Tail-Feathers, who was a powerful decoyer, had long been urging our chiefs that we use the *piskan* there, and at last they had given in to his plea. He was a great warrior as well as a decoyer. He was married to three sisters; my mother, the eldest one, was his sits-beside-him-wife.

We made camp on the north side of the river, opposite the *piskan* on its south side. On the following morning my father and our chiefs climbed to the top of the sacred butte for a look at the country, and I followed them. We arrived upon its flat top. There, long since, some of our Sun's men had, with many white stones, made a figure, very large, of Old Man (a powerful but mischievous god of the Blackfoot tribes). Yes, it was a very large figure of him, his arms and legs outstretched. When we stopped before it my father made a prayer. "*Haiyu*, Old Man!" he chanted. "Pity us, help us to prosper. Our *piskan*, there close below us, help me fill it with buffalo." And as one man the others chanted: "*Haiyu*, Old Man! Help us to prosper! Give to us long and full life."

We then sat down and looked off. In all directions, near and far, the plain was dotted with herds of buffalo and antelope, some grazing, some resting, others going to and from water. Said my father: "Sun is good to us; just see how plentiful are the animals that he created for our use. Let us smoke and pray to him."

Four pipefuls, sacred number, they smoked one after another as they prayed to Him, sang His sacred songs, and then we returned to camp. Many of our people, with their horses, were drawing old logs and tree branches out to repair and heighten the *piskan*. Not a cliff *piskan*, it was at the mouth of a small, short coulee running down from the plain, and the cut bank at its inner side was just high enough to prevent the buffalo jumping back out of it. From the head of the coulee, of course, ran the two ever-diverging lines of rock piles, and just beyond them was the little ridge so necessary for preventing a herd, farther out, from seeing the decoyer and the frighteners hurrying out to take their various places.

Came night, and in our lodge my father and some of his friends smoked and prayed Sun for quick success at the *piskan*. *Ha!* Before the middle of next day our watchers came hurrying down from Old

Man Lying Butte with news that a herd of buffalo were resting close out from the decoyer's ridge. At once the frighteners began running out to take their places, I going with my mother and almost-mothers. With a few others we dropped down at a rock pile of the right line and well out from the *piskan*. Then came my father, but not afoot as had been the far-back decoying way. He was riding a brown horse upon whose head he had fastened the dried head-skin and fur and horns, and even the chin whiskers, of a buffalo bull, and he was wearing a buffalo robe, fur side out. Swiftly he rode past us and up the ridge. Nearing its top, he bent over flat upon the horse to imitate the hump of a buffalo. So, arriving upon the top of the ridge, he appeared to the resting herd beyond to be one of their kind. Shouting "Whoo hoo! Whoo hoo! Whoo hoo!" he rode down toward them a way, then turned and hurried back, up and over the ridge and out of their sight. Again and again he repeated that going and coming and whoo-hooing, all of us frighteners closely watching him as we prayed Sun to give him success, to keep us safe. There was always danger for the frighteners; more than once an oncoming herd had swerved, broken through a line of them, and trampled several of them to death. My mother gave me a scared feeling, made my eyes wet as she prayed, "Oh Sun! This day I give you my new beaded dress. So is it that I pray you to give my man success. And we poor ones, oh Sun! Make the buffalo run straight to the *piskan*. Oh, prevent them from turning and cutting us to pieces with their sharp hooves."

Six times my father ran down the ridge a little way, whoo-hooing to the herd and then as he came back over it he did not stop; on he came, fiercely quirting his horse, and over the ridge came the buffalo after him. As soon as they were well within the lines of rock piles the frighteners began rising and yelling and wrap-waving at them. They had come down off the ridge well scattered, but now, terribly frightened, they bunched close together and ran ever faster, the thudding of their hooves like thunder in our ears. Soon my father turned his horse, rode out through the left line of the frighteners, but the buffalo were no longer after him. What they did see and

314

fear was the shouting and waving of us frighteners, continually rising upon their either side and running after them. So on they ran, straight ahead, down into the little coulee and jumped off the cutbank into the *piskan*, we frighteners singing and yelling, hurrying thither. Oh, what a satisfying sight it was, that great *piskan* filled with buffalo, as later counted, 181 of them; our hunters on top of the *piskan*, with guns and with bows and arrows shooting them. I climbed up onto the *piskan* beside my father, reloading his flintlock gun. "Give it to me. Let me kill one!" I yelled.

"No! You are too young for that," he said. But I grasped his arm, hung onto it, pleaded hard, and at last he handed me the gun. I aimed it at a yearling close by; aimed for the ball to pierce the lungs. I pulled the trigger, and down off the *piskan* that gun kicked me flat upon my back. My father and the others near by laughed at me. I climbed back upon the *piskan* and looked down: my yearling was dead.

"Laugh, you crazy ones; I don't care. I have killed a buffalo," l yelled.

Said my father as he recovered his gun: "So you have, my son. Next time hold the gun tight against your shoulder and it will not kick you."

Men and women, boys and girls, we all worked hard the rest of that day in butchering the many buffalo, and with pack horses and travois horses getting the meat and hides across the river to camp. And then what a happy evening for us all! My father's friends were constantly coming to our lodge to smoke with him and praise him for his decoying of the herd. There was feasting and smoking and singing in nearly every lodge. Some of the warrior societies, the Crazy Dogs, Raven Carriers, Kit Foxes, and others, sang and danced. I sneaked into the lodge of the Raven Carriers society to see them dance, hear their powerful heart-stirring songs. Their leader, Eagle Head, had recently led a war party on a raid against the Crows, and they had returned with many horses and scalps. He, himself, had killed three of the Crows. He noticed me sneaking into the lodge and I thought that he would tell me to leave. But, no. He signed to me to come and sit upon his couch. I did so and he patted my shoulder. Said to me: "Your father, what a Sun-favored man he is. What a powerful decoyer. It is because of him, his success, that we dance tonight."

He was so friendly that I said to him: "Killer of Crows, I want to be a member of you Raven Carriers."

"So you shall be when you grow up," he answered. And then as the drummers and singers began again the society's dance song, he sprang up, raised me up, and said: "Come, you shall dance with us." I did so. I danced out from the circle of them, danced close around the fire; and, clapping their hands, they said that I was a perfect dancer. I went home very proud of myself: I was to be a Raven Carrier. In our lodge all were asleep when I entered it. I noiselessly got upon my couch and slept, too.

Daybreak was near when loud shouting awakened us. A man was shouting: "Get up! Get up, you people! Our *piskan* is burning! Hurry! Hurry! We must put out the fire."

Cried my mother: "Our man. He is out there. Where can he be?" We all rushed out. The *piskan* was a very large fire.

"Enemies are burning it," our head chief, Lone Walker, shouted. "You warriors, all of you get your weapons, get upon your horses and we will make those enemies to cry."

Again my mother cried: "Our man, oh where can he be? I know not when he got up, went out."

As our many warriors were hurrying to obey Lone Walker's order, lo! my father appeared. He was coming from the river, carrying his leggings and moccasins; and when he had come close he signed to the crowd of us: "Be quiet. Be quiet." And then said loudly: "Retie your horses, put away your weapons. I set fire to the *piskan*. You cannot save it."

"*Ha*, you set it afire. Why did you do it? Are you crazy?"

"No, not crazy. I did it because of my vision, my powerful vision," he answered.

"That vision—what was it?"

"I cannot tell you about it now. I am very tired. I must rest," he said, and turned, walked slowly to our lodge and into it, my mother, almost-mothers, and I following, hearing the people all about us angrily talking, saying that the fire-setter should be made to suffer.

My father sat down upon his couch, put on his leggings and moccasins. My mother, building up the fire, asked what he would eat: pemmican, broiled ribs, berry soup, or what?

"Nothing. Nothing at all," he almost whispered, lay down, turning his back to us. And sadly, worriedly, we looked at him, and obeying my mother's signs to us went outside and sat at one side of the doorway of the lodge. Foodless, silent, long we sat there. From afar the people stared at us, came not near us. We were very sad.

Sun was near the middle of the blue when my father came out to us. He had not washed, rebraided his hair, nor painted his face with sacred red. Very poor looking he was. "I am going to Lone Walker's lodge to tell of my vision; you better come; sit outside," he said to us. We got up and followed him, sat down close outside the lodge where we could hear all that would be said within.

After a few words with my father, Lone Walker came out and shouted to this and that one of our chiefs and Sun's men to come to him. They soon entered the lodge, and a big crowd of our people surrounded it, also sat down to listen.

Then soon my father began, loudly speaking: "My friends, my vision was powerful. As I slept I, my shadow, went forth upon discovery of whatever I might see. It was that, as I was walking in a valley strange to me, a buffalo bull came out from a grove, came toward me, stopped and raised high a right forefoot, making as it were, the sign for peace. So, peace I also signed, and he came on. Soon we met and he said to me: 'I have been looking for you. It is that I must give you warning about something you and your kind are doing that is very wrong. It is that with your *piskans* you are rapidly killing off us buffalo. If you keep on doing it you will soon put an end to the very last ones of us. So this I say: stop using your *piskans* if you would prevent something dreadful happening to all of your kind.'

" 'What would it be, that dreadful thing?' I asked.

" 'I have warned you; I will say no more,' he answered and turned and walked back the way he had come. With that I awoke, my body wet with sweat. I felt that I must at once prove to my vision buffalo that I accepted his warning, accepted it not only for myself but for all of us. So was it that I hurried across to the *piskan* and set it afire."

Said Lone Walker low heartedly—we outside could barely hear him: "My friend, you did right; you had to do it. As our Sun-given visions tell us to do, so must we do if we are to survive the dangers that beset us."

"Yes. Yes. Yes. True. So ends our *piskan* killings," cried the others there within. And with that we all arose and strolled off our various ways.

Visiting us at the time were several members of our brother tribes, the Blackfeet and the Bloods. At once they hurried home to tell of my father's vision. So was it that they too ceased using *piskans* for obtaining food. *Ha!* Of all those present at that last killing of buffalo in Old Man Lying *piskan*, Mountain Chief and I are the only ones now alive.

So ended my old friend Many-Tail-Feathers' tale of the *piskans* in the long-ago.

In recent years a few Montanans have been digging into the sites of some of the *piskans* and finding quantities of flint and obsidian arrow and spear points, flint knives, stone mauls and axes, bone fleshers and scrapers, and other prehistoric artifacts in layer upon layer of buffalo bones and even buffalo fur. There are *piskan* sites near all of the Montana towns east of the Rockies. A favorite one of the Blackfoot tribes was that on Wolf Creek, two miles above Wolf Creek Town, called Wolf-Also-Jumped *piskan*. It was so named because a wolf, close following a buffalo herd that was being decoyed, also went off the cliff. On the Blackfoot Indian Reservation, Montana, north side of Two Medicine River Valley, and two miles down a branch road from U.S. Highway 89 is a *piskan* site that near-by Indians will gladly point out to the tourist. It lies at the foot of a very high cliff, and its layers of buffalo bones are all of two hundred feet in circumference. It was that, after decoying and killing of a herd, the bones and offal left by the butchers would be covered by a wash of earth from the plain before another decoying would occur; hence the layers of them. A very interesting *piskan* site on this reservation is one in Cut Bank River Valley, a mile above the Indian boarding school. The school children recently exploited it and found its lowest layer of buffalo bones at a depth of four feet.[1] On the Blood, the Blackfoot, and the North Piegan Indian reservations in Alberta there are also many *piskans*, few of which have ever been dug into.

[1] It was scientifically excavated in the summer of 1958 by an expedition under the direction of Thomas F. Kehoe, then curator of the Museum of the Plains Indian at Browning.

CHAPTER TWENTY-TWO

Bison Skulls on Chief Mountain[1]
(Told by *Ahko Pitsu*)

IT WAS IN 1902, if I rightly remember, that Henry L. Stimson and William H. Seward III decided to climb Chief Mountain at the east edge of the region which was in 1910 to become Glacier National Park. But disdaining the easy ascent to its summit from the west, they chose to climb its south, precipitous side. Accompanied by their guide, *Paiota Satsiko* ("Comes-with-Rattles"), they set out early of an autumn morning and with great risk of their lives made the ascent, arriving at the summit at noon. There, to their great surprise, where buffalo could not possibly come, owing to a last, clifflike rise of the ridge on the west, they found three buffalo skulls: two of them very old and weather worn, the other one still in a good state of preservation.

Stimson mused: "It is strange that these buffalo skulls should be here. Long-ago Indians must have brought them up, but why? What reason could they have had for doing it?"

Said Comes-with-Rattles: "They came here to fast, to pray for visions as they slept, and brought these buffalo skulls for pillows. That much I know about it."

But though Stimson and Seward questioned him, he could tell them no more. When of but few years, his father had been killed in the Baker Massacre of 1870, and his brothers-in-law, Kipp and Upham, had raised him, kept him with them, so he knew but little of the lore of his Pikuni people.

[1] Published in *The Great Falls Tribune* (January 23, 1938).

At the time I was camped at St. Mary lakes with George Bird Grinnell, and when the climbers returned and told of their find of the skulls on top of the mountain, I determined to learn if possible who the men were that had carried them there, and what had been the result of their fasts. I felt sure that *Ahko Pitsu*, my close friend and a notable historian of the three Blackfoot tribes, would have the answers for me. Come winter, I would ask him about it.

In our cabin on Two Medicine Lodges River, *Ahko Pitsu* ("Returns-with-Plenty") was a frequent visitor. So one evening after my wife, Fine Shield Woman, had served us a good meal of beef stew, bread, and coffee, and we were enjoying a smoke of *l'herbe* and tobacco in front of our fire, I mentioned the climb of the two white men led by Comes-with-Rattles, how they had found three buffalo skulls on top of Chief Mountain and were wondering how they got there. Two of the skulls were so very old that the black sheaths of their horns had been worn away by winds and storms, and the sheaths of the other horns had turned from black to yellowish white.

"Long, long ago, one of those skulls was taken up there," *Ahko Pitsu* said. "Strange you should ask me about it now. Last night I had a dream, and in it my old friend *Miah* came to me. That is all I remember of my dream. I have been thinking about *Miah* (obsolete word) all day. He was my close friend and adviser in my youthful days. No doubt you remember him. He died in that last summer that many of us Pikunis were camping at Raven Quiver's trading house on Bear River."

"Yes, I remember *Miah*. Tell me something about him, about his stories of his youthful adventures. I remember he was a very old man when he died."

He drew several lengthy, satisfied whiffs from the pipe which I had filled for him and said: "Now. I begin."

This is the story he told:

Never was there a man of our tribes who endured so much bad luck as he did for many winters. Then, because of a vision he obtained upon the top of Chief Mountain, with a buffalo skull that he carried up there for a pillow, he thereafter had great success in all of his undertakings.

Miah told of finding two buffalo skulls when he arrived at the top of Chief Mountain. One of them, he said, had been the fasting pillow of that powerful, long-ago warrior, Eagle Head; but none knew who had carried the other skull up there. He had been, of course, some very, very long-ago warrior of our people.

Miah in his old age loved to tell of his many terrible experiences, how he failed in everything that he attempted to do, and how, at last, he obtained the power to overcome his continuous bad luck. I well remember the last time I heard him tell of it. A number of us were gathered in Heavy Runner's lodge, *Miah* one of our circle, and Heavy Runner, who had just returned with some of his friends from an unsuccessful raid upon the herds of the Cutthroats, was telling of their bad luck.

Said *Miah*, when Heavy Runner had finished his sorrowful tale: "Friend, your bad luck was as nothing compared with the continuous failures of my undertakings for many winters, the last one worst of all. I had become so talked about for my failures in all that I did that the leaders of our war parties would not let me join them from fear that I would cause them trouble. My closest friends would not go hunting with me. Even my two wives ceased liking me. They did not smile when I was with them. Silently, cold eyed with set lips, they cared for our lodge, placed food before me. Oh, how unhappy, how sad I was.

"At last on a day of early summer I said to my wives: 'At once make for me two pairs of moccasins, plain ones. Put them, an awl, sinew thread, sacred paint, flint and steel, some pemmican in my war sack. I am going to try to take Cutthroat scalps and horses.'

"Said my sits-beside-me-wife, Mink Woman: 'What a thoughtless one you are, leaving us with barely enough meat for two more days. Before starting off to war, you bring in the meat of a fat buffalo cow for us to cut up and dry for future use.'

" 'Should I go hunting, my horse would probably stumble, fall, and kill or cripple me. I leave it to your brothers to keep you supplied with meat,' I answered, and tearfully, with never another word to me, they set about their work.

"I did not ask a sacred-pipe man to give me a going-away sweat-lodge bath. No use of that. Time and time again they had done it for me, and always had Sun and his Above Ones failed to heed their fervent prayers for my success against the enemy.

"Night came. Silently my wives watched me sling on my war sack and my shield, take up my gun, and leave them. We were camped, our whole tribe of Pikuni Blackfeet, where Bear (Marias) River joins Big (Missouri) River. Taking up onto the plain, I traveled on eastward, heading the long, deep, and timbered coulees running down into Big River. Old Woman (Night Red Light) came up big and round. The Seven Persons (constellation Ursa Major) were brightly shining and turning in the northern sky, marking the passing of the night.

"Well, one did not need to pray to them for help, I thought. Different from Sun and the other Above Ones, there they were, always helpful when not cloud hidden, plainly telling how long it was since night had come and how far off was the coming of a new day. I was feeling so sad that I had to force myself to walk. What was the trouble with me, what had I done that the Above Ones had failed to hear my prayers to them for success against the enemy, for success in all my activities? They heeded the prayers and the offerings of other men, helped them to be successful in their raids upon our enemies, to become rich from their takings of enemy horses. In all I had been upon eleven raids against the Crows, Cutthroats, Parted Hairs (Sioux), and other enemies, and never yet had I taken an enemy scalp, or even an enemy horse. No wonder that our warriors and hunters shunned me, that my wives lived with me only because they had to. Well, upon this, my twelfth war trail, I would make a successful raid upon the enemy, or die trying, I said to myself, and with that went on more forcefully.

"Herds of buffalo, bands of antelope fled as I approached them. Wolves and coyotes howled and shrilly yelped. A kit fox began following me and I was pleased, thinking it might be a sign of coming good luck. I turned about and stopped. It stopped, sat on its haunches, and I spoke to it. 'Sinopah,' I said, 'you, your whole kind are wise. When you are hungry you never fail to catch and kill food, birds and the various small animals; and you all are runners so swift that you always escape from your many enemies who try to kill you. Sinopah, pity me. Ask your far-back ancestors' shadows (spirits, souls), they who lived in that long-ago time when all of the various animals and men spoke together, to pity me, help me to be successful in my undertakings. Keep on following me, Sinopah, and I will do something for you. I shall presently kill an animal of some kind, and you shall have all that you can eat of it.'

"With that I went on, and seeing that Sinopah still followed me I was more than ever pleased. He is going to help me, give me of his power, I thought.

"I felt stronger, walked faster, on and on along the rim of the plain, often looking up at the Seven Persons constantly turning in the northern sky. At last they gave me to know that the new day was near. The eastern sky began to whiten, then to redden. Sinopah was still following me. Oh, what a good-luck sign. Haiya! Just as Sun was coming up I heard a sudden tearing sound like that of a dead, loose-barked tree in fierce wind, and looking back, I saw a big eagle swoop down upon Sinopah and with one claw in the back of his neck, the other in his loin, rise and fly off with him, Sinopah shrilly crying. Haiya! Haiya! Even he, his kind, wise and swift though they were, had enemies still more wise and swift, big birds that seized and carried them off for food for their young. Gone my hope for help from Sinopah. Sad, feeling weak, I turned off the plain, sped down the long slope to Big River, and drank thirstily of its muddy water.

"I was hungry. My pemmican was for a time when I would be close to an enemy camp. Some whitetail deer came to the shore to drink. Should I shoot one, enemies somewhere about might hear the boom of my gun and come searching for me. But I must take that risk. I killed a yearling doe, built a fire, broiled and ate my fill of its meat, broiled more, enough to last several days, then crept into thick brush and slept until night came again.

"Again I took up onto the plain and traveled eastward, heading the deep coulees running down into the valley of Big River. The Seven Persons gave me to know that it was midnight when I came to where the river turned to the south. I then went on east of north, and as Sun was reddening the sky I arrived at the foot of the Bear Paw Mountains, drank from a little spring, climbed the steep slope, and stopped in the edge of a grove of pine for my daily rest.

"Near and far down on the plain, herds of buffalo and antelope were grazing, resting, heading for water. How peaceful it all was. I ate some of my broiled meat, lay down, and slept. But not for long. Loud, forceful singing awakened me. I sat up, looking down the slope through the branches of the little pines. There at the spring where I had drunk, a war party of many men, with many horses, were gathering to drink and rest. Five of the men were waving scalps laced to forked sticks in time with the fierce, triumphant war song that all were singing. Most of them had an eagle tail feather tied straight up at the back of their heads. So. They were Cutthroats or some other tribe of Parted Hairs (Sioux).

"They had come from the west to the spring. Probably the scalps and the horses that they had were scalps and horses of my own people—perhaps of my own close relatives. How sad and how angry I felt as I looked down at them. Three pipefuls they smoked after they had drunk at the spring and eaten plenty of broiled meat, and then rode on eastward, lashing and shouting at their big band of stealings, keeping them going at a swift pace. Sun had not helped in my past doings, but perhaps he would now. 'Sun! oh Sun! Pity me. Help me to come upon the camp of my enemies, there going, and do them harm,' I pleaded.

"That night and on the following night I traveled eastward along the foot of the Bear Paws. On the next night I crossed the valley of Middle Creek (Cow Creek) and stopped for the day at the west end of the Wolf Mountains (Little Rockies). Three mornings later I climbed to the top of that butte at the east end of the Wolf Mountains, the Hairy Cap, for my daily rest. *Ha!* The Hairy Cap. Very tall and slender, its upper part thickly pine grown, the most beautiful butte in all of our great country. Rightly our far-off fathers named it Hairy Cap. It was very slowly, with great caution, that I made the steep climb, for its summit was a lookout stopping place of war parties of many tribes traveling in that part of our country.

"I had often heard our warriors tell of stopping there and looking off upon the plain for traveling enemies, or for signs of them. As I had expected, I found upon the summit a waist-high, large circle of rocks that some long-ago war party had piled up for shelter from the wind. It was a warm, still morning. But had the wind been blowing ever so cold and fierce, I would not have taken shelter from it within that circle, for enemies might have built it up and left within it their sacred power to do later users of it great harm.

"From the top of Hairy Cap on that still, clear morning, I carefully scanned the great plain for sight of any enemies who might be traveling upon it, but could see none. And near and far, north to Little River and beyond, to the east, and south to the dark breaks of Big River, the many herds of buffalo and of antelope were quiet. A war party could not travel anywhere off there without frightening some of the herds and putting them to swift flight. Contentedly I filled my pipe and smoked it, then lay down to sleep, noticing as I did so two ravens flying to their nest in a near pine tree and carrying in their beaks some kind of food for their squawking, hungry young ones.

"I did not sleep long. The loud, hoarse croaking of the father and mother ravens flying round and round above their nest awoke me, and I seized my gun and sat up just as three whitetail deer came leaping up the east side of the butte, closely passed me, and turned down its north side. It was not the deer, I well knew, that had alarmed the ravens; they would pay no attention to their coming and going. My concern was the cause of the flight of the deer; which of their enemies—men, wolves, or mountain lions—had been after them. On hands and knees I crept through the grass and brush until I could look down whence the deer had come. *Haiya!* Only a little way below me, so close that I could plainly see them, some men were climbing the steep slope.

"Their leader, tall, heavy bodied, had an eagle tail feather at the back of his head. They were another war party of Parted Hairs. I crept back a little way, then got up and turned down the west side of the butte as fast as I could go without making any noise, and in the lower edge of the timber forced my way into a thick growth of berry brush and sat down. I was sweating, breathing hard from my run. My heart was fast beating. For a long time I kept looking up at the way I had come, but the enemy did not appear, nor could I hear anything of them. Without doubt they did not know of my presence there on the butte. But for the excited, croaking ravens they would have come upon me, killed me as I slept. This, I felt, was a sign that my luck had turned, that my bad luck was ended. 'Oh, you Ravens,' I said. 'You saved me from those Parted Hairs. Give me of your power. Continue to help me. I will help you. Yes, I will leave always some of the meat of my killings for you and your raven kind to eat.'

"From Hairy Cap it had been my intention to go north to Little River and follow it down in quest of the camp of the Cutthroats. But now as I sat there on the slope of the butte I saw, well to the south from me, a herd of buffalo suddenly bunch up and then run swiftly toward the breaks of Big River. Soon appeared the cause of their flight: thirty or forty sitting-on-tops (horsemen) riding eastward, now at a trot, again at a lope—another homeward-bound war party, probably Cutthroats. I decided that, come night, I would take to their trail.

"I did so and three mornings later, from the edge of a grove on Big River, I discovered the enemy camp. It was in a big, open bottom where Little River joins Big River; and its three hundred and more lodges were set in a circle just above the mouth of Little River. *Ha!* At last I had come upon that which I sought. I was glad. Sun was just rising and already the people were building their early fires and stirring about, men turning loose their fast buffalo horses to graze, women going for water, for wood, children running hither and thither and happily yelling. And out from the camp, all over the big bottom, band after band of horses were grazing. How easy, come night, for me to drive off many of them. But no. Those common ones I did not want. For me, only the fast, valuable ones that the hunters and warriors tied before their lodges for better safety during the night.

"I drank at the river, ate some of the pemmican that I had so care-fully saved, crept into a thick, high growth of rose brush, and slept now and then during the day, hearing when awake the many noises of the near, big camp of Cutthroats. Came night. Again I ate a little pemmican, drank at the river, then stole down along its shore until I was opposite the center of the camp. It was not a good night for that which I had to do. Night-Light (Moon) was big and round in the sky, making the night almost the same as day. Well, I would remain right where I was until the lodge fires all died out and the people slept, then go in and take out one by one a few of the fast buffalo horses that I had seen brought in and tied at the lodges of their owners. There was but a thin growth of timber there lining the rivershore, a scattering of small trees, some brush. I sat in the inner edge of it, the swirling, whispering current of the river close before me. I was so near the camp that I could plainly hear the talk-ing, singing, drumming of its people.

"They were happy. Well, why shouldn't they be so? They had plenty of buffalo meat, their war parties had made some successful raids, doubtless upon the herd of my own Pikuni people. Thinking of that, I got angry, more and more angry, and at last thought that just taking a few of their best horses was not enough punishment for them. No. I would take but one horse, rope-bridle it, then shoot into one of the lodges, kill one of its occupants, and mount and ride away, Yes. Yes. That I would do.

"After long sitting, there at the shore, it seemed to me that I could hear several people, very low talking, come from the camp into the timber; but they did not appear, and at last I decided that I had been mistaken. I stood up and looked. Many of the lodges were still lit by the fires within them. Well, I would go to the outer edge of the timber and there sit until the last one of them should become dark. Slowly, noiselessly I moved out, closely eyeing the bright lodges, not looking where I stepped; and so going, stumbled upon a pair of out-hiding sweethearts. It was the soft, yielding body of the woman that my foot struck. She sprang up yelling, and so did the man. I fired at him, missed, and as they ran off shouting, men at once began coming from the lodges, yelling to one another as they came on toward the timber.

"They were so very many that I could not possibly hide from them in the thinness of it. There was but one thing for me to do and I did it. I ran to the river, waded in, and tried swimming down it, gun in hand. But that I couldn't do. I needed both of my arms and hands. I tried to thrust the gun under my belt, sank as I fumbled with it, began to choke, to drown. I had to let the gun go. Gasping, sputtering, I came up, swam back up and slowly, only my nose and eyes above the water.

"The Cutthroats were swarming in the timber, yelling to one another. The women and children in the camp were screaming and crying. I constantly expected to be shot at by some of the searchers, but it must have been that they never looked out upon the river, did not think that I would take to it. Suddenly I was swimming, drifting another way. The swift incoming water from Little River was pushing me out. I had passed beyond the Cutthroat searchers, below their camp. With the little strength that I had left I somehow managed to swim in and draw out upon the shore a little way below the mouth of Little River; and there, for long I lay, so tired that I could not move. And so very, very sad.

"Again I had failed in my attempts against the enemy. Failed worse than ever, for there I was, many nights' travel from my people, and without a gun. Wearily, and with little hope that I would ever again see them, I set out up Little River Valley to try to rejoin them.

"I was not far above the camp of the Cutthroats when morning came, and, climbing up to the top of the north slope of Little River Valley, I came to rest in a growth of cherry brush. I opened my war sack, spread out its wet contents to dry. I had still enough pemmican to last, with care, three days. And what then? Well, I had flint and steel for making fires, but of what use were fires if I could get no meat? And again I thought what use anyhow for me to struggle on? Bad luck has ever been and will continue to be mine in all that I attempt to do.

"Sun coming up in the blue warmed me and I slept, but not for long. The singing and talking of people awakened me and I sat up. *Ha!* Many riders were coming up the valley—the Cutthroats again, a hunting party of them, for women on their travois horses were trailing the men. Happy, eager for their hunt, they passed on up the valley, around a bend of it, and out of my sight. Again I stretched out, lay half-asleep. After a time I heard shooting up in the west, the Cutthroats, of course, making a big killing of buffalo. Well, they would leave some of the poorer meat of their killings. There would be plenty for me if I could find it, but in the night that would be impossible. I had, now, to see them at their butchering. I ran down into the valley, into the timber and up it. How I ran. Tearing on and on through the brush, sweating. I ran as I never had before in all of my life.

"After long running, at last I stopped short in a point of timber, for in a big bottom ahead the Cutthroats were here and there loading their horses and travois with meat and hides. Soon they finished, got together and came back down the valley, passing so close to me that I could see their eyes. I then went to the river, drank, ate all that I wanted of my pemmican, and slept.

"Sun was setting when I started up the bottom to the remains of the Cutthroats' hunt. They had killed many buffalo, and, as I had thought, they had taken the tongues, but had left untouched the meat of the heads. This meat was good. I took all of it that I could carry in my robe, staggered to the timber with it, built a fire—though I knew that to be risky—and was nearly the whole night cutting the meat into very thin pieces and drying them in the heat of the blaze. When I finished, I had more than enough of it to last until I could get back to my people. As I lay down to rest this was my thought: my enemies, when I was weaponless, had furnished me plenty of food. Was that, oh, was it possibly a sign that my bad-luck experiences were ended?

"Anyhow, I had no bad luck on my homeward way. On a warm morning I walked into our camp and into my lodge. '*Nayeyah*' cried my sits-beside-me-wife as I entered. 'He returns and without even his gun.'

"Said my younger woman, 'Oh, how thin you are. Rest here upon your couch and I will feed you.'

" 'I have meat of my own. The Cutthroats provided me with meat,' I answered, and took from my war sack several pieces of it.

" 'So! You have become friendly with our worst enemies. Yet you come without your gun and without horses. Your new friends must be stingy.'

"I did not reply to that for just then came crowding in my brothers-in-law and others to smoke with me and hear what I would tell of my experiences during my long absence from them. I told it all, and they had great pity for me because of my bad luck. When I told of my flight into the river and there losing my gun, both of my women wept.

"My brothers-in-law had kept my women well supplied with meat and had taken good care of my horses. I rested, did nothing for several days, then rode out to hunt, alone as always, and with a gun that that powerful medicine man, Talks-with-the-Buffalo, loaned me. With it, I soon killed an antelope. Then, on my homeward way with the meat and hide, I sighted a big real-bear (grizzly). He was in a little grassy clear place in the timber, eating of the carcass of a deer that had somehow died there. Should I attempt to kill him? With the guns of that time, the one of them that I had, a powder-and-balls-and-cap gun, shooting at real-bears was very dangerous. If I only wounded him, he would probably kill me.

"I got down from my horse and considered what to do about it, and at last this was my thought: I had survived the loss of my gun in the river, my enemies had fed me. And just now, and easily, I had killed an antelope. These, perhaps, were good signs. Well, anyhow, I would chance it.

"Down into the timber I slid, slowly, noiselessly, walked on toward the grassy place and soon sighted the bear. He was sideways to me, tearing ribs from the carcass and crunching them, meat, bones, and all, in his powerful jaws. I crept on through the brush until I was no more than thirty steps from him, and, oh, how big he looked! Almost as big as a buffalo bull.

"I put my gun to my shoulder, carefully aimed it at his side, where the ball would go into his heart, and fired. With terrible, thundering roaring, real-bear swung his head around, attempted to bite at his wound, and I saw that it was almost at the top of his back. And then, as I was putting powder into the muzzle of the gun, he saw my movements and came for me.

"Close at my back was a small cottonwood tree. I dropped the gun and began climbing it. Came real-bear and sprang up, tried to grab me. One of his long-clawed paws raked the calf of my right leg, tearing open my blanket legging, tearing deep gashes in my flesh, almost pulled me down from the tree. I managed to climb higher, out of his reach. He ran round and round the tree, looking up at me, woof-woofing, and now and then attempting to bite at the wound in the top of his back. Was it the fault of my aim or the fault of the gun that the ball had not gone in where I intended it to go, straight into his heart?

"The tree that I was clinging to was very slender. My weight made it bend and sway. I feared that it would break and drop me down on the real-bear. My claw-torn leg was bleeding and very painful. I was becoming weak. I was thinking this was to be the end for me when, with a last look up at me and a snort, real-bear walked off, head down, and fast. I watched him go into the willows bordering the river, and then slid to the ground, took up the gun, limped up the slope to my horse, and rode back to camp.

"By that time I was so weak that my women had to help me into the lodge and to my couch. But when they had washed my torn leg and greased it, I felt better. I half slept. After a time I heard my woman outside talking. Said Spear Woman, my younger wife: 'Well, anyhow, he brought us meat.' And said my sits-beside-me-wife, Mink Woman: 'He just happened to kill the antelope and then had more bad luck. Poor man. Poor you and me. Never will he be the great warrior, the great meat-getter that we thought he would be when we married him.'

"That they said of me was true and it hurt. I lay there thinking of it and at last decided to make one more effort to be rid of my continuous bad luck. Came evening and I limped to the lodge of Talks-with-the-Buffalo, handed him his gun, told of my bad luck with the real-bear, besought him as he loved his women and children, for help. Said he: 'I have been thinking about your troubles, your failures in hunting and in your raids upon our enemies. Now, tell me something that you will not like to tell, but that I must know if I am to help you. It is this. In your youth—your before-marriage time —you endured your sacred fast. Well, what was the helpful vision that you then had?'

"His request surprised me. It is between the gods and the sacred faster, the vision that they give him. But this was different. Talks-with-the-Buffalo was a very powerful sacred-pipe man, close to the gods. He would not ask of me anything that would do me harm. Anyhow, I would risk it. So I gave him the name of the animal that had come to me in my vision and promised to help me in all that I should do. 'What did that animal tell you that you should do in return for his help?'

"When I had told him of that, and fully, he asked if I had always done as the animal had said I must do, and I had to confess that I had once failed. I had forgotten to make a certain sacrifice to the Above Ones, and a dog had eaten it.

"'*Ha!* And thereafter your bad-luck times began. You should have told me of it long ago. And now it is that you will have to endure another sacred fast, try to obtain another powerful helper. Yes, and I know the very place for it. The top of Chief Mountain. There where Eagle Head obtained the vision that enabled him to become the most powerful warrior and successful hunter that our tribe ever had. Yes. There you must fast, taking up there with you, as he did, a buffalo head for your pillow.'

"'I do not like to go so far from our people to fast,' I answered.

"'We will move up close to the mountain. I will advise Big Lake and our other chiefs to do it,' he said.

"The chiefs willingly granted his request, and three days later we made camp on Many Chiefs' River (St. Mary) and not far from the foot of Chief Mountain. On the following day Talks-with-the-Buffalo had a sweat lodge made, and in it, as we perspired, he prayed Sun and all the Above Ones, and his own sacred helper, too, to give me strength to endure a sacred fast and to give me a helpful vision. And again he loaned me his gun.

333

"So on the next morning we mounted our horses and set out for the mountain, Talks-with-the-Buffalo, my two women, and I. Upon our way to it, I took up the whitened, dry head of a buffalo bull that had been killed in the run of a herd that our hunters had made three summers back. Arrived at the mountain, we rode up the west slope of it as far as our horses could carry us and then, leaving them, climbed up to the summit, arriving there a little after Sun had passed the center of the blue. In a small, level place on the very top of the mountain, we found the buffalo head that Eagle Head had used for a pillow and another head brought up there by some far-back sacred faster of our people.

"My women had brought along my bedding, two buffalo robes and a blanket. They went back down the slope, got some pine branches and made a good bed for me, placing the buffalo head at the west end of it so that I could see Sun as he came every morning to travel across the blue. Then Talks-with-the-Buffalo again prayed for me, and, crying, my women joined him in singing some sacred songs. And then they left me. For a little I stood, looking off at our great plain, at our Pine Needles Buttes (Sweetgrass Hills), at our Bear Paw Mountains, much farther to the east. Would I ever camp and hunt among them again? Earnestly I prayed Sun for help, for a good vision, and stretched out upon my couch.

"I slept continuously, had no vision on that night. Awoke hungry and thirsty, became more so as the day wore on. For two more nights I lay there, sleeping at times, becoming weak from want of food and water, often praying the Above Ones for help. At last they took pity on me. On my fourth night there they gave me a very sacred vision. Came to me a certain animal that frequents the water, all but lives in it, and said that he would help me in all of my undertakings; and that in return for his help I should do certain things for him in the way of prayers and sacrifices. Oh, how pleased I was. Although so weak that I could hardly stand, still I felt that I had power to do great deeds.

"As they had agreed to do, next morning came Talks-with-the-Buffalo and my women to learn how I was getting along, and pleased

334

they were when I told them that, at last, on my fourth night, I had obtained a powerful vision, that a certain water animal was to be my helper.

"Then my sits-beside-me-wife asked: 'Tell us, was it one of the long-bodied, short-legged fish eaters, or was it one of the smaller, fluffy-furred kind that eats both fish and birds?'

" 'Oh, you woman,' Talks-with-the-Buffalo yelled at her, 'Are you crazy that you would have him name his vision animal and so break the power that it has given him?' And he went on scolding her until she cried.

"Well, they half carried me down to the horse that they had brought for me to ride, and, oh, how I did drink of the water of the first spring that we came to. And then, in my lodge, how good it was to rest upon my soft couch and eat good meat, and smoke with the many friends who came in to visit with me. I told them about the powerful vision that the Above Ones had given me, there on top of sacred Chief Mountain, and then that great warrior, Three Bears, said that he was so sure of it that he wanted me to join a war party that he was about to lead against the Crows. *Ha!* How glad I was to know that he was sure that my bad-luck times were ended. How strong to go I felt.

"There were thirty in our party, Three Bears our leader, and Talks-with-the-Buffalo our sacred-pipe man. I carried a gun and a pistol that my brothers-in-law loaned me. Many nights we traveled southward, rafting across Big River, fording Yellow (Judith) River and Other-Side Bear (Musselshell) River, at last rafting across Elk (Yellowstone) River and following up Bighorn River. As with every war party, our sacred-pipe man rested and slept away from us, praying the Above Ones and his own sacred helper for a revealing vision of what was ahead of good or bad for us.

"Came the evening of our second day of rest up in Bighorn River Valley, and when Talks-with-the-Buffalo joined us to eat the meat that I had broiled for him, he said that enemies were not far ahead of us, that we must proceed very cautiously for the Above Ones had given him a vision. In his sleep he had seen two parties of men fighting one another and one of the parties had turned and run, the other party pursuing them. They had been far from him, but the pursuing party had appeared to have been of our own Pikuni tribe.

"So was it that all through the night we went on more watchfully than ever, and with the first faint white light of morning, went into hiding in the upper end of a grove on the west side of the valley, our leader sending two scouts to the top of its slope to watch any movements of enemies. As we ate some meat that we had broiled on the previous day, Talks-with-the-Buffalo said that he would not rest and sleep off by himself for he had the feeling that danger threatened us, was near. Yes, and his vision had warned him of it. He was right.

"Sun was not halfway up in the blue when our scouts came running in, awakened us, and said that a war party of more than twenty men, afoot, was coming down the valley. We hurried to the upper end of the grove in which we had stopped, and, sure enough, there the enemy were, out in the open bottom and coming straight toward us. We stood still until they were within close gunshot of us, and then began shooting at them. A few fell. The others ran to the willows bordering the river, jumping from a cut bank down into them.

"We reloaded our guns, went to the cut bank, and, cautiously looking down from its rim, could see some of the enemy and were able to shoot more of them. At last we could see no living ones but were sure that a few, unhurt, remained there in hiding. So our leader divided us into two parties, one to start at the lower end of the willows, the other one at their upper end, and so go in and hunt for the living. I was with the upper party. As we moved in, I, the one of us closest to the river, kept praying, 'Haiya, Sun! Haiya, Sun! Haiya, you powerful water animal of my vision! Pity me. Keep me safe. Help me to make to cry these our enemies.'

"Suddenly there was shooting and yelling ahead of us, and then seven of the enemy came running and shooting at us. I shot down one of them; another one, tall and heavy bodied, turned and ran for the river, I after him. He dropped his empty gun as he took to the water. I dropped mine, swam, took after him, overtook him, and we slashed at one another with our knives. I stabbed him in the breast, in his heart, drew him ashore, scalped him, then scalped the other one I had killed. And then I knew, oh, I knew that my luck had turned, that my bad-luck times were over. And so said Talks-with-the-Buffalo and others.

"Thereafter all war leaders were eager for me to join their war parties, and after a time I myself became a leader and had great success against our enemies. As you all know, eleven enemies I have killed, and more than one hundred enemy horses, taken. All that because of my vision on top of Chief Mountain."

"And so, *Apikuni*, friend, you now know how and why two of the buffalo skulls on top of Chief Mountain were placed there. *Haiya!* How powerful, how they were helped by the Above Ones, our Pikuni warriors of the long-ago," ended my friend, Returns-with-Plenty, and signed me to fill another pipe.

CHAPTER TWENTY-THREE

The Faith of *Ahko Pitsu*[1]
(Told by *Ahko Pitsu*)

AHKO PITSU ("Returns-with-Plenty"), a wise member of the Pikuni tribe of the Blackfoot Indian Confederacy, has seen seventy-one winters. We have been close friends since the long-ago time of the buffalo. With his wife and grandchildren he lives in a comfortable house furnished him by the Indian agency in Browning, Montana. Though almost blind and quite feeble, he daily feels his way up the road to my home to visit with me. I fill an ancient, blackstone-bowled, long-stemmed pipe with his favorite mixture of tobacco and *l'herbe*, and we smoke and talk. Mostly, he talks and I listen.

As we smoked our first pipe on a recent afternoon, he began: "Of course you remember that Black Robe whom we named Noon Eater, he who spoke and well understood our language."

"Yes, I well remember him. He died long ago in a place of many houses west of the mountains," I answered. He was the Rev. Father Prando, S. J., and a most zealous missionary.

"Well, I once had great argument with Noon Eater and got the

[1] *Ahko Pitsu* is one of the very few surviving friends of Schultz's life in the days of the buffalo. Like many Indians of the old days, he has another name, Chewing Black Bone (*Sikochkeka*), by which he is today universally known and honored on the Blackfoot Reservation. The grandson of two great chiefs of the Pikunis, Only Chief (also called Lame Bull) and Sits-in-the-Middle (known also as Middle Sitter), first and tenth Pikuni signers of the Treaty of 1855, he represents the finest tradition of his noble tribe. The editor of this volume is his adopted son, whom he honored with the name of his paternal grandfather Sits-in-the-Middle (*Ichtutsikiaupi*). Chewing Black Bone is now (autumn of 1961) in his late nineties but, except for blindness, retains all his faculties, and is able to recount with vigor and feeling the stories of his youth and the religious lore of his people.

best of it," my old friend continued. "He came into my lodge, sat down beside me, and said, 'Ahko Pitsu, my real friend, I have just now learned that you Pikunis believe that, in the very long-ago, one of your ancestors went with the help of certain animals and visited the sun. My friend, such a belief is craziness. No one, white nor Indian, ever did that. It could not possibly be done.'

" 'Noon Eater,' I answered, 'Though you whites are very wise, you are pitifully ignorant about some things that we Indians absolutely know. One of our kind did go to Sun, got great help from him, as I shall now tell you.'

"In that long ago time there was a poor young man whose face was badly scarred. He loved a beautiful girl, and after long seeking for the chance met her one day as she was going to the river for water and said: 'Oh, beautiful one, I love you. I want you to be my wife.'

"Said the girl: 'Oh, you poor, nothing-man, you make me laugh. Well, this I tell you: Get the scars off your face, get it smooth, then I will marry you.' And with that, happily singing, she went on to the river and forgot the poor one's request.

"The poor young man was very sad. After long thinking of his trouble, he said to himself: 'I can get no help here; even our most sacred, powerful, Sun's men cannot help me. I will leave. Travel far. Ask all whom I meet to pity me; smooth my face. Perhaps some one of them will do so.'

"Telling none of his intention, not even his poor father and mother, he set off, traveling west. It was in that very long-ago time when people and animals had a common language. So, meeting a wolverine, he said: 'Oh, you beautifully furred, powerful meat-getter. As you love your woman, your children, I beg you to pity me; help me to get my scarred face smoothed.'

"Said Wolverine: 'Man, that I cannot do. I am sorry that I can't help you. But there are others who have great power. Go see Lynx. Maybe he can help you.'

"Scar-Face met, one after another, Chief Lynx, Chief Elk, Chief Buffalo, and other four-footed chiefs, but not one of them could help him. At last he met Chief Badger, and that striped-faced, wise

339

one said: 'Poor man, I haven't the power to smooth your face, but I know of one who can do it: Sun, himself. Keep on going westward, and somewhere off there you will find him.'

"Day after day that poor Scar-Face traveled on and at last arrived at the shore of a lake. It was so large that, look as he would, he could see no land to the west, the north, the south, so farther he could not go. He sat down upon the shore and wept. This was the end for him, he thought. Useless to turn back home, there to keep on seeing that beautiful girl, never to be his wife. Better, far better for him to die right here. As he sadly wept, came swimming close to shore two swans, and one of them said to him: 'Man, why are you weeping, why so sad?'

"Said Scar-Face: 'It is that I have traveled far, seeking someone of power to smooth my face, but none whom I met could do it. At last, however, I met Chief Badger and he advised me to go to Sun; said that most powerful one would help me. But here I am, at the end of land, can go no farther, never meet Sun to ask his aid. So is it that here I die.'

"Said the male swan: 'Not so. You shall not die here. Take courage. Get up on our backs and we will take you to Sun, to his island home, out there.'

"Scar-Face waded out to the swans, lay across their backs, and they swam off with him. Swam a long time; swam far into the West, and at last brought him to the shore of an island in that Everywhere Water, told him that there Sun lived. As he stepped out upon the shore, came running toward him a beautiful young man, pursued by some huge, long sharp-billed birds, and the young man shouted to him, 'Help me! Help me! These angry birds are about to kill me!'

"Scar Face ran and met the birds, began stabbing them with his spear, soon killed them all. Then came the handsome youth and said to him: 'You have saved my life. Who are you, why are you here?'

" 'I am a poor man of the plains. I am here to try to meet Sun,' Scar-Face answered.

" 'Good! You are brave; you saved my life. I am Morning Star. Sun is my father; Night-Light (Moon) is my mother, is in our lodge.

Come, we will cut off the heads of these bad birds and take them to her.'

"When Scar-Face saw the lodge it was so large, so perfectly made, and painted with birds and animals so strange that he could hardly believe his eyes. Before its doorway, Morning Star called out: 'Mother, I have with me a young man from the earth. Those big bad birds were chasing me, about to overtake me, but he ran and met them and killed them all.'

"Said Night-Light: 'Oh, my son! How often your father and I have told you never to go near those powerful birds! But now this stranger has killed them and you are forever safe from them. Bring him in, the brave one.'

"They went in, dropped the birds' heads before the fireplace. Night-Light, wearing a beautiful gown, was sitting upon her couch. She was perfect of form and face; her hair was long, and smoothly braided. She sprang up, hugged and kissed Scar-Face. Said to him: 'Oh, earth man! You have done a great favor to us this day. Tell me, why are you here?'

" 'It is that I want to meet Sun; ask him to help me,' Scar-Face answered.

" 'Meet him you shall, but we must be very cautious about it. Just do as I tell you, and I think that all will be well.' she told him. Then she set food before him and Morning Star. When they had finished eating night was near, and she made Scar-Face lie down, covered him with a soft tanned robe of strange fur, and told him to be quiet.

"From his day's travel across the blue Sun came home; in the doorway of the lodge stopped short, sniffed, and said, '*Ha!* A strange odor in here. It is the odor of earth people. I don't like it.'

"Said Night-Light: 'An earth man is here, but you must not be angry. He is a young man and you must pity him, for he saved our son from those terrible, long-billed birds. They were chasing him, were almost upon him, when this newly come youth ran and stopped them, killed them all. See, there are their heads before you.'

" 'That is good; our son can now safely wander everywhere about. This newly come one, where is he?'

" 'Here. Here he is,' Night-Light answered and pulled the robe off Scar-Face. He sat up, and there stood Sun, the best appearing man that he had ever seen. His skin was white, his hair yellow, his face and hands red painted. He was tall, slender. His white, soft leather shirt, leggings, and robe were beautifully painted and fringed with ermine skins. His quilled moccasins were red painted. His weapon was a long spear. He moved on to his couch, sat down, and said to Scar-Face: 'I am glad that you are here with us. I know why you came. Well, I will help you, I will remove your scars, but you must remain with us for some time as I have much to teach you, that you, in turn, must teach your people, so that they may have long and successful lives.'

"So! Evening after evening Sun taught Scar-Face how he and his people should pray to him for help; how sacrifice to him of their belongings; how to build, every summer, to honor him. White buffalo, he said, belonged to him alone. When the people killed one of them, they were to make a soft tanned robe of its hide and tie it to the center post of the next sacred lodge that they would build for him. Also, they were never to eat the meat of a white buffalo; they must leave its carcass right where they killed it, saying that they sacrificed it to him and praying for his help.

"Finally, Sun had Night-Light build a small sweat lodge, and that evening he went into it with Scar-Face, and Night-Light rolled into a pit in its center some stones that she had heated. Sun then sprinkled them with water, and as steam arose from them and filled the lodge he rubbed some black medicine on the young man's scarred face, taught him some sweat-lodge songs and prayers. Day after day, Night-Light built three more sweat lodges, and in the evenings, in them, Sun rubbed more black medicine on the young man's scars, taught him more sweat-lodge songs and prayers. Then, in the fourth and last one of the sweat lodges, He said to him: 'Four is my number; it is sacred. When, in every summer, you, your people, select the place for building the great lodge for me, you will put up and use a sweat lodge to the north of it; on the following day, have a sweat lodge to the south of it; on the third day, a sweat lodge to the west of it; and finally, one to the east of it; and so, lastly, you will build the big lodge.

The Faith of Ahko Pitsu

"During those four sweat-lodge evenings Sun taught Scar-Face much else that would be for his benefit, for the long life and happiness of his people. After he had for the fourth time put on the black medicine, he told him to go wash his face. The young man did so, then felt of his face. *Ha!* Its scars were gone; it was as smooth as on the day he had been born.

"Came then the time for the cured one to return to his people. Night-Light had made beautiful clothes for him, Morning Star had given him a shield, and Sun said that such were to be the war clothes of the people, and shields their protectors in battle. 'So now you go,' he said, and with Night-Light and Morning Star led him to a very large turnip not far from the lodge. Sun grasped it, pulled it out from the ground, told the cured one to look down into the hole he had made. *Ha!* That hole went down clear through the ground, and below it the Wolves' Trail (the Milky Way) was plainly in sight.

" 'You are to take to that trail, follow it; so will you go to your people. And now shut your eyes,' Sun said to the cured one. He did so, Sun lifted him, dropped him into the hole, and when he opened his eyes, oh, wonderful! Wonderful! There he was upon the white shining trail. Swiftly, happily he followed it, and near morning came down upon the earth, not far from the camp of his people, his own Pikuni people. Day had come when he entered it, and men, women, and children, they stared at him, did not recognize him, now smooth of face and wearing strange and beautiful clothes. He had to tell them who he was; where he had been; and all that Sun, Night-Light, and Morning Star had done for him. Then soon he had the girl who had refused to marry him because of his scars. Soon had a lodge of his own. And having taught the people all that Sun had taught him, they prospered in all ways.[2]

[2] Several versions of the legend of Scar-Face have been recorded, each one differing in many details from the others. See George Bird Grinnell, *Blackfoot Lodge Tales* (London, 1893), 93 ff.; Clark Wissler and D. C. Duvall, *Mythology of the Blackfoot Indians* (New York, 1908), 61 ff.; Walter McClintock, *The Old North Trail* (London, 1910), 491–501; C. C. Uhlenbeck, *Original Blackfoot Texts* (Amsterdam, 1911), 50–57 (with Blackfoot and English texts in parallel columns); J. P. B. de Josselin de Jong, *Blackfoot Texts* (Amsterdam, 1914), 80–82.
Walter McClintock, *op. cit.*, 518–19, relates how he induced Arthur Nevin to compose an opera on the theme; "Poia" was completed in the spring of 1906, with a

"That, *Apikuni,* is what I told to Noon Eater, the Black Robe. And then I said to him: 'Noon Eater, you whites are very wise, but of course you don't know everything. You said that no white, no Indian, ever went to Sun. Well, I have now proven to you that one of our ancestors actually did visit him and his family in their island home. So now you can tell your Black Robe and other white friends about it. People are always glad to learn the truth about the various matters that interest them.'

"*Ha!* That Noon Eater! He realized that I had bested him. He looked at me, and strangely, then arose and silently went upon his way. I really felt sorry for him."

Again I filled the big pipe with the fragrant mixture, passed it to my friend to light. A match would not do: it was not sacred fire. He knelt before the fireplace, with a pair of willow tongs plucked out a coal, placed it upon the pipe, drew in smoke, wafted it skyward, and solemnly chanted: "Oh, Sun! Oh, you Above People! Have pity on us. Give to my friend *Apikuni* here long and full life. Help me to go to my Blackfoot friends when summer comes; be with them when they plant their sacred gardens, for they will then powerfully pray for me."

"So you intend to go up there," I said.

"If I possibly can go. My friend Running Rabbit, a member of the Planters' Society, has invited me. As you know, I suffer from pains in my breast. Daily I pray Sun to give me strength to make the journey."

My friend's prayer requires explanation. It is that, from remote time, the Blackfoot Indians have annually planted and harvested, with most impressive ceremonies, a variety of tobacco that they call "*meahwakosis*" (*nicotiana attenuata*). The Blackfoot historians relate that the Mandan Indians, living on the Missouri at the mouth of Knife River, were the original planters and users of it, that the Crow

---

libretto by Randolph Hartley, was played first in concert form on January 16, 1907, in Pittsburgh, and produced in Berlin by the Royal Opera House. The premier performance there was on April 23, 1910, while the second was attended by the Crown Prince and Crown Princess. The opera had an Indian setting, used Indian musical themes, and was "superbly staged, both as to scenery and costumes."

Indians obtained its seeds from them and began planting them, and that finally the Blackfeet got seeds of the sacred plant from the latter tribe.

The Blackfoot Tobacco Planters are a society of Sun priests—so-called medicine men—and the leader of them is the owner of the Water, or Beaver, bundle, consisting of the prime-furred hides of beaver, otter, mink, and other water animals. The ceremonies preparatory for planting the seeds are held in his lodge—four days and four nights of prayers and songs to Sun and all of the Above People. Prayers more fervent, inspiring than any offered by the most zealous of Methodist preachers. Songs deeply solemn, soul lifting; truly as classic as the music of Mendelssohn and Beethoven. During this time the sick are welcomed in the lodge, and, after painting their faces and hands with Sun's sacred color, red ocher, the Planters pray for their recovery and prosperous long life—prayers believed to be ever efficacious except through some fault of the sick one.

Each member of the Planters society having selected the place for his garden, his women and children burn the brush and weeds upon it, make it ready for planting. On the fourth and last day of the ceremonies a large, buffalo rawhide vessel shaped like a dishpan is brought into the lodge and filled with a mixture of manure and serviceberry soup, and then the tobacco seeds are stirred into it. The vessel is then taken to the gardens—in a large cottonwood grove bordering Bow River—and each Planter drops pinches of its contents into holes in his plot that he has made with a sharp-pointed stick, then fills the holes with loose earth.

During the four days' ceremonies, the sits-beside-him-wife of each Planter has made two images—one of a man, the other of a woman. Each of them has an extra pair of moccasins and a little pouch of pemmican. For the closing rite of the ceremonies, the Planters pray to their images, entreat them to guard carefully their plantings from all depredations, and then place them at the heads of their gardens. And finally the people are warned not to go to or even near the gardens, lest the images do them grievous harm. Long ago, a crazy young man of the tribe, singing a song of defiance, went to the gardens and stole some of the sacred tobacco leaves, with the result that he soon choked to death. Also, three summers back, a white rancher living near the reservation, disregarding the warnings of the Planters, sneaked into the gardens, had a good look at them, took one of the tobacco plants, and then at the agency bragged of what he had done. With the result that, upon his homeward way, his horse threw him and he died of a broken neck.

Incidentally, because I have been a member of the Pikuni tribe of the Blackfoot Indian Confederacy for more than fifty years, and because my wife is an active member of the *Mahtokiks*, the womens' secret society of its Blood tribe, we were two summers ago invited to take part in the ceremonial rites of the Tobacco Planters and visit their sacred gardens. We were the only white persons ever given that privilege. It was a vastly interesting experience.

But to return to the visit of my friend, *Ahko Pitsu:* We smoked a fourth pipe—four, the sacred number—and then he said to me: "*Apikuni*, friend, write a letter for me, a letter to my Tobacco Planters friend.'

"Yes. Wait until I put a thin leaf in my writing machine. There. Begin."

> *Running Rabbit, my very close friend.*
>
> I have not forgotten your invitation. I am not well. I have pains in my breast. But daily, nightly I pray Sun to keep me alive, at least to enable me to be with you sacred ones when you have your to-bacco-planting ceremonies; for I know that your prayers for me will be favored by the Above Ones, so that I will become well and strong again. Yesterday my son drove me over to a grove on Two Medicine Lodges River. There I sacrificed my otter-fur cap to Sun. I tied it to a tree limb and prayed the powerful one to give me strength to go to you when comes next New-Grass Moon (April).
>
> My wife, my children, my grandchildren are well. We hope that you and your loved ones are also well.
>
> Your friend,
AHKO PITSU

Such is the faith of my friend *Ahko Pitsu* and all the other full-blood members of the three Blackfoot tribes. The missionaries of the various white religious sects have made no least dent in it.

346

CHAPTER TWENTY-FOUR

A Bride for Morning Star
(Told by Charles Rivois)

ONE OF MY DEAR FRIENDS of the long-ago buffalo days was Charles Rivois, affectionately named by the Blackfoot "*Utsena Pwoyit*" ("Gros Ventre Talker").[1] Born in St. Louis in 1803, he spent most of his long life on the northwestern plains, and died at the age of ninety-six on the Blackfoot Indian Reservation. He was a fascinating storyteller, and here is one of his best:

"Men for the war trail, women for the home lodge." An old, old saying of the Blackfoot Indian tribes, and true, as I well know. Because of a woman member of a war party that I once joined, we all got into plenty of trouble, as you shall learn.

I had been wandering, hunting, trapping with the Pikunis for four years when, in the spring of 1856, we moved in to Fort Benton to trade our winter gatherings of furs and buffalo robes for white men's goods. Soon after we arrived there *Pinukwiim* ("Far-Off-in-Sight"), with whom I was living, decided to organize a war party to raid the horse herds of the far-south tribes, and asked me to join it. I would likely have refused had it not been for a fine and forceful Tewa Indian, a great wanderer, named Far Pine, who had been with us for two years. He had told me much about the southern tribes, and I was eager to see them, see their ancient pueblos, learn something of their ways of life; so, as he was going, I would, too. The camp crier spread word of the war party; and came in to us, among others, Red Wolf,

---

[1] See "Charles Rivois' Tale of Hardship," in *Friends of My Life as an Indian*, 134–47, where his Blackfoot name is given as *Utsenakwan* ("Gros Ventre Man").

a brave warrior of twenty-five, and his eighteen-year-old, beautiful sister, Lance Woman, and said that they wanted to join the party.

Said *Pinukwiim:* "Lance Woman, my almost-daughter— I call you that because Three Bears, your father, is my very close friend—the long and dangerous war trail that we are to follow is not for such as you, but glad I am to have your brother join us.

Said the girl: "In the very long-age there was a woman warrior, a leader of warriors, to whom, because of her bravery and success, the chiefs gave a man's name, 'Running Eagle' . . . ."

"Yes. And what became of her?" *Pinukwiim* interrupted.

"Raiding a camp of the Kutenais, she was killed. No, almost-daughter not for you the war trail, you so soon to marry brave, good-hearted Young Bull."

At mention of that name, Lance Woman drooped, sighed; then straightening up, she loudly said: "I cannot marry him because of a vision that I have had—a vision that I belong to Morning Star, and must go to war."

At that all stared at her, and said *Pinukwiim:* "What? A vision, do you say?"

"Yes. In my sleep last night, came to me a tall, beautiful war-clothed man, light shining from him, and said: 'I am Morning Star. I have long watched you. You are mine. You must not marry unless I in my own way give you consent. I want you to paint your fore-head as mine is painted and go to war, take many horses.' Then as suddenly as he appeared he was gone."

Loud were the exclamations of her hearers when she finished. How wonderful, how very powerful was her vision. Surely that great sky god, chief of warriors, favored her, favored the Pikunis. Said *Pinukwiim* to her: "Morning Star, next to Sun, is the most powerful of the sky gods. So. He vanished. You awoke. What then?"

"I felt very strange. I thought and thought about my vision, kept it to myself until, my brother saying he would join your war party, I told him of it and that I, too, must go."

"So you shall," *Pinukwiim* assured her. "Yes, and we will do our best to teach you the ways of war. For as the gods direct, so must we do."

Tall, handsome, proud Young Bull had entered and stood just within the doorway listening. Lance Woman turned and saw him, sadly said: "Oh, my sweetheart! You heard then. *Kyaiyo! Kyaiyo!* We are not to set up a lodge together."

"Yes, I heard. It is true that, as the gods direct, so must we do. Well, though we cannot marry, I shall be ever with you on your war trails," he answered, and that, too, had the loud approval of our circle.

Proud, pleased was Lance Woman's crippled father when, returning home, she told him of her vision and that she was to follow *Pinukwiim* to war. Chiefs, medicine men, staid old warriors hurried to Three Bears' lodge to be told in full the vision and recount the brave deeds and sing the songs of that long-ago woman warrior, Running Eagle; and tell Lance Woman that she must be such another virgin leader of Pikuni warriors.

(As you well know, dreams—visions, as they call them—powerfully influence the lives of Blackfoot people. To them, dreams are actual experiences that enable them to learn what the future has in store for them of good or ill. For instance, if one dreams of green grass, it is that he will live to see the new-growing grass of another summer.)

Came the day for us to go, and we were ten men and one woman busily preparing to follow *Pinukwiim* into the far-south land. Of these there was one, White Antelope, whom the chiefs hesitated to accept, for he had long been a persistent and unsuccessful suitor of Lance Woman. However, because of his well-known bravery, *Pinukwiim* finally told him that he could go. He was tall, eagle-beak nosed, fierce appearing, of some twenty-five winters. My main preparation for the long trail was to go to the fort, where I had a good sum to my credit, and draw out two hundred dollars in gold for possible emergencies. The bourgeois, forceful, friendly Alexander Culbertson, head of the American Fur Company in the Upper Missouri River country, advised me not to go. His good wife, Sacred Snake Woman, said that she was glad that I was going, as I could do much to protect her good young friend, Lance Woman.

Sun was near setting when with our saddled and pouches-laden horses we gathered before *Pinukwiim*'s lodge to sing, as was the custom of all war parties when ready to leave. From their father's lodge came Red Wolf and Lance Woman, and all eyes were at once upon her, for she wore the clothing and accouterments of a man: buckskin shirt and leggings, blue breechcloth, beaded moccasins, red blanket wrap, powder horn and ball pouch at her sides, sheath knife in her belt, light smoothbore gun in her hand. Red painted were her cheeks, and on her forehead, in blue paint, was a +, the symbol of Morning Star. At once several of the women around us began voicing disapproval of her costume, whereat *Pinukwiim* roared: "My friends, our young woman companion is dressed as I requested, for in woman's clothing she would be the one of us most wanted by our enemies. You all know that to them the capture of a fine young woman is more than the taking of many scalps."

In answer to that we heard on all sides shouts of approval: "Take courage, Lance Woman." "Perfectly clothed one, heed not the talk of these few jealous women."

"And now the Wolf Songs," *Pinukwiim* ordered, and we sang them with good will, for they were believed to bring good luck. Lastly we sang the Going-Away Song, very solemn, very slow, the burden of which was: "We go. But still the women will bear children; our tribe shall not end." With that we mounted our horses and were off. None of us spoke, and silent was the crowd watching our departure. Sun was setting as we passed the fort, its inmates gathered before it to see us pass and doubtless wondering as did we—myself, anyhow—how many of us would ever return. Fording the river just above the fort, we climbed up onto the plain and struck off southeast for Arrow Creek. Night came on clear, almost frosty. A full moon enabled us to see the herds of buffalo and bands of antelope that now and then fled from our approach. The howling of wolves and the muffled barking of coyotes were ever in our ears.

It was dawn when we turned down into the deep and narrow valley of Arrow Creek, killed a cow buffalo, took some of its meat, and unsaddled in a grove of cottonwoods. Over a fire of dry, all but smokeless wood, we broiled and ate our fill of the meat, Lance Woman broiling the tongue of the cow for *Pinukwiim*. Very happy she was as she waited on him. She was of goodly height; slender, rounded figure; beautiful, womanly face. To us all, oldsters and youngsters alike, she was very dear. The meal ended, *Pinukwiim* named one of our number to go back up onto the rim of the plain, to watch that no enemy war party surprise us; named another to herd our grazing horses. Both herder and watcher were to be relieved at noon. We then spread our meager bedding and lay down for a good rest and sleep—Lance Woman on one side and I on the other side of her brother; *Pinukwiim* going to some little distance from us, where undisturbed he would pray for a vision that would reveal what the future had in store for us.

Such was our daily and nightly procedure upon this southward trail—a trail that had been followed for more than a hundred years by war parties of the Blackfoot tribes in quest of Spanish horses, shirts of mail, and big-knives (swords). Twice had *Pinukwiim* and another member of our party, Talks-with-the-Buffalo, followed it and with great success. And the Tewa, Far Pine, knew it well. He knew practically all of the great West from Mexico north to the Saskatchewan; was at home with many of its Indian tribes, and spoke their various languages, as well as English and Spanish. He had trapped with Kit Carson and Jim Bridger, and told me many tales of those two mighty men. We would, he said, meet Carson at a Spanish town named Taos in the far-south land.

We were soon sorry that *Pinukwiim* had allowed White Antelope to join our party. At our first stop on Arrow Creek he began paying unwanted attention to Lance Woman, sitting beside her, trying to get her to talk with him, boasting of his success in war. We arranged for her to sit within the row of Red Wolf, Young Bull, and me, so that he could not get close to her. But still he kept on staring at her, advising her about this and that, though she made no reply. It made us all nervous. Privately, *Pinukwiim* told Red Wolf and Young Bull that they must endure it so long as White Antelope did no more than talk. I often saw Lance Woman and Young Bull look lovingly, sadly, at one another. At one of our day-stops I heard her say to him, in answer to something that he had said: "No, we can never marry, but I shall always dearly love you." And then he: "I want no other woman. I shall live only to be of help to you."

Crossing the Yellowstone, we followed up the long length of Big-horn River through the country of bitter enemies, the Crows, and were unseen by them. Then crossing the Rockies through South Pass, we rode down Green River a long way, turned over a low divide and for some nights followed down a stream that, Far Pine said, was the Río Dolores. Leaving it, our way was in high, timbered country, across streams running southwest and then southeast, and so we re-crossed the Rockies. At dawn of our fortieth day from Fort Benton we turned from the high mountains down into a fine, wide valley; and there before us was a great mass of brown, adobe buildings, several of them of five or six stories and so built together that they appeared to be one huge house with roofs of varying height. It was the pueblo of Far Pine's friends, the Taos Indians. *Pinukwiim* and Talks-with-the-Buffalo had seen it before, but we others of the north, staring at it, could hardly believe that it had been built by Indians. Far Pine said that they would welcome us, so we rode on and soon perceived that the great structure was of two parts, divided by the little river running down the valley.

We approached the entrance to the south part and the crowd of men and women standing outside it and staring at us. Far Pine told them who we were as we got down from our horses, and they gave us hearty greeting, escorted us inside; the chief, *Tua* (Bear), gave us a fine room for our stay and had some of his young men take our horses out to graze. Women brought us a feast of corn and meat stew, hot with chili—food new to us that burned our throats. They were greatly taken with Lance Woman, and in the sign language invited her to go and visit with them. After the feast we smoked and, Far Pine interpreting for them, *Tua* and *Pinukwiim* had a long talk, in the course of which *Tua* said that he envied us our far-north, plenty-of-buffalo country. His people and all the Pueblo tribes had once been prosperous and happy. But the Spaniards had come in, killed many of them, and seized their best lands, so they were now very poor. In the end we gladly accepted *Tua*'s invitation to rest and visit with him for several days.

Came morning, more chilied stew, and then we rode with Far Pine down to near-by Taos town to meet Little Chief (Kit Carson), his long-time friend. Nearing the town, we saw that a number of Indians were encamped a little farther down the timber-lined stream, their shelters temporary ones of poles and skins and brush. They were Picuri Indians from their big house far down the river, and here to trade, Far Pine said.

Entering the adobe-houses town, we passed some stores and came to a house of several rooms, before which a number of Picuri men were gathered. To a post of its wide piazza was nailed a sign which read: "United States Indian Agency." We dismounted, tied our horses to a long hitching rail, had a short talk with the Picuris, Far Pine interpreting, and they invited us to visit them in their near-by camp. We then filed into the big room of the agency. At sight of us, a man rose from a desk at which he was sitting and came hurrying to meet Far Pine. Not possible that this could be Kit Carson, I thought, this slender, bow-legged, thin-haired, freckled little man. But it was. Kit Carson, himself! So different from what I had imagined him to be, a giant of fierce appearance. Uneasy I stood as, talking with Far Pine, the great man's eyes were often upon me. How were we to explain to him, an Indian agent, our presence there in that far-south country, I wondered; and was relieved when Far Pine said that we were upon our way with him to visit his Tewa people.

Presently the two came to us standing stiffly near the doorway, and Far Pine said to him: "Little Chief, this is Gros Ventre Talker."

"Charles Rivois," I hurriedly explained, and quizzical was his expression as he shook hands with me. I hurriedly introduced him to the others, to Lance Woman last. Intently he looked at her and said, more to himself than to us: "In men's clothing! A beautiful young woman, too."

"It is that she is to be a warrior-woman," Far Pine explained. Carson shook his head, exclaiming: "These Blackfeet! These Blackfeet! What terrors they are. Even their women take to war."

"Not Blackfeet. These are Pikunis," I explained.

"Oh, yes, Piegans. Fiercest one of the Blackfoot tribes. Don't I know it! Haven't I fought war parties of them several times. The worst wound I ever got was in a fight with the Piegans."

Came hurrying in just then two excited white men to talk to Carson, and he told us that we must come in later to visit with him. So we withdrew and, leading our horses, strolled down to the camp of the Picuris and had a long visit with them—Far Pine, of course, interpreting. Their women made much of Lance Woman—one particularly, who was a good sign talker. Like the Taos Indians, our new acquaintances complained bitterly of the wrongs that they had suffered under Spanish rule, and we could only answer: "Too bad. Too bad."

As we were preparing to move on, Lance Woman came to us, greatly excited, and displaying a fine Navajo blanket that had been given her. "They like me, these different kind of women, and I like them. Very much I like them. They ask me to stop with them for the night, and I shall," she said.

"Shall not. You go with us back to the big house in which we are stopping," Red Wolf answered.

"But I shall be as safe with them as with you all. I want much to know these women. Let me stop with them just this one night. Brother, do say yes, she pleaded, and with insistent look and nod of head to me, demanded my aid. Her new friends meantime were earnestly talking to Far Pine. He turned to us and said: "Very much they want her to stop with them tonight. They will give her more presents, take good care of her."

"Well then, stay. I will take your horse, come for you tomorrow," Red Wolf told her.

As she was turning happily away, White Antelope said to her brother: "Crazy you are to let her remain here." And then shouted: "Lance Woman, come back. You must not stop here."

Whirling around and pointing to him, she cried: "Cease bothering me. This I tell you and do not forget it: Now and forever, cease talking to me." With that she went on with her friends, and muttering I knew not what, White Antelope sprang into his saddle and rode up the valley. The Picuri men stared after him, shook their heads. Asked us to have one more smoke with them. So we remained with them a little longer, talking of this and that, and they mentioned that a small party of men of the Wolf People had arrived and were encamped a little farther down the stream. In interpreting that, Far

Pine said in an aside to me that the Wolf People were the tribe that the whites called the "Pawnees." *Pinukwiim* said that a war party he was once with had raided a camp of the Wolf People, far below the mouth of the Yellowstone, killed a few of them, and taken a large band of horses. Wolf People men were easiest of all to scalp, for they shaved their heads, all but a round patch on top, which they tied to stand up like a horn. Curious about them, I proposed that we go down and visit in their camp, but *Pinukwiim* was against it.

Returning to the agency, we found Kit Carson busy with several white men and Spaniards, so Far Pine told him that we would visit him on the following day. At Taos pueblo we found White Antelope talking in the sign language with *Tua*. He would not look at us, which didn't matter in the least.

The evening passed pleasantly with talk of the events of the day until we were told that a group of Picuri men had arrived and would have talk with us. They must speak with Far Pine, and at once. From the excited manner of their talk, we knew that there had been trouble in their camp. Then Far Pine explained that, early in the evening, three of the Wolf People men had visited in the Picuri camp and taken great interest in Lance Woman. In sign language they had asked her why she had Morning Star painted on her forehead. They had talked with her for some time before returning to their camp. Then suddenly the whole party of them had appeared upon their horses and one, springing down, had seized the girl, passed her up to one holding out his arms, though she had fought hard against it, and off they had gone with her in the darkness. It had been done very quickly, the Picuri men powerless to prevent it, for they had been scattered here and there in the camp; and anyhow they had been too few to fight her captors. They had hurried to their agent, Little Chief, about it, and he had said that we must at once be notified. He awaited our coming.

The young Taos herders brought in our horses and, leaving Lance Woman's horse and belongings with *Tua*—for to lead it would slow us up—we were off, soon with Carson in his office, and long was our talk with him, for Far Pine and I had to turn into Black-foot and English all that was said. *Pinukwiim* and Talks-with-the-

Buffalo wanted a lot of information from Little Chief, and he gave us much advice. He could not possibly go with us and demand the girl for he was having a lot of trouble with the Spaniards. They were robbing, sometimes killing the whites coming into the country. It looked as though there would soon be war between the United States and Mexico.

Well, at last it was decided just what we should do. We were all to go up near the Pawnee village on Loup River, some ten or twelve days' travel to the north, and, while our companions concealed themselves somewhere close to it, Far Pine and I were to go into the village as traders and try to work out some way to save the girl. Carson even offered to furnish the goods that we would need, but I had plenty of money to buy them. Far Pine in his wanderings had several times visited the Pawnee villages, so knew the way to them, but for my better understanding, Carson drew a map of the route to them; all stared at it as, I interpreting, he explained it, repeatedly saying that the village of the Skidi, or Wolf band of the tribe, on Loup River was the one to which Lance Woman would be taken.

As Lance Woman's horse would now be needed to carry the trade goods, we returned to the Taos pueblo to get it and pass the remainder of the night. There, when we had lain down to rest in the room that *Tua* had given us, White Antelope broke out with: "This is wrong; this is craziness; we stopping here when we should have gone on in pursuit of Lance Woman's captors. By this time, we might have overtaken them. Oh, I am against, very much against this your slow plan, your crazy plan to rescue her. Well I believe that I can do better than that." To which none replied.

We were early up and back in Taos town, and when one of the stores opened I bought tobacco, Navajo blankets, bracelets and rings, knives, scissors, vermilion, needles and thread for trade. Then, tobacco, powder, balls, and caps for my companions. White Antelope did not go into the store with us, and when we went out with our purchases he was nowhere in sight. A couple of Picuri men standing near the store told Far Pine that he had signed to them: "My companions are very slow. I am going on fast and from the Wolf People get my woman." That did worry us, for, as Far Pine said, he might in some way interfere in what we were to do and get us into serious trouble. As we were packing Lance Woman's horse with our purchases, Carson came to have a few last words with us. He asked Far Pine if he remembered a Skidi man named High Eagle, who had been with them that time they had trapped the headwaters of the Platte and the Bighorn rivers. Far Pine answered that he did and that he had been thinking he might be of help to us. "My thought exactly; it came to me in the night. Well, good luck to you all," said Carson, and with that we were off.

Leaving Taos, we ascended the Río San Carlos; crossed the Arkansas River, and then the Platte, after which we traveled at night. So going, and worried, unhappy, for *Pinukwiim* was getting no revealing visions of any kind, on our twelfth morning out from Taos we stopped upon a wooded bluff and saw the Skidi village about four miles below us on the Loup. It was a village of many large earth lodges in the midst of fields of growing corn. Far Pine assured our companions that Lance Woman was in one of the lodges and was being well fed, beautifully clothed, and waited upon as though she were really the wife of Morning Star. He advised that they remain in the timber on the bluff where they would be safe from discovery, as at this time the Wolf People, preparing for the sacrifice that they intended to make of their captive, would not be coming out to hunt. And as we could, he and I would come to inform them what progress we were making toward her rescue. So with our pack-horse load of goods we circled down and approached the village from the southeast, as though we were really coming from Far Pine's Tewa country. As we neared it, he said to me: "Ain't you afraid?"

"Yes, plenty afraid."

"So am I; but in we go, my friend."

A number of men and women at the edge of the village were watching our approach and several of them, recognizing Far Pine, came forward and shook hands with him, and then with me. Haltingly in their language, but plainly in sign language, he said that we were come to trade with them and asked for his friend, High Eagle. A boy was sent for him and he soon came, a man of about fifty, tall, well built, of kindly face, and with a thick, long, stiff horn of hair

rising from the top of his head. Eagerly he greeted Far Pine; pleasantly, me; and invited us to his lodge. Its entrance, like all the others,
faced the east, and was about ten feet long, six feet wide, and six
feet high; it was built of posts, poles, and brush. His wife and several
children helped carry in our belongings, took our horses off to graze,
and we were soon comfortably seated inside. The size of the lodge
surprised me. It was all of fifty feet in diameter, its floor four feet
below the surface of the ground, and it was most comfortably furnished with sleeping compartments, mats of rushes, and buffalo robes.
The roof, of poles thatched with grass and covered with a couple of
feet of earth, had a large, square opening that was both its smoke
hole and its window. The whole interior was clean and neatly kept.

I hurried to give High Eagle a couple of pounds of tobacco and
so pleased him. We smoked, he and Far Pine talked, and from their
constant use of the sign language I understood all that they said. They
spoke of their good friend, Little Chief (Carson); Far Pine told of
his wanderings; and then High Eagle gave his big news: Some men
of the tribe, going to Taos to trade, had there captured a young
Painted Cheeks (Pikuni) woman, and four mornings hence the medicine men were going to give her to Morning Star, kill her with their
very ancient sacred arrow.

"So. She really is here. How are we to save her?" I said to Far
Pine in English.

"Be patient. I think we find some way to do it," he answered.

High Eagle's wife came in to give us food, and with her came my
first customer, wanting tobacco in exchange for a beaverskin. Then
came others with beaver, otter, mink, and fox skins, and I traded
for them—skins that would never be of benefit to me. High Eagle and
Far Pine went out and were gone all afternoon. I finally signed to
High Eagle's wife and one or two waiting customers that I was
through trading for the day and went out and sat on top of the lodge;
looked at the people going about their various affairs; wondered in
which one of the lodges Lance Woman was confined. Women were
carrying the furnishings of a very large one into other near ones.
They finished, and then men began going into it with bundles like
the medicine bundles of the Blackfoot tribes. I suspected that this

had to do with Lance Woman, and then saw her and quickly shielded my face with my capote, lest she recognize me and cry out. She was walking between two women; walking lightly, freely, as though she had no suspicion of the fate for which she was intended. They had done away with her man's clothing and dressed her in a buckskin gown that had embroidered upon its back, in bright-colored quills, the symbol of Morning Star. The three went straight to the entrance of the lodge into which the men had carried their medicine bundles, and her companions signed to her to enter and followed her in. Then, as they began praying and singing in there, Far Pine joined me and said that they had begun the four days and nights of ceremonies that would end with the sacrificing of the captive. He too had seen Lance Woman going into the lodge and had been careful that she did not see him.

High Eagle's wife called us in to eat of stewed corn and dried buffalo meat. Then as we smoked he told us, at my request, why his people made human sacrifices to Morning Star. Briefly, it was that one named *Tirawa* made the earth and the stars, and the stars were really human beings; those in the west were women, those in the east were men. In time, and after overcoming many difficulties, Morning Star married Evening Star, Sun married Moon, and all four lived in the eastern sky. Each couple had a child, a boy and a girl, and they took them down to earth to grow up, breed, and people the earth. The people rapidly increased, became various tribes. Came a time when the Skidis were starving, and Morning Star appeared to one of them as he slept and told him what must be done to end their suffering. They were to capture a pure young woman and after certain ceremonies sacrifice her to him, their chief god. That they did, and at once all was well again with them.

Then High Eagle went on to say that for many summers back no sacrifice had been made to Morning Star. The son of the head chief of the Skidis had objected to the killing of the woman captured for the purpose, saying that it was very wrong, very cruel, and not necessary for the welfare of the tribe. A few others had also been of that opinion and had agreed with him upon what should be done about it. So, when the girl had been tied to the sacred scaffold, and the medicine men had gone down into the coulee back of it to pray over the arrow that was to kill her, the chief's son had run forward, cut her bindings, lifted her up onto his horse, and carried her back to her tribe. Though the preparations for this sacrifice had come to naught, though the one captured for it had escaped, the tribe had anyhow prospered, and now some of the people were against the sacrificing of this captive. High Eagle, himself, was very much against it. There probably never would have been any thought of making another sacrifice to Morning Star had not the keeper of the sacred arrow, Spotted Elk, come upon this young woman at Taos. Seeing the symbol of Morning Star painted upon her forehead, learning from her that it was because of a vision that she had had of the sky god, he was sure that it was meant for him to seize her, sacrifice her. His companions had thought likewise and had helped to carry her off.

Said I to Far Pine when High Eagle had finished: "Let's tell him why we are here."

"Yes. I am sure that he will help us. But his woman, his children must not hear. Always talking, always telling all that they know, women and children. I will ask him to go sit on top of lodge with us."

Sun was near setting when we perched upon the roof. As briefly as possible, Far Pine told his friend of the war party, our purpose in the country, how we had been turned from it by the seizure of our woman companion, and then asked him, straight out, in some way to help us save her. Then, before he could reply, I added that I would give him all of the furs for which I traded and all the goods that I might have left. Smiling, he replied: "Though you gave me nothing, still would I help, for I hate this killing of young women by my people. Now let me think, try to see what will be best for us to do."

It was dark when we accepted High Eagle's plan for the rescue, and I had a gone, sick feeling inside me because of the part that I was to have in it.

We were called in to eat and had a good meal of stewed, cracked corn and dry buffalo meat. Then, until late, men and women came stringing in to trade with me. I disposed of the last of my goods and had a large pile of beaver- and other skins to leave with our friend. Stepping out for a moment, we saw a crowd of villagers upon the roof and surrounding the lodge in which Lance Woman was confined. High Eagle said that her captor, Spotted Elk, and a number of medicine men were in the lodge, and Spotted Elk, impersonating Morning Star, was enacting all of the difficulties that the sky god had encountered and overcome in traveling into the west to take Evening Star for his wife.

Sometime after midnight we were awakened by the shrieking of women and yelling of men near by, and ran out to learn the cause of it. High Eagle soon informed us that the women guarding Lance Woman kept a fire going all night, one and another of them occasionally getting up to replenish it. So resting, dozing, one of them had discovered a man, a stranger wearing a white blanket coat, stepping cautiously from the entrance down into the lodge, and when she and then the others sprang up shrieking, he had turned and run away. The men of the near-by lodges, aroused by their cries, had come out too late to see him or learn what way he had gone. That worried Far Pine and me, for well we knew that the wearer of the white capote was White Antelope. We had often talked of him, wondered where he was, what he was doing. And now what next would he do, perhaps to cause us trouble?

Came into the lodge, as we were eating our morning meal, a man dressed in most peculiar fashion. He had on a black-striped buckskin shirt, black leather leggings and moccasins, and a fanlike band of eagle tail feathers stuck straight out from the back of his head. His face, hands, and horn of hair were red painted. He barely glanced at Far Pine and me as High Eagle's wife handed him a little sack of black paint and another of red paint, and at once he turned and was gone. He was, we learned, Spotted Elk, keeper of the sacred arrow, and Lance Woman's captor, and therefore the one to sacrifice her to Morning Star. He was going the round of the village collecting paints for the fence to which she would be tied. Tall, powerfully built, with eagle-beak nose and outthrust chin, he had a most fierce appearance. Said Far Pine to me in English: "I have a bullet that I would like to give him."

We were anxious to communicate with our companions, now that our plan to rescue Lance Woman was made, so on the following morning we saddled our horses and were off, High Eagle letting it be known that we were going antelope hunting. The men of the village were doing no riding, not even looking after their bands of horses, grazing far and wide, so intent were they upon the preparatory, almost continuous rites for the coming sacrifice; so we rode straight to the wooded bluff in which we left our friends and found them anxiously awaiting our coming.

They were loud in their denunciation of the Wolf People when we told what they were preparing to do to Lance Woman, and Red Wolf and Young Bull were particularly put out that they could not accompany us to the village and help in our attempt to rescue her. We all went out to the edge of the bluff, and with my telescope they each had a close-up view of the village, the knoll upon which the sacrificial fence was to be built, and its surroundings. I then fully explained what Far Pine and I were to do in our attempt to make the rescue, and it was agreed that, two nights hence, they would round up a fine band of the Wolf People's horses and then, before daylight, come to the head of the coulee back of the knoll and be ready to rush in and help us at our call.

Next I told of White Antelope's attempt to enter the lodge in which Lance Woman was held, and Red Wolf said that he and Young Bull had seen him. In the previous night and on foot they had gone down to the village hoping to get word with us, at least see us, but so many people were moving about among their big, earth lodges that they had been unable to go close in. Returning the way they had come, keeping well within the timber bordering the stream, they had seen a rider cross the trail that they were following; seen him indistinctly, but had made out that he was upon his spotted horse, its hip a big spot of white in the darkness. They had had but a glimpse of him. He had startled them. When too late, they realized that they should have called out to him, made him go with them.

We were a gloomy party, fearful of what the future had in store for us. Far Pine and I did not long remain there. As we were leaving, *Pinukwiim* said to us: "I have been unable to get a vision of the future. Be wise, be cautious in all that you do, my friends."

And said Red Wolf; "Watch out for that White Antelope. Crazy he is, and crazy ones make trouble."

Upon our way back to the village we rode through every grove along the stream but found no least sign of the man. Re-picketing our horses in High Eagle's field, and caching our saddles under a pile of old cornstalks, we sauntered in to the village and into High Eagle's lodge, in which were a number of visitors. For their benefit he signed to us: "Not bloody your hands?"

"No. We saw no antelope," I answered.

"Far off the antelope, the buffalo. But we shall soon give Morning Star another woman, and he will send them back close to us," one of the visitors remarked.

The remainder of our stay in that Skidi village was very trying to Far Pine and me, so anxious were we about what would be the outcome of it. Day and night weird ceremonies were going on in the lodge in which Lance Woman was confined—rites in which only the medicine men and certain medicine women participated. On the fourth and last afternoon of the doings, High Eagle had us go with him to see the building of the fence, the scaffold upon which Lance Woman was to be sacrificed. He led us down near the knoll and told us to sit. Many others were there and very quiet. It seemed not a time for gossip. Soon two medicine men and a warrior appeared upon the knoll. The medicine men stood about ten feet apart, and the other, in front of them, loudly gave the Skidi war cry. In answer to it a medicine man came running from the village with a bow and two arrows and shot them into the ground close in front of the two standing medicine men. Then came four more medicine men, dug a pit between the arrows, and lined it with handfuls of white, downy feathers. The pit, High Eagle told us, represented Evening Star's garden in the western sky, and the feathers were for the plentiful milk of women and of corn. Then as the work went on he explained the meaning of it all.

Came two girls, and where the two arrows stuck in the ground they dug holes for the posts of the scaffold. Appeared then some men with material for it, their leader black-clothed, befeathered Spotted Elk, Lance Woman's captor. They set the two posts firmly in the

363

holes that had been dug, and one by one lashed four poles to them, and painted them. The lower one, black, represented the northeast and the god of that direction, the bear; the next pole, red, was the southeast and the wolf; the third pole, yellow, was for the northwest and the mountain lion; the fourth one, white, was for the southwest and the lynx. All of the animals represented had been fought and overcome by Morning Star when upon his way to take Evening Star for his wife. A fifth pole was then lashed in place, high above the fourth one, and painted white and black, colors for the clouds and rain, and to it the captive's wrists were to be lashed, she standing upon the fourth pole.

The work finished, the medicine men and the spectators strolled back to the village, but we three sat on for a time, smoking a pipe that High Eagle produced. Said he, ending our talk: "I hate that fence; hate what the medicine men intend to do there. It must be the last one built by them. You two and your friends, you must do your best to save this poor, captive woman. Myself, I shall do all that I can to help you and so will others to whom I have talked."

There was to be no sleep for Far Pine and me that night. Side by side we lay and worried, and in English went over and over just what we were to do. It was well after midnight when High Eagle got up, started a blaze in the fireplace, awakened his wife and children and told them to prepare to go down to see the coming sacrifice. After they had gone, we three, with Lance Woman's saddle, bridle, and saddle pad, went up to the entrance of the lodge and, watching for the chance, managed to slip out of the village unobserved. Then, hurrying to our horses, we saddled them, rode down through the timber until opposite and near the scaffold; and there leaving them with Far Pine, High Eagle and I slipped back to the upper end of the village and joined the crowd going down to see the sacrifice to Morning Star. I had left my rifle slung to the horn of my saddle, as I would need both hands for what I was to do.

We sat down in the front line of the crowd, and there followed on my part a terribly anxious and seemingly endless time of waiting. But at last, with the first faint light of coming day, subdued murmurings of those behind us evidenced that it was ended; and a moment later Lance Woman, in the custody of two medicine men holding her wrists, went closely past us. I gathered from the way she walked, freely, lightly, that she had not the least inkling of the purpose for which she was being led. And now she had a black robe around her shoulders, her moccasins were black, and a fanlike band of eagle tail feathers was on her head. The three were closely followed by a number of medicine men who carried the sacred bow-and-arrow bundle and another one that, High Eagle said, contained a human skull and a flint knife. All paused before the scaffold; then Lance Woman's escort mounted it, lifted her up between them, and bound her wrists to the top cross pole, she standing upon the one next below it. That done, they and the medicine men passed on and disappeared in the wooded coulee just beyond the knoll, there to build a fire for their concluding sacred-arrow rite. At once I made to rise, but High Eagle held me back, furtively signed: "Wait. A little wait."

The eastern sky was now white with the light of the new day, and Morning Star was shining brightly. I was so nervous that I could hardly breathe. I wanted to be up and at what I was to do, whatever the result of it might be. Lance Woman was motionless there upon the scaffold, powerless to move. Suddenly she began wailing, praying: "Oh, Sun, have pity. From these Wolf People free me." And then with knife in hand and shouting *"Ikákimat!"* ("Take courage!"), I was running to her, and the villagers, shrieking, yelling, shouting to one another, were springing up, many of the men coming against High Eagle, and others trying to hold them back.

As I was cutting Lance Woman's bindings, Young Bull came to the edge of the scaffold; she dropped into his arms and he rode off with her. I sprang down and made for my horse. Red Wolf had joined Far Pine, and they, with High Eagle and his friends, were striving hard to hold back the furious trying to get at me. One of them struck my right shoulder with a heavy stick. I dropped my knife, staggered, almost fell, would never have reached my horse had not Red Wolf struck the man down with the barrel of his gun. I somehow got up into my saddle and we joined our companions, coming to assist us. The black-clothed medicine man, Lance Woman's captor, had killed our young friend New Robe; and *Pinukwiim* killing him, the others had run back down into the coulee. So gone was the power of the sacred bow and sacred arrow.

The yelling, angry crowd of men was coming hot after us; High Eagle was signing to us: "Go! Go! Go!" We fled; Young Bull with Lance Woman in his arms was well ahead of us, making up the valley. Suddenly a rider came from the timber, made swiftly toward them— a rider with a white-spotted horse. White Antelope. As we quirted our horses to faster pace, Lance Woman dropped to the ground, and Young Bull turned to meet him. White Antelope fired on him, and then he fired, and White Antelope slumped from his horse, his mean life ended. We had no desire to bury him. Lance Woman got up onto her horse, and we hurried on up the valley to the fine herd of Wolf People horses that Red Wolf and others had rounded up in the night. Young Red Bird's Tail was holding them, awaiting our coming. We changed our worn-out, sore-footed horses for fresh ones and pushed on as fast as was possible with so large a herd. We expected that in time some of the Wolf People would be hot on our trail. All through the day we kept looking back for them, but none came. As we long afterward learned, they believed that Morning Star was angry at them, had refused to accept the girl that Spotted Elk had captured to sacrifice to him, and so had caused her to be freed, the captor killed. Not for them to avenge his death, they decided, nor attempt to recover the horses that we had driven off.

Late in the afternoon—oh, cheering sight!—we came again to buffalo, herds and herds of them scattered widely upon the plain. Killing a young cow, we built a fire at the edge of a stream and sat around it, broiling and eating the fat meat. All day long Lance Woman had been sad and silent, and now she sat drooped over, without appetite for the meaty rib that she had broiled. We ceased our chatter. Concernedly *Pinukwiim* eyed her and said: "Lance Woman, almost-daughter, of course you know that, there where the Wolf People tied you, they were about to kill you, give you to Morning Star for another wife. But now you are safe. Now tell us about your capture and then forget it, be again our happy young warrior-woman companion."

Said she: "When I was carried off from that far-south camp, I wanted to die for I thought that the man who had seized me, that black-clothed one whom you killed, was taking me to be his woman. But when we stopped to eat, and then to sleep, he and his companions lay down in a circle, I in the center, and none came near me. So was it all the way to their earth-lodges village. And I wondered. I was not to be manned; why then had they captured me?

"There in that earth lodge in which I was kept the women who ever were at my side were good to me. They gave me good food, a beautiful gown to wear; said that they were preparing me to meet their sky god, Morning Star. Those Wolf People men, what strange ceremonies they had before me. I could not understand them, but knew that they were very powerful, sacred, and I thought that they might bring Morning Star to meet me. I kept thinking of you all; hoping that you would in some way come and take me from them. This morning, when the women put this black wrap, these black moccasins upon me, and the men led me out, I still was not frightened, not until they lifted me up onto that fence of painted poles, tied my wrists to the topmost one of them, and that black-clothed one, with bow in hand, came and stared up at me and passed on. Then I felt sure that they were going to harm, perhaps kill, me. I almost died of fright. And then suddenly came Gros Ventre Talker and Young Bull, and then you all, and saved me from them. And now you tell me to forget it. I never can forget it, the terror of it. And I don't want to be a warrior-woman. I want to be a real woman. I want to have what all real women have, a lodge of my own. And oh, poor me. Because of my vision, I cannot have it. *Kyaiyo! Kyaiyo!*"

Said *Pinukwiim*: "Almost-daughter, so that is the way you feel about it. Well, cheer up. You don't have to be a warrior-woman. Your escape from that sacrificial fence, the death of your black-clothed captor, so ending the power of his sacred arrow, was Morning Star's way of telling you that you can marry, have a lodge of your own . . . ."

"Oh, *Pinukwiim!* Do you really think that? Can it be true?" she cried.

Said Young Bull, before the chief could answer: "Lance Woman, it is plainly true. Morning Star has given you to me. The lodge that you want will be yours and mine." And unabashed, there before us all, he put his arms around her, and she leaned close to him and smiled.

Some three weeks later, in the Pikuni camp on Shonkin Creek, I saw their fine, new lodge set up.

Glossary of Geographical Names
English and Blackfoot

❦❦❦❦❦❦❦❦❦❦❦❦❦❦❦❦❦❦❦❦❦❦❦❦❦❦❦❦❦

Alhambra Hot Springs: *Kisto Ksiskum* ("Hot Springs").
Antelope Creek: *Áhwakas Isisakta* ("Antelope Creek").
Armell Creek: *Itsískiotsop* ("It-Crushed-Them Creek").
Arrow Creek: *Ápsisakta* ("White Creek").
Augusta: *Spitsí* ("High Grove").

Badger Creek: *Mísinski Tsisakta* ("Striped Face").
Baker Massacre Bottom: *Itomótahpi Pikúni* ("Killed-Off-the-Pikunis").
   The river bottom of the north side of the Marias River, twenty miles
   below Fort Conrad, was the place where the Baker Massacre occurred,
   January 23, 1870.
Bear Paw Mountains: *Kyai Ochisistukiks* ("Bear Hand Mountains").
Bear Tooth Mountains: *Mahkwí Opikínah* ("Wolf Tooth").
Beaver Creek: *Ksístuki Ituktai* ("Beaver Creek").
Beaverhead River: *Ksístuki Otkátsi* ("The Beaverhead").
Belly River: *Mókwamski* ("The Belly").
Belt Mountains: *Mapsí Istuk* ("Belt Mountain"). The mountain range is
   named from a butte at the head of Belt Creek which has a circular rim
   of rock around it part way to the top.
Big Coulee Creek: *Sinopaks Ótsitsipumotsi*. It was here that the Kit Fox
   warrior society gave their sacred medicine to Buffalo Painted Lodge,
   the chief.
Big Horn Mountains: *Míki Istúkists* ("Red Mountains").
Bighorn River: *Amúkikini Isisakta* ("Bighorn River").
Big Sandy Creek: *Áhmi Saptsiko* ("Sandy Up").
Birch Creek: *Síhokini Isisakta* ("Birch Creek").

Bird-Tail Butte: *Súatsi Istuki* ("Eagle-Tail Butte").

Black Butte: *Iswátoyis* ("Sweet Pine Butte against the Judith Mountains").

Black Leaf Creek: *Siksoyo Pokskwo* ("Black Leaf").

Blood Creek: *Ahkiks Ótsitótsipi* ("Where the Women Swam"). The story goes that the women of a party, while swimming in this stream, began to fight and their blood colored the water. White men saw the water and so called it "Blood Creek."

Blue River: *Natoyí Isisákta* ("Sun [Holy] River"). Along the banks of this stream were places where blue ocher was dug and used for paint.

Boulder River: *Ústaiyi Tuktai* ("Diving Creek"). This stream was so named because it zigzags swiftly down.

Box Elder: *Pahksípiskwi* ("Box Elder").

Buffalo Fall, nine miles above the town of Choteau: *Ahkaksuwachis Otsitotop* ("Many-Tail-Feathers Burned It"). This is the very last place that the Pikunis used a buffalo fall. For the story of Many-Tail-Feathers' burning of it, see Chapter 21 of this volume.

Buffalo Lake: *Ómuk Inískim* ("Big Buffalo Stone"). The buffalo stone was a joint of a fossil plant which was held sacred by the Indians. Its use was to charm the buffalo into coming near. Some years ago Mr. Richard Sanderville of Browning, Montana, found what was left of a camp on this lake. The tipi circle was there and the tipis had faced east. To the south of the door of one was a large stone to represent the rising sun. At the back of the tipi, directly opposite the door, was the buffalo stone. On the north side, traced in rocks, was the figure of a man lying down. Directly in the center was the fireplace. On the north side of the fireplace, set in a semicircle, were the horns of seven buffalo bulls; back of them in a semicircle also were the bones of the forelegs of eight buffalo cows. In the same manner on the south side of the fireplace were the horns of eight buffalo cows; and in back of them, the bones of the forelegs of seven buffalo bulls. This camp was there many, many years ago. The buffalo stone found there was last in the possession of Mr. Sanderville, who intended to give it to the Museum of the Plains Indian at Browning.

Bull Mountains: *Istúmik Istukiks* ("Snake's Nose"). At the west end of this range of mountains is a ledge of rocks that the Pikunis called the "Snake's Nose."

Butte: *Nitúmo* ("A Butte").

Bynum Reservoir: *Nitókitsi* ("Grove in Sight").

Choteau: *Nissué Tupi* ("Four Persons"). A party of Blackfeet met four Crow Indians at this point; a battle followed, and the four Crows were killed.

Cone Butte: *Inuksi Toyis* ("Little Pine").

Conrad: *Ahkai Ókwitokskwi Ksískum* ("The Many Rocks Spring"). About ten miles east of Conrad is this spring. Here the Pikuni hunting parties camped, especially in the winter because it was not necessary to chop ice to get water.

Cow Creek: *Stáksi Tuktai* ("Middle Creek").

Cow Island: *Imíni* ("Buffalo Island"). This is one of the historical places of Montana. There in low water the steamboats unloaded their freight for Fort Benton and the mining camps beyond. In 1877 the Nez Percés on their way to Canada had a fight with some freighters near the island and did considerable damage to them and their freight train. They took the stock and burned the freight trains of James Pickett, O. G. Cooper, and Fred Barker.

Crazy Mountains: *Pahtsís Stuksi* ("Unfaithful Mountains"). So many of the Pikuni were killed near these mountains that they came to call them the "Unfaithful Mountains."

Crazy Mountains Pass: *Kómonoyi* ("Blue").

Crooked Creek: *Mutsiníks Itiawáapi Pistsa* ("Where We Ran Away from Our Killings"). The Pikunis had killed many buffalo and were preparing them to take to camp when they thought they saw the enemy coming; then they all ran away home, leaving the kill.

Crown Butte: *Satsáwanahksa* ("Flat Rattle Butte"). Woman's Arm Man, a Shoshoni Indian, was captured by the Pikuni over in Idaho and brought to this country where he grew to manhood and lived with the Pikunis. On a hunting party at this butte he was set upon by a Shoshoni war party and was killed.

Cut Bank Creek, mouth of: *Inópisi* ("Hung Themselves Down"). A war party of Gros Ventres with Dog Takes Gun, their chief, let themselves down over a cliff with ropes and took a party of Pikunis by surprise.

Cut Bank River: *Piksáksin Otsiskum* ("Snake Spring").

Dearborn River: *Áhwotan Ótsitamistsi* ("Where the Shield Floated Down"). The Pikunis were moving camp, and while crossing the river a shield fell and floated down the river.

Deep Creek: *Pístun Isisakta* ("Deep Creek").

Dunkirk: *Itsipótmawp* ("Battle Ground"). In the year 1874 a war party of Crees fought with the Pikunis and three Crees were killed, one of whom was Little Gun. The Pikunis were camped in the shadow of a bluff which they called the "Ever-Shadow." They fought up on the hill.

Dupuyer Creek: *Osaks Ituktai* ("Backfat Creek").

Eagle Butte: *Pitai Tumo* ("Eagle Butte"). A nest of eagles on a high cliff gave the Indians a name for this butte.

Ear Mountain: *Itská Nanitumó* ("The Danger Butte"). Danger Butte is near Ear Mountain and was so named because the Pikunis had two battles there. They went to this butte for safety and to hide, but they were always afraid that the enemy might be there before them. The Pikunis also had a war house there built of logs and covered with brush and timber.

East Butte: *Mouyístsimokam* ("Hairy Cap").

Flat Willow Creek: *Ahpúkwi Tsipiska* ("Broad Willow").

Fort Benton: *Ahkápi Oyis* ("Many-Houses").

Fort Conrad: *Sisukikaiyi Istsimokan* ("Spotted Cap," Charles Conrad). It was built in the year 1875 by I. G. Baker and Company and named for Charles Conrad, one of the members of the firm. It was managed by Alfred B. Hamilton and bought by Joseph Kipp in 1878. The site of the fort is now an island in the Marias River about one hundred yards above the Great Northern Railroad crossing of the stream.

Frenchman's Ridge: *Nápio Pahwakwi* ("The Old Man's Ridge"). On the east end of this ridge there was a point that the Pikunis called the "Hunter's Lookout" (*Sam Issupi*).

Giant Springs: *Sokwí Otsiskum* ("Big Mouth Spring").

Gold Butte: *Apoyi Kiniko* ("The White Grass Butte").

Goose Bill: *Misa Okokensi* ("Hard Gooseneck").

Grayling Creek: *Iksíkkominkini* ("White Fin Creek"). This stream is so named because the grayling fish, native to that river, have a long white back fin. Incidentally, this stream is the only one west of the streams of Wisconsin in which the grayling are native.

Great Falls: *Ipumí Stukskwi* ("Rock Ridge Across").

Greenfields Lake: *Ikítskimi* ("Alkali Lake").

Headlight Butte: *Áhwakas Otskina* ("Antelope Horns"). From a distance this butte looks like an antelope head. The Crows and Pikunis engaged in a battle on top of this butte, and the Pikunis were victorious.

Heart Butte: *Úskitsipupi Istúki* ("Heart Butte"). In 1872 the Pikunis had been stealing horses from the Crows near the Sweetgrass Hills, and the Crows followed the Pikunis looking for their horses. They lost the tracks of the party they were following, but just below Heart Butte, along a stream, they came upon a war party of Blackfeet and killed three. They never did find the Pikunis or the horses.

Heavy Breast School: *Kutoyókan* ("Sweet Pine Medicine Lodge").

Helena: *Ohkótokwatsis Sakum* ("Many Sharp Points [Cactus] Ground").

Highwood Mountains: *Sitosis Tuksi* ("Middle Mountains"). This range has mountains on all sides of it so the Indians called the range the "Middle Mountins."

Hudson Bay Divide: *Appukitsuaskwi* ("Broad Timber").

Jefferson River: *Oki Tuktai* ("Medicine Lodge Creek"). During the medicine-lodge ceremonies there the medicine woman was riding a horse which stampeded and threw her to the ground; thus, the Pikunis called this stream "Medicine Lodge Creek."

John Joe Spring: *Masto Ksiskum* ("Raven Spring").

Judith Gap: *Itsipótsi Stukwi* ("Where the Mountains Come from Both Sides").

Judith Mountains: *Otokwi Istuki* ("Yellow Mountains").

Judith River: *Otokwi Tuktai* ("Yellow River"). It was at the mouth of this river in 1855 that the government made its first treaty with the Blackfoot tribes, whereby it was agreed that these tribes owned all the country between the Canadian border and the Musselshell River, from the summit of the Rocky Mountains eastward for an average width of four hundred miles.

Knees, the: *Mutóksisiko* ("The Knees").

Lame Deer: *Omúk Itumo* ("Big Butte").

Lee's Creek: *Sákaimaupi* ("Rope-Stretched-Across").

Little Bighorn River: *Khpaksí Tuktai* ("Ash River"). This was one of the places where the Pikunis got wood to make their bows and arrows. They also used the wood of the ash for their pipestems.

Little Rocky Mountains: *Mahkwyi Stukists* ("Wolf Mountains").

Lodge Creek: *Nitsi Kupwi Issakta* ("Double Creek").

Long Butte: *Itsipáh Wunah* ("Perpendicular Rattle").

Lonesome Lake: *Imoyíkini* ("Hairy Lake"). The grass around the lake is fine and looks like hair. All different tribes of Indians, both war parties and hunting parties, made it a point to go to this lake to camp and to meet with other parties. There were many skirmishes there among the different Indians in early days.

McDonald Creek: *Kaíyo Ahtiwapiksi* ("Where-the-Bear-Wagged-His-Tail Creek").

Marias River: *Kaíyi Isisakta* ("Bear River").

Marias River, bluff on: *Awyi Kaitsi* ("Ever-Shadow Bluff"). About five miles below the dry fork, this bluff was where the Pikunis were camped when the Crees surprised them before the battle at Dunkirk *(q.v.)*

Marias River, dry fork of: *Amiyátsisko* ("Head of the Creek Timber").

Milk River: *Kinuk Sisakta* ("Little River").

Milk River, north fork of: *Ahksiomai Piskán* ("The Good-Gathering-Buffalo Falls").

Milk River, south fork of: *Ahkákoksistuko* ("Cut Bank with a Point of Rocks").

Mud Creek: *Paksikwi Kitaktai* ("The Creek").

Muddy Creek: *Kaksinútsipwi Ituktai* ("Scattering Standing Trees").

Musselshell River: *Kaíyi Tsisísakto* ("Bear River"). The upper part of the river is known to the Indians by the name of "Shell River" (*Otsistsi Tuktai*).

Pondera Creek: *Omúk Amyatsisko* ("The Big Timbered Creek").

Porcupine Creek: *Kiskáp Ituktai* ("Porcupine Creek").

Powder River: *Satsópachis Ituktai* ("Powder River").

Priest's Butte: *Mikápi Otsistsi* ("Where Red Old Man Was Buried").

Pryor Creek: *Ápsi Tuktai* ("Arrow Creek"). Along this stream is a high cliff with a hole in the rock near the top. Long ago the Indians shot arrows into the hole as a gift to the rock with prayers for good luck. The stream took its name from this.

Pryor Mountains: *Ahwáhpitsi Istúkiks* ("Lonesome Mountains"). These mountains were so rough and barren that the Indians called them the "Lonesome Mountains."

Red River: *Ahmóki Tuktai* ("Red River").

Red Old Man's Butte: see Priest's Butte.

Rekap: *Ahkwinimakan* ("Pipestone Bend"). The first bend of the Missouri river below Three Forks has an outcropping of black stone; there the Blackfoot tribes used to go to get the black stone to make their pipes.

Rocky Spring Ridge: *Ahkó Ksiskumiks* ("Many Springs").

Rosebud River: *Ahkókinikskwo Ituktai* ("Many Rosebuds River").

Round Butte: *Sisístotokis* ("Owl's Ears").

Round Butte: *Ahnúts Kimikoi* ("Pretty Butte").

St. Ignatius: *Spítukskwo* ("High Timber").

St. Mary Lake: *Púhtomuksi Kimiks* ("Lakes Inside").

St. Mary River: *Púhtomuksi Kimiks Atuktai* ("Lakes Inside River").

St. Peter: *Manokyópahn* ("Feathered Ends of Arrows"). A war party of Crows were making arrows there when the Pikunis surprised them and killed them all.

Shelby: *Niyítsan Kahwakwo* ("Yellow Paint Coulee"). The Pikunis there found deposits of yellow earth which they dug and used for paint.

Shonkin Creek: *Páhksi Piskwo* ("Box Elder Creek").

Silver City: *Sikíkskim Ituktai* ("Black Metal Creek").

Smith River: *Apúm Pistún Sisakta* ("Other-Side Deep Creek"). Named so for the reason that there is another Deep Creek on the other side of the Missouri near Choteau.

Smith River: *Maaúyi Ituktai* ("Mouth Creek").

Snake Butte: *Istsiksin Otsinutsi* ("Looks Like a Snake's Nose"). Just below this butte in a coulee the Pikunis and a Crow war party fought, and the Pikunis defeated the enemy.

Square Butte: *Aisitupi Namiks* ("Looks Like Two Persons").

Square Butte: *Ahwanáhksa* ("Rattle Butte"). There are three buttes in this vicinity all named for the rattles used by the Pikunis in religious ceremonials. They are made of rawhide with long handles and have gravel inside.

Square Butte: *Sahúnio Kachis* ("Lower Bear Paw").

Square Butte: *Ksisto Nimán* ("Roached-Hair Butte").

Sun River: *Kaksístukskwi Ituktai* ("Pile-[Point?-]of-Rocks River").

Sun's Fort: *Natós Okwoi* ("Sun's House"). This was a fort built by W. G. Conrad in 1868 and was the first trading post built on the Marias River. It was at the mouth of Medicine Rock Coulee. At the head of this coulee the Pikunis found a rock which looked to them like a person sitting down, and they thought it was a person turned into stone. They made offerings to the rock and prayed to it for their safety and long life. A party of Blood Indians came along and made fun of the Pikunis for worshiping the rock and said it was just a rock and shot at it; then they went on their way, but a little later they met an enemy and the entire party of Blood Indians were killed. The Indian name of the rock and the translation of it is *Okwitak Owhkwotau* ("Rock That We Give to").

Sweetgrass Creek: *Sipútsimo Tuktai* ("Sweetgrass Creek").

Sweetgrass Hills: *Kutoyísiks* ("Sweet Pines").

Teton Ridge: *Ótsatchis* ("Meat Strings"). Meat strings were used by the Pikunis to tie two pieces of meat together to hang over the back of a horse.

Teton River: *Múnikis Isisakta* ("The Breast").

Teton River, south bend of: *Ikinitskátah* ("Soft Earth Bend"). The bottom is impassable in wet weather. Weasel Horn, a Pikuni war chief, died there in 1872. In 1874 a party of Flathead Indians stole a horse from the Pikunis there. The Pikunis recovered it and one of the Flatheads was killed.

Three Forks: *Ahkaítowaktai* ("Many Come Together").

Timber Creek: *Mastó Omúksim Otsitówatsaps* ("Big Raven Went Crazy Here"). Big Raven was a Pikuni chief. He took off his clothes and went swimming in this stream. He came back singing but he was crazy and he never again put on his clothes.

Tongue River: *Mutsini Ituktai* ("Tongue River").

Two Medicine Lake: *Mátoki Okás Omúksikimi* ("Two Medicine Lodges Lake").

Two Medicine Lodges River: *Mátoki Okás* ("Two Medicine Lodges").

Valier: *Sawkí Ahsokaíyis* ("Prairie Trunk").

Wilder, formerly called "Rocky Point": *Okwítaksi Piskátah* ("Rocky Point"). This was the regular landing place for freight to Fort Assiniboine. Broadwater and Pepin had a trading post at this point in the years 1880, 1881, 1882, and 1883. Five miles below on the south bank of the river at a place called Carroll, Joseph Kipp had a trading post during those years.

Willow Creek, head of: *Nitók Itsi* ("Grove in Sight").

Wolf Creek: *Utsina Itómatsa* ("Where the Gros Ventres Were Massacred by the Pikunis").

Wolf Creek: *Mahkwíyi Istikiop* ("Where the Wolf Fell Down"). There was a buffalo fall here, and a buffalo at the end of the herd went over taking a wolf with him. Just above the town of Wolf Creek, on the north side of the stream, was the ranch of Malcolm Clark who was really the cause of the Baker Massacre.

Wolf Point: *Mahkwi Piskátah* ("Wolf Point").

Yellowstone Park: *Aisítsi* ("Many Smokes"). A war party of Pikunis traveling south came upon what is now the park and saw what they thought was the smoke of many campfires, but when the night came there were no fires. They learned afterward that what they had seen was the mist from the hot springs.

Yellowstone River: *Ponoká Isisakta* ("Elk River").

Index

Index

Index